I Think of You Constantly with Love

ALSO AVAILABLE FROM BLOOMSBURY

Wittgenstein's Family Letters, edited by Brian McGuinness
Portraits of Wittgenstein, edited by F.A. Flowers III and Ian Ground

I Think of You Constantly with Love: The Letters of Ludwig Wittgenstein and Ben Richards

Edited by
Gabriel Citron &
Alfred Schmidt

BLOOMSBURY ACADEMIC
LONDON • NEW YORK • OXFORD • NEW DELHI • SYDNEY

BLOOMSBURY ACADEMIC

Bloomsbury Publishing Plc, 50 Bedford Square, London, WC1B 3DP, UK
Bloomsbury Publishing Inc, 1359 Broadway, New York, NY 10018, USA
Bloomsbury Publishing Ireland, 29 Earlsfort Terrace, Dublin 2, D02 AY28, Ireland

BLOOMSBURY, BLOOMSBURY ACADEMIC and the Diana logo are trademarks of
Bloomsbury Publishing Plc

First published in Great Britain 2026

Copyright © Gabriel Citron and Alfred Schmidt, 2026

Gabriel Citron and Alfred Schmidt have asserted their right under the Copyright, Designs and Patents Act, 1988, to be identified as Authors of this work.

For legal purposes the Acknowledgements on p. ix constitute an extension of this copyright page.

Cover design by Darren Rumney @rumneydesign.co.uk

All rights reserved. No part of this publication may be: i) reproduced or transmitted in any form, electronic or mechanical, including photocopying, recording or by means of any information storage or retrieval system without prior permission in writing from the publishers; or ii) used or reproduced in any way for the training, development or operation of artificial intelligence (AI) technologies, including generative AI technologies. The rights holders expressly reserve this publication from the text and data mining exception as per Article 4(3) of the Digital Single Market Directive (EU) 2019/790.

Bloomsbury Publishing Plc does not have any control over, or responsibility for, any third-party websites referred to or in this book. All internet addresses given in this book were correct at the time of going to press. The author and publisher regret any inconvenience caused if addresses have changed or sites have ceased to exist, but can accept no responsibility for any such changes.

A catalogue record for this book is available from the British Library.

Library of Congress Cataloging-in-Publication Data

ISBN: HB: 978-1-3500-2646-9
ePDF: 978-13500-2648-3
eBook: 978-13-500-2647-6

Typeset by RefineCatch Limited, Bungay, Suffolk
Printed and bound in Great Britain

For product safety related questions contact productsafety@bloomsbury.com.

To find out more about our authors and books visit www.bloomsbury.com
and sign up for our newsletters.

Contents

Editorial Note vi
Acknowledgements ix
Foreword by Ray Monk xi
Introduction xiii
Short Biographies of Frequently Mentioned Family and Friends xlviii
List of Wittgenstein's Frequently Used Abbreviations lii

Letters

I   In Cambridge and Swansea (June 1946 – July 1947)   1

II   In Ireland (August 1947 – July 1949)   77

III   With the Malcolms in Ithaca, NY (July – October 1949)   207

IV   With the von Wrights in Cambridge, & in Vienna (November 1949 – April 1950)   235

V   With Elizabeth Anscombe in Oxford (May 1950 – February 1951)   267

VI   With the Bevans in Cambridge (February – April 1951)   323

VII   Undatable Letters and Cards, & Notes from 'John Smith'   347

Timeline 361
Bibliography 367
Index of Names 371

Editorial Note

After Ben Richards' death in 1995, the Austrian National Library acquired from Richards' widow – Tara Richards – 150 letters from Wittgenstein to her late husband. These letters dated from August 1947 to just a few days before Wittgenstein's death, at the end of April 1951. In accordance with Ben Richards' will, these letters remained sealed for 25 years – until the end of 2020. Much to our astonishment, as we were preparing an edition of these 150 letters, we were told by Miranda Richards – Ben's and Tara's daughter – that many more letters between Wittgenstein and her father existed. These ended up being over 100 further letters from Wittgenstein to Richards and about 90 letters from Richards to Wittgenstein. These additional letters now brought back the date of the correspondence's start to July 1946, and gave us – for the first time – a glimpse of Richards' side of the friendship in his own words, in addition to Wittgenstein's. Moreover, this new cache of documents also included numerous greetings cards, telegrams, photographs, and a handful of letters from Wittgenstein to Angela Richards (one of Ben's younger sisters). Miranda Richards wanted the full correspondence safeguarded for posterity by being brought under one roof, and so – in 2021 – the Austrian National Library duly acquired this second trove of documents and photographs. It is not clear why, or by whom, the correspondence was originally divided into two parts. But fortunately, all 373 pieces are now united into a single collection and are published here for the first time in their original form.[1]

Scans of all the original manuscripts can be accessed through the Austrian National Library's website (you can find them by doing a catalogue search for 'Wittgenstein Richards Korrespondenz'). The original manuscripts themselves are held in the Department of Manuscripts and Rare Books in the Austrian National Library,[2] accessible under the call marks:

---

[1] A German translation appeared in 2023 as: *"I think of you constantly with love ..." Briefwechsel Ludwig Wittgenstein – Ben Richards 1946–1951*, ed. Alfred Schmidt in collaboration with Gabriel Citron, trans. Alfred Schmidt, Innsbruck, Haymon Verlag.

[2] The only exceptions are some of Wittgenstein's letters and cards to Angela Richards, which are in the possession of Gabriel Citron.

Autogr. 1840/1 to 33
Autogr. 1841/1 to 35
Autogr. 1842/1 to 34
Autogr. 1843/1 to 40
Autogr. 1844/1 to 45
Autogr. 1845/ 5 to 8, and 21
Autogr. 1900/1 to 35

This volume is a complete edition of the collection – including all the letters, cards, telegrams, and photographs. The material is divided chronologically into six chapters, each one covering a distinctive period of Wittgenstein's life, defined by where he was based at that time. We have started a new chapter for each time he made a major move. A final – seventh – chapter contains the letters and cards which were undated and whose dates we were unable to estimate through contextual evidence. These undatable letters include a couple of notes which Wittgenstein wrote for Richards using the playful pseudonym 'John Smith'.

The brief introduction at the head of each chapter provides a biographical overview of the period that the chapter covers, and furnishes whatever broad background information is needed to set the letters in context. The running footnotes aim to provide enough information to explain the context, references, and allusions of each particular letter. The main introductory chapter provides more detailed context for – and an overview of – the entire collection. All translations which appear in the various introductions and footnotes are by us, unless they are attributed to a particular translation edition.

Most of the letters in this collection were dated by Wittgenstein. Often, when Wittgenstein did not date a letter, the originals have had a date added in pencil. These dates were presumably added by Richards, usually marking the date he received the letter. When letters were undated by either Wittgenstein or Richards, we have dated them either using postmarks (when available), or by means of contextual evidence (in which case we briefly lay out our reasoning in the footnotes).

We have transcribed the letters here as faithfully as possible. This means that – in contrast to almost all previous editions of Wittgenstein's letters – we have accurately reproduced Wittgenstein's idiosyncratic (and often just poor) spelling and punctuation. For the most part they do not present any difficulty for understanding. Because these mistakes are ubiquitous, we have done this without comment, rather than inserting an intrusive 'sic' on every occasion. Similarly, we have retained Wittgenstein's orthographic idiosyncrasies – such as his consistent use of '&' for 'and', and his frequent, long strings of abbreviations for many of his endearments to Richards (for expansions of which see the list on pp. lii–liii). We have reproduced Wittgenstein's underlinings as such (rather than converting them into italics). And where Wittgenstein or Richards have added a word, phrase, or sentence, above or below the line (usually indicating where it should be inserted into the sentence by an arrow) we have inserted it in the place that the arrow indicates and marked the insertion by enclosing it between slashes /like this/. Everything written by Wittgenstein and Richards appears in serif font, and any text included in the letters but not written by them – such as pre-printed greetings card messages, letterheads, or telegram formulae – are reproduced in sans-serif font to distinguish them from Wittgenstein's and Richards' own words. Editorial insertions – such as the informational line which titles each letter and enclosure, and picture captions – are all in italics.

The small sketches and drawings with which both correspondents would sometimes embellish their letters are reproduced here, as far as possible in their original positions. So too, the dried flowers and plants which Wittgenstein often included with – or attached to – his letters, have been included here (whenever they have survived) by means of photographs. We have included photographs of all the picture postcards and illustrated greetings cards as well, and – where possible – we have reproduced some of the images to which Wittgenstein refers in the letters.

If readers spot any mistakes in our transcription, when comparing our edition to the online scans of the letters, we would be very grateful if you could let one of us know, so that we can correct any errors in future editions. We can be contacted at: gabrielcitron@gmail.com and alfred.schmidt77@gmail.com

Acknowledgements

For permission to publish Wittgenstein's letters we are grateful to both The Master and Fellows of Trinity College Cambridge and also the representatives of the Wittgenstein family: Andreas Sjögren, Florian Stockert, and Pierre Stonborough. And for permission to publish Richards' letters we are grateful to Miranda Richards.

We would like to thank Johanna Rachinger, Director General of the Austrian National Library, for her invaluable support in purchasing the second part of the correspondence for the library; Andreas Fingernagel, former head of the manuscript collection of the Austrian National Library, and his colleague Katrin Jilek, who supported the project from the very beginning; Ernst Gamillscheg for purchasing the first part of the correspondence; and Ray Monk for contributing a foreword to this volume.

For valuable help and information – especially in connection with the many and varied footnotes – we are grateful to: Nicolas Bell (Wren Library, Cambridge); John Berkman (Regis College, University of Toronto); Jacqueline Cox (Cambridge University Archives); Julia Creuer (Ben Richards' youngest sister); Anthony Gottlieb (New York Institute for the Humanities); Eran Guter (Max Stern Yezreel Valley College); Inbal Guter (University of Haifa); Richard and Jennifer Kingston (descendants of Wittgenstein's hosts in Kilpatrick House); Benjamin Lipscomb (Houghton University); Patricia McGuire (King's College, Cambridge, Archive Centre); Philip and Julia Mortimer (descendants of Wittgenstein's neighbours in Rosroe); Bernt Östermann (The Von Wright and Wittgenstein Archives in Helsinki); Kjell Petersen (The National Library of Finland); Alois Pichler (The Wittgenstein Archives at the University of Bergen); Alan Sandry (Swansea University); Joachim Schulte (University of Zurich); Radmila Schweitzer (Wittgenstein Initiative); Arend Smilde (of the Lewisiana blog); Jonathan Smith (Wren Library, Trinity College, Cambridge), Jim Stockton (Boise State University); Bent Sofus Tranøy (Knut Erik Tranøy's son); Harald Vatne (author of *Ludwig Wittgenstein and the People of Skjolden*); and an anonymous reviewer for Bloomsbury Publishing.

Our thanks, also, to Colleen Coalter, Aimee Brown, Suzie Nash, Merv Honeywood, Niamh Rogerson, and the rest of the Bloomsbury team, for all their excellent work on this edition of the book. And finally, I (G.C.) would like to thank Chelsea Adewunmi for her support, encouragement, and forbearance above and beyond, through the long process of this book's preparation; and I (A.S.) want to thank my wife Selis for her patience and understanding.

Foreword

"It is the mark of a true love that one thinks of what the other person suffers. For he suffers too, is also a poor devil."[1]

So Wittgenstein wrote in a notebook in August 1946. The "true love" that he had in mind was that which he felt for Ben Richards, a student at King's College, Cambridge, whom he had met towards the end of 1945. Wittgenstein had been in love several times before, but, as this moving and captivating collection of letters shows, his relationship with Richards was special. It was not only the last love of his life, it was also the happiest.

In researching my biography of Wittgenstein, I met Richards at his house in Hemel Hempstead several times, but he never confided in me that he was in possession of this delightful set of love letters. When Alfred Schmidt showed them to me, therefore, they came as a wonderful revelation.

With his first love, David Pinsent, Wittgenstein could often be (as Pinsent records in his diaries for 1912-13) surly, argumentative and judgmental, and with Marguerite Respinger (whom, in 1929, Wittgenstein had wanted to marry), he could be severe and controlling. Francis Skinner, with whom Wittgenstein lived for several years in the 1930s, was completely dominated by him. In these letters to Richards, however, we see a very different Wittgenstein, one who is, indeed, thinking of what the *other* is thinking and feeling. "I wish I knew," Wittgenstein writes to Richards, "a little more about how happy, &/or unhappy, you're feeling in your work."[2] When Richards is anxious about his medical exams, Wittgenstein suffers with him and wants to help. When Wittgenstein sees something beautiful, he wants to share it with Richards. When he hears a piece of music that has particularly impressed him, he recommends it to Richards in the hope that when he listens to it too, he will think of Wittgenstein. He sends him flowers to brighten his day. He wants to make Richards *happy*.

---

1 MS 131, p. 41-2 (trans. R.M.).
2 Wittgenstein's letter to Richards of April 19, 1951.

He was, too, constantly aware of how happy Richards made *him*. "All is happiness," he wrote on 8 October 1946. "I could not write like this now if I had not spent the last 2 weeks with B[en]."³ A few weeks later, he wrote: "love is a joy."⁴

That joy comes across vividly in these beautifully simple and warm letters, many of which were written with a single aim: "I want to tell you how much I love you & how much I need you."⁵ Perhaps the most poignant of these letters is the one written shortly before his death. He knew that he did not have long to live and there was something he felt he *had* to say:

> "There is one thing I want to tell you. Whatever happens to me now, I want you to know that you have given me more than I could possibly ever have hoped for. You have given me happiness & joy which I never deserved & made my life different altogether from what it would have been without you. Thanks for all you did to me. /You are at the background of all my happiness./"⁶

As he lay dying, he was told that his close friends, including Richards, would be coming to visit him the following day. He knew that he would not survive long enough to see them, so before losing consciousness he said: "Tell them I've had a wonderful life." Some people have been puzzled by this. How could someone who had experienced such intense torment and angst that he had repeatedly considered committing suicide describe his life as "wonderful"? These letters make his final words seem rather less puzzling, and Alfred Schmidt and Gabriel Citron are to be congratulated for their meticulous work in allowing us all a glimpse of a side of Wittgenstein's life that was indeed wonderful.

Ray Monk

---

3   MS 132, p. 147 (trans. R.M.).
4   MS 133, p. 8 (trans. R.M.)
5   Wittgenstein's letter to Richards of April 7, 1951.
6   Wittgenstein's letter to Richards of April 11, 1951.

Introduction

At the start of the new academic year of 1945-46, Ben Richards – a recently graduated medical student at Cambridge – appeared in Ludwig Wittgenstein's lecture course on the philosophy of psychology.[1] This proved to be a pivotal event for both men, and the friendship which developed between them – and which is both played out and recorded in these letters – decisively coloured every aspect of the last six years of Wittgenstein's life.

"Man's greatest happiness is love", wrote Wittgenstein in his philosophical notebook in December 1948.[2] This correspondence is a testament to what was perhaps the greatest happiness of Wittgenstein's life. And yet, if it was a deep happiness, it was also a profoundly difficult one – for the letters also show us a lonely and vulnerable man, painfully aware of his dependence on the care and affection of his beloved friend at every moment, and painfully aware of the fragility of their connection.

Wittgenstein called himself Richards' "loving friend",[3] and he wanted Richards to be a "loving friend" to him in return.[4] Wittgenstein spoke of their "relation": how important "the depth & warmth of our relation" was to him,[5] and how much he feared "a lopsided relation" in which his love and need for Richards was stronger than Richards' love and need for him.[6]

---

1 One of Richards' obituaries explicitly states that he attended lectures by Wittgenstein (*King's College Annual Report* 1995: 73); and see also Klagge 2019: 54.
2 MS 127, p. 130a
3 See Wittgenstein's letter to Richards of February 17, 1947.
4 See Wittgenstein's letter to Richards of November 26, 1949.
5 See Wittgenstein's letter to Richards of June 31, 1946 (and also of September 6, 1946).
6 See Wittgenstein's letter to Richards of June 16, 1948 (and also of November 16, 1947, and June 8, 1948).

Wittgenstein sometimes referred to the two of them as "companions" for one another.[7] But most frequently, he simply spoke of the two of them as "friends".[8] And from the records that we have, this seems to have been Richards' chosen descriptor too: "You know I am your friend and will always be unless I change very greatly," he wrote to Wittgenstein in 1947.[9] In this book, therefore, we will follow both Wittgenstein's and Richards' lead in speaking of them as *friends*.

We know what this friendship meant to Wittgenstein: "I love you & need you",[10] "I long to be with you & love you always",[11] "I think of you constantly with love & gratitude",[12] "Nothing I do, or look at, is as enjoyable as when you're with me",[13] "You are at the background of all my happiness".[14] Unfortunately, we have no equivalently revealing statements from Richards. He wrote fewer and shorter letters to Wittgenstein than Wittgenstein did to him, and of those, many have not been preserved.[15] And while we have Wittgenstein's manuscript notebooks to act as companions and guides to the feelings and concerns which lay behind his letters, we have no such documents in Richards' case.

Certainly, both Wittgenstein and Richards expressed love for one another from early on. The first letters we have from each to the other – from the summer of 1946 – are both signed identically:

"With love – always,
                Ludwig"[16]

"With love
        always
                Ben"[17]

---

7   See Wittgenstein's letter to Richards of November 17, 1948 (and also of February 7, 1949, May 6, 1950, and July 3, 1950.
8   See, for example, Wittgenstein's letters to Richards of February 17, 1947, September 13, 1949, and many other places.
9   Richards' letter to Wittgenstein of March 1 or 2, 1947. See, also, the quotation that Wittgenstein copied into his manuscript notebook, from a letter from Richards that has not survived (MS 133, October 26, 1946, p. 8r; quoted below on p. xxiv).
10 Wittgenstein's letter to Richards of June 16, 1948.
11 Wittgenstein's letter to Richards of April 25, 1951.
12 Wittgenstein's letter to Richards of May 25, 1948.
13 Wittgenstein's letter to Richards of August 2, 1949.
14 Wittgenstein's letter to Richards of April 11, 1951.
15 None of Richards' letters at all have survive from the whole period of mid-October 1947 until early July 1949, and many of his letters from the other periods are missing too.
16 Wittgenstein's card to Richards of around June 23, 1946.
17 Richards' letter to Wittgenstein of June 26, 1946.

And the correspondence is punctuated repeatedly by statements of missing and longing, and the declaration from each to the other that: "I think of you constantly with love" (in multiple variations).[18] But these declarations come far more frequently and much more intensely and insistently from Wittgenstein's side than from Richards', and it was almost always Wittgenstein who was taking the lead. It is no wonder, therefore, that Wittgenstein was often deeply anxious about what Richards truly felt and where they stood in relation to one another. While his friendship with Richards was the great 'love story' ('*Liebesgeschichte*')[19] of Wittgenstein's life, it is much harder to know – as Wittgenstein himself felt all too painfully – how exactly Richards saw their friendship: what it meant to him, and what role it played in his life. In the end, Richards' surviving letters will have to speak for themselves.[20]

This collection of letters between Wittgenstein and Richards is not only the single largest correspondence of Wittgenstein's that has survived, but – more importantly – it is by far the most significant and revealing cache of letters between Wittgenstein and someone whom he loved romantically.[21] As such, they offer an entirely new window onto Wittgenstein's inner life. They are a profound and moving testament to his emotional and intellectual concerns in his last years. And in addition to their human and biographical significance, they are – like all of Wittgenstein's writings – shot through with opinions and insights, delivered in Wittgenstein's typically sharp and powerful manner. In short, this is a most remarkable collection of documents – both for those interested in Wittgenstein's philosophy, and for those interested in his life.

---

18 This phrase first appears in Richards' letter to Wittgenstein of November 27, 1946, and is then echoed by Wittgenstein in his letter to Richards of January 21, 1947, and from then on, many times.
19 See Wittgenstein's MS 130, p. 185.
20 As to whether there was a sexual relationship between Wittgenstein and Richards, see the discussion below, on pp. xxx-xxxv.
21 Of the people with whom Wittgenstein had a romantic relationship, or in whom he had a romantic interest, we have only one letter from Wittgenstein to David Pinsent (and about 15 from Pinsent to Wittgenstein); we have only three letters from Wittgenstein to Marguerite Respinger (and about 45 from Respinger to Wittgenstein); we have no letters at all from Wittgenstein to Francis Skinner (though we have about 100 letters from Skinner to Wittgenstein); and we have no letters from Wittgenstein to Keith Kirk (though we have about 10 from Kirk to Wittgenstein).

Ben Richards

Ben Richards, probably taken by Wittgenstein with the camera which Richards gave him for Christmas 1946

Ben (Robert Benedict Oliver) Richards was born on June 23, 1924, to a family of London doctors. His father, William Arthur Richards (1895-1962), was a general practitioner in Uxbridge, a suburb in the northwest of London; and his mother, Noel Richards (née Olivier, 1892-1969), was a paediatrician at the Westminster Hospital.

Brought up in a (socially) progressive and (politically) socialist home, Noel was a particularly colourful figure, along with her three older sisters, Margery, Brynhild, and Daphne.[22] The four Olivier sisters (Ben's mother and aunts) had been – in their youth – part of a social set which Virgina Woolf dubbed the 'Neo-Pagans' on account of their nature-loving and permissive lifestyle.[23] A notable member of this circle was the celebrated poet Rupert Brooke, who fell in love with Noel in 1907 when she was 15, and carried on a correspondence with her until his death at war in 1915.[24] The sisters were also part of the broader literary and artistic scenes – close friends with members of the

---

[22] See Sarah Watling's biography of the four Olivier sisters: *Noble savages: The Olivier sisters – Four Lives in Seven Fragments*, London, Jonathan Cape, 2019.
[23] See Watling 2019: 36-7 and Delany 1987: 39-59.
[24] Noel Olivier's correspondence with Rupert Brooke appeared in 1991 under the title: *Song of Love: the Letters of Rupert Brooke and Noël Olivier (1909-1915)*, ed. Pippa Harris, New York, Crown Publishing, 1991.

overlapping Bloomsbury Group (in London) and Apostles Conversazione Society (in Cambridge). Interestingly, Wittgenstein – who was around the same age as Noel – was also involved in these circles at around the time that the Olivier sisters were, during his first years in Cambridge (1911-1913).[25] Being a member of the Apostles himself, Wittgenstein had multiple friends in common with Noel and her sisters, such as John Maynard Keynes and Lytton Strachey. But though their circles overlapped, there's no evidence that Wittgenstein and Noel met until decades later, as a result of his friendship with Ben.[26]

William and Noel Richards had five children. Ben was the oldest (born in 1924), followed by four girls: Angela (b. 1929), Virginia (b. 1931), Isabella (b. 1933), and Julia (b. 1940). The Bloomsbury connections continued from Noel into the next generation, for while Noel had been a close friend of James Strachey,[27] Angela ended up collaborating with Strachey on his enormous project of issuing Freud's collected works in English.[28]

Ben Richards attended the prestigious Beltane School in London, then began his university studies at King's College, Cambridge, in November 1942.[29] Cambridge undergraduate studies are usually divided into two consecutive parts, known as 'Part I of the tripos' and 'Part II of the tripos'. After completing the courses and examinations of their chosen Part I, students either take Part II in a more specialized area of the same field, or they take the opportunity to study a different subject for Part II. For his Part I, Richards studied Natural Sciences, focussing on medicine. He sat exams in Physiology,

---

25 See McGuinness 2005: 118-41, and Monk 1990: 47-69.
26 That said, Wittgenstein had made such an impression on this segment of Cambridge society in the years immediately preceding the First World War, that it's likely he would have been much discussed in Noel's circles. Indeed, we know that Ferenc Békássy – one of the younger Apostles at that time, along with Wittgenstein – had mentioned Wittgenstein in a letter to Noel in 1912 (though not by name): "I don't know if you've heard of the Austrian who is here; he is 20 and last term, after much deliberation, decided not to go in for aeronautics and to take moral science here? He now utterly confounds Russell and Moore; the latter says he can't understand his arguments, but sees by the way in which they are spoken that they are true! Norton has seen him and is quite gone on – his intellect" (Békássy 2016: 87-8; letter of May 5, 1912). We don't know whether Noel remembered him and made a connection between the Cambridge professor who was now so close with her son and this remarkable young Austrian of 35 years earlier.
27 See Rosenbaum 1998: 188f.
28 The 24 volumes of *The Standard Edition of the Complete Psychological Works of Sigmund Freud*, London, The Hogarth Press, under the general editorship of James Strachey.
29 Most of the information in the remainder of this section is derived from the Cambridge University Archives (provided to us by Jacqueline Cox, Keeper of University Archives), and two short obituaries of Richards: Richards & Benjamin 1995: 870; and *King's College Annual Report* 1995: 73-4.

Anatomy, Biochemistry, Pathology, and Vertebrate Zoology, and – as was possible at the time, but not any longer – he was awarded a BA degree in June 1945 after passing just those Part I exams. After graduating, however, he stayed on in Cambridge for a further year and undertook his Part II in Moral Sciences (i.e. philosophy), which was when he attended one of Wittgenstein's courses. He passed his exams for this tripos in the Easter Term of 1946. After this brief foray into philosophy, Richards returned to his medical studies, spending most of the next four years as a student doctor in various hospitals, and passing his final Cambridge M.B. (*Medicinae Baccalaureus*) examinations in 1950. To complete his medical training, Richards took residencies at a number of hospitals over the following two years. Once fully qualified, he served as a doctor in the Royal Navy from 1952 to 1954. And after that he practiced for many years as an associate specialist in orthopaedics and rheumatology at Watford General Hospital (in Hertfordshire).

In addition to his career as a doctor, Richards was a keen trekker and climber, an avid theatre goer, and was passionate about music. He played the viola in an amateur string ensemble and sang in choirs (first the King's College Choir, then later the London University Choir). He remained lifelong friends with a number of Wittgenstein's closest friends and students, such as Elizabeth Anscombe and Georg Henrik von Wright.[30] And his correspondence with von Wright over many years makes clear that he retained a serious and active interest in philosophy.[31] Indeed, later in life he obtained a further B.A. – from the Open University – taking courses in subjects as wide-ranging as geology, quantum mechanics, and Wittgenstein's philosophy.

Richards married Tara in 1976, and they had a daughter, Miranda. He died of cancer on January 22, 1995, being survived by his wife, daughter, and his four younger sisters.

---

[30] Regarding both Anscombe and von Wright see the 'Short Biographies of Frequently Mentioned Family and Friends'.

[31] On March 31, 1969, Richards sent a lengthy essay on the subject of time logic to von Wright (Richards' letters to G.H. von Wright are in the von Wright Archives of the Finnish National Library in Helsinki, call mark COLL.714.202).

Story of a friendship

Richards and Wittgenstein walking together in London, taken by a street photographer

The period of Wittgenstein's life in which he met Ben Richards was marked by recurring depressions and a pervasive sense of loneliness: "I suffer greatly from fear of the total loneliness that now threatens me" he wrote in February 1942.[32] The loneliness was both personal and social.

On the personal side, his partner of more than eight years – Francis Skinner – had died suddenly in October 1941, leaving Wittgenstein shocked and utterly bereft.[33] And on the social side, as the Second World War progressed, then turned, and the Allies started to push through Europe towards victory, Wittgenstein was taken aback and deeply alienated by what he felt to be a spirit of vengeful anti-Germanism in England all around him.[34]

In 1942 – in the wake of Skinner's death – Wittgenstein had left Cambridge and thrown himself into war work; first as a porter at Guy's Hospital in London, and then with a medical research team in Newcastle. When – in February 1944 – the research team left for France to continue their study with wounded soldiers, Wittgenstein returned to his philosophical work. Then, with the start of the new academic year – in October 1944 – he returned to Cambridge to start teaching again.

---

[32] MS 125, 36v.
[33] As with Richards, Wittgenstein had met Skinner when the latter was a student in Wittgenstein's lectures – in the 1931-32 academic year. By 1933 they seem (judging by Skinner's letters to Wittgenstein) to have been a couple, and they eventually lived together in Cambridge in 1938 and 1939 (see Monk 1990: 402). For more on Wittgenstein's and Skinner's relationship, see Monk 1990: 331ff, and the further discussion below, on pp. xxxii-xxxiv. For more on Wittgenstein's immediate reaction to Skinner's death see Monk 1990: 427-33.
[34] See Wittgenstein, MS 151, pp. 46-7, and Venturinha & Smith 2018.

It was in October 1945 – exactly a year after his return to Cambridge, and at the height of his loneliness and sense of alienation – that Wittgenstein met Richards, who was a student in his class that Michaelmas Term. Wittgenstein was 56 years old, and Richards – 35 years his junior – was 21. We know nothing about the first eight months of their acquaintance and growing closeness, as it left no written traces. The record of their friendship begins with the first surviving letters of their correspondence, dating from the end of June 1946. And references to Richards start appearing as asides in Wittgenstein's philosophical notebooks very shortly after that. The first such entry is a desperate accounting written in July of that year:

> *MS 130 (July 22, 1946):* "I am terribly depressed. Completely unclear about my future. My love story [*Liebesgeschichte*][35] with R[ichards] has utterly exhausted me. It has held me fast, like a madness almost, for the last 9 months. It is as though I have been running after a phenomenon with all my strength; sometimes in the hope of catching it, more often still in fear or despair. But I cannot blame myself, i.e. I don't reproach myself. Was it good, was it bad? I don't know. I will only say: it was an awful fate."[36]

In the ensuing weeks the remarks about Richards pile up – often a similar mix of love, desperation, and fear for the coming loss that feels inevitable:

> *MS 130 (August 8, 1946)*: "I am very sad, very often sad. I feel as though this is the end of my life now. And yet it is possible that my life will go on for years; how? God knows. The <u>one</u> thing that love for B[en] has done for me is: it has pushed the other petty worries, those concerning position and work, into the background; at least for a short time. I sometimes see that it is more important to live than to have this and that position."[37]

Despairing as he was about the prospects of a successful relationship, Wittgenstein found that the strength of his love for Richards – quite independent of what it may or may not come to – was radically rearranging his sense of what mattered in his life.

A week later Wittgenstein moved from reflecting on his love for Richards to reflecting on what he felt to be Richards' love for him. He believed that Richards did indeed have love for him, but that this love was almost bound to fade and disappear. So Wittgenstein found himself struggling both to find the right perspective from which to understand

---

35 Or equally: 'love affair'. This paragraph as a whole was written normally, but this single word – '*Liebesgeschichte*' – was written in the substitution code which Wittgenstein often used for the personal passages in his notebooks.
36 MS 130, p. 185.
37 MS 130, p. 287.

the nature of their relation, and to take up the right attitude towards the fact that it seemed doomed sooner or later to collapse:[38]

> *MS 131 (August 12, 1946)*: "May the heartache lead me to the right <u>action</u>. Can you not think the following: that B[en] is growing <u>entirely</u> out of his love for you; just as, for example, in the way that as a boy one no longer remembers what one felt as a little child & forgets every childhood affection, without disloyalty."[39]
>
> *MS 131 (August 14, 1946)*: "Upset. Don't hear from R[ichards]. I think about it daily, and that I should gain the right stance towards this loss. Nothing seems more likely to me than that he has left me, or is about to do so, & nothing, in a sense, more natural. Yes, I also feel that I must give this event free rein, that I have done what I could & that it is now out of my hands. And yet, every morning, when I don't find a letter again, I feel <u>eerie</u>. I feel as though there's something I have not yet <u>realised</u>; as though I must find a standpoint from which more truth can be seen."[40]

Again and again – in these months – Wittgenstein interrupted the philosophical notes in his working notebooks to add a reflection on his (usually poor) mental state, and on where he stood with Richards. Almost always these remarks were written in the simple substitution code he often used for private matters in his notebooks.[41] His intense and

---

38 It is notable that Wittgenstein's reflections on his relationship with Marguerite Respinger – with whom he had a rather turbulent, on-again/off-again relationship, especially between 1929 and 1931 – strike a somewhat similar tone in May 1930, one of the periods during which Wittgenstein thought that Respinger was going to definitively choose her other love interest over him: "I am very much in love with R[espinger], have been for a long time of course, but it is especially strong now. And yet I know that the matter is in all probability hopeless. That is, I must be braced that she might get engaged & married any moment. And I know that this will be <u>very</u> painful for me. I therefore know that I should not hang my whole weight on this one rope since I know that eventually it will give. That is I should remain standing with both feet on firm ground & only hold the rope but not hang on it. But that is difficult. It is difficult to love so unselfishly that one holds on to love & does not want to be held by it. — It is difficult to hold on to love in such a way that, when things go wrong one does not have to consider it a lost game but can say: I was prepared for that & this is also alright. One could say 'If you never sit on the horse and thus entrust yourself to it completely, then of course you can never be thrown but also never hope ever to ride. ['] And all one can say to that is: You must wholly dedicate yourself to the horse & yet be braced that you may be thrown at any time." (MS 183, pp. 26-7; Wittgenstein 2003: 33-5). For more on Wittgenstein's and Respinger's relationship see Prokop 2003: 172-211, and the further discussion below, on pp. xxxi-xxxii.
39 MS 131, p. 26.
40 MS 131, pp. 37-38.
41 The code involved inverting the alphabet – replacing 'a' with 'z', 'b' with 'y', and so on (so that, for example, the word 'Ich' would be written: 'Rxs'). Wittgenstein could write fluently in this code, and had used it extensively since – at least – his First World War notebooks (see MSS 101ff) and probably much earlier. His periodic use of the code throughout his notebooks seems to have been intended partly as a safeguard for his privacy (though only from casually prying eyes, rather than from his executors – to whom he left instructions in the code itself), and partly just to set the coded matters off from the rest of his philosophical work (whether they were diary-like notes, thoughts on religion or art, or trivial observations). For a detailed discussion of Wittgenstein's use of code in his notebooks see Somavilla 2010.

unremitting anxiety over his friendship with Richards and its prospects (or lack thereof), exhausted him and pushed him almost to breaking. Wittgenstein often suffered from periods in which he feared for his sanity – in which he felt that madness was perilously close – and this now became one of those periods:

> *MS 131 (August 18, 1946)*: "I feel, my mental health is hanging by a thin thread. It is of course the anxiety & angst about B[en] that has worn me down so much. And yet even this could not have happened if I were not highly inflammable."[42]

> *MS 131 (September 8, 1946)*: "I am often very afraid for my mental equilibrium. It's a strange state. It's just as though the ground were moving a little. Just enough to make you realize that the foundation is volcanic. I have a very slight headache in the front. At the same time, I feel a certain tiredness, an <u>eerie</u> tiredness, actually as if all cheerfulness had ceased for me, as if it had been extinguished, as usually only happens in death. As if the dark powers were taking possession of me, as they would if I took my own life."[43]

In the midst of all this – towards the end of the summer break, a little before Wittgenstein would need to start teaching again – Wittgenstein and Richards took a two-week holiday together in Swansea. The time together (and away from Cambridge) did Wittgenstein a world of good, and he returned to Cambridge at the beginning of October 1946 in a much better state. He even found – to his happy surprise – that he was able to make progress with his philosophical work. A few days after his return, in the middle of a cascade of philosophical notes on aspect perception, he briefly switched into his code to record what seems to have been a gratitude-infused realization about the contingency of his current good state – how it could so easily not have been, and how the fact that it was, depended wholly on the good fortune of things having gone so well with Richards:

> *MS 132 (October 8, 1946)*: "Everything is luck! I couldn't be writing like this now if I hadn't spent the last two weeks with B[en]. And I could not have spent them like that if illness or some accident had intervened. – (!!!)"[44]

---

42 MS 131, pp. 65-66; Wittgenstein provided his own translation for the last phrase.
43 MS 131, p. 220. See also Wittgenstein's letter to his friend Rudolf Koder from about a month later (October 14, 1946): "As far as I can tell, my mind is not significantly less lively than it was. I still have thoughts that seem interesting to me. But I keep falling into a state that bears some resemblance to great tiredness, but is not ordinary tiredness. Then I feel as if I were very close to a mental catastrophe, close to some form of madness; as if I could no longer resist the mental derangement. Sort of like I was on a very slippery slope & could only hold on to a few blades of grass. I have days & weeks without these terrors & days where I hear very little reminder of them. God knows where it will lead – whether I can really recover, or whether what I feared will really happen."
44 MS 132, p. 147.

But all was not solved. Within just a few weeks of returning, the agonizing doubt and anxiety in relation to Richards were back, and Wittgenstein used his notebook to try to work through what he should do – for on the one hand, if he leant into the friendship as strongly as he felt he needed to, this may be too much for Richards and cause the friendship to collapse; but on the other hand, if he held himself back for fear of that collapse, he would thereby be being untrue to himself, and this unnaturalness would be incompatible with genuine love. His thinking echoed an exhortation he had written for himself in his notebook some weeks earlier: "Be neither overconfident nor submissive in your love!"[45] He concluded that he needed courage, faithfulness, and piety:

MS 132 (October 21, 1946): "I am too little <u>faithful</u> and too little <u>courageous</u> in love. Surely, one must be careful not to hurt the other, but you should confidently lean on him, and if he cannot bear that, then he is not your friend. But I am easily hurt and fear being hurt, and protecting oneself in <u>this</u> way is the death of all love. True love requires <u>courage</u>. But that also means, one must have the courage to break off and renounce, thus the courage to endure a mortal wound. But I can only hope that I will be spared the most terrible."[46]

MS 133 (October 25, 1946): "I have neither the courage, nor the strength & clarity, to look the facts of my life straight in the face. – B[en] has a <u>pre</u>-love [*Vor-Liebe*] for me. Something that cannot last. <u>How</u> this will wither, of course I do not know. Nor do I know how <u>something</u> of it could be kept, alive, not pressed in a book as a memento. It is infinitely unlikely that this love, if pressed by another or by other circumstances, will have enough resilience to not tear. This is now a terrible difficulty in my life. I don't know if and how I will be able to endure continuing <u>this</u> relationship with <u>this</u> prospect. But I do not have the clarity or the strength to break it off. When I imagine that I would have broken it off, I fear the loneliness; having to tell myself that I have unfaithfully and impatiently torn apart a bond that was a great and extraordinarily strange gift from heaven, <u>and that I did not know how to use for good</u>. It will seem to me that here, when I could never have expected it, an opportunity was offered to me, and I, instead of making <u>good</u> use of it, threw it away. That is <u>difficult</u>: If I want to use this affection, I can only do so by suffering a lot. – And whether it will work <u>then</u>, I do not know, nor whether I can endure this pain.

---

45 MS 131, p. 163.
46 MS 132, p. 205.

Demons have woven this bond and hold it in their hands. They can tear it apart, or let it live."[47]

MS 133 (October 26, 1946): "Love is happiness. Perhaps happiness with pain, but happiness nonetheless. If the happiness is missing, or shrinks to a brief flicker, then love is missing. – In love, I must be able to <u>rest</u> securely. – But can you turn away a warm heart? Is it a heart that beats warmly for <u>me</u>? – 'I'll rather do anything than to hurt the soul of friendship.'[48] – I must know – he won't hurt <u>our friendship</u>. A person cannot step out of their own skin. I cannot give up a demand that lies deeply within me, rooted in my entire life. For <u>love</u> is connected with nature; and if I became unnatural, love would cease. – Can I say: 'I will be reasonable, and no longer demand this'? For some, it is possible. Perhaps it is possible for most, <u>for a time</u>. But only as a means to an end, not as an end itself. I can say: Let him have his way – it will be different one day. – <u>Love</u> is the pearl of great price that you hold close to your heart, that you value above everything and would not trade for <u>anything</u>.[49] It <u>shows</u> one – if one has it – what great value <u>is</u>. One learns what it <u>means</u>: to recognize value. One learns what it means: to separate one precious metal from all the others. The immense preference it evokes teaches us the concept of unique value. The immense <u>preference</u> leads us to see: it is our <u>duty</u> to defend it. The preference leads us to seriousness. The passion, to seriousness. – If the preference does not do this, then it is not love.

The terrible thing is the uncertainty. And in the uncertainty, my mind is always busy imagining possibilities, and almost always bad ones. Sometimes that is right, but mostly it is wrong. "Trust in God". But I am far from trusting in God. It is a <u>long</u> way from where I am to trusting in God.

Joyful hope and fear are twinned. I cannot have one without it bordering on the other."[50]

MS 133 (November 27, 1946): "Can you not be cheerful even without his love? <u>Must</u> you sink into grief without this love? Can you not live without this support? For that is the question: can you not walk upright without leaning on this staff? Or can you not <u>bring yourself</u> to give it up? Or is it both? – You <u>mustn't</u> always expect letters that don't come! But how can I change this?

---

[47] MS 133, pp. 7r–8r.
[48] This seems to be a quotation from Richards – perhaps from a conversation, or more likely from a letter of his that has not been preserved.
[49] See Matthew 13:46.
[50] MS 133, pp. 8r–9r.

It is not love that draws me to this support, but rather that I cannot stand securely on my two feet alone."[51]

And in a similar vein a little later:

> *MS 134 (April 10, 1947)*: "You cannot simply shift your own problems onto the other person. Consider what you may demand of him, & should demand, & demand that; & you must come to terms with the consequences."[52]

Wittgenstein's love for Richards was teaching him seriousness in life and calling him to courage. But even so, he couldn't shake his gloom. And as he looked to the future, he did so with a despondency and despair which settled over every aspect of his life:

> *MS 133 (November 19, 1946)*: "I foresee a bad end for my life. Loneliness, perhaps madness. My lectures go well, they will never go better. But what effect do they have? Am I helping anyone? Certainly no <u>more</u> than if I were a great actor, performing tragedies for them. What they learn is not worth learning; & the personal impression is of no use to them. This applies to everyone, with <u>maybe</u> one or two exceptions."

> *MS 133 (November 20, 1946)*: "In a bad state."

> *MS 133 (November 22, 1946)*: "Looking to the future with despair. My life seems to lie like a wasteland. And I can't find it in myself to accept it that way. I am always brooding, to absolutely no avail, over a favorable change."

> *MS 133 (November 23, 1946)*: "Some people are sick their whole lives and know only the happiness felt by those who, after long, intense pain, have a few painless hours. (It is a blessed sigh of relief.)"[53]

But the bond didn't break, and their friendship did not wither, as Wittgenstein had so feared it would. On the contrary, Richards remained a steadfast and loving friend to Wittgenstein until the very end – treating him with great care and generosity. And when Wittgenstein's anxiety ran away with him (as it also continued to do for the entirety of their friendship), Richards did his best to calm it – as Wittgenstein poignantly described in a letter to Richards from some years later:

---

51 MS 133, pp. 42v-43r.
52 MS 134, p. 131.
53 MS 133, pp. 41r-42r

> *Wittgenstein to Richards (May 6, 1950)*: "It was wonderful for me to be with you last weekend, as it always is. You know how intensely I enjoyed being with you.
>
> I'm afraid I acted very foolishly when once, on walking to Mrs. Rhees's place with you, I gave vent to my anxiety about what would happen if one day you felt I was no longer a satisfying companion for you. It was foolish of me to talk as I did, but it wasn't in my power /at the time/ to shut off these thoughts & fears, – I was /then/ overpowered by them. Some kind words of yours made me stop & brought me to my senses."

But though Wittgenstein never shook his propensity for being periodically overwhelmed by anxiety, the fact that he did not break off their friendship out of a sheer inability to tolerate the discomfort of his fear (and the fragility from which it derived) shows that he must have succeeded in finding a way to cope with this discomfort. Part of this capacity may have come from an insight of Goethe's which he took as his mantra:

> *MS 132 (September 29, 1946)*: " 'For desires veil from us the very thing desired. The gifts come down in their own forms, etc.'[54] This is what I say to myself when I receive B[en]'s love. For that it is the great, rare gift, I well know; that it is a rare gem, I well know, – and also, that it is not entirely of the kind I had dreamed of."[55]

Perhaps Wittgenstein had dreamt of a secure love, and a love that made him feel secure in the face of life's vicissitudes. What he got instead was a love that made him feel life's fragility *more* sharply rather than less. And now he had to learn to accept this gift as the precious jewel that it was – despite its being so profoundly different from (and so much more difficult than) what he had hoped for.

For most of 1947 Wittgenstein was living and teaching in Cambridge, while Richards was a medical student training at St. Bartholomew's ('Bart's') Hospital in London, living with his parents and sisters in their house in Ickenham (a suburb in Uxbridge, in northwest London). Wittgenstein and Richards would spend a weekend together every few weeks or so – with either Wittgenstein travelling down to London or Richards visiting Cambridge. When Wittgenstein came to London he would usually stay in the Richards family home, and thereby got to know Ben's parents and sisters fairly well. Indeed, he seems to have been such a regular fixture at the house that he kept some

---

54 This is a very slightly misremembered quotation from Goethe's *Hermann and Dorothea* (see Goethe 1987: 274 [lnn. 917-8]).
55 MS 132 p. 77.

clothes and toiletries there rather than bring them with him each time.[56] Wittgenstein was grateful to Ben's parents for their hospitality on these occasions, and would sometimes send flowers to Noel Richards as a 'thank you'.[57] But even so, these stays were not without their tensions. For one thing, Wittgenstein found the small-talk inherent in family life to be difficult, as Elizabeth Anscombe later recalled:

> "[Wittgenstein] told me that listening to people's talk – e.g. in a family circle – gave him a hazy feeling, sent him into a haze. This he told me about the general family conversation in Ben's family. He added that it had been the same in his own, so that sometimes he would be asked 'Why did you have such a terrible expression?' "[58]

More significant, however, was the tension that sometimes emerged between Wittgenstein and Ben's mother. From the letters we get only oblique glimpses of it, with the details never fully spelled out. Near the beginning of 1949, for example, Wittgenstein seems to have got the sense that perhaps Noel Richards disliked him – or disliked having him stay at the house – so Ben spoke with her to find out more. She seems to have responded with surprise, and said that this was not the case at all. Wittgenstein felt reassured enough to continue visiting, but he was not entirely convinced.[59] There's also a telling letter from June 1947.[60] Wittgenstein was hoping to stay with Ben in the family home in August – when the rest of the family would be away on holiday – but Wittgenstein was worried that Ben's parents might have invited a relative to stay with Ben to keep him company (and to act as a chaperone?). Wittgenstein wrote that having a stranger there would destroy the kind of (stay-at-home) holiday with Ben that he was hoping for. Sometimes Wittgenstein tried to clear up tensions with Noel by letter – but we only hear of these indirectly, through his reports to Ben:

> *Wittgenstein to Richards (November 26, 1947):* "I have written a short letter to your mother. I wrote her two longer ones but tore them up. May she understand my letter as it's meant. That's difficult, as our languages (her's & mine) are so different."

---

56 See, for example, Wittgenstein's letter to Richards of December 16, 1947.
57 See, for example, Richards' letter to Wittgenstein of January 18, 1947, and Wittgenstein's letter to Richards of March 25, 1947.
58 Anscombe 2025: 121.
59 This is a speculative reconstruction of what likely happened, based on Wittgenstein's letter to Richards of March 27, 1949.
60 Wittgenstein's letter to Richards of June 30, 1947.

Wittgenstein to Richards (December 16, 1947): "I had a very nice letter from your mother two days ago & answered it before I had your letter."[61]

Unfortunately, none of these letters to or from Noel Richards have survived. (By contrast, a number of letters from Wittgenstein to Angela Richards – the eldest of Ben's four younger sisters – have survived, and are included in this volume. Wittgenstein had initially got to know her from his stays with the family in Ickenham, but then got to know her much better in 1950, when she was studying at Oxford and Wittgenstein was living there.)

Thus, for most of 1947 Wittgenstein and Richards were shuttling back and forth between Cambridge and London to see each other. But in the autumn of that year this routine was interrupted because of a major change in Wittgenstein's life. He had been considering resigning his position at the university for some years, but in the summer of 1947 he finally decided that the time had come to take the leap. As he wrote to his friend Norman Malcolm[62] in August:

Wittgenstein to Malcolm (August 27, 1947): "I'ld like to be alone somewhere & try to write & to make at least one part of my book publishable. I'll never be able to do it while I'm teaching at Cambridge. Also I think that, quite apart from writing, I need a longish spell of thinking <u>alone</u>, without having to talk to anybody."

Wittgenstein had been working to get his new thinking into publishable form since 1931[63] – but so far without success. Towards the end of 1936 the beginnings of a book finally started to take shape, but in the eleven years since then he had nonetheless not been able to bring it to completion. Resigning his professorship would free him from his teaching obligations and allow him to live somewhere he could think and work undisturbed. Perhaps then he'd be able to bring his book – or at least part of it – into publishable form. Eventually he chose Ireland as the place that would be best suited to this task. He officially tendered his resignation in October 1947, and he headed for Ireland at the end of November.

From that November it would be almost exactly two years until Wittgenstein was living back in England again (spending most of that time in Ireland and the last few

---

61 See also Wittgenstein's intervening letter to Richards of December 7, 1947, which fills in a little more context.
62 Regarding Malcolm see the 'Short Biographies of Frequently Mentioned Family and Friends'.
63 On October 30, 1931, Wittgenstein wrote to his old student and friend William Heriot Watson: "I hope to publish something in less than a year's time."

months of it in America). This significantly changed the pattern of the friendship. Though Richards visited Wittgenstein in Ireland four times, and Wittgenstein visited Richards in England twice, for these next two years it was mainly their letters which had to bear the friendship's weight. And in Wittgenstein's case, the weight was considerable. He found himself waiting eagerly for every letter and often pleading for more. Thinking of Richards and re-reading his letters was his solace. When a new letter arrived it either brought joy:

> *Wittgenstein to Richards (January 13, 1948)*: "Getting your letter made me feel <u>very happy</u>. /In fact I seem to get more than my proper share of happiness./ Thanks for everything. God bless you always."

or it allayed disaster:

> *Wittgenstein to Richards (January 31, 1948)*: "[T]hen the boy brought me your letter. When I read your kind words the nightmare left me & I felt happy & felt that now I wanted to go out & and enjoy the sun, which I did. God bless you!"

In either case, as Wittgenstein told Richards: "Your letters are food & drink for a whole week /& and that's <u>no</u> exaggeration/. . . . I have often been thinking that if it weren't for you I couldn't live here at all" (June 2, 1948).

But Wittgenstein's hunger for letters from Richards – in part simply as a mode of ongoing contact, but perhaps even more as tokens and reassurances of Richards' continued friendship – often turned Wittgenstein's responses from thanks to pleading. Wittgenstein felt himself wholly dependent on Richards' love, but often deeply unsure of whether Richards loved him (or *still* loved him) enough to balance the strength of his need. If the love was still there, then Wittgenstein implored Richards to express it in more regular letters; and if not, then he implored him – just as earnestly – to tell him honestly, so that he would no longer be leaning on a phantom:

> *Wittgenstein to Richards (January 19, 1949)*: "I've often said to you that your letters 'keep me going', & that wasn't just a façon de parler. I need them; & if they keep me waiting /for some days/ after the week's past, I spend these days in constant anxiety, feeling wretched, mentally & physically. – <u>That's the truth.</u> ...
>
> Imagine you had bought a dog. For a time you give him his food regularly, & you enjoy his pleasure & gratitude. Then, may be, it gets monotonous, & you're busy & feed him at odd times when it suits you. You make the animal wretched & ill. – Now there is no reason why you should keep such a delicate animal (on the other hand, it's not the animal's fault that it is like that). If you feel that you haven't bargained for all that regularity in feeding him, you must get rid of him without delay."

Or as Wittgenstein powerfully put it a little later: "[I]f I want to lean on you & and take refuge in our friendship I must know that I have a right to do so. For untruth is the worst of all, however sad the truth may be" (November 26, 1949).

But Wittgenstein's simultaneous pleading for both more love and absolute honesty put Richards in a difficult position. He was being asked for perfect candour, but the stakes of this candour were being continually raised and stressed. This made it very hard for Richards to state his position and his feelings plainly. We see this dynamic causing friction in October 1948. Wittgenstein had been to Vienna to visit his family, and was returning to Ireland via England. The plan was for Richards to travel to Ireland with him so that they could spend some time there together. Wittgenstein was tasked with making the boat bookings, and he assumed that it would be okay to book one cabin for the two of them to share. As it turned out, Richards was not happy with this – but he seems not to have managed to convey his discomfort explicitly. Wittgenstein eventually picked up on it nonetheless and made a change to the booking – and found himself again stressing how important Richards' frankness was to him:

Wittgenstein to Richards (October 3, 1948): "I wish you'd been more frank with me at the station the other day. Whichever way you feel about it I <u>will</u> be frank & explain <u>why</u> I made the suggestion that we might share a cabin for two. (I thought on Friday my reasons were obvious but suppose the weren't.)

   a) M^iss Parker had told me that she wouldn't be able to get me a cabin for one ~~person~~.
   b) I should prefer sharing a cabin with you to sharing it with a stranger.
   c) I thought (stupidly) that you too might not mind sharing it if it was with <u>me</u>.
   d) M^iss Parker said ~~she thought~~ she might be able to get a cabin for two for us.

Only when I mentioned the matter to you at the station did I notice that I'd been thoughtless in assuming <u>c</u>; but had you told me straightforwardly that you didn't like the idea of sharing a cabin with me <u>I think</u> I'd have had sense enough to understand it & to drop that idea. As it was, your tone put me off & I didn't know where I stood. For I <u>hate</u> to have to ~~read~~ /guess/ a friend's meaning from his tone. That's all right in a drawing room /where one mustn't say things outright/ but not between you & me: I wish you understood that."

Given the information we have, it's impossible to say whether or not there was a sexual relationship between Wittgenstein and Richards. It's clear from the letters that when each visited the other they always had separate accommodations or separate rooms (indeed, the task of finding appropriate rooms for the other to stay in is one of the recurrent practical themes of the correspondence). And this incident with the cabin booking brings this point home. More than this, though, we do not know.

In this context a few contextual considerations should be kept in mind. First, sex between men was illegal in the United Kingdom at the time, and harshly punishable ('sodomy' by up to life imprisonment, and 'gross indecency' between men by up to two years' hard labour);[64] and it was similarly illegal in Ireland and Norway, the other countries where Wittgenstein and Richards spent time together. This led to an understandable lack of openness and explicitness about sexual relationships between men, especially in communications which could fall into the wrong hands.[65] Secondly, both Wittgenstein and Richards were familiar with (and had varying degrees of connection with) communities in which sexual relationships between men were nonetheless common and even celebrated – including between men with significant age gaps and status differences, such as between Cambridge fellows and their undergraduate students (a practice that was especially notable in King's College, Cambridge, where Richards was a student).[66] These communities included the overlapping circles of Bloomsbury and the Apostles in London and Cambridge, to which Wittgenstein and Richards both had connections (though it's relevant that Wittgenstein seems to have strongly disapproved of the atmosphere of 'sexual intrigue' – among numerous other things – that he found among the Apostles).[67] And thirdly, these communities also recognized intense, passionate, and even romantic, relationships between men that were not sexual – or at least which were not necessarily sexual. 'Romantic friendship' between men – which might involve no physical elements at all, or which might involve physical intimacies (such as hand-holding, embracing, and even kissing) without a further sexual element – was a paradigm of intimate same-sex friendship that would have been much more familiar at that time than it is today.[68] These three considerations make it especially difficult to speculate with any certainty about the presence or otherwise of a sexual element in Wittgenstein's and Richards' friendship.

When it comes to Wittgenstein's two earlier significant romantic relationships – with Marguerite Respinger in the period from the mid-1920s to the early 1930s; and with

---

64 See, for example, Weeks 2018: 106-109.
65 See, for example, Taddeo 2002: 32 & 45.
66 See, for example, Goldhill 2025: 23-4, 82-91 and 157-68.
67 See Monk 1990: 47-9 and McGuinness 2005: 146-52.
68 See, for example, Taddeo 2002: 15-49; and – for an indirect but relevant discussion – see also, Faderman 1993.

Francis Skinner from the early 1930s to the early 1940s – we don't know much about their sexual aspect, but we do know something.[69]

Wittgenstein had a fraught relationship with Respinger, who was romantically torn between Wittgenstein and a younger friend of the Wittgenstein family, Talla Sjögren. Respinger sometimes favoured Wittgenstein, but more often favoured Sjögren – keeping them both on (alternating) tenterhooks for multiple years. During the vacillating periods when Wittgenstein and Respinger were close, and when they were in the same country, we know from Wittgenstein's diaries that they would often kiss. And when they were apart, Wittgenstein longed to hold her and kiss her (and all the more painfully when he feared he was about to lose her):

> *MS 183 (October 2, 1930)*: "By the evening of that day, our relationship was as good & intimate as it had been in earlier days. I held her in my arms & we kissed <u>for a long time</u> & I was glad to have stayed. The next day, however, a letter arrived from Talla, and it caused a reversal, or setback in the mood."[70]

> *MS 132 (May 9, 1930)*: "I think: Will I ever again be able to hold R[espinger] in my arms & kiss her? And I must also be prepared for & able to come to terms with the fact that it will not happen."[71]

On the other hand, when Wittgenstein raised the possibility of marriage with Respinger in late 1929, it seems that what he proposed was a Platonic and childless union.[72] Indeed, this was a significant part of the reason why Respinger eventually married Sjögren rather than Wittgenstein.[73]

Wittgenstein's relationship with Skinner was far steadier and more consistent. But as was the case with all of Wittgenstein's romantic relationships, much of their time was

---

[69] Before Wittgenstein met Richards, Wittgenstein himself singled out these two relationships in his life, seeing fit to pair them together and compare them. Thus, in the middle of his relationship with Francis – in 1937 – he wrote in his notebook: "Think of my earlier love, or infatuation, for Marguerite and of my love for Francis. It is a bad sign for me that my feelings for Marguerite could grow so completely cold! Admittedly, there is a difference here; but <u>my coldness of heart</u> remains. May it be forgiven me; but that is to say: may it be possible for me to be sincere and loving" (MS 120, p. 26v; December 1, 1937). And the next day he added: "Masturbated tonight. Pangs of conscience, but also the conviction that I am too weak to resist the urge and the temptation, when such-and-such mental images present themselves to me, without my being able to <u>flee</u> into other ones. Yet <u>yesterday evening</u> I had thoughts about the necessity of the purity of my lifestyle! (I thought of Marguerite and Francis) —" (MS 120, pp. 26v-27r; December 2, 1937).
[70] MS 183, p. 36.
[71] MS 183, p. 28; and see also: MS 183, pp. 1-2 & 31-40, and Villon-Lechner 1989: 57b-c.
[72] See Monk 1990: 258, and Prokop 2003: 193.
[73] See Villon-Lechner 1989: 57d.

spent in different countries to one another. Wittgenstein periodically recorded in his notebooks his 'sensual feelings' towards Skinner when they were apart (and especially when he hadn't heard from him for a while):

> *MS 120 (January 4, 1938)*: "As is often the case when I am cold and unwell, I am once again very susceptible to sensual thoughts, i.e., highly sexually excitable. I have not heard from Francis for a long time; I am worried."[74]

> *MS 120 (January 5, 1938)*: "Sometimes worried that I have not heard from Francis. Always prepared for the worst. Think of him with sensual desires, and that is bad, but that's how it is now."[75]

When Skinner came to visit Wittgenstein in Norway towards the end of 1937, Wittgenstein took the two-day boat trip down the Sognefjord to meet him at the port in Bergen and accompany him back up to his cabin just outside Skjolden, where Skinner would stay with Wittgenstein for the next week and a half.[76] Wittgenstein records his longing for Skinner on his journey to meet him, and their sleeping together upon their arrival in Skjolden (with his usual conflictedness when it came to almost all sexual matters):[77]

---

74 MS 120, p. 57r.
75 MS 120, p. 57r. The only other person for whom similarly sensual feelings are recorded in Wittgenstein's surviving notebooks is David Pinsent, more than twenty years earlier, in Wittgenstein's First World War Diaries. For example: "Still no news from David. More sensual in recent weeks" (MS 102, p. 51v; January 16, 1915); "Yesterday a lovely letter from David! … Replied to David. Very sensual" (MS 102, p. 68v; March 18, 1915); "Very sensual. M[asturbate] every day. Haven't heard from David in a long time" (MS 102, p. 70v; April 16, 1915). Wittgenstein and Pinsent had become close in Cambridge in the years just before the war. Wittgenstein seems to have been in love with Pinsent, though it's not at all clear that Pinsent was fully aware of how Wittgenstein felt.
76 See Monk 1990: 375-7.
77 Wittgenstein seems not to have had a problem with sex or sensuality in themselves, including homosexual sex and sensuality. This can be illustrated by two anecdotes. Maurice O'Connor Drury recorded the following from 1943: "As we walked by the river at Durham I began to tell him some of my experiences in Egypt. How on one occasion, when I had a period of leave, I had travelled down to see the temples at Luxor. A wonderful experience. /DRURY: 'One thing did surprise me and rather shocked me. On going into one of the temples there was on the wall a bas-relief of the god Horus with an erect phallus in the act of ejaculation and collecting the semen in a bowl!' / WITTGENSTEIN: 'Why in the world shouldn't they have regarded with awe and reverence that act by which the human race is perpetuated? Not every religion has to have St Augustine's attitude to sex. Why, even in our culture marriages are celebrated in a church; everyone present knows what is going to happen that night, but that doesn't prevent it being a religious ceremony'" (Drury 1984: 148). And Elizabeth Anscombe recorded the following: "I remember once speaking to [Wittgenstein] of a woman who was supposed to be a serious Catholic and an active lesbian, marvelling how she could combine them. 'How can you be so bornée [narrow-minded]!' he said with weary impatience" (Anscombe 2025: 155). But while he did not frown upon sex or sensuality in themselves, he was deeply troubled by the decency or otherwise of his own sensuality on any given occasion. What seemed most often to worry him was whether the *spirit* of his sexual relationships was good or bad, whether it was morally serious or not – and this is what often comes out in his sceptical comments in his notebooks about his sensuality, masturbation, and sex.

MS 118 (September 18, 1937): "Traveling today to Bergen to meet Francis. Am again very sensual; in the night, when I can't sleep, sensual fantasies. A year ago I was much more decent, I mean: my mind was much more directed toward improvement, more <u>serious</u>."[78]

MS 118 (September 22, 1937): "Brought Francis from Bergen. On the way there wrote a lot, full of thoughts. Then sensual, excitable, indecent with F[rancis]. Lay with him two or three times. Always first with the feeling that it was nothing bad, <u>then</u> with shame."[79]

This is the only reference Wittgenstein made to having sex in the entirety of his surviving corpus.[80] We have no other note like this – whether in connection with Skinner or anyone else.[81] But we know that about seven months later, in April 1938 – after Wittgenstein had left Norway (and spent some time in Vienna and then Dublin) – he returned to Cambridge and moved in with Skinner, at Skinner's flat on East Road above the Barbrooke's grocery shop.[82] They lived there together for almost a year and a half – though Wittgenstein eventually moved out and back into his old rooms in Trinity College, while their relationship continued with a bit more distance until Skinner's death in 1941.[83]

These (and a few other similar passages) are pretty much all the documentary evidence we have regarding the physical and sexual aspects of Wittgenstein's two most significant relationships prior to his friendship with Richards. It's hardly very much, but it's something. With Richards there is even less. No mention of kissing or holding, sensual thoughts or lying together – neither in the surviving notebooks nor in the surviving letters. Instead, a single piece of indecisive evidence: a telling but ambivalent

---

78 MS 118, p. 104r.
79 MS 118, p. 105v.
80 Skinner's undated letter to Wittgenstein of a few months earlier – probably from March 1937, and probably referring back to Wittgenstein's stay in Cambridge in January 1937 – seems likely to allude to earlier sexual relations between them: "I often wish I could be with you and I think of you a lot… I often remember all the things we have done together in the past and also the things we did here in Cambridge. This makes me long for you, sometimes very violently."
81 The only other direct piece of evidence we have in this connection is from Rowland Hutt's recollection of Wittgenstein's 1937 'confession', in which he recalled Wittgenstein to have said something along the lines of: "Most people would think that I have had no relationship with women, but I have". Hutt understood him to have meant that "although most people would have taken him to be a virgin, he was not so: as a young man he had had sexual relations with a woman" (see Monk 1990: 369).
82 See Monk 1990: 402.
83 See Monk 1990: 426; and see also: Skinner's letter to Wittgenstein of October 11, 1939, and Wittgenstein's letters to Raymond Townsend of September 30 and October 15, 1939.

remark in Wittgenstein's notebook of August 1946 (in the middle of his cascade of despairing comments about his love for Richards):

> *MS 131 (August 21, 1946)*: "One can hesitate and procrastinate when it comes to touching a loved one; but in the end one must <u>act</u>, because even hesitation and procrastination is an action! And beware of sparing yourself too much, or else you will act <u>unnaturally</u>."

Whether Wittgenstein hesitated and procrastinated with Richards for five years, however, we do not know. Nor what Richards' reaction was or might have been if Wittgenstein did reach out.

To return to late 1948 and the story of Wittgenstein's and Richards' friendship, it's clear that Wittgenstein's repeated pleas for total honesty and frankness from Richards – and his reassurance that this was truly what he wanted "however sad the truth may be" – were not sufficient to enable it (and perhaps quite the opposite). It would be exactly a year from the incident with the cabin booking, before this dynamic came to a head.

In the summer of 1949, despite not being in the best of health, Wittgenstein finally decided to accept a long-standing invitation from his friend and old student Norman Malcolm, to stay with him and his family for a while in Ithaca, in upstate New York. Interestingly, in the letter to Malcolm in which he confirmed that he had booked his passage to come over in a few months' time, Wittgenstein sounded a note familiar from many of his letters to Richards:

> *Wittgenstein to Malcolm (April 1, 1949)*: "There is one more thing I want to say: In this life one doesn't know what's going to happen; & so, supposing later on you were inclined, <u>for whatever reason</u>, to change your mind about the desirability of my visit, please <u>don't hesitate</u> to tell me so. I'm told that I can have <u>all</u> my money for the ticket refunded (except 10 s, which is nothing)."

It was not only with Richards that Wittgenstein wanted continually to be sure that he was standing on precisely the ground that he hoped to be. The Malcolms replied with due encouragement, and Wittgenstein set sail in late July 1949, with tickets to return to England in late October. From about half way through his stay Wittgenstein's health started to deteriorate – with a severe pain in his shoulder and general weakness. By October, Wittgenstein was very relieved to be heading back to England.[84]

---

84 For an account of Wittgenstein's trip to America, see Malcolm 1984: 66-77, and Pinch & Swedberg: 2013.

A week or so before his departure, however, a crisis erupted between Wittgenstein and Richards – played out by post and telegram – which could easily have spelled the end of their friendship. Around October 9 or 10, Wittgenstein received a letter from Richards that mentioned – by the by, in a postscript – that he was growing a beard. Wittgenstein reacted with surprising – and quite shocking – vehemence:

Wittgenstein to Richards (October 10, 1949): "Your P.S. about letting your beard grow was a <u>shock</u> for me, & it's difficult for me to write about it. The best I can say is this: If one <u>loves</u> someone that person's face becomes a <u>symbol</u> which one can't arbitrarily change without hurting the person who has come to love it. If you had an accident which changed your face this would be different, I could then always see your old face in your mutilated one. Or if you had a skin disease that made it impossible for you to shave, again it wouldn't matter. But to let your beard grow <u>without serious reason</u> is a <u>wanton</u> way of playing about with something which, if you love /somebody/, is not quite yours/own/. – As I said, it's difficult for me to write about this because I feel so strongly about it. This is <u>not</u> an aesthetic matter for me. – You know that I have always looked at your face with delight. When I felt bad, & depressed I looked forward to seeing it, & when I saw it I felt good again. I say again: if your face were mutilated by sickness or accident, it wouldn't matter in the slightest. But your face is something <u>sacred</u> to the person who loves you & if you play about with it you <u>play</u> with something that's sacred to me. – I mean every word of this."

Richards must have been taken aback by this reaction, and affronted, as he responded immediately with a telegram:

Richards to Wittgenstein (October 14, 1949): "Don't come back for me. Writing. Ben."[85]

We do not have a copy of the letter that followed. It seems likely that Wittgenstein destroyed it (along with Richards' initial letter announcing the beard). But we can infer at least some of what Richards must have said from Wittgenstein's various reactions to it.[86] Wittgenstein likely received Richards' letter only just before leaving Ithaca for his return journey, as his reply is posted from the ship itself:

Wittgenstein to Richards (October 20, 1949): "I had your letter to-day. I <u>understand</u> what you say & I <u>believe</u> it. – I don't think there is anything for me to forgive. I think

---

85 The telegram has not survived, but Wittgenstein quotes it in his letter of October 13, 1949.
86 His immediate reaction in his letter to Richards of October 20, 1949, and also his later references to the incident in his letters of November 15/16, 1949 and January 19, 1950.

I understand how you could have been maneuvered by me into a false position. I can't feel the slightest resentment.

I don't think that it is right for us to break with each other, I feel it's wrong, unless you can't any more see me without some bad feelings."

It seems that Wittgenstein's violent reaction to Richards' beard was either the straw that broke the camel's back or the lens which brought into focus what Richards had long been feeling. Or perhaps a combination of both, in that it was so egregious and overbearing an overstep on Wittgenstein's part that it made Richards feel that he simply could not keep silent any longer about the dissonance that he'd been feeling for a while. We can surmise from Wittgenstein's response the general outline of what Richards must have written. Roughly, that he didn't think he was able to inhabit the role that Wittgenstein seemed to continually be pushing onto him, and that he had allowed himself to be maneuvered by Wittgenstein's pressure into a position that did not actually feel natural to him. Perhaps Richards apologized for that fact itself, or perhaps for the fact that he had not said this – or realized it – earlier. He seems not to have concluded that they should therefore break off their friendship entirely. It's possible that he even signed off in the same way as he had in his recent letters: "Love, always".[87] But the spectre of a total break had been raised – if not in the letter, then at least in the shorter and sharper telegram that had preceded it. Wittgenstein's response was that for his own part he certainly did not think that they should "break with each other", and that if Richards felt able to do so without ill feeling, he should come to meet Wittgenstein's boat or train so that they could see each other and talk.

Richards did come to meet him, and a decisive break was averted. They spent time together in London repairing their friendship and setting it on this new footing of greater honesty and realism. At some point during that time together Richards reflected along the lines that he "thought it was right that we had stuck together",[88] and Wittgenstein replied that indeed he "was sure that it had been the only natural thing to do". On later reflection, however, Wittgenstein apologized for this response: "I ought not to have said that, because I can't decide what is really natural for you".[89] This self-correction was directly relevant to the issue at hand: that Wittgenstein stop presuming or imposing a particular shape on Richards' side of their friendship. Thus, though it was difficult for him, it seems as though Wittgenstein really was trying to learn a new way of being – and of letting be – in the friendship.

---

87 See, for example, Richards' letters to Wittgenstein of September 27 and October 9, 1949.
88 Wittgenstein quotes this remark of Richards' in his letter of November 15/16, 1949 (though he notes that those were not Richards' exact words).
89 Ibid.

It clearly took some time for Wittgenstein to fully digest what Richards had told him, because almost three months later Wittgenstein made another reference to Richards' post-telegram letter, which gives us an even clearer sense of what it must have said:

> *Wittgenstein to Richards (January 19, 1950)*: "One thing I now see clearly is how very hard & difficult it must have been for you to write to me that last letter you sent to America, & and how wonderful it was that you had the strength to do it. Thank God. –
>
> Not only had I nothing to forgive you but you have to forgive me all the many occasions on which – without fully realizing it – I ~~have~~ exerted pressure on you & your feelings. I wish that I now could make amends for all this, & I can only say that I will never again want you to see me, or write to me, more often than you feel is good for you; & if you feel that you'd rather not see me, or write to me, that, too, is perfectly all right. (Not that my feeling for you is less strong /now/! On the contrary.) – I'm always in your debt!"

The honesty of Richards' last letter to Wittgenstein in America – and Wittgenstein's apologetic and conciliatory response – rather than spelling the friendship's end, helped to guide it onto a new and better footing. And it even seems that Richards became a little more effusive in his expressions of feeling (at least periodically) after the incident than he had been before it:[90]

> *Richards to Wittgenstein (January 21, 1950)*: "I miss you very much."
> *Richards to Wittgenstein (May 9, 1950)*: "I long to see you again."
> *Richards to Wittgenstein (Feb 25, 1951)*: "I miss you terribly."
> *Richards to Wittgenstein (April 16, 1951)*: "I long to see you again and think of you constantly."

Indeed, even Wittgenstein seemed – at one point – to have noted a change, for he replied to the third of the above expressions by saying: "It felt good to read that you miss me, because that makes us a little more equal".[91]

---

90 Though it is certainly possible to find all these sentiments expressed in Richards' earlier letters, sometimes, too (see, for example, his letters to Wittgenstein of the end of May 1947, and August 5, 1949).

91 Wittgenstein's letter to Richards of February 27, 1951. That said, Wittgenstein often still feared that their friendship was not evenly weighted, and he sometimes could not help but revert to exerting the same kind of pleading and cajoling pressure that he had eschewed in the wake of Richards' last letter to him in America (see, for example, Wittgenstein's letters to Richards of November 15/16, 1949, November 26, 1949, February 24, 1950, and May 6, 1950). This would prove to be an almost impossible dynamic for Wittgenstein to give up entirely, though he seems to have genuinely tried to be more aware of it and to keep it in check.

Another element that may well also have factored into the strength of Richards' expressions of feeling in the final year and a half of their friendship, was Wittgenstein's significantly deteriorating health. Within weeks of his return from America, Wittgenstein was diagnosed with prostate cancer. The cancer had apparently already metastasized, and this was the explanation for Wittgenstein's long-standing anaemia and periodic weakness and pains. He was put on a regimen of hormones to slow the cancer's growth and spread. Wittgenstein had already been feeling rather depressed, but this news made him despondent. He wrote to Richards: "If I could see you, that could give me some strength; for in many years my only happy hours were connected /in some way/ with you" (November 29, 1949).

Despite Wittgenstein's failing health, he and Richards undertook a trip to Norway in October and November of 1950 – to stay in the mountainside cabin which Wittgenstein had had built for himself, just outside of the village of Skjolden, back in 1914. They had planned to go in the summer of 1950, but had to cancel as Richards failed some of his medical exams and had to re-sit them. This was an important trip for Wittgenstein. It was a matter of sharing a significant part of himself with the person he loved. He had similarly taken the two people he'd previously been in romantic relationships with to see or stay in his cabin – Marguerite Respinger in 1931, and Francis Skinner in 1937. Now he would get to show Richards the place where he had done some of his most important philosophical work, and where he had undergone some of his most significant spiritual ferments.[92]

Wittgenstein had a horror of dying in a hospital, so his doctor Edward Bevan – with remarkable generosity – invited him to spend his last weeks or months in his and his wife's home in Cambridge.[93] Wittgenstein moved in with Edward and Joan Bevan in February 1951, and shortly thereafter stopped taking the hormones that he had been taking for the past year and a bit, but which had by this point stopped being of much use. He was preparing to die. Unfortunately, at around the same time Richards started a new job at Derby City Hospital – which meant that he was both farther away and significantly more busy getting to grips with his new position and his greater degree of

---

92 See his diaries from Skjolden for 1936-7, in MS 183. Richards had already seen the cabin once, without Wittgenstein – for when he took a trip to Norway in 1946 and was due to be nearby, Wittgenstein suggested that Richards visit Skjolden too, to see his cabin and meet some of his local friends (see Wittgenstein's letter to Richards of August 3, 1946).
93 See Anscombe 2025: 182, Drury 1984: 169, and Malcolm 1984: 79-80. Regarding Bevan see the 'Short Biographies of Frequently Mentioned Family and Friends'.

patient responsibility. Richards managed to get away, however, for a weekend towards the end of March. Of that trip Wittgenstein wrote: "every moment I was with you was wonderful for me" (March 27, 1951), to which Richards replied: "You can guess what it meant to me to be with you again. … I long for the next time I can see you" (April 2, 1951).

After that, Wittgenstein's health deteriorated quite rapidly, and his letters took on an air of farewell. In his penultimate letter to Richards, Wittgenstein movingly summed up his feelings of gratitude towards his loving friend:

Wittgenstein to Richards (April 11, 1951): "There is one thing I want to tell you. Whatever happens to me now, I want you to know that you have given me more than I could possibly ever have hoped for. You have given me happiness & joy which I never deserved & made my life different altogether from what it would have been without you. Thanks for all you did to me. /You are at the background of all my happiness./ I can't express /completely/ what I want to say, but if I could, I know you wouldn't dislike it. I long to see you again, & I hope that I shall at least once more be with you, see your old face, etc. etc.."

On Saturday April 28, 1951, Wittgenstein was slipping in and out of consciousness. Dr Bevan called Wittgenstein's closest friends to his bedside – Elizabeth Anscombe and Yorick Smythies (from Oxford), Maurice Drury (from Dublin), and of course, Richards (from Derby). None of them managed to arrive before Wittgenstein lost full consciousness that night. But they were all by his bedside the next day – Wittgenstein's last. Anscombe reports that during that day Wittgenstein largely lay with his eyes shut. But at one point he opened his eyes and flung his arms out, then shut his eyes again. Richards and Anscombe each held one of Wittgenstein's hands. If they let go, he reached out for his hand to be held again. Just before Wittgenstein died, Drury arrived from Ireland and took Anscombe's place. But Ben held Ludwig's hand till the end.[94]

In the list of people to whom Wittgenstein left "gifts of specific articles or chattels" in his will, Richards appears first, as follows:

"To Dr. Benedict Richards my French Travelling Clock my Fur Coat my complete Edition of Grimm's Fairy Tales and my book "Hernach" by W. Busch"[95]

---

94 See Anscombe 2025: 185.
95 Wittgenstein's 'Last Will', pp. 1-2 (a copy is held in the Wren Library, Trinity College, Cambridge).

This final will was written on January 29, 1951, just before Wittgenstein moved to the Bevans. Only days earlier Richards had written to Wittgenstein saying: "It was wonderful to be able to see you and read Busch & Grimm again" (January 26, 1951). This, perhaps, was Wittgenstein's way of extending that wonderful experience.

The Content of the Letters

Wittgenstein's and Richards' letters are dominated by mundane matters and everyday news. There is much planning of the date of their next meeting (or trip), and there are continual arrangements to be made for Wittgenstein's accommodation in London or for Richards' in Cambridge, and the like. There are reports of their day-to-day activities – on Richards' side his medical studies, exams, and his first hospital internships, and on Wittgenstein's side his writing and teaching, and later on, his slowly deteriorating health. On both sides there are reports of their fluctuating moods. But beyond the everyday, a number of other themes run consistently through the correspondence too.

Music: The importance of music in Wittgenstein's life can hardly be overestimated. He once said to his friend Maurice Drury: "It is impossible for me to say one word in my book about all that music has meant in my life. How then can I hope to be understood?"[96] In Richards he found a friend with whom he could share the music that was most meaningful to him and enjoy their joint appreciation for it. Thus we hear – in the letters – about the music they are planning to play together at their next meeting (especially Schubert).[97] We're told about the records and concerts they have listened to while apart and the impressions that they made (Bruckner, Brahms, and others).[98] We're told about the choral performances for which Richards was rehearsing and Wittgenstein's opinions about the various performance programmes (Bach's masses and Mozart's Requiem).[99] We hear about the scores and records which Wittgenstein gave Richards as gifts on various occasions (Schumann, Bruckner, Bach, and others).[100] And we even hear about particular pieces – or small parts of pieces – which Wittgenstein especially liked or

---

96 See Drury 1984: 79 & 160.
97 See, for example, Richards' letters to Wittgenstein of June 26 and September 1, 1946.
98 See, for example, Richards' letter to Wittgenstein of December 30, 1946; and Wittgenstein's letter to Richards of September 16, 1947, and September 16, 1948.
99 See Wittgenstein's letters to Richards of February 25, 1948, and of February 1st, 1949.
100 See, for example, Wittgenstein's letters to Richards of, December 31, 1946, January 1, 1948, and March 17, 1951.

found especially notable (such as in Bruckner's 8th symphony, Mozart's Requiem, and Reincke's children's songs).[101]

Books: Their exchanges about reading followed much the same pattern. We find, in the letters, their plans for what they will read together during their next visit (such as Grimm, Tolstoy, and Wilhelm Busch);[102] and we find reports and recommendations of the things they read for themselves while apart (such as Agatha Christie and Desmond Young).[103] No one book or author gets a long analysis, but there are plenty of short but fascinating critical remarks (such as about *Hadji Murad*, *Howards End*, and *Moby Dick*).[104] As far as philosophical reading was concerned, Richards had distinctive tastes, which Wittgenstein appreciated – as Elizabeth Anscombe later recalled:

> "The oddest thing I knew about Ben was that he read *Principia Ethica*[105] through with immense enjoyment, a thing which I am sure was always happening to people fifty years before – but it was surprising in the late nineteen forties. I said this to Wittgenstein and he replied 'Oh, Ben is *extremely* old fashioned.'"[106]

Nature: Descriptions of nature are another dominant theme of the correspondence. Wittgenstein often took pleasure in sharing with Richards the places he was living, by sending him finely observed descriptions of the flora and fauna he would come across on his walks. This was especially the case during his periods in Ireland and in Ithaca.[107] In Dublin he was a regular visitor to the Botanic Gardens in Glasnevin, where the large glasshouses provided a pleasant climate for his work during the winter, and he would send Richards reports of the latest exotic plant or flower he had seen.[108] While living on the west coast of Ireland, in County Galway, he took a particular interest in the local birds – learning to identify them with the help of an illustrated book of birds which

---

101 See, for example, Wittgenstein's letter to Richards of January 8 and 22, 1948, July 1, 1948, and February 1, 1949.
102 See, for example, Wittgenstein's letters to Richards of February 23, 1949, September 6, 1946, and September 12, 1950, and see Richards' letter to Wittgenstein of September 20, 1949 along with Wittgenstein's reply of October 6, 1949.
103 See, for example, Richards' letter to Wittgenstein of September 20, 1949 and Wittgenstein's reply of October 6, 1949, and see Wittgenstein's letter to Richards of March 12-14, 1951.
104 See, for example, Wittgenstein's letters to Richards of May 2, 1948, February 12 and 23, 1949, and February 21, 1951.
105 George Edward Moore, *Principia Ethica*, Cambridge, Cambridge University Press, 1903; it had captivated and profoundly influenced many of the members of the Bloomsbury Group at the turn of the 1900s.
106 Anscombe 2025: 159.
107 See chapters 2 and 3 respectively.
108 See, for example, Wittgenstein's letters to Richards of December 6, 1948, and June 7, 1949.

Richards had sent him, and sending Richards detailed descriptions and diagrams as his identifications proceeded.[109] During his stay with the Malcolms in upstate New York, Wittgenstein marveled at the wholly foreign local trees. Even from his less exotic locales – such as Cambridge – he sent Richards updates on the fate of the flowers in his window-box at Trinity College.[110] And perhaps one of the most striking physical aspects of the correspondence: both Wittgenstein and Richards repeatedly enclosed dried flowers and leaves in their letters to each other – many of which still survive with (or stuck onto) the letters.

Philosophical updates: Though Wittgenstein does not discuss the details of his philosophical work in his letters to Richards, he frequently reports on how well or poorly his work has been progressing, and his feelings about that. By 1945 Wittgenstein had essentially completed work on Part I of the *Philosophical Investigations* (§§1-693). In the ensuing years – the years of this correspondence – he developed his ideas in the manuscript volumes which have been numbered 130-138, and the pocket notebooks which have been numbered 167-177. In these years he traversed many topics and areas, but one particularly important project was his work on the grammar of psychological terms and phenomena such as 'aspect seeing', which made up what was posthumously published at Part II of the *Philosophical Investigations*, of which he produced a fair copy in 1949 (MS 144).[111]

Wittgenstein frequently reported to Richards that his philosophical work was moving painfully slowly or stalling.[112] And when this happened, Wittgenstein often feared that he may be witnessing the final and decisive waning of his philosophical capacities altogether.[113] In that case he felt he must simply carry on until he could do no more, and then he would just need to find a non-philosophical job (perhaps teaching German).[114] Sometimes, however, Wittgenstein was able to report that he was making good progress (or at least good progress under the circumstances).[115] But even when his work was going well his progress was never fast, for – as he described it to Richards – his

---

109 See, for example, Wittgenstein's letters to Richards of June 16 and 18, 1948, and July 1, 1948.
110 See Wittgenstein's letter to Richards on March 17, 1947.
111 This has more recently been published not as 'Part II' of the *Philosophical Investigations*, but instead as the more self-standing 'Philosophy of Psychology – A Fragment' (Wittgenstein 2009: 182-243).
112 See, for example, Wittgenstein's letter to Richards of January 25, 1949, and April 22-24, 1950.
113 See, for example, Wittgenstein's letter to Richards of October 6, 1946.
114 See, for example, Wittgenstein's letter to Richards of June 1, 1948.
115 See, for example, Wittgenstein's letters to Richards of December 1, 1948, and April 11, 1951.

forward movement was helical, such that he had to traverse many full circles to inch even a little way forward.[116]

Wittgenstein also periodically described his teaching – both in his formal lectures and at his 'at homes' (informal philosophical discussions he held with students on Saturdays).[117] And perhaps even more revealingly, he describes – in some detail – a number of significant philosophical meetings. These included the occasion when Wittgenstein spoke at Oxford's Jowett Society,[118] the occasion when Elizabeth Anscombe and C.S. Lewis engaged in a (now legendary) debate at Oxford's Socratic Club (and in this case Wittgenstein enclosed for Richards a letter that Anscombe had sent to him describing the occasion in detail),[119] and the occasion when J.L. Austin spoke at the Cambridge Moral Science Club.[120] Wittgenstein's accounts of the Moral Science Club meetings in general are almost uniformly negative: the talks were superficial and the discussions didn't get anywhere. He took the problem not to lie in the club narrowly, but more deeply in the misguided approach of the other Cambridge faculty members – and perhaps even in the very project of trying to do philosophy in a university context.[121] All this contributed to his eventual resignation of his chair towards the end of 1947.

Critique and advice: Another recurring theme of the correspondence – as with all of Wittgenstein's correspondences with those to whom he was close – is that of moral reproach and exhortation[122] (or what Wittgenstein sometimes – self-deprecatingly – called his 'preaching').[123] This happens very frequently in the context of Wittgenstein's repeated entreaties that if Richards' feelings for him are no longer as strong as they once were then he should tell Wittgenstein truthfully, whereas if Richards' feelings are still strong and serious then he should write more frequently and make time for more visits. In these contexts Wittgenstein has much to say about what true friendship means and

---

116 See Wittgenstein's letters to Richards of March 12, 1948 (he had used the same image to describe his movement of thought much earlier too – back in 1931, in MS 110, p. 82).
117 See, for example, Wittgenstein's letters to Richards of October 18, and November 19, 1946.
118 See Wittgenstein's letter to Richards of May 17, 1947.
119 See Wittgenstein's letters to Richards of January 31, and February 11, 1948 (and the letter from Anscombe enclosed in the latter).
120 See Wittgenstein's letter to Richards of November 1, 1946. While this club is usually called the 'Moral Sciences Club' today (with 'sciences' in the plural), at the time of this correspondence it was more often called the 'Moral Science Club' (with 'science' in the singular).
121 See, for example, Wittgenstein's letters to Richards of November 1 and 10, 1946, and May 2, 1947.
122 See Wittgenstein's letter to Richards of February 24, 1950.
123 See, for example, Wittgenstein's letter to Richards of July 30, 1950 (and compare also – for example – his letters to Norman Malcolm of November 16, 1944, and to Rush Rhees of April 30, 1947).

what responsibilities it brings with it.[124] But it also happens more broadly – for example, when Wittgenstein notices what he takes to be a certain stinginess on Richards' part,[125] or a certain carelessness in the opinions Richards expresses.[126] For the most part, Richards is very gracious in his openness to Wittgenstein's moral interventions (and even takes himself to have grown as a result of them).[127] But it's significant that Richards also feels free to push back against Wittgenstein's critiques when he feels them to have been misplaced or unjust,[128] and even gives Wittgenstein some moral critique of his own when he feels it appropriate.[129]

Sometimes Wittgenstein simply gives Richards advice (rather than moral critique). Significantly, in his advice-giving Wittgenstein returns multiple times to the 'old saying' about piety (in the face of good fortune) and courage (in the face of bad) that serves as the motto for the first edition of Schumann's *Davidsbündlertänze* – a motto which, at one point, Wittgenstein even copied out for Richards on a separate piece of paper.[130] But his advice is far more wide-ranging than this – and indeed, Wittgenstein's advice regarding Richards' attitude to his hospital work is the main theme of their very last exchange. In Richards' final letter to Wittgenstein he complains that he sometimes lacks enthusiasm for his work, and worries about what this means for his vocation.[131] Wittgenstein's final letter to Richards – written just a few days before he died – becomes an exercise in encouragement, reassurance, and the passing on of an insight about how even those times that he finds himself without motivation or enthusiasm can be deeply meaningful regardless.[132]

Humour: One of the things which drew Wittgenstein and Richards together was their shared sense of humour. As Elizabeth Anscombe later recalled:

> "[Wittgenstein] liked the riddle: What is the difference between a hairdresser and a sculptor? – the first curls up and dyes, and the second makes faces and busts. The

---

124 See, for example, Wittgenstein's letters to Richards of June 31, 1946, February 4, 1947, January 19, 1949, and February 24, 1950.
125 See, for example, Wittgenstein's letter to Richards of July 8, 1947.
126 See, for example, Wittgenstein's letter to Richards of August 21, 1946.
127 See, for example, Richards' letters to Wittgenstein of October 23, 1946, and the end of May 1947.
128 See, for example, Richards' letter to Wittgenstein of mid-July 1947.
129 See, for example, the reference in Wittgenstein's letter to Richards of October 22, 1947.
130 See Wittgenstein's letters to Richards of December 28, 1946, January 19, 1950, and February 13, 1951.
131 Richards' letter to Wittgenstein of April 23, 1951.
132 Wittgenstein's letter to Richards of April 25, 1951.

collapse of meaning, I mean the revolution in the transition from noun to verb. He got that from Ben Richards, on whose affection, with that of Con Drury, he so much relied in the last years of his life. Ben was mostly rather silent but he enjoyed many of the same sorts of things as Wittgenstein and particularly the same sorts of jokes. ...

I remember Ben Richards, in commenting on Norman Malcolm's memoir,[133] of which I said that it made too grim and cramped an impression, said 'Yes, you couldn't imagine that character speechless with laughter.'"[134]

With Richards, Wittgenstein would – apparently – sometimes be taken over with uproarious laughter. Throughout these letters we get a sampling of the kinds of things that they found funny. Wittgenstein's humour came in a few varieties. He enjoyed indulging in the ridiculous or the absurd (for example, when he wrote 'P.T.O.' on both sides of the paper in one of his letters so as to generate an infinite loop,[135] or when he pasted onto his letter a small picture cut from one of his pulp detective magazines and then wrote as though it was an original Dürer engraving).[136] Perhaps his series of letters written under the name of his supposed lawyer and representative – John Smith, K.C. – fall into this class too.[137] He also liked to spoof the pomposities and the unwitting absurdities of others (such as in his ironic use of unnecessarily fancy or archaic words like 'perpend',[138] or the occasion on which he drew stick-figures of himself in various poses into the scenes on the front of his postcard to mock a photo-shoot for which the public intellectual C.E.M. Joad had sat).[139] Related to this are the occasions on which Wittgenstein and Richards shared with each other examples of unwittingly absurd things written or said in all seriousness by others – sometimes by means of quotes, but usually by enclosing a cutting from a newspaper or magazine.[140] Most often, though,

---

133 Norman Malcolm's memoir of Wittgenstein – *Ludwig Wittgenstein: A Memoir* – was first published by Oxford University Press in 1958 (referred to in this volume as: Malcolm 1984).
134 Anscombe 2025: 158–9 & 162.
135 See Wittgenstein's letter to Richards of February 4, 1947.
136 See Wittgenstein's letters to Richards of July 8 and 17, 1948.
137 See the 'John Smith' letters gathered in chapter VII, and also the one of (probably) late September 1946 (in chapter I).
138 See, for example, Wittgenstein's letter to Richards of probably December 9, 1946.
139 See Wittgenstein's postcard to Richards of April 19, 1948.
140 See, for example, Wittgenstein's letters to Richards of January 25, 1949, and 12th-14th March 1951, and Richards' letter to Wittgenstein of the end of May 1947. Indeed, many of Wittgenstein's close friends and family knew that he delighted in such cuttings, and they would send him choice examples, the best of which he kept in his so-called 'Nonsense Collection'.

Wittgenstein's sense of humour was essentially that of groan-worthy 'dad jokes' (such as saying that he had better not enclose a hail-stone from the storm outside lest it shatter in the post, warning Richards against doing wheelies in his car, observing that the water in his jugs that morning had been damp, and the like).[141]

Another example of a jocular – though also prescient – remark comes in a letter of Wittgenstein's from the end of 1946:

> *Wittgenstein to Richards (November 28, 1946):* "A slight difficulty has arisen about our correspondence. I saw a publisher the other day who said he'ld print all our letters when we're dead. But, he said, reproducing your pictures would make the book too expensive for the common reader. He said you should limit yourself entirely to straight lines in the future, as this would come cheaper. –"

This remark was prompted by the fact that Richards would often decorate his letters with small drawings and cartoons. As much as the idea of the publication of their correspondence was a joke, it was clearly a joke that was playing on his mind around this time. Just a few days earlier he had written to his friend Roy Fouracre:

> *Wittgenstein to Fouracre (November 22, 1946):* "You say you haven't heard from me again for some time, but I'm writing pretty regularly. It's the Censor who keeps my letters; & I don't blame him either, because they're so full of wit & wisdom. It must be difficult for him to read one of them & then let it go again. I'm sure he collects them & one day they'll all be published."[142]

But for all that the letters touch on these many and important themes, even the most cursory reading makes clear that pervading the whole correspondence is Wittgenstein's love for Richards and his need for him, which he declared and expressed over and over. Whatever else Wittgenstein's letters are, they are *love* letters. And as such they are among the most heartfelt, revealing, and vulnerable writings of Wittgenstein's that we have.

---

141 See, for example, Wittgenstein's letters to Richards of November 26, 1947, February 1, 1949, and June 1, 1949. And for an example of Richards indulging in just this kind of humour too, see Richards' addition at the end of their joint postcard to Angela Richards of May 19, 1948.

142 In these years, more generally, we see Wittgenstein coming to terms with the prospect of his – at this point, seemingly inevitable – posthumous fame. Compare his – again, jocular but knowing – remark to Norman Malcolm from the previous year, upon giving him a book as a gift: "If you don't like the book throw it away. Only first cut out the leaf with my dedication. For when I shall become very famous it'll become very valuable as an autograph, & your grandchildren may be able to sell it for a lot of "dough" " (Wittgenstein to Malcolm, October 6, 1945).

Short Biographies of Frequently Mentioned Family and Friends

Anscombe, Gertrude Elizabeth Margaret (1919-2001): Known by her middle name, 'Elizabeth', and usually referred to by Wittgenstein as 'Miss A.'. A student and then close friend of Wittgenstein's. From 1942, as a graduate student at Cambridge, Anscombe regularly attended Wittgenstein's lectures. In 1946 she received a research fellowship at Somerville College in Oxford, and in 1970 she was appointed Chair of Philosophy at Cambridge. Together with Rush Rhees and Georg Henrik von Wright, Anscombe was one of the three literary trustees appointed by Wittgenstein in his will in 1951, and she was co-editor of many of his posthumously published works. Wittgenstein lived in her house in Oxford, 27 St. John Street, from April 1950 to February 1951.

Bevan, Edward (1907–1988): A friend of two of Wittgenstein's close friends, Maurice O'Connor Drury and Georg Henrik von Wright – through these connections, Bevan became Wittgenstein's primary doctor in Cambridge for the last year and a half of Wittgenstein's life. Bevan had been an Olympic rower, and had a joint medical practice in Cambridge for many years with the Olympic shot putter, Rex Woods. He had many Cambridge dons as patients. Wittgenstein spent the last months of his life in the home of Edward and his wife Joan Bevan, at 76 Storey's Way, Cambridge. Wittgenstein thought very highly of Dr. Bevan, and recommended that Ben Richards also take his advice.

Con: The nickname of Maurice O'Connor Drury (see his entry below).

Drury, Maurice O'Connor (1907-1976): Usually called 'Con'. A student and then close friend of Wittgenstein's. Drury studied philosophy in Cambridge, where he met Wittgenstein in 1929. He gave up his original intention of becoming an Anglican priest under Wittgenstein's influence and began studying medicine in 1933, which Wittgenstein partly financed. Wittgenstein followed the progress of Drury's medical career with great interest. Drury completed his medical studies in 1939 and then completed specialist training in psychiatry. From 1947 Drury worked as a psychiatrist at St. Patrick's Hospital in Dublin, and from 1969 as head physician of the psychiatric department. Drury's presence in Dublin was one of the draws that Wittgenstein felt to the city, and one of the reasons he spent time there in 1947 and 1948.

Heshe: The family nickname of Julia Richards (see her entry below).

Jinny: The family nickname of Virginia Richards (see her entry below).

Malcolm, Norman (1911-1990): A student and then close friend of Wittgenstein's. Malcolm had arrived in Cambridge in 1938 chiefly to study with G.E. Moore, but also attended Wittgenstein's lectures and soon became close with him. He received his doctorate from Harvard in 1940. He taught briefly at Princeton, joined the U.S. Navy for the Second World War, then returned to Cambridge to attend Wittgenstein's lectures in 1946-47. After that he taught at Cornell University from 1947 until his retirement in 1978. Wittgenstein spent three months living with Malcolm and his wife Leonida ('Lee') in their home in Ithaca (NY) in the summer and autumn of 1949.

Moore, George Edward (1873-1958): An important English philosopher, and one of the founders of analytic philosophy. He taught philosophy at Cambridge from 1898, and was Professor of Philosophy there from 1925 to 1939 (after which, Wittgenstein succeeded him in this prestigious chair). Moore and Wittgenstein got to know one another in 1912, when Wittgenstein began to attend Moore's lectures as a student. And when Wittgenstein returned to Cambridge as a faculty member in 1929, Moore attended his lectures in turn. They became close, and when Wittgenstein was in Cambridge they would meet regularly for philosophical discussion.

Rhees, Jean (1903-1981, née Henderson): The wife of Wittgenstein's old student and friend, Rush Rhees (though for many years she lived in London while he lived in Swansea). Jean Rhees worked as a Jungian analyst in London, was active as a member of the Society of Analytical Psychology, and played a role in founding Child Analytic Training in the United Kingdom. She had grown up in Italy, studied English literature as an undergraduate, knew multiple languages, was highly musical, and had an interest in art. During many of Wittgenstein's short stays in London in the 1940's, Jean Rhees would put him up in her flat at 104 Goldhurst Terrace, NW6.

Rhees, Rush (1905-1989): A student and then close friend of Wittgenstein's. Rush Rhees first studied philosophy at Edinburgh, Manchester, and Innsbruck, before attending Cambridge as a graduate student in 1933 to study under G.E. Moore. Rhees started attending Wittgenstein's lectures in 1933, but it wasn't until 1936 that he became close with Wittgenstein, and indeed became one of his favourite conversation partners. From 1940 to 1966, Rhees taught at the University of Swansea, and between 1942 and 1947 Wittgenstein regularly visited him in Swansea during the holidays. Together with Elizabeth Anscombe and Georg Henrik von Wright, Rhees was one of the three literary trustees appointed by Wittgenstein in his will in 1951, and he was co-editor of many of Wittgenstein's posthumous works.

Richards, Angela (1928 –): The eldest of Ben Richards' four younger sisters. She studied at Oxford as an undergraduate, so Wittgenstein met up with her periodically when he lived in Oxford from April 1950 until February 1951. A number of letters and cards from Wittgenstein to Angela Richards have survived, and are included in this volume.

Richards, Isabella (1931 –): The second youngest of Ben Richards' four younger sisters, and often called 'Tazza' by the family.

Richards, Virginia (1929 –): The second oldest of Ben Richards' four younger sisters, and often called 'Jinny' by the family.

Richards, Julia (1940 –): The youngest of Ben Richards' four younger sisters, and often called 'Heshe' by the family.

Salzer, Helene (1879–1956, née Wittgenstein): The middle of Ludwig Wittgenstein's three older sisters. She was married to Max Salzer, and lived in Vienna.

Smythies, Yorick (1917–1980): A student and then close friend of Wittgenstein's. Smythies came to Cambridge in 1935 and continued to attend Wittgenstein's lectures long after he graduated (taking copious notes). He worked in Oxford, first as a researcher at Nuffield College and then as a librarian at the Cambridge Philosophical Society, at the Department of Forestry, and later at the Department of Social Studies. During the period of this correspondence, Smythies was married to Diana ('Polly') Pollard. They lived at 22 Banbury Road, Oxford, and Wittgenstein stayed with them there on a few occasions for short periods.

Stonborough-Wittgenstein, Margaret (1882-1958, née Wittgenstein): The youngest of Ludwig Wittgenstein's three older sisters. She was married to Jerome Stonborough, and lived between Vienna, Berlin, New York, Switzerland, and England. Ludwig Wittgenstein designed and built the Wittgenstein House for her on the Kundmanngasse in Vienna's 3rd district in the 1920s.

Tazza: The family nickname of Isabella Richards (see her entry above).

Wittgenstein, Hermine (1874-1950): The eldest of Ludwig Wittgenstein's three older sisters. She lived in Vienna.

Wright, Georg Henrik von (1916-2003): A student and then close friend of Wittgenstein's. Von Wright studied philosophy in Helsinki, and from 1939 also in Cambridge under G.E. Moore and Wittgenstein. He and Wittgenstein became close, and when in the same city would hold wide-ranging discussions. Wittgenstein greatly respected von Wright's philosophical acumen, and in 1948 – after Wittgenstein resigned his chair – von Wright was appointed to succeed him as Professor of Philosophy at Cambridge (for which Wittgenstein had written him a letter of recommendation). Wittgenstein spent several months living with von Wright and his wife Maria Elisabeth in their home in Cambridge from November 1949 to April 1950. Together with Elizabeth Anscombe and Rush Rhees, von Wright was one of the three literary trustees appointed by Wittgenstein in his will in 1951, and he was co-editor of many of Wittgenstein's posthumous works.

List of Wittgenstein's Frequently Used Abbreviations

Wittgenstein often used abbreviations for his most common endearments to Richards, combining them in multiple permutations. Here is a list of the abbreviations he used most frequently.[1]

a. a.	as always
b. o.	bloody old
b. o. f.	bloody old face
bl....	bloody
d. h.	dear heart
d. o. h.	dear old heart
G. b. y. (G. bl. y.)	God bless you
G. b. y. a. (G. bl. y. a.)	God bless you always
L.	Ludwig
l. L.	love Ludwig
l. a.	love always
l. a. L.	love always Ludwig
l. y. a.	love you always
m. d. h.	my dear heart

---

1 Though Wittgenstein usually used abbreviations for these repeated phrases, he did sometimes write them out in full. These unabbreviated phrases give us the key to interpreting the more idiosyncratic of his abbreviations when they are used in similar contexts to the fully spelled-out counterparts. For a sample of occasions on which he wrote these phrases unabbreviated, see: Wittgenstein's letter to Richards of June 23, 1946 ("God bless you", and "With love – always, Ludwig"); Wittgenstein's letter to Richards of August 15, 1946 ("As always, with love Ludwig"); Wittgenstein's letter to Richards of October 6, 1946 ("dear old heart", and "God bless you, always"); Wittgenstein's letter to Richards of June 24, 1948 ("I think of you constantly with love"); and Wittgenstein's first undatable 'John Smith' note to Richards ("your bloody old face"); as well as multiple others. Richards periodically used similar abbreviations as well (see, for example, his letter to Wittgenstein of September 13, 1949), but much less frequently.

o. h.	old heart
P. T. O.	Please turn over
t. o. y. (th. o. y.)	think of you
t. o. y. c.	think of you constantly
w. l.	with love
w. l. a.	with love always

I. In Cambridge and Swansea

(June 1946 – July 1947)

After his return from Newcastle, where he had been doing war work as part of a medical research team, Wittgenstein began to teach regularly again at Cambridge from Michaelmas Term (i.e. October) 1944. A year later – in October 1945 – he met the 21-year-old Ben Richards, a student at King's College, who was attending Wittgenstein's lectures on the philosophy of psychology. Wittgenstein soon fell deeply in love with Richards, which profoundly unsettled him (as can be seen from the entries in his manuscript notebooks from July 1946 onwards). Over the ensuing months a loving friendship developed between them, which lasted until the end of Wittgenstein's life (see the Introduction).

The preserved correspondence begins in June 1946. At this time Wittgenstein was living in Cambridge while Richards was completing his practical medical training at 'Bart's' (St. Bartholomew's Hospital) in London. Every few weekends one of them would visit the other, and they would write letters between visits. Wittgenstein spent the summer of 1946 in Swansea, as usual (seeing a lot of his friend and old student, Rush Rhees, who lived there). In July 1946 Wittgenstein and Richards visited Maurice O'Connor Drury – another friend and old student of Wittgenstein's – for a few days in Exeter. Shortly thereafter Richards went on a climbing holiday to Turtagrø, Jotunheimen, one of Norway's most popular mountain regions not far from Skjolden, where Wittgenstein had a small mountainside cabin, and where he had lived for varying lengths of time in 1913/14, 1921, 1931 and 1936/37.[1] In advance of Richards' trip, Wittgenstein wrote to his friend Anna Rebni, in Skjolden, asking her to welcome Richards when he arrived: "Please be nice & kind to him, & think you're doing it for me".[2] Many years later Richards recalled his trip to Norway in the summer of 1946, as follows:

---

1 See Johannessen, Larsen, & Åmås (1994) and Vatne (2016).
2 Wittgenstein to Rebni, July 18, 1946; a facsimile of this letter is printed in Vatne 2016: 81.

"I had been… in Norway, with the Climbers Club in July-August 1946 to climb in the Horungtinder, staying in Turtagrø which is reached via Skjolden. Wittgenstein had given me Frøken Raebni's address among others and one day I came down from Turtagrø to visit her. /Someone on the bus pointed out the hut and told me it had been built by "an eccentric Englishman"./ She told me then how during the wartime occupation with Germans stationed in Skjolden less than a mile away, she used to take in British airmen and others on their way across the mountains to the coast to escape to Britain."[3]

At the end of September 1946 – shortly before the new academic year began – Richards and Wittgenstein spent a two-week holiday together in Swansea. The Easter Term of 1947 was the last in which Wittgenstein taught at Cambridge. His lecturing had increasingly become a burden to him and he felt that he needed time and solitude to work on his book. He also found the academic atmosphere in Cambridge to be stultifying (as he wrote to Richards in October 1946: "The worst thing about this place is the cold, inhuman atmosphere which makes me feel lonely & as though I were condemned to live with wax-works"). Wittgenstein therefore escaped to Swansea as often as possible, and spent the Christmas holidays of 1946/47 there. During his stays in Swansea he at first lodged with a Reverend Wynford Morgan and his wife, and later – from April 1947 – with their neighbors, the Clement family (on Cwmdonkin Terrace, Uplands).

During this period Wittgenstein was working intensively – especially during his stays in Wales – producing what are now known as manuscripts 130 to 134.

---

3 Richards' letter to von Wright of August 15, 1990 (Von Wright Archives of the National Library of Finland in Helsinki, call mark: COLL. 714.202).

Ludwig Wittgenstein to Ben Richards, Birthday Card (around June 23, 1946)[4]

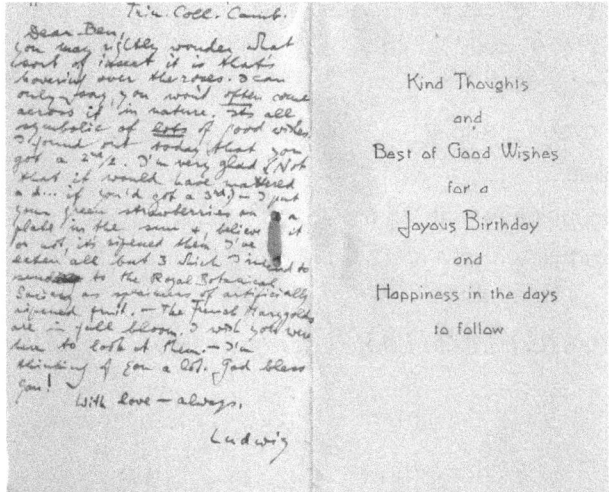

Trin. Coll. Camb.

Dear Ben,

You may rightly wonder what sort of insect it is that's hovering over the roses. I can only say, you won't <u>often</u> come across it in nature. It's all symbolic of <u>lots</u> of good wishes. I found out to-day that you got an 2nd/2.[5] I'm very glad. (Not a d…[6] if you'd got a 3rd.) – I put your green strawberries on a plate in the sun &, believe it or not, it's ripened them. I've eaten all but 3 which I intend to sending to the Royal Botanical Society as specimens of artificially ripened fruit. – The French Marigolds are in full bloom. I wish you were here to look at them. – I'm thinking of you a lot. God bless you!

    With love – always,

        Ludwig

---

4   Wittgenstein did not date this card, and Richards did not add a date either (though he usually did when Wittgenstein hadn't). The date can be inferred, however, from the fact that Richards' birthday was on June 23; and the year can be inferred from the reference to Richards' exam result coupled with the fact that the only result of this sort which Richards received after he had got to know Wittgenstein was in 1946 (see the relevant footnote below).

5   In the Easter Term of 1946 – the end of Richards' year of study of Moral Sciences, for Part II of the tripos – Richards took an exam in 'Section C: Psychology', and received a lower second class pass (i.e. a 2nd/2). The range of degree classes at Cambridge begin with 'first class' at the top, then 'upper second class', then 'lower second class', then 'third class' (the latter being the lowest passing grade). As a member of the Moral Science faculty, it's possible that Wittgenstein could have come to know of Richards' result independently of Richards.

6   Stands for: 'damn'.

Kind Thoughts
and
Best of Good Wishes
for a
Joyous Birthday
and
Happiness in the days
to follow[7]

Ben Richards to Ludwig Wittgenstein, June 26, 1946

Robertson Lamb Hut
Great Langdale
Nr. Ambleside
26.6.46

Dear Ludwig,

Thank you very much for sending the book. I shall bring it to Exeter & we can read it together. I'll borrow the Schubert songs too.[8] Please would you let me know when would be the best time for me to come. I had better be at home for a few days before the 20th of July to prepare for the journey.[9] I'll be back at home by the end of next week.

It drizzled & poured this morning & is now fine. It looks as if I shall have a good time here, but I wish you were here to share it.

I am looking forward very much to meeting Drury.[10]

With love
always
Ben

---

7 Wittgenstein seemed to enjoy kitschy greetings cards, with especially sentimental messages (compare Norman Malcolm: "Wittgenstein always bought extremely florid Xmas and Easter cards: they had to be 'soupy' " (Malcolm 1984: 101, fn. 2).

8 See Wittgenstein's letter to Richards of July 20, 1946.

9 Richards was due to travel to Norway for a climbing holiday on July 20 (see his letter to Wittgenstein of July 24, 1946).

10 Maurice O'Connor Drury; see the 'Short Biographies of Frequently Mentioned Family and Friends'.

Ludwig Wittgenstein to Ben Richards, June 28, 1946

As from: c/o Rev. Morgan[11]
2 Cwmdonkin Terrace
Swansea
28.6.[12]

Dear Ben,

Please write to me, don't delay it any longer. Please think of the feelings & thoughts I'm liable to have if I don't hear from you; don't give me a bad time; & may you have a good & happy time yourself!

    With love, always

        Ludwig

Ludwig Wittgenstein to Ben Richards, July 1, 1946

c/o Rev. Morgan
2 Cwmdonkin Terrace
Swansea
1.7.46.

My dear Ben,

I was glad to hear from you. I'm thinking of you a <u>lot</u>. – Why do you ask "What would be the best time" for you to come? We arranged in Cambridge that you'd come to Exeter on July 12th & stay 6 days, till the 18th. Drury has taken rooms for us in a hotel (the 'Royal Clarendon'). Please, don't change these plans, if you can <u>possibly</u> help it! – Do your very best! Drury is coming to Swansea on July 8th, & he & I will leave here early on the 12th & be in Exeter in the afternoon. So, if you get to Exeter in the evening I'll be at the station. I'll write you the exact times of trains later.

The weather here has been abominable, so far – fog, rain & cold. I <u>hope</u> it's better where you are! & also that it'll be better in Exeter. (Though we'll be all right in bad weather, too). My dear, please let there be no hitch & no disappointment.

    God bless you! Let me hear from you.

    With love, always

        Ludwig

---

11 Wittgenstein was lodging in the home of Reverend Wynford Morgan, a Methodist minister, and his wife – as he had often done in the last years. During a stay back in 1944 Wittgenstein had written to Rowland Hutt: "I'm not staying with Rhees, but a very kindly, good-natured parson has put me up, & it's very peaceful here" (Wittgenstein to Hutt, December 28, 1944).

12 The year is taken from the postmark: June 30, 1946

Enclosure included with the letter of July 1, 1946:

[Along the top of the postcard, with an arrow pointing to the picture of the Swansea Civic Centre in the top left of the card, Wittgenstein has written:] "This abomination is the joy & pride of Swansea."

Ludwig Wittgenstein to Ben Richards, Postcard, July 2, 1946

[Written on the backside:]

c/o Rev. Morgan
2 Cwmdonkin Terrace
Swansea
2.7.46

Dear Ben, This is just a postscript to the letter I sent you yesterday. First I want to say, that, if it is <u>absolutely</u> necessary for you to change our plans, rather come a day earlier to Exeter than cut short your visit. But, if <u>at all possible</u>, don't alter our arrangements. Only let me know about it as soon as possible.
Secondly, the weather has cleared up a bit. It's muggy now, but one can go out & that's damn good. – Thirdly I hope that you're having a good time.
Fourthly, I'm looking forward a lot to seeing you. Fifthly, I thought that you might like to see a little more of our Civic Centre. – Look after yourself, be careful, & be good!

God bless you.

    With love

        Ludwig

Ludwig Wittgenstein to Ben Richards, July 8, 1946[13]

        c/o. Rev. Morgan, 2 Cwmdonkin Terr.

        Swansea

        Monday

My dear Ben, This is my new note-paper. I've had /it/ made specially for our correspondence. – Drury & I are arriving in Exeter on Friday afternoon.[14] Please take the train which leaves Waterloo at 2.50p.m. & gets into Exeter at 6.43p.m. I shall meet that train. <u>There is a diner in that train.</u> I'm looking forward <u>a lot</u> to seeing you! God bless you! With love

Name   Ludwig[15]

Address   exactly nowhere

City   of wrath

State   pretty lousy

P.S. Our hotel at Exeter is not 'Royal Clarendon' as I wrote, but 'Royal Clarence'.

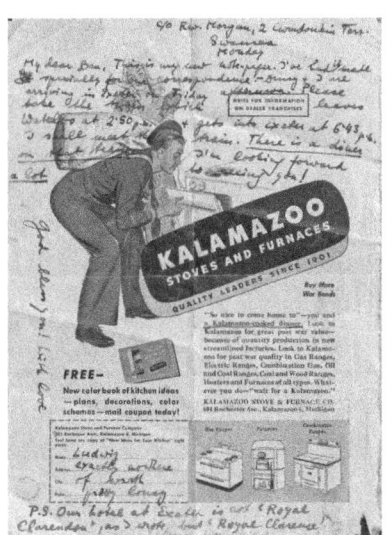

---

13 The date is taken from the postmark – July 8, 1946 – which was a Monday that year, and therefore presumably the day the letter was written. Wittgenstein used a torn sheet from a magazine for this letter.

14 Friday, July 12, 1946; Wittgenstein, Richards, and Drury remained in Exeter until July 18, 1946.

15 The magazine page on which Wittgenstein wrote this letter has an 'order form' on the bottom left corner. The 'Name', 'Address', etc, categories that Wittgenstein is facetiously completing are from that form.

Ludwig Wittgenstein to Ben Richards (postmarked: July 20, 1946)

c/o Morgan

2 Cwmdonkin Terrace, Swansea

Saturday

My dear Ben, O.H.,

I got the enclosed letter yesterday; too late to reach you at Uxbridge. I also enclose a card I obtained from "Isis" "The eye that sees all" for a penny. Study it carefully, please. I should have liked to enclose some grass seed, for you to throw it at yourself in my name, but there isn't any about where I'm writing. I left /Exeter/ yesterday afternoon. I was with Drury on Thursday afternoon & yesterday until I left. I always hummed[16] myself that song we did last but one, "Der Kreuzzug".[17] I enjoyed doing that with you almost more than /I did/ the others. I don't know why /though I enjoyed them all/. – The chocolate you gave me is lovely; only I'm liable to eat too much of it. – I had to go out for a moment just now & found some grass seed; but it's not the right kind. So take it as a symbol.

I am thinking of you a lot; with a lot of deep & good wishes, &

God bless you!

W. l., always,

Ludwig

First enclosure included with the letter of July 20, 1946:

> THE MIRROR SEES—you are impetuous, do not jump at decisions and do not lightly reject sound friendly advice.
>
> You are capable, able to get things done and with more stability should go far. Lovable disposition and well liked by your friends.
>
> Study this personal reading in conjunction with the "characteristics" of your birth month overleaf.
>
> ISIS.

---

16 A small piece of the bottom left corner of this page is torn off here, and it looks like a single word has been torn off with it. If so, that word would have appeared here, between 'hummed' and 'myself. It's not clear whether this happened by mistake after Wittgenstein wrote the letter, or whether Wittgenstein tore it off himself to delete the word in question.

17 The song *Der Kreuzzug* [The Crusade] (D. 932) by Franz Schubert was written in November 1832, using a text by Karl Gottfried von Leitner.

Second enclosure included with the letter of July 20, 1946:[18]

Ben Richards to Ludwig Wittgenstein, July 24, 1946

Hotel Turtagrö[19]
Norway
24/7/46

Dear Ludwig

I reached here at 1.0 this morning in the bus from Leikanger & to-day, which has been very wet, we had a short walk to the foot of the Skagastöls Glacier & back. We had a very smooth crossing of the North Sea & went ashore at Stavanger for an hour or two on Sunday evening. Our ship – the m/v "Astrea" called next at Hangesund, & reached Bergen at about 8.30 on Monday morning where we wandered about & shopped a bit – some went up the hills, on foot or by the railway – until 10.30 P.M. when the fjord steamer – the "Fanaraaken" – sailed. I woke up when we reached Vadheim off the Sognefjord. We continued all day up the Sogn, stopping at about half a dozen places & arrived at Leikanger at 7.0. It was midnight when we passed your house, & although it was still dusk I could not really see it. There was a shadow in about the right position, across the lake, which could have been either a house or a rock. It was too late to deliver your letters, but in a few days I shall take an off-day & go down to Skjolden in the bus.

---

18 Wittgenstein has underlined April and June – his birth month and Richards' respectively.
19 This was where Richards stayed on the climbing holiday which he took in Norway, near Skjolden, where Wittgenstein had lived periodically and had a cabin; see the introduction to this chapter.

It has been misty & rather wet but I was very impressed by some of the scenery in the fjord. I hope it will be clearer on the return journey – we go by bus to Hermansvaeste & take the steamer to Flaam.

I hope you are well.

I very much enjoyed that week in Exeter and I am very glad you introduced me to Drury.

    With love, always

        Ben

Ludwig Wittgenstein to Ben Richards, July 28, 1946[20]

        c/o Rev. Morgan

        2 Cwmdonkin Terrace

        Swansea

        28.7.46

My dear Ben,

I've been for a lot of very lovely walks lately, many of them quite new to me. I'm doing a moderate amount of work[21] & I hope I'll be doing more & more as time goes on. I sometimes think that perhaps I'll publish soon after all.[22] It's good to be away from Cambridge & to be here, & among friendly people.[23] The weather is very changeable; rain almost every day, but part of the day fine. – I think of you a <u>great</u> deal. <u>God bless you, always</u>!

    With love

        Ludwig

I hope you have good weather! L. L.

---

20 Wittgenstein dated this letter July 28, but it was postmarked July 29.

21 At this time Wittgenstein was working in MS 130. This is the manuscript notebook that contains the first of his remarks on Richards, which begin on July 22, 1946 (p. 186).

22 At this time, Wittgenstein was apparently thinking of publishing as a stand-alone book what later became known as 'Part I' of *Philosophical Investigations*. He did not manage to publish any of his later philosophy himself, in the end.

23 Wittgenstein had expressed a similar attitude the previous year, a letter to Norman Malcom: "I'm in Swansea again over Christmas & probably over New Year. The weather's foul. but I enjoy not being in Cambridge. I know quite a number of people here whom I like. I seem to find it more easy to get along with them here than in England. I feel much more often like smiling, e.g. when I walk in the street, or when I see children, etc." (Wittgenstein to Malcolm, December 15th, 1945)

Ludwig Wittgenstein to Ben Richards, August 3, 1946

c/o. Rev. Morgan

2 Cwmdonkin Terrace

Swansea 3.8.46.

My dear Ben,

This is only, or almost only, to say that I had your letter at the beginning of the week. It was good to hear from you. I hope you're having <u>some</u> sunshine! We have a little, occasionally, but mostly rain, & it's pretty cold. I imagine you've been to Skjolden by now & have seen my house &, I hope, my friends. Please write me about it. – The person I was fondest of in Skjolden, Arne Draegni died at the beginning of the year.[24] I wish you could have seen him. – I'm keeping well & working a moderate amount. I wish the weather were nicer. Look after yourself, & be good! <u>God bless you</u>!

With love, always

Ludwig

I enclose some mint from our garden. Let me know if it still smells when it arrives in Norway.

Ludwig Wittgenstein to Ben Richards, August 15, 1946

2 Cwmdonkin Terrace

Swansea

15.8.46.

My dear Ben,

I don't really imagine that any letters of ours have gone astray. But as such things have happened, I want to say that I sent you three letters to Norway & had one from you, dated Aug. 24th[25] After that I had nothing.[26] I don't want to write more to-day, except, that <u>I'm thinking of you</u> & wondering if you're well.[27]

---

24 Arne Drægni (1871-1946) lived in Skjolden, and was the postman in charge of the sometimes dangerous route between the various local villages (Vatne 2016: 99-101). In the letter which Wittgenstein had given to Richards to deliver to Anna Rebni he had expressed his sorrow at Arne's recent passing: "I was extremely sorry to hear of Arne Drægni's death. He was the best friend I had in Skjolden" (Wittgenstein to Rebni, July 18, 1946); see the introduction to this chapter.

25 Wittgenstein miswrote the month, and presumably meant Richards' letter from *July* 24, 1946.

26 As it turned out, Richards had not yet received all of Wittgenstein's letters, and they only ended up arriving a couple of weeks later (see Richards' letter to Wittgenstein of September 1, 1946).

27 Wittgenstein was very troubled by Richards' long silence, as evidenced by the remark he made in his manuscript notebook on August 14, 1946, the day before he wrote this letter: "Upset. Don't hear from R[ichards]. I think about it every day, & that I should gain the right position on this loss. Nothing seems more probable to me than that he has left me, or is about to do so, & nothing, in a sense, more natural. Yes, I also feel that I must give this event free rein, that I have done what I could & it is now out of my hands. And yet, every morning, when I again find no letter, I have an ominous feeling. I feel as if I have not yet <u>realized</u> something; as if I must find a point of view from which more truth can be seen" (MS 131, p. 37).

God bless you & keep you! As always, with love

Ludwig

Ben Richards to Ludwig Wittgenstein (undated, second half August 1946)

c/o Mrs Michell
Boswinger
Near St Austell
Cornwall

Dear Ludwig,

I have returned from Norway as you see, and am camping with my family ~~near~~ on the South coast of Cornwall. I enjoyed myself very much at Turtagrö in spite of the weather which, in the west of Norway was the wettest there has been in July & August, for many years. Inland & further North it was fine & last Summer there were many weeks sunshine with no rain. We had some good rock climbing, and quite a lot of experience on glaciers & snow which of course I have never had before. I went down twice to Skjolden and went to see Frk. Rebni.[28] She was very kind to me. She gave up the farm in February this year because of the work, but she still works very hard about the house. At the beginning of the ~~war~~/occupation/ she sheltered several Englishmen and helped them escape. The Germans did not occupy Skjolden permanently but came from time to time, & when they did, the English had to hide up the valley & in the woods. She said they were hunted like animals, and if she had been discovered helping them she would have been shot and her farm burnt.

I was unable to visit Fru Holme[29] as she was away in Bergen all the time I was at Turtagrö, with her mother who had an operation and is recovering. I left the letter in Skjoden for her.

I saw your house across the lake and have a picture postcard of it. No one lives there at present.

We had rather a rough homeward crossing and most of the party, including me, were seasick.

I came straight here after getting home. It is raining & blowing hard as I am writing in my tent, but we have had three fine days out of five. Yesterday we went to see the

---

28 Anna Rebni (1869-1970) was one of Wittgenstein's close friends in Skjolden; she owned the Eide farm and also ran a guesthouse there where Wittgenstein often stayed (Vatne 2016: 70).

29 Kari Holme was the daughter of Hans and Sofia Klingenberg (and Sofia, née Drægni, was Arne Drægni's sister). During his first stay in Skjolden in 1912-13, Wittgenstein had lodged with the Klingenberg family.

annual swimming gala in the harbour at Mevagissey – there were swimming races, diving contests & water polo. Jimmy Kelly of Mevagissey won the championship of Cornwall for swimming. I like this part of Cornwall very much. I was here last when I was ten.

I am looking forward to seeing you in Swansea. I think of you a lot.

I am enclosing a letter Frk. Rebni gave me for you. She wants to know the address of a lady friend[30] who stayed in Skjolden when you were there.

  With all my love
    always, Ben

Ludwig Wittgenstein to Ben Richards, August 21, 1946

    2 Cwmdonkin Terrace
    Swansea
    21.8.

My dear Ben,

Thanks for your letter which arrived yesterday. I'm glad you had an enjoyable time in Norway & that you like it in Cornwall. The weather here is frightfully changeable & rainy; but perhaps that means that it'll be fine when you'll be here. – There where two things that struck me about your letter. One – that you didn't <u>mention</u> any of the 4 letters I wrote to you.[31] That isn't a <u>good</u> idea. For everyone wants to know wheather a friend has received his letter. It's even customary to thank for a friendly letter; & it's a good custom; for a friendly letter is an act of kindness, & to thank for it is not a dictate of politeness, but of kindness. — The other thing that struck me was this. You write Anna Rebni told you that the Englishmen she was hiding were hunted by the Germans 'like animals'. Like animals? – Like <u>enemies</u>! Like any hiddening enemy is hunted in a war. The Germans may have been wicked, but this was none of their special wickedness. I'm not surprised, of course, that Frk. Rebni felt it that way. She – naturally – <u>hated</u> the German occupation & the Germans – who hunted a few harmless & very friendly Englishmen.

---

30 This was Marguerite Respinger (with whom Wittgenstein had been in a complicated intermittent relationship in the late 1920s and early 1930s). In the summer of 1931 they had visited Skjolden together, with Respinger staying in Rebni's guesthouse while Wittgenstein stayed in his cabin. She eventually married Talla Sjögren in December 1933.

31 As mentioned above, Richards had not yet received all of Wittgenstein's letters, and they only ended up arriving a week or so later (see Richards' letter to Wittgenstein of September 1, 1946).

In case I've overlooked something in my criticisms, <u>please</u> correct me & forgive me! I very much want you to come to Swansea on Sept. 12th, or 13th (if possible 12th). I don't know for certain if I'll be able to stay here until the 30th. Even if I am, I'd <u>very</u> much like you to stay with me till then, though it's 3 days over a fortnight. It's important for me.

I'm looking forward to seeing you, going for walks, etc, etc.

Please acknowledge this letter & also the others, if you've had them. This isn't bullying. I <u>really</u> want to know if you received my letters, & even if you liked getting them. Look after yourself & be good! God bless you.

  With love, always
    Ludwig

I'm glad Anna Rebni was kind to you. I know she can be. I'm sending her the address she asked for.[32] L. L.

Ben Richards to Ludwig Wittgenstein, August 23, 1946

    C/o Mrs Michell
    Boswanger Near St Austell
    Cornwall
    23.8.46

Dear Ludwig,

Thank you very much for your letters. Of course I loved getting them. I am very grateful for any criticisms you make. I know I am very apt to be thoughtless, and I know you won't hesitate to tell me when I am – please don't! I am always really sorry when I have caused you pain. I hope I did not say I thought there was anything specially bad in the Germans hunting the British in Norway – I do not feel this is any worse than most other aspects of war. I am glad you sent Frk. Rebni the address. I am very well, and having a good time in spite of the weather. I have been helping a little to get in the harvest. I hope you too are well & happy.

  Bless you always – with love
    from Ben

---

32 On the same day as Wittgenstein write this letter to Richards he replied to Rebni's letter, providing her with an address at which she could reach Respinger.

Ludwig Wittgenstein to Ben Richards, August 31, 1946

2, Cwmdonkin Terrace
Swansea
31.8.46.

My dear Ben,

Thanks for your letter! You say you're very apt to be thoughtless. I suppose that's so. But whether it, alone, explains your not writing to me for a month, knowing what you knew — I won't say. – Please judge yourself. You can do it better than I. – When you come to Swansea I want you to have a good time. And you know, of course, that a good time with us (no matter whether we are serious or just fooling around) rests entirely on the depth & warmth of our relation. If that's there I'll undertake to promise you a good time. If it isn't, don't come. Whichever way it is – God bless you! May you become, as time goes on, a bit less thoughtless, less selfish, more kind, & more reliable. And please forgive me if I've hurt you through being stupid & nasty myself!
Let me know if, & when you're coming.

With love, as always

Ludwig

Please read this letter through once more slowly. L. L.
God bless you! again.

Ben Richards to Ludwig Wittgenstein, September 1, 1946

GREENOGE
40, SWAKELEYS ROAD
ICKENHAM
UXBRIDGE
RUISLIP 2114
September 1st 1946

Dear Ludwig,

I hope you are very well & happy. I have just received two more letters from you, forwarded from Norway; one dated August 3rd and containing some mint which still smells quite strongly, and the other a postcard dated July 2nd, of Swansea Civic Centre (/round/ which no doubt you will be eager to show me) which was sent first to Langdale, then to King's College, then to Ickenham, then to Turtagrö, then back to Ickenham and finally down to Cornwall. I was very glad to get them both – thank you very much!
The weather in Cornwall has continued as bad as ever. On Tuesday night seven out of eight dozen lobster pots were battered to bits in a storm which blew down most of our

tents. Next day we moved all our camping things into Mr. Michell's barn, & room was found for everyone to sleep indoors. Some fellow campers the same night had their tent-pole broken for the second time in three weeks, & they gave up & went home on Thursday. I am going to Skye for a week now where it is normally pretty wet.

I hope to see you on the 12th. Please can you let me know what ~~you~~ trains you advise, and what your plans are? I can bring Schubert again, and I should like to do some reading with you as well as on my own, and go for some long walks. Can you get Wm. James' book[33] again or have you suggestions for books I could bring?

With love always,

Ben

Ludwig Wittgenstein to Ben Richards, September 6, 1946

2 Cwmdonkin Terrace

Swansea

6.9.46.

My dear Ben,

Thanks for your letter from Uxbridge. I'm <u>very</u> sorry you had such rotten luck with the weather in Cornwall. Of course it's been atrocious here too, only I've had a solid roof over my head.

Unfortunately I sent you a letter[34] to Cornwall on Sunday 1st which can't have reached you & may perhaps be sent on a wild goose chase again. This is unfortunate, because the letter was important to me. I meant every word I wrote very seriously. One thing I wrote I want to repeat here, in case you don't get the letter. I said I want you to have a <u>really</u> good time when you come to Swansea, & that, /as you know/, a good time with us rests on the depth & on the warmth of our relation; that if <u>that</u>'s there we'll have a <u>good</u> time, & if not you shouldn't come; & that, whichever way you feel, God bless you! If you come on the 12th it'll be great. Your best train, I think, is the 1^{55} p.m. from Paddington. (Make sure, though.) It arrives here about 7 p.m. & I'll be at the station. – I have no psychological books here. In fact I think it <u>might</u> be better if I didn't read psychology with you now, because my brain is often <u>very</u> tired. I've been working a fair amount & am still doing so[35] & I might have to relax.

---

33 Richards was probably referring here to William James' *The Principles of Psychology*. In the lectures on the grammar of psychological concepts that Wittgenstein was about to deliver over the coming academic year, he often discussed James' views in these books (Wittgenstein 1988).

34 This was presumably Wittgenstein's letter dated August 31, 1946.

35 At this time Wittgenstein was working in MS 131.

I'd like to read Tolstoy with you, say 'Hadshi Murat'[36] or 'The Death of Ivan Ilitch'. Could you bring it along? (And, if you like, some psychology, just in case?)

My mind, as I've said, feels sometimes a bit exhausted & I shall have to make use a great deal of your leniency, your patience & kindness.

Let me know if you'll come, &, if so, what time. Just wire. – Should I, in some <u>unforeseen</u> way, be prevented from meeting your train, please take a bus Nº 74 at the station (everybody will show you where it stops) & tell the conductor you want to get off at "Uplands". From there it's 2 to 3 minutes walk (& anyone will direct you).

 Again: God bless you. I think of you with love always.

Ludwig

The weather has been better last two days. Not far from Swansea there's a place where lots of horses & foals are grazing. The foals are /lovely &/ so tame one can get near them, pat them, etc. The other day when I talked to one of them, I found myself using the same words I often use when I talk to you. That's a fact, Love Ludwig

Enclosure included with the letter of September 6, 1946:

---

36 Wittgenstein had admired Tolstoy's novella since 1912, when he praised it highly to Bertrand Russell: "I have just read 'Hadji Murat' by Tolstoy! Have you ever read it? If not, you ought to for it is wonderful" (Wittgenstein to Russell, undated, summer 1912). See also his letters to Rush Rhees (of June 25, 1945), to Norman Malcolm (of June 26, 1945), and his later letters to Richards (of May 2, 1948 and February 23, 1949).

Ludwig Wittgenstein to Ben Richards (undated, September 12, 1946)[37]

As from: the bathroom[38]

2 Cwmdonkin Terrace

My dear Ben,

This is to welcome you heartily in my humble /sitting/ room.

I am in the bathroom shaving:

So long!

        W. l. a.,

            Ludwig

Ludwig Wittgenstein to Ben Richards (undated, probably late September 1946)[39]

2 Cwmdonkin Terrace

'The Sitting room'

Dear Mr Richards,

As Professor Wittgensteins Attorney I welcome you heartily in his sitting room. He much regrets to be unable to greet you himself on your arrival as he had an urgent business call to the lavatory & bathroom /where he will be detained for some little time/. However, he hopes that, after transacting the necessary & important deals there, he will be able to see you before your departure.

I remain, dear Sir,

your obedient servant

John Smith[40]

---

[37] The date of this letter can be inferred from the fact that Richards only visited Wittgenstein once while he was staying at 2 Cwmdonkin Terrace, and on that trip he arrived on September 12, 1946.

[38] Wittgenstein wrote Richards a number of notes like this, but he later came to playfully sign them from 'John Smith, K.C.' (Wittgenstein's 'attorney'), as can be seen in the letter following this one which was likely written later in Richards' visit to Swansea that September (and see also the other such letters included in chapter VII).

[39] The rough date of this letter can be derived from the fact that during his stays in Swansea, Wittgenstein only stayed with Rev. Morgan at 2 Cwmdonkin Terrace, until April 1947, so this must date from before then. More specifically, though, since in this letter Wittgenstein explains who 'John Smith' (the 'signatory') *is* – i.e. Wittgenstein's attorney – this was likely the first of his playful John Smith letters; and since Richards refers to John Smith in his letter to Wittgenstein of October 23, 1946, this letter must date from before then. It therefore most likely dates from Richards' visit to Swansea for the second half of September 1946.

[40] This was the persona in whose name Wittgenstein came to leave notes for Richards, if Wittgenstein was going to be in the bathroom when Richards arrived at Wittgenstein's lodgings. Compare his similar note to Richards of September 12, 1946, which is in his own name; and for further examples of 'John Smith' notes see chapter VII.

Ben Richards to Ludwig Wittgenstein, October 5, 1946

GREENOGE
40, SWAKELEYS ROAD
ICKENHAM
UXBRIDGE
RUISLIP 2114
5/10/46

Dear Ludwig,

I hope you and your case got safely back to Cambridge – I believe the porters' strike did not last long.

I started the term on Tuesday. We have a three months introductory course of lectures, demonstrations and ward rounds before we are ourselves responsible for examining and talking to patients. We have a good deal of free time to visit the different departments of the hospital or read or do anything we like. I have been to one minor operation on the jaw joint. It did not disturb me at all in the way of making me feel queer, but I was very interested in the technique or organisation of the theatre; in how to dress up in the green coat cap and mask, and in the way everything is kept aseptic.

I hope you don't have too bad a time in Cambridge this year and that you find your class on the whole intelligent & not superficial.

I loved it down in Canterbury – thank you for everything!

Please sleep well and be happy as much as you can.

With love

always

Ben

Ludwig Wittgenstein to Ben Richards, October 6, 1946

Trinity College Cambridge

6.10.46.

Dear Ben, dear old heart,

I got here on Monday after a comfortable journey. I don't like it here at all, but I haven't decided to do anything about it.[41] I'll start lecturing on Friday.[42] Smythies[43] won't come as his library hours are now till 6 p.m. M^{iss} Anscombe[44] will come once a week from Oxford for a kind of supervision. I'll also have Hijab[45] & Dr Malcolm,[46] all separately.[47] How it'll work, God knows. I'm at present writing & want very much to go on doing it until my brain dries up again.[48] What I'm afraid of most is the college noise, especially the music. That's the one thing which makes it completely impossible for me to work properly. As Term hasn't yet begun, the music hasn't either, at least not all of it. Well, all I can do now is wait & see, & hope to God that I'll act intelligently before it's too late. – I am in the old rooms, of course, & I have a new neighbor who is a quiet man.[49] — Drury is in Dublin. He tried to get suitable work in England while reading for his exam, but he couldn't get anything. He seems to feel quite well in Dublin, & I understand that. He'll come back about Christmas.

---

41 On the day he had arrived – Monday, September 30, 1946 – Wittgenstein had written in his manuscript notebook: "Arrived in Cambridge today. Everything in the place repels me. The stiffness, artificiality, complacency of the people. The university atmosphere is disgusting to me" (MS 132, p. 85). Wittgenstein had long felt disgusted with and alienated from Cambridge academic society, as he expressed to his student Desmond Lee in the early 1930s: "[Wittgenstein] spoke of the Cambridge atmosphere as lacking in oxygen (though he said he was able to provide his own): he disliked the conversation and society of High Table, and after he was made a fellow soon gave up dining there. He had an intense dislike of anything he regarded as affectation, and thought he found much of it in the rather self-consciously intellectual society of Cambridge. ... [H]e complained that there was little true kindness in Cambridge society..." (Lee 1979: 216)
42 Starting on Friday October 11, 1946, Wittgenstein gave his lectures in Whewell's Court twice a week – on Mondays and Fridays – from 5pm to 7pm. Notes of these lectures by three different students have been published as Wittgenstein 1988.
43 Yorick Smythies; see the 'Short Biographies of Frequently Mentioned Family and Friends'.
44 Elizabeth Anscombe; see the 'Short Biographies of Frequently Mentioned Family and Friends'.
45 Wasfi Hijab (1919-2004) was a mathematician from Palestine and a student of Wittgenstein's from 1945 until 1947. During this time he was also secretary of the Moral Science Club in Cambridge.
46 Norman Malcolm; see the 'Short Biographies of Frequently Mentioned Family and Friends'.
47 Norman Malcolm recalled: "Wittgenstein devoted a great deal of time to students that year. There were his two weekly classes of two hours each, his weekly at-home of two hours, a whole afternoon spent with me, another whole afternoon spent with Elizabeth Anscombe and W. A. Hijab, and finally the weekly evening meeting of the Moral Science Club which he usually attended" (Malcolm 1984: 46).
48 At this time Wittgenstein was working in MS 132 (see around pp. 123 ff).
49 Wittgenstein's neighbour at the time was the later well-known physicist and mathematician, Freeman Dyson (see Malcom 1958: 64).

I am thinking of you a lot, & of our time in Swansea with gratitude. God bless you always! May you be able to live, in the great dangers & uncongenial surroundings, with a warm & kind heart.

May you help me again as you helped me before to be moderately human myself! God bless you, always!

With love

Ludwig

P.S. Please write to me soon, if you can. If you think that I'm a bl ... nuisance say so, too. I should like to repeat the same old words again & again. L. L.

P.P.S. The worst thing about this place is the cold, inhuman atmosphere which makes me feel lonely & as though I were condemned to live with wax-works.[50]

A. a. L.

Ludwig Wittgenstein to Ben Richards, October 18, 1946

Trinity College, Cambridge

18.10.46.

My dear Ben, o. h., –

It seems quite a time that I haven't heard from you. Thing around me & and in me seem so very unsatisfactory & and it would be particularly good now to hear from you. My lectures, so far, haven't been bad, but there's a huge crowed (about 30) coming to them, & lecturing feels too much like giving a performance & not enough like talking to human beings.[51] (Altogether, my job & my life don't seem human enough.) I am on the ascending branch of a cold just now, but I felt just as low before it started two days ago. I was in London /on Wednesday/ to see my sister who was on her way back to New York.[52] She had contrived, with unbelievable difficulties, to enter Austria & to see

---

50 On October 15, 1946 Wittgenstein wrote to Rhees in a very similar way: "I dislike this place intensely, & the worst part of it is that I haven't got a real friend here, i.e., someone who'd go out of his way to do something for me."

51 Compare Wittgenstein's letter to Rush Rhees from a few days earlier: "I've had two lectures so far. There's a crowd coming to them as always at the beginning of the year when they don't know what to expect. Still my lectures went quite well, except for the fact that during my second lecture I sometimes got so exhausted that I could hardly speak. But my brain, oddly enough, was very active. What's to become of it all I don't know" (Wittgenstein to Rhees, October 15, 1946). As to feeling that his lectures were mere performance rather than genuine philosophical engagement with those who were attending, Rhees later recalled the following remarks from probably somewhere around this time: "I was walking with him in Swansea once when he was feeling the hopelessness and futility of his lectures. Students came because they thought it was interesting: they wanted to know what was being said. It was only rarely that anyone came because he was troubled by the sorts of difficulties Wittgenstein was discussing" (Wittgenstein & Rhees 2015: 61).

52 Wittgenstein's sister, Margaret Stonborough-Wittgenstein, had emigrated to America in January 1940 (see Prokop 2003: 235); see the 'Short Biographies of Frequently Mentioned Family and Friends'.

her two sisters in Innsbruck for about a week. Her aim is now to pull all the strings she can think of to be allowed to go to Austria for good. I hope she'll succeed. – She asked me to give you all her good wishes. She'll arrive in New York to-day.

I wonder how you are & what your work feels like. Do you think you could come to Cambridge for a week-end? E.g. the one after this? If you could come on Saturday I could reserve a room for you, if you let me know soon. I'ld promise you good weather, good food & all sorts of other good things. – This letter is pretty stupid – but then, so am I. Please forgive me, <u>always</u>.

Would you like a 'Cambridge Diary'?[53] If so, I'll send you one, or give it to you.

Be good, & God bless you whatever you do!

With love, always

    Ludwig

I'm being painfully reminded of you about every two minutes /now/, because I'm blowing my nose into the handkerchiefs you gave me.

There are still a few Marygolds in my window-box flowering. I'm enclosing one as proof. Note my crested envelopes! L. L.

Ben Richards to Ludwig Wittgenstein (undated, October 1946)

GREENOGE

40, SWAKELEYS ROAD

ICKENHAM

UXBRIDGE

RUISLIP 2114

Dear Ludwig,

Thanks very much for your letters – I have just received the last one. A very unlucky thing happened about the second letter you wrote – in reply to mine: I started reading it at breakfast and took it out ~~to~~ in the train & found it wasn't in the envelope – it must have dropped out somewhere. I never found it again and will never know what you said unless you can remember.

I think I could manage to come up to Cambridge next week-end, on Saturday evening and return Sunday evening, so will you try and get me a room somewhere for Saturday night. I think I could find a place to stay all right if you found any difficulty. I shall love seeing you again.

---

53 Wittgenstein used these Cambridge Pocket Diaries for many years to keep a record of his various appointments (see Nedo 2012: 267 and 275).

I like the work fairly well but I think I shall like it better after Christmas when I am clerking and will be more in contact with the patients. At present I go to the out-patient's classes question times[54] and the patients are brought in for ¼ of an hour and their case discussed while we sit and listen or crowd round to examine the patient. On the whole it seems the patients are treated kindly and the students well behaved, – but I have no idea what it all feels like to the patient. In the wards it is better: We are a smaller group, all beginners. Most of our time otherwise is taken by lectures and practical pathology.
I am writing with one of these patent pens – supposed not to blot or smudge even on wet paper & to last 80 hours continuous writing without refilling etc etc – it is not very satisfactory as you see – the writings looks rather ugly and often it refuses to mark the paper, also it costs 5/- to refill. Please thank your sister for her kind wishes and give her mine when you write – I am glad she was able to get to Austria. I have written to Con Drury to be forwarded from Exeter as I don't know his Dublin address.

    Love always

      Ben

Ludwig Wittgenstein to Ben Richards, October 21, 1946

Trinity College

Cambridge

21.10.46.

My dear Ben,

Thanks for your letter. I'll have a room for you on Saturday. It's not quite certain yet where it'll be, but there will be a room, I hope in Trinity, – so be sure to come! Please, if you can, let me know the time of your arrival. I'll meet the train. In case I'm prevented in some way, you'll come straight to my room, won't you?

Now I think I must ask you a question. It may be that the answer is quite simple & trivial, & maybe it isn't. I, <u>honestly</u>, don't know. Please give <u>yourself</u> the answer anyway – though I wish you'd also tell <u>me</u>. Here goes. – When you had lost my letter (the one I wrote a fortnight ago) why didn't you let me know sooner? – There was nothing in that letter that can't wait till I see you in a few days, though what I wrote was <u>important</u> to me. But how did you know that there wasn't something in it I wanted you to know <u>urgently</u>? I might have asked you to do me a favour, e.g.. Wouldn't that have mattered? I'm <u>not</u> writing this with a reproachful face, or with reproachful thoughts. But doesn't this question make sense? If it's foolish, forgive me. –

---

54 These last two words are uncertain as the handwriting is hard to read.

God bless you! Please come without fail.

There are lots of things I'd like to say, e.g., all I wrote in that letter, but I'll save them up till Saturday.

Be always good!

>With love, always
>
>>Ludwig

Ben Richards to Ludwig Wittgenstein, October 23, 1946[55]

>>GREENOGE
>>
>>40, SWAKELEYS ROAD
>>
>>ICKENHAM
>>
>>UXBRIDGE
>>
>>RUISLIP 2114
>>
>>Wednesday 23rd October

Dear Ludwig

I have not yet found out the train times to Cambridge. I will, I hope, come up after lunch. There is a friend I very much want to visit who lives near the station, but I promise to come to your room between 6.0 and 7.0.

I am sorry I did not answer your letter sooner. I confess it had not occurred to me that it might contain something <u>immediately</u> urgent, I will make no excuses. I hope you will forgive as always. My faults are slow in being cured, but I do believe some of them have diminished a little since I have known you.

I went to the dentist yesterday and he opened my tooth and said the pulp was infected. He put penicillin on and, if it gives no more trouble, will stop it on Monday. It is behaving well now.

It will be lovely to see you again.

With love always

>your bloody old[56] ——
>
>>Ben

P.S. Please convey my kind regards to Mr. John Smith.[57]

---

55 Because this letter responds directly to Wittgenstein's letter of October 21st, it almost certainly fits here; and this is bolstered by the fact that October 23rd was a Wednesday in 1946.

56 This was likely an endearment that Richards had adopted from Wittgenstein. 'Bloody' was one of Wittgenstein's favourite slang terms, and he used it frequently, and in all manner of unusual forms, contexts, and ways (for many examples see his correspondence with Gilbert Pattisson throughout the 1930s). The word comes to be so ubiquitous in this correspondence that it is usually abbreviated to 'b.' or 'bl.'

57 This refers to the persona in whose name Wittgenstein sometimes left notes for Richards, if Wittgenstein was going to be in the bathroom when Richards arrived at Wittgenstein's lodgings. See Wittgenstein's 'John Smith' note to Richards of (probably) late September 1946 (and see chapter VII for further examples).

Ludwig Wittgenstein to Ben Richards, November 1, 1946

Trinity College
Cambridge
1.11.46.

My dear Ben,

Before you go on, note the writing paper. You will see on the back of it that it is very expensive. (Also see what the stamp says.)[58] I can only use it for special letters & have to compress all I have to say to the utmost, giving you, as it were, only the quintessence of my thoughts. Here goes. – Immediately after your train had left & while I was still walking down the platform the second half rolled in. It was <u>by far</u> emptier than the first & I said to myself that you'ld ~~have~~ been wise to wait a little. — It was good to see you. To talk nonsense, to talk sense, to walk, & <u>everything</u>. — When you'd gone I thought of a use you <u>might</u> make of <u>those</u> Michael Angelos[59] you don't like to keep. I think you have a small sister,[60] & children sometimes like to play with water colours. You might let her use some of the leaves if she likes to. (It doesn't matter that they are great pictures, as long as she happens to like them.) I needn't say, that I don't mean it as an education, & perhaps the pictures aren't suitable in other respects. (I don't really remember) I hope you won't think me nuts. — We had a Moral Science Club Meeting yesterday.[61] It was

---

58 This letter is written on what seems to be a scrap piece of cardboard, which is white on the front and bold red on the back (that is the 'expensive back' that Wittgenstein refers to). The back is imprinted with the following stamp (to which Wittgenstein added the word 'sheet' covering over the stamped word underneath it): "THIS *sheet* IS THE PROPERTY OF SEA WAR LIBRARY SERVICE, 3 ENDSLEIGH STREET LONDON, WC1. ENGLAND, TO WHOM IT SHOULD BE RETURNED WHEN NO LONGER REQUIRED."

59 Presumably: Michelangelo.

60 Richards had four younger sisters (see the book's Introduction). Wittgenstein was presumably here thinking of the youngest – Julia – who was 6 years old at the time.

61 On October 31, 1946, J.L. (John Langshaw) Austin – one of the leading philosophers at Oxford – presented a paper to the Moral Science Club entitled 'Nondescription'. Wasfi Hijab's minutes of the meeting read as follows: "Third Meeting [of 1946-47 academic year]   Oct. 31ˢᵗ, 1946.
Mr. J. L. Austin: Nondescription.
In Mr. Braithwaite's Rooms at King's.
The aim of his paper, Mr. Austin said, was to point out a phenomenon of our language which is not usually recognised by grammarians. The latter do recognise such different parts of speech as, "question", "exclamation", "interjection", etc. But there is a large class of first-person-singular-present-indicative-verb expressions which are, for the lack of a better word, non descriptive; and, as such, they should be distinguished from the normal descriptive use of the indicative mood. Such expressions, which may be called ceremonial or contractual, are characterized by the fact that their utterance is part of an act or by means of which an act is performed. E.g., "I name this ship Queen Elizabeth", "I do" in a marriage ceremony, "I declare this meeting open", etc… A characteristic feature of this way of using the indicative mood is that no question of truth or falsehood would arise; a lawyer may say the act was null and void. Mr. Austin gave examples of expressions where one would say they do sometimes describe and sometimes not, or where one wouldn't know what to say. In the discussion Mr. Austin agreed that there is a temptation to use "true" or "false" in the case of christening the ship, but he insisted that we should resist the temptation. A not very successful attempt was made to separate linguistic from philosophic considerations. Prof. Wittgenstein was in the chair.
Wasfi Hijab Sec" (Cambridge University Archives, Min.IX.44 [C.U.M.S.C. Minute Book, 1935-1952] fol. 146).

awful. A man, Austin, from Oxford read a [I can't continue on another sheet of this kind. It would be too expensive] paper which <u>could</u> have been worse, except that it was superficial, & might have led to an interesting discussion, – but <u>didn't</u>. I left early, about 10, with the feeling that trying to do philosophy at a university is a completely hopeless job. (To-day I feel less violently about it.) There was W. & Br[62] & the atmosphere was shallow, vain & nasty; I too was vain & rather stupid.[63]

By the way, I thought again about "dynasty" & wondered whether my pronunciation was American. I looked it up in Webster, & it gave as pronunciation: dīn asťi or (esp. Brit.) dˇinˇasťi. So I wasn't as wrong, nor you as right, all that, after all. Except that you might say, I have no business to pronounce a word the American way; & if you say that you're right, I suppose.

My dear, take care of yourself & be good & God bless you.

Thanks for coming, & for everything.

  With love, always

    Ludwig

P.S. My lectures are going quite well, so far, & my body feels o.k., & I sleep pretty well. This morning I thought: – may you always improve your judgment & your understanding of human beings, & not let <u>anyone</u> – <u>not me either</u> – bamboozle you into superficial, or wrong judgments. If you use <u>your own head</u> you may go wrong (<u>as everybody</u>) but if you <u>go on</u> doing it you have some hope of getting out of the fog. – You said the other day that it was easy for you to run away from 'being sorry for people'. Of course that's so (& on that road one's always in plenty of company, which makes it so easy). I know it, ~~strongly~~ because running away is, & has always been, a large part of my life. Even in any ordinary philosophical discussion it costs me quite an effort to discuss things about which I feel <u>seriously unclear</u>. Think of me, & God bless you. L. L.

---

62 This perhaps refers to various other members of faculty: John Wisdom and either Richard Braithwaite or C. D. Broad.

63 On the same day as he wrote this letter, Wittgenstein commented similarly in his manuscript notebook: "Yesterday 'Moral Science Club': I myself vain & also stupid. The 'atmosphere' miserable. – Shall I go on teaching?" (MS 133, p. 13r). Interestingly, Wittgenstein doesn't mention the (now infamous) 'poker incident' at the Moral Science Club meeting with Karl Popper that had taken place just a few days earlier on October 26, 1946.

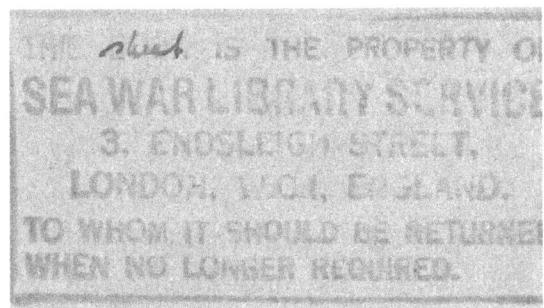

The stamp on the back of the piece of card on which the letter of November 1, 1946, was written

Ben Richards to Ludwig Wittgenstein, November 2, 1946

GREENOGE
40, SWAKELEYS ROAD
ICKENHAM
UXBRIDGE
RUISLIP 2114
2/11/46

Dear Ludwig,

I loved seeing you again. Thanks a lot for arranging about the room. Thank you very much for the present. I am very glad now that I took it, it means a lot to me. ~~No~~ I am thinking of you a lot. I have heard from Con Drury again.

I hope the vitamin B.[64] is working well & that you really feel good, and sleep well.

    Love always
        Ben

---

64 The doctor had recommended that Wittgenstein take Vitamin B to combat his exhaustion, as he had written to Rush Rhees a few days earlier: "This is only to let you know that the doctor's advice, to take vitamin B, seems to have been a good one. The fact is that several hours after taking it for the first time ('Benerva', Roche) I felt much less exhausted, in spite of hardish work, & I haven't had another of my queer attacks since. (I'm taking it regularly now). Try it; it might do you good & it can't harm you. Of course, it's only 5 days since I started" (Wittgenstein to Rhees, October 28, 1946).

Ludwig Wittgenstein to Ben Richards, November 10, 1946

Trinity College
Cambridge
10.11.46.

Dear Ben – d. o. h.,

Thanks for your letter which I got on Tuesday. It's good reading a letter from you. My health is very good & I'm all tanked up with Vit. B. – Yesterday (Sat.) I had an 'at-home'![65] The Mor. Sc. Club is very bad these days, & the disease is incurable because the macro-organisms that cause it can't be killed off. It's against the law. – So I thought I might <u>try</u> to provide some discussions for people by having at-homes (Sat. from 5 to 7). It is just an <u>experiment</u>. About 10 turned up yesterday & things didn't go <u>too</u> bad. (Far better than in the M. Sc. Cl. – but that doesn't mean much.) – My dear, I wish I saw you with the eyes of my body, & not only with the eyes of my mind, – as I'm doing just now (& you look like an ape-man)! — It may interest you to hear that the Marygolds in my window-box are still flowering & one is just getting a new flower. When it's out I'll send it, or give it to you. — I've been to two P.o.W.[66] camps a few days ago to find out what sort of things one should buy for the inmates.[67] /One camp was a/ sad sight. They aren't fed, or treated, <u>badly</u>, but they lack many simple comforts (toothbrushes, paper, thread & needles, books, etc.) & some have been prisoners for over 4 years! They lead a rotten life. — I am thinking of you <u>a lot</u>. God bless you.

With love, <u>always</u>
Ludwig

---

65 'At-homes' were regular gatherings at a member of faculty's home, intended for less formal discussion than would take place in regular lectures or classes. In the 1946-47 academic year Wittgenstein held his 'at-homes' on Saturdays from 5-7pm, and the discussion would be on a topic suggested by one of the students attending. See Malcolm's description of these sessions in his 1984: 45; and find Gilbert Harris Edwards' notes of some of these meetings in Wittgenstein 2003: 401-5.

66 Prisoner of war.

67 By late 1946 there were more than 400,000 German prisoners of war in the United Kingdom in various camps across the country. The process of repatriation had finally begun in September 1946 – only a couple of months before Wittgenstein wrote this letter – but it was very slow, and many prisoners remained until as late as 1948 (see Sullivan 1979). Wittgenstein had himself been a prisoner of war for about ten months in Italy after the First World War.

Ben Richards to Ludwig Wittgenstein, November 17, 1946

GREENOGE
40, SWAKELEYS ROAD
ICKENHAM
UXBRIDGE
RUISLIP 2114

Sunday 17/11/46

Dear Ludwig

Thank you for two letters. It must be awful to be a prisoner of war for a long time even if one isn't ill-treated. I expect a lot depends on the officer in charge of the camp. I went away last week-end, climbing for 3 days – North Wales. I enjoyed it very much – I wish I could have taken you up some climbs; you feel much safer on solid rock with good holds than on the edge of a crumbling cliff. But you might not like it as the district is popular with climbers, walkers & tourists, though less so at this time of year. I expect you would find it nice & warm there around January.

There is a poster up in tube stations "compassion to <u>all</u> animals m<u>us</u>t come before peace to mankind" with a picture something like this: [sketch] – I have been wondering to whom it is addressed.

I hope your "at home" discussions continue to go well. I wish I could do some philosophy still.

    With much love
        always your ape-man[68]
            Ben

---

68 An allusion to Wittgenstein's remark in the previous letter from October 11, 1946, which seems to refer to an unknown prior shared joke.

Ludwig Wittgenstein to Ben Richards, November 19, 1946

Trinity College
Cambridge
19.11.46

My dear Ben,

I was <u>glad</u> to get your letter this moment for I was all set to send you a short & sad ~~letter~~ one saying how I felt about not hearing from you. (If, by any chance, you think that I am a bloody so & so, just say so.) Now I must tell you that I am very worried about Drury. He is in an <u>exceedingly</u> bad state with his nerves.[69] He has been suffering for insomnia (not more than 2 hours sleep) for over 2 months. I think you know that he went to Dublin to get his M.D.. His nerves were in a <u>bad</u> state <u>before</u> he went & got much worse there. About a fortnight ago he accepted an invitation from a friend of his who has a farm in Ireland to stay & do some work at the farm. Drury, very foolishly, plunged into heavy physical work to which he is not accustomed, & his nerves got worse & his sleep did <u>not</u> improve. The dissertation which he had written for the M.D.[70] was, to his surprise, accepted in Dublin & he is to go there on Dec. 3rd & to take his exam. How this will be possible in his present state & and what consequences the strain might have God knows! Drury intends to return to England in December, to spend Christmas in Exeter & possibly to take a job as resident physician in Taunton again. I want him to stay part of the Xmas eve with me in Swansea; for, although I can't help him much, he can talk to me about his troubles better, probably, than to anyone else (except maybe his sister Mary who is in Africa). — My health is good & my classes & "at-homes" are going all right – though they don't <u>deeply</u> satisfy me. My dear, I think of you a <u>lot</u> & very much want to see you & to talk to you about a lot of things (also /possibly/ about Drury). I could chuck an at-home & come to London on a Saturday & return on Sunday, or I could come to London on a Wednesday &

---

69 The previous month Drury had described his situation to his friend Raymond Townsend (another of Wittgenstein's old students and friends) as follows: "Since we last met great fear came over me, this wasn't just that I couldn't decide what to do, but that all my life seemed empty and my thinking quite vain. I felt that I would be glad to die, but not in such a way that I thought of suicide... I hadn't been over here more than a few days... when I had suddenly to go and make a full confession to the priest at St. John's, the first I had made in 15 years. Since then I have been much more at peace and able to rejoice and thank God for the fear he sent me. It seems to me that I had never really believed in God before, but that now I do" (Drury to Townsend, October 13, 1946, quoted in Hayes 2017: 29-30).

70 Drury's dissertation was entitled: *The Significance of Posture in the Aetiology and Treatment of Chronic Disease* (see Hayes 2017: 29).

return on Thursday, or we could both go to some place /other than/ London or Cambridge, or you could come to Cambridge & I'd get you a room /a nicer one than the last time, I hope/. God, how difficult everything is!

You say you wish you could do some philosophy still. So would I, for, though I am a bum-philosopher, still it would be good to see your face among the crowd in my room.

I have an idea that this is a pretty bloody letter! Still, I better send it off.

May you have strength & courage & kindness, & God bless you. Write soon (don't curse me).

    With love, always

        Ludwig

P.S. I enclose the flower I promised you.

<u>Whatever</u> you write to me always means a great deal to me. Even your works of art[71] are included in this remark

    God bless you.

        L. L.

---

71 This is a reference to the drawings and illustrations with which Richards would sometimes decorate his letters.

Ben Richards to Ludwig Wittgenstein, November 27, 1946

GREENOGE
40, SWAKELEYS ROAD
ICKENHAM
UXBRIDGE
RUISLIP 2114
27/11/46

Dear Ludwig

Thank you for the letter and the flower – is it from the same plant as the one which had offspring?

I was very sorry to hear that Drury was in so bad a state. I hope his exam goes well and will not have too serious effects, and that he will get better with a good rest at Christmas. I expect he has tried most of the remedies for insomnia which he recommended for you. By the way, is the vitamin B, still working well?

I am applying to do medical clerking rather than surgical dressing for my first 3 months clinical appointment in January.

I am not sure how much time we get off at Christmas; I think the medicine & surgery go on for another two or three weeks. The pathology /course/ started about a fortnight late and will probably go on longer. The clinical appointments start on January the first. I can arrange to come up to Cambridge for a weekend, before Christmas. I want to see you very much.

I expect the Cambridge term ends in a week or so. I hope it has not gone t_oo_ badly for you, and that there are one or two new people you are glad to have in your class. Have you been able to get on well with the book.

I think of you constantly,
      with love
           Ben

P.S. I append a Work of Art.⁷²

Ludwig Wittgenstein to Ben Richards, November 28, 1946

Trinity College
Cambridge
28.11.46

My dear Ben,

Thanks for your letter of Nov. 27ᵗʰ. First I want to tell you that I have better news from Drury. His insomnia seems to have subsided. I had a letter from him yesterday, saying that he could now get 6 hours sleep (with luminal, though). He is also much quieter. He is leaving the farm & going to Dublin & doing a locum there until his exam. He is obviously still pretty shaby but apparently on the way to recovery. In January he will start in Taunton again, in his old position.

I /want if possible/ to come to London next Wednesday afternoon or evening & stay the night. I should <u>very</u> much like to see you for an hour or two /or longer/ on Thursday (Dec. 5ᵗʰ) before going back to Cambridge – mainly to arrange with you about seeing each other. This is <u>very</u> important to me. Now this is the position: A lady, a radiologist at Guy's,⁷³ ~~has~~ in the past sometimes put me up for a night & she may do

---

72 Richards has written 'The Worm's Head' at the bottom of his drawing of a sea serpent just off a coastal cliff. This is presumably a reference to Worm's Head, a tidal island just off the coast to the west of Swansea, which Richards and Wittgenstein had likely visited together during their Swansea holiday. Its name comes from the word 'wyrm', the Old English word for a sea serpent (probably because the island is shaped a bit like one).

73 This was Naomi Wilkinson, who was a radiographer at Guy's Hospital, where Wittgenstein had worked between 1941 and 1943. They had got to know one another through the gramophone recitals that she had organized at the hospital in the waiting-time between air-raids (see Kinlen 2016: 723).

so again on Wednesday night next week. If she does I want to attend a certain meeting on Thursday morning at 11, which will take about two hours, I Imagine. From about 1 p.m. I'ld be free. Please let me know as soon as possible (e.g. by wire) whether you can spend part, or all, of Thursday afternoon with me, & if part <u>which</u> part. If M^{iss} Wilkinson the radiologist, <u>can't</u> put me up but you can spend an <u>appreciable</u> time with me on Thursday afternoon I'll still come to London by an early train on Thursday.

A slight difficulty has arisen about our correspondence. I saw a publisher the other day who said he'ld print all our letters when we're dead. But, he said, reproducing your pictures would make the book too expensive for the common reader. He said you should limit yourself entirely to straight lines in the future, as this would come cheaper. –

Please let me hear from you /soon/ about Thursday.

<u>God bless you!</u>

With love always

Ludwig

P.S. The rest of this page & the next page you can use to jot down your impressions after reading this letter. L. L.

Ben Richards to Ludwig Wittgenstein, December 1, 1946

GREENOGE

40, SWAKELEYS ROAD

ICKENHAM

UXBRIDGE

RUISLIP 2114

Sunday (Dec 1st ?)[74]

Dear Ludwig,

I was very glad to hear from you ~~and~~. I am free most of Wednesday afternoon and could meet you then or in the evening. On Thursday I have from 1 to 2 off for lunch and finish work at about 4. If you will let me know when and where to meet you, I shall be there. Lectures, etc. finish on December 19th but there may be a special department class (eye dept, e.g.) on the following Monday morning.

---

[74] Because this letter responds directly to Wittgenstein's letter of November 28, it almost certainly fits here; and this is bolstered by the fact that December 1 was a Sunday in 1946.

I am very glad Drury is better – he will be starting his exam in a day or two; I hope it goes well.

I am looking forward to seeing your B. o. F.; love always,

Ben

Ludwig Wittgenstein to Ben Richards, (undated, probably December 9, 1946)

Trinity Coll.
Camb.
Monday[75]

My dear Ben,

Thanks for your letter. It seems Miss Wilkinson can't put me up & I have an idea London is pretty full just now; so I better come on Thursday (unless you happen to know a place where I can sleep). I could meet you on Thursday at 4 p.m. say at the National Galery on top of the front stairs where it's sheltered, or in the lobby. If you know a place where I could stay Wednesday night, let me know at once. In this – unlikely – case I'll arrive at L.pool Street[76] Wednesday at $2^{.39}$ p.m. & you can have the pleasure of my company as long as you'll like. Please wire your reply.

Looking forward to seeing you, <u>d. o. h.</u> with love, always

Ludwig

Do you know which is better: a slave-driver, a bus driver, or a pile driver? Perpend this![77] If you've got nothing better to do.

Ludwig Wittgenstein to Ben Richards, December 24, 1946

2 Cwmdonkin Terrace
Swansea
24.12.46.

My dear Ben,

This is chiefly to say that I am thinking of you a very great deal. – Thank you for the X-mas card.[78] We've had awful weather here until last night: first terribly cold, so that I

---

75 Because this letter follows on directly from the previous two, it almost certainly fits here. The most likely Monday that this would therefore be referring to is December 9, 1946.
76 Stands for: Liverpool Street.
77 Wittgenstein uses the word 'perpend' and the dramatic phrase 'perpend this' a few times in his correspondence with Richards, and it seems to have been a joke between them. For the possible allusion see Wittgenstein's letter to Richards of February 2, 1947, and the relevant footnote there.
78 Three undated Christmas cards from Richards to Wittgenstein have survived (see Chapter VII). This is possibly one of those.

felt really wretched, & then rain. But to-day was beautiful. I went to Langland Bay by bus & then walked along the cliffs to Caswell & and on to Pull Du.[79] I wished you were with me. – By the way, if anyone asks you "How are you?" answer him: "Thank you, fine! We eat crunchy Ryvita as our daily bread."[80] –

I hope I'll hear from you soon!

God bless you!

With love, always

Ludwig

P.S. I've had no news from Drury since I saw you last. I wish I knew how he is!

    Be always good! L. L.

P.P.S. If you're puzzled why I gave you the Mozart Quartett, look at its 3rd movement. L. L.

Ben Richards to Ludwig Wittgenstein (undated, Christmas 1946)

GREENOGE

40, SWAKELEYS ROAD

ICKENHAM

UXBRIDGE

RUISLIP 2114

Dear Ludwig,

Please accept this poor quality, rather mouldy camera with my love. I couldn't get a case for it either.

I hope you will have a really happy Christmas in Swansea. I am looking forward to opening your parcels.

I have a feeling I never put the names in that card to Mrs. Davies' family after all. Anyway, please give my love to them to Mr. Morgan and to the Clements.[81]

    Love always

    Ben

---

79 This should be 'Pwll Du' (a village on the Welsh coast near Swansea).

80 Ryvita is the brand name of an English rye crispbread. This is probably a quotation of – or variation upon – an advertising slogan.

81 Mr Morgan was Wynford Morgan in whose house Wittgenstein was lodging. The Clements were the family who lived next door, to whom Wittgenstein became close – Albert and Mary, and their young daughters Joan and Barbara (see Monk 1990: 464-5). The Davies appear also to have been neighbours.

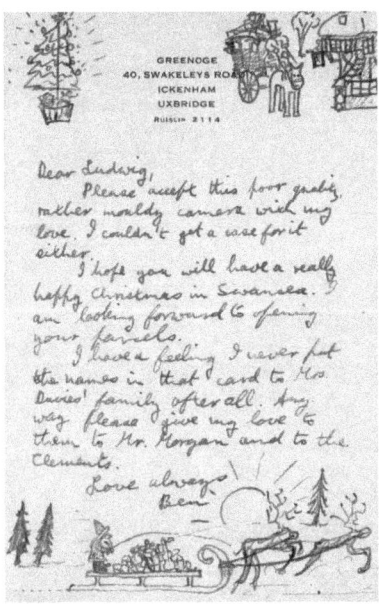

Ludwig Wittgenstein to Ben Richards, December 28, 1946

2 Cwmdonkin Terrace
Swansea
28.12.46

My dear Ben, O. H.,

I just now got your lovely present, it's <u>much</u> too nice for me! Thanks! & thanks for your /Xmas-/ letter. (You did write the names on the card you sent to Hugh Davies. He & his parents were most delighted with the theatre.) To come back to your letter: you say that you're looking forward to opening my parcels. Well now you know that they contained junk, but my heart went with it.

The German motto I wrote into the Davidsbündler Tänze[82] in the correct version. What I wrote down for you some time ago /from memory/ wasn't right. (The word "seyd" instead of "seid" is merely an old spelling, though) – I got <u>a lot</u> of pleasure out of your letter. Please write to me again soon. I need it <u>very</u> much. The Morgans & the

---

82 The motto with which Robert Schumann prefaced the first edition of his 'Davidsbündlertänze' ['Dances of the League of David'] (op. 6) is: 'Alter Spruch: /In all und jeder Zeit/ Verknüpft sich Lust und Leid /Bleibt fromm in Lust und seyd/ Dem Leid mit Mut bereit' ('Old saying: /In each and every age/ pleasure and suffering are intertwined /Remain pious in pleasure and be/ ready for suffering with courage'). Wittgenstein returns to this motto again in his letters of January 19, 1950 and February 13, 1951.

neighbours send their love. I had X-mas dinner next door & went to Tumble[83] to Mrs Morgan on Boxing Day. It's very pleasant there. – I'm looking forward to seeing you before long & to hearing from you before seeing you.

Thanks, & God bless you!

 With love, always

   Ludwig

This is the first snapshot I took with your camera. It was a pretty terrifying experience! L. L.[84]

Ben Richards to Ludwig Wittgenstein, December 30, 1946

   GREENOGE
   40, SWAKELEYS ROAD
   ICKENHAM
   UXBRIDGE
   RUISLIP 2114
   30.12.46

Dear Ludwig

Thank you very much indeed for the masses of presents, and for the two letters. Why did you call them "junk"? They are all things I shall always want to keep for themselves as well as because they come from you. I had already recognized the

---

83 A small village about 25km north of Swansea.
84 Wittgenstein taped onto the letter – just below where he had signed his name – what looks to be an illustration which he had cut out of one of the detective magazines which he liked to read, then he added a final 'explanatory' sentence beneath it.

movement in the Mozart quartet, and I was going to ask you about the different wording of the motto to the Schumann. With all these hadkerchiefs, I can keep a cold going for a very long time.

If the camera will take photographs like that without any ill-effects it will stand a lot. I am glad you have enjoyed Christmas – I have very much.

One of my best presents was a recording by the Roismann quartet[85] of Beethoven quartet in B♭ op. 130, from my mother. A very happy New Year to you and also to the Clements, Davies's & Morgans.

  Love always

    Ben

Ludwig Wittgenstein to Ben Richards, December 31, 1946

            2 Cwmdonkin Terr.

            Swansea

            31.12.46.

My dear Ben,

Thanks for your letter. I have heard from Drury now. He is better. He was kept under until the 24th, I believe. He was allowed to get up for lunch on Sunday & is to go into the country before long for a rest. I hope he'll recover <u>completely</u>!

I took my first photos today & have used up the roll of film you sent me. The first two pictures are no good. I know, because I had trouble with the finder. One of the finders doesnt work, I think it's been damaged on the transport. The upright one works. I took Mrs Morgan & Morgan & Mrs Clement.[86] This is all just a preparation for taking you from all <u>possible</u> angles. – There is one more thing I'd like to say, although it may sound queer. I'd <u>very much</u> like you to play some of the Schumann. In particular I'd like you to try the "Kreisleriana"[87] (which is hellishly difficult). (Try the second part; it's easier.) I'm almost afraid that you mightn't <u>really</u> care for it, but perhaps you will. I'm <u>extremely</u> fond of it.

---

85 Better known as the 'Budapest String Quartet', in which Joseph Roismann played first violin from 1932. It became particularly known for its recordings of Beethoven's chamber music works.

86 Richards pasted these photos onto a sheet of lined of paper and tentatively labelled them.

87 The Kreisleriana (op. 16) is a piano cycle by Robert Schumann written in 1838. Wittgenstein refers to this again a couple of weeks later in a letter to his sister, Helene: "For Christmas I gave a friend who plays <u>a little</u> piano some piano works by Schumann & he played me a few bars of the Kreisleriana. I thought: How extraordinarily noble!" (Wittgenstein to Helene Salzer, January 16, 1947).

I think of you a lot!

Phob llwyddiant y flwyddyn Newydd,[88] as I always say when I'm speaking Welsh.

God bless you!

With love always

      Ludwig

Hearing from you makes me feel pretty good.

These are probably the photos of Mrs Morgan, her husband Reverend Wynford Morgan, and Mrs Clement, to which Wittgenstein was referring in his letter of December 12, 1946

Ludwig Wittgenstein to Ben Richards, January 7, 1947

                2 Cwmdonkin Terrace

                      Swansea

                      7.1.47.

My dear Ben,

When I saw you off at Cambridge before the vac you mentioned that I might stay a night in Ickenham again, & we talked tentatively about this being done on Monday next (Jan. 13th). Now I very much want to see you & I could leave here either on Saturday, Sunday, or Monday. (Term begins on Tuesday.) If you're engaged on Sunday I could come on Monday, arriving at Paddington about 1.30 p.m.; if you're free I could come on Saturday evening & leave on Sunday night. Or I could come some time on

---

88 This is Wittgenstein's slightly mistaken Welsh for 'Every success in the New Year' (more correctly it should have been: 'Pob llwyddiant yn y Flwyddyn Newydd').

Sunday. (Coming & seeing you on Monday has the disadvantage that I <u>may</u> be rather tired form the journey & liable to be depressed.)

Please write to me, or wire, what you'd like me to do. There are <u>no end</u> of things I'd like to talk to you about!

  With love, always,
    Ludwig

I won't write more now because I hope to see you. L. L.

Ludwig Wittgenstein to Ben Richards, January 10, 1947

                2 Cwmdonkin Terr.[89]
                     Swansea
                       9 10.1.47.

My dear Ben,

I wrote to you a few days ago & I assume that you have received my letter, but I haven't had an answer. Meanwhile I've had to change my plans. I am leaving here in a few minutes & going to Ryde on the Isle of Wight. where I shall stay near Ryde in Quarr Abbey until Monday morning. I'll arrive at <u>Waterloo</u> at $1^{.1}$ p.m.. So I can only see you on Monday afternoon, after all, I'm sorry to say. Now I want you to let me know the following things. a) Can you see me on Monday afternoon & evening? b) Can you meet the train at Waterloo at $1^{.1}$ p.m.? c) If you can't meet the train, where can we meet? d) Can I stay in Ickenham over night? Please <u>wire</u> the reply <u>as soon as possible</u> to me c/o Rev.

/Father/ Prior Guestmaster

Quarr near Ryde

Isle of Wight

I've got to know as soon as possible whether I'll return to Cambridge on Monday or on Tuesday, & this depends on you.

I'll explain my visit to Quarr Abbey when I'll see you.

  Be good, & God bless you.
    With love
      Ludwig

I shall post this letter in London. I wish I had heard from you before leaving Swansea /I would feel more cheerful/! I'm writing this P.S. in the train. L. L.

---

89 The word 'Express' has been written in pencil in the top left of the page. This was probably added by Richards.

Ben Richards to Ludwig Wittgenstein, January 18, 1947

GREENOGE
40, SWAKELEYS ROAD
ICKENHAM
UXBRIDGE
RUISLIP 2114
Jan 18th 1947

Dear Ludwig,

My mother has asked me to write to say thank you for sending the flowers. The red and yellow tulips remind her of some little lilies which used to grow in Jamaica[90] which she liked very much; and the mimosa makes her think of the south in France of which she has very vivid & agreeable visions although she has never been there. So the whole effect is very happy. The bottle of bubbles arrived safely, and Heshe is delighted: wafting them all over the house. No doubt, one day she will thank you herself. She apologises for not writing herself, but is glad to say her doctor has advised her to not to exert herself in any way.

It was wonderful to see you again. I hope you will come & stay here again when my mother is well. She is still much the same, and is still starting to have injections of penicillin – I don't know how much good that will do.

I hope the lectures will go well.

      Love always

        Ben

Ludwig Wittgenstein to Ben Richards (not fully dated, probably January 21, 1947)

Tuesday ?.1.46[91]

/47/[92]

Dear Ben, O.H.!

It was good to get your letter. I had hoped /& longed/ to hear from you soon & it was good to have that hope come true.

---

90 Ben Richards' mother, Noel, spent a number of her teenage years in Jamaica, as her father – Sydney H. (Baron) Olivier (1859-1943) – was the English governor of Jamaica from 1907-1913.

91 Wittgenstein wrote '46' for the year, but Richards corrected this to '47' just underneath (Wittgenstein made the common January mistake of dating to the previous year). Wittgenstein's first two classes in Michaelmas Term 1947 were January 17 and 20, and the next day was a Tuesday. So given the content of the letter, this was presumably written on Tuesday January 21, 1947.

92 This correction was added by Richards.

The first two lectures passed without catastrophe.[93] I must say that always before I lectured I felt that I wouldn't be able to say <u>anything</u> worth saying, but after I had talked for a while some idea came into my head which I could work out. May my luck hold for a while! Yesterday I had to lecture in the Old Combination Room. On Sunday evening my stove suddenly started to give off fumes & on Monday (yesterday) they got so awful & sickening that it would have been impossible to have my class in the room; so we moved. The trouble was, I think, dirt in the anthracite. I am now trying clean stuff & we shall see. – I had a letter from Drury /this morning/ which sounds better than the one before. He sends you his love.
I hope your mother will soon recover!
It was <u>lovely</u> to see you.
I think of you constantly.
  God bless you.
  With love Ludwig

Ludwig Wittgenstein to Ben Richards, January 27, 1947

Trinity College
Cambridge
27.1.47.

My dear Ben,
I wrote you that my stove started to give trouble a week ago. I thought the cause was the dirty anthracite which I was then using, but the fact was: the cylinder that contains the anthracite had rusted through & the fumes were coming through the hole. So the stove had to be removed, & now (when it's as cold as hell) I've only got the electric fire. I hope the stove will be back in a few days, though.
I don't know if it's the sudden cold or something else that makes me so stupid – but my mind is a complete blanc & I'm very worried about how to go on lecturing. My last (3rd) lecture was bad. I have only corpses of thoughts in my mind which I'm ashamed to trot out. – I'm thinking of you a <u>great</u> deal. I hope that the penicillin may

---

93 See Klagge 2019: 56ff.

have done your mother some good & that the cold isn't doing her harm. – I hope I'll soon hear from you because that always bucks me up a lot. – I know this letter is pretty deadly. It reflects the state of my brains. Forgive me for being /such/ a sad sack & look at the enclosure which shows how romance can be brought about by Thin Gillette –

Wish me luck. God bless you.

    With love, always

                Ludwig

Enclosure included with the letter of January 27, 1947:

Ben Richards to Ludwig Wittgenstein, January 28, 1947

                GREENOGE
            40, SWAKELEYS ROAD
                 ICKENHAM
                  UXBRIDGE
              RUISLIP 2114
                   28.1.47

Dear Ludwig

Thanks for both letters. I am very sorry to hear about the stove – it's bad it should happen just now while it's freezing cold. I hope you will have it back very soon; and that your lectures will go well again. Have you many new people in your class this term?

My mother is very much better – she would have got up to-day but for the weather. Heshe has been tobogganing on the pond which has been frozen since Saturday. I have joined the London University choir who are rehearsing Bach's B minor Mass[94] – I have been to one rehearsal on Thursday, and we are reading it through.
Thank you for sending that very moving story about the gillette blade. With unerring inevitability it conjures forth the whole gamut of human emotions, don't you think?
It is very good to hear from you. I do hope things will not go badly for you this term.
    Love always
      Ben

Ludwig Wittgenstein to Ben Richards, February 2, 1947

Trinity College
Cambridge
2.2.47.

My dear Ben,

There are a good many things I want to write. First, thanks for your letter; it was good seeing it! – I enclose the three best pictures of the six passable ones of the 16 shots I've taken so far (Three of them turned out complete blancs – though <u>why</u> I don't know – & two showed traces of things but not distinct enough to make prints worth while.) I hope you like the ones I'm sending. – Now I want to make a confession. I said it was good seeing your letter, but this was an understatement: I <u>longed</u> to hear from you. You see – I'm very dependent upon you, that's the trouble. And I'm <u>not</u> saying this in order to entreat you to go on writing to me a lot, though of course that's what I'd like, – but I'm saying it because if there's something wrong, or even repellant about it I should like you to see it. It's simply that I have a strong wish & yet would rather have it denied right out than fulfilled when this means, in some sense, <u>preying</u> on you. Because then the wish isn't fulfilled, after all. Please perpend this, as 'Q' would say.[95]

---

94 Johann Sebastian Bach's Mass in B minor (BWV 232), completed in 1749.
95 Wittgenstein uses the word 'perpend' and the phrase 'perpend this' a few times in his correspondence with Richards, and it seems to have been a joke between them. It's unclear what it derives from – and who the relevant 'Q' was – but one possibility is that they had been looking at Arthur Quiller-Couch's *On The Art of Writing* (Cambridge, Cambridge University Press, 1919), which was an edition of lectures he had delivered at Cambridge in 1913-14. In that book he uses the phrase on a couple of occasions, and Wittgenstein perhaps found it affectedly archaic and over-dramatic. Namely: "Perpend this then, and do not too hastily deride my plea that you should practise verse-writing" (p. 38, Lecture II), and "Perpend this, Gentlemen, and maybe you will not hereafter set it down to my reproach that I wasted an hour of a May morning in a denunciation of Jargon" (p. 103, Lecture V).

I'd like you to see me as I am (at least up to a point), & then to make your decision, – & God bless you, always. – My stove is back & my room is now comfortable as usual. My brain is more lively again (for reasons unknown) & the lectures last week went all right. My at-homes always do, & I think you would approve of them if you could hear them. (Oddly enough, <u>after</u> them I /often/ feel tired & empty.) – Would you mind coming to Cambridge before long? say the weekend after next? I'll get the best rooms, & the best food, etc. (Please let me know soon.) – I heard from Drury a few days ago. He has left the hospital & is now in a convalescing home somewhere near Dublin. He writes he's sleeping all right again 'but is still given insulin every morning'. I don't know what this means. I didn't know he had been given insulin. (Was it some sort of shock treatment?) – I'm glad to hear your mother is better again.

That's all for to-day.

      With love, as always

           Ludwig

P. S. As it's important not to waste any paper I want to say that I have 20 students[96] in my class only one of which is new (& not very bright). – I'm having these aluminum envelopes made for my best letters only. G. b. y.. – One of the photos shows me. I wonder if you can find me.

Ludwig Wittgenstein to Ben Richards, February 4, 1947

                                            Trinity College

                                                Cambridge

                                                     4.2.47.

Dear Ben,

Thanks for your letter. I reserved a room for you in Trinity a week ago. If I'd waited till you wrote there might not have been one. (I mean, a room.) I took it for Friday (7th) & Saturday (8th) night, thinking that you might possibly be able to come on Friday evening. If you are, <u>come</u>. If you do I won't cancel my at-home. If you come on Saturday I'll /probably/ cancel it. I'll explain my reasons when I see you. – <u>May a good</u>

---

96 Among them were: Norman Malcolm, Peter Geach, Wasfi Hijab, A. C. Jackson, Kanti Shah, Georg Kreisel, Miss H. Martini, J. R. Jones, E. Bruce Hunt, Stephen Toulmin, Georg Henrik von Wright, Elizabeth Anscombe, Yorick Smythies, Gilbert Harris Edwards, Peter Munz, John Vinelott, Stephen Plaister, R.O.C. Winkler, Evangelos Christou, and Jani Christou (see Klagge 2019: 56).

spirit work in you! May you be my friend the way I mean it: not only in words but in actions.

    With love, always
             Ludwig

P.S.

R.S.V.P.[97] by wire L. L.

                                              P.T.O.[98]

P.T.O.

Ben Richards to Ludwig Wittgenstein, February 8, 1947

            GREENOGE
        40, SWAKELEYS ROAD
             ICKENHAM
             UXBRIDGE
          RUISLIP 2114
              8.2.47

Dear Ludwig,

The photos have come out very well, haven't they? – Particularly Mrs. Clements & Morgan; somehow the ones of Mrs Morgan don't look quite like her. I see your head on Mrs Morgan's shoulder in the picture with Mrs Clements, but it flatters you too much.[99]

I have been in bed a few days with a cold and had better say I won't come to Cambridge next week-end. I want to come up before long; and go to your 'at home', & see you again. I am glad your stove is back. We ran out of coke again but we have got some more now. The snow is thicker than before.

Ann Phillips, our housekeeper, went up to North Wales because her father was ill. He died before she got there.

I wonder why Drury is having insulin. Have you heard again from him?

I hope you get on well with your lectures and your book.

    Love always
        from Ben

---

97 French: Répondez s'il vous plaît (Please reply).

98 Stands for: 'Please turn over'. Wittgenstein's letter fills one side of the paper, and he wrote 'P. T. O.' at the foot of that side; but all there is on the other side of the page is a second – playful – 'P. T. O.'.

99 See Wittgenstein's letter to Richards of December 31, 1946.

Ben Richards to Ludwig Wittgenstein (undated, between February 13 and 15, 1947)[100]

GREENOGE
40, SWAKELEYS ROAD
ICKENHAM
UXBRIDGE
RUISLIP 2114

Dear Ludwig

I am up and quite well again. Now my sister has twisted her knees and in addition feels a bit sick, so she is staying in bed now! Dr. Wheatly, my father's assistant was in bed for a week with an sore throat – which kept my father pretty busy[101] – but he is back now. I hope you are keeping well – do you sleep all right now?

Next week-end I have visitors & engagements, and the following one is my sisters' half-term, but I hope to be able to come to Cambridge the one after that (March 8th), but I will confirm this.

I hope you have good news from Drury.

God bless you always

    with love from

        Ben

Ludwig Wittgenstein to Ben Richards, February 17, 1947

Trinity College
Cambridge
17.2.47

Dear Ben,

I think of you a very great deal & when I do I have many great wishes & hopes. One is that you're in good health /again/ & that you're moderately lucky all round. Another &, I confess, even deeper one is this: may you <u>not</u> be superficial; not in your thoughts & and not in your feelings. – A third is: may you have a kind & understanding heart.

---

100 This letter is undated, but the following three letters (two from Wittgenstein and then one from Richards) indicate that it fits here in the sequence; and the specific date (or date-range) can be arrived at by working backwards from March 8th which is mentioned in the letter, along with the fact that Wittgenstein replied to this letter on February 17, 1947.

101 Richards' father – William Arthur Richards (1895-1962) – was a general practitioner with a practice in Ickenham, near the family home.

(& not, e. g., put pride before kindness). – That I also should like you to be my friend, – you know. And that, <u>if</u> you are, I should like you to come & see me soon, you know, too. And, of course, I'd like you to be kind to me: if you're my friend, then <u>as a friend</u>; & if you're not, then by just saying so. – As long as I regard you as I do now I will make <u>demands</u> on you; & if I cease making them you will know that my feeling has changed.

I heard from Drury again some days ago. He is still in the convalescing home & is still given insulin. I'd rather, just now, not ask him why.

Please read this letter once more & read it carefully.

  May God be with you!

    With love, as always

      Ludwig

P. S. I want to write a post-script to this letter. And now listen. Please don't think that in what I am going to say I'm sentimental. Because I'm not. – What would I like (& long) to do with you if you came here? The usual things, & walking, & talking. What about? Apart from <u>all</u> the nonsense I'd like to say – about music, about my work, about your's, about Drury, & no end of things. [<u>Of course</u> I'd cancel my at-home unless you specially wished to hear it.]¹⁰² And I'd find this <u>most pleasant</u>; <u>good</u>; <u>useful</u> (for both).

BUT – all this (in our case, at any rate) presupposes something else on which these things can float, which supports them. Without <u>it</u> for me to think of them, to wish for them, to look forward, is merely building castles in the air. All these nice things presuppose something else, & without it they can't exist. Am I beefing? No. But I long to speak the truth to you about it & to make you see it!

  Your loving friend

    Ludwig

P.P.S. I must say, I find the picture of Mrs Morgan (alone) rather good! But perhaps you're right & it is too momentary an expression. Still, I rather like it.

---

102 The square brackets are Wittgenstein's own.

Ludwig Wittgenstein to Ben Richards, February 27, 1947

Trinity College
Cambridge
27.2.47

My dear Ben,

I wonder if you've thrown away my last letter yet &, in case you haven't, if you could make it do for a little longer by reading it again. In this age of power-cuts we've got to be oeconomical, & what I wrote then expresses very much just what is in my heart (at least, as well as I <u>can</u> express it). One thing, perhaps, I ought to add. When I wrote, I wanted you to be kind to me "if you're my friend, then <u>as my friend</u>...", by what I underlined I meant: in action. Apart from that I only wish to say that I'm thinking of you with love –

Ludwig

Ben Richards to Ludwig Wittgenstein (undated, probably around March 1, 1947)[103]

GREENOGE
40, SWAKELEYS ROAD
ICKENHAM
UXBRIDGE
RUISLIP 2114

Dear Ludwig,

I was very glad to get your letters. You know I am your friend and will always be unless I change very greatly.

I am coming up to Cambridge next week-end – the 8th – I hope; can you get a room for me? Please don't cancel your "at-home": I want very much to come to it.

It is a beautiful sunny day – I hope it will be like this next week-end – though still a bit cold. My two sisters[104] /(whom you haven't seen)/ are home from school for half-term this week-end. Most of the snow is gone now; a week ago we had some very good tobogganing. We have also done a little skating, but not much: my skates /(boots)/ are rather small and the ice surface is not very smooth.

We are very well now, and I hope you are the same and that your work and classes are going well. I hope Drury is better; I have not heard from him.

---

103 This letter is undated, but given its mention of a March 8,1947 visit and Wittgenstein's 'at homes', it clearly fits here in the sequence; and the rough date can be arrived at by working backwards from March 8.

104 Presumably Ben's two youngest sisters: Isabella and Julia.

It will be wonderful to see you.
Love always
>Your B. O. F.[105]
>>Ben

Ludwig Wittgenstein to Ben Richards, March 15, 1947

TRINITY COLL. CAMB 15.3.47.

Dear Ben,

Soon after you left me on Sunday I began to feel rather queer & it seems this was the beginning of a slight gastric 'flu. I stayed in bed for 3 days, but I'm up now, only rather weak & shaky. The thought of you & how lovely it was seeing you was with me <u>the whole time</u> & helped no end. – Please write about next week-end <u>soon</u>. I think I'll be quite strong again by then.

I hope you haven't been ill, too! – There are lots of things I'ld like to say, but I'll wait with them till I see you. Some are very intelligent & <u>some</u> not at all: for, like Mr B.,[106] I am a gourmet & like to think something absolutely stupid before /thinking/ something immensely intelligent, just to enjoy the contrast. – Let me hear from you soon & God bless you.

Always with love
Ludwig
P.T.O.

P.S. This is a scene I witnessed the other day.[107]

---

105 This would usually stand for 'bloody old face'; but perhaps in this context – both in the sentence and in the letter more generally – it stands for 'bloody old friend'.
106 It's unclear who this is a reference to.
107 Wittgenstein pasted onto the back of his letter what looks to be an illustration which he had cut out of one of the detective magazines which he liked to read and added a handwritten comment on it.

Ludwig Wittgenstein to Ben Richards, March 17, 1947

TRINITY COLL. CAMB.

17.3.47

Dear Ben,

W.W.P.[108] I shall arrive at Liverpool Street on Saturday at 12.37 p.m. (Twelve thirty seven.) I'll look out for you on the platform & in the waiting room. I'm still weak, but I'll be pretty fit by then. We had a terrific gale last night & I'm told the Backs[109] are under water. A lot of earth was blown out of my window-box, a disaster which dwarfs the blowing away of mere roofs, etc. – One of my Crocuses is beginning to flower & the Cyclamen has 5 blossoms & a 6th almost open. – That's all the news. – I'm looking forward to seeing you. God bless you.

    With love

        Ludwig

Ludwig Wittgenstein to Ben Richards, March 25, 1947

Trinity College
Cambridge
25.3.47.

An alleged seal of power.[110]

Dear Ben,

It's been lovely being with you. I wanted to send flowers to your mother from London but there was no time; so I had them sent from here.

I heard from Mrs Clement. She will put me up.[111] I intend to leave here on Monday. Friday /(this week)/ I shall have two roots extracted (<u>not</u> $\sqrt{2}$). I'll arrive at Liverpool

---

108 Probably: 'Wind and weather permitting'.
109 The 'Backs' refers to a grassy area between the back of a number of Cambridge colleges and the River Cam.
110 Wittgenstein cut out this seal, pasted it onto the top left corner of the first page of the letter, and wrote this underneath.
111 For the previous few years, whenever Wittgenstein was in Swansea, he would lodge with Reverend and Mrs Morgan, at 2 Cwmdonkin Terrace. During his stays there he got to know the neighbouring Clement family, who lived at No. 1. From this visit, Wittgenstein began to lodge with the Clement family rather than with the Morgans (see Monk 1990: 464-5).

Str. at 10.³⁶ a.m. & my train to Swansea leaves Paddington at 1.⁵⁵ p.m.. I don't suppose you'll have time to see me. But, just in case, I'll look for you on the platform at L'pool Street. For it would be <u>pretty</u> good to see your <u>b.</u> old face again. My address in Swansea will be

1, Cwmdonkin Terrace (This is an /undisguised/ hint.)

My crocuses are very nice. Only three are in flower but there are about 80 plants coming altogether. The 6 cyclamen flowers are still on their stalks, but not for long now.

As I said: it's been lovely being with you. God bless you. – With love

       Ludwig

P.S. Give my love to all.

Ben Richards to Ludwig Wittgenstein (undated, around February or March 1947)[112]

GREENOGE
40, SWAKELEYS ROAD
ICKENHAM
UXBRIDGE
RUISLIP 2114

Dear Ludwig

Ann[113] was very pleased indeed to get the flowers. They came on Wednesday and in good condition.

We did our performance of the Mass in B minor[114] last night, and it went very well. The tenor was the only one of the professional soloists who was any good. The bass was just feeble but the two ladies were horrible – their vibrato and rubato combined to make it almost impossible to hear ~~what~~ the melody they were supposed to be singing. We had not rehearsed with them before.

I am looking forward to seeing you at the week-end. Will you meet me as before at Barts between 12 & 12.15?

---

112 This letter is undated, but a rough date can be estimated from the context. At the end of January 1947 Richards was rehearsing for a performance of Bach's Mass (see his letter to Wittgenstein of January 28, 1947), and since this letters reports having done the performance, this letter is likely from some time in February or March 1947.
113 Ann Phillips was the Richards family housekeeper.
114 Johann Sebastian Bach's Mass in B minor (BWV 232); see Richards' letter to Wittgenstein, of January 28, 1947.

Please let me know your plans.

Thanks for your letter.

    With love al<u>wa</u>ys

        Ben.

Ludwig Wittgenstein to Ben Richards, April 1, 1947

            c/o Clement (not Clement<u>s</u>)

            1 Cwmdonkin Terrace

            Swansea 1.4.47.

My dear Ben,

I had your book & the card this morning. Thanks! Thanks a lot! It was good of you to come to Paddington; & sad that we didn't see each other. I had a sort of idea you might possibly come to Paddington & I looked round for you. I sat in the carriage next to the engine (because it's least crowded there) & probably you never went as far forward as that. If you had you'ld have been repaid for the lot of trouble you took by seeing how much I enjoyed seeing you. God bless you for doing what you did; & next time we'll make better arrangements.

As you see, I'm staying with the Clements, & they are as nice as always. The weather's moderate just now. – I had a letter from Drury the other day, saying that he's leaving the Home today & going to Devon where he'll spend his holidays with his family. After that he will return to St. Patricks in Dublin, but not as a patient but as assistant to Dr Moore[115] (who has treated him). He'll stay there, I think, till Christmas.

My dear, please let me hear from you soon again, as that keeps me going. I hope to have a good rest here & to do some moderately decent work as well. I hope to see you before long!

God bless you, again.

    With love

        Ludwig

P.S. Give the /enclosed/ paper bag to Angela[116] with my <u>best</u> wishes & tell her to read it carefully, & to treasure it. Give my <u>best</u> wishes to everybody.

---

115 Dr John Norman Parker Moore (1911-1996) had shortly before taken over as medical director at St. Patrick's Hospital in Dublin.

116 The oldest of Richards' four younger sisters.

Ludwig Wittgenstein to Ben Richards, April 10, 1947

c/o Clement
1, Cwmdonkin Terrace
Swansea
10.4.47.

Dear Ben,

I wish you'd write to me, give your friend a break in the vacation. – He needs it. – Drury intended to come here before the 18th. He's staying with his mother in North Devon & thought he could come over by boat. But boats aren't running yet & he rather dreads the long train journey, so he asked me to come to Exeter next Tuesday & stay with him at 3 Colleton Crescent till Friday, 18th, when Term begins. So I'll be there /c/o Drury/ from the 15th to the 18th. (I'd rather have seen him here, of course.) – The weather's been very fine for the last 2 days & I'm taking walks along the cliffs. I've also been working a fair amount.[117] – May you have a good time & be happy, & not miss that /brand of/ pleasure either which comes from giving others happiness.

I'm thinking of you with love.

Ludwig

Enclosure included with the letter of April 10, 1947:

---

117 At this time Wittgenstein was working in MS 134 (see around pp. 131ff).

Ben Richards to Ludwig Wittgenstein (undated, around April 10, 1947)[118]

GREENOGE
40, SWAKELEYS ROAD
ICKENHAM
UXBRIDGE
RUISLIP 2114

Dear Ludwig

Thank you very much for the easter card and letters. Angela was very grateful for your kind gift, and has been studying it with great care ever since I gave it to her.

I am glad you are going to see Drury. I hope he is well; please give him my love. I am glad too that you are getting some good walks – I wish I were there with you – and that your work is going well.

Since starting my appointment at the surgical unit (April 1st) I have been working, for me, quite hard. Two or three days a week we are operating from 9.0 or 1.30 till 5.0 or 7.30, when we are supposed to be in the theatre for all operations, & be ready to assist on our own patients. Besides examining our patients there is a good deal to do in the way of changing dressings, removing stiches & so on. So far I have done evening duty three times, and night duty once. I am enjoying the work very much & find it even more interesting than the medical wards, though I am not yet a very efficient worker. Please give my best wishes to the Clements, Morgans & Davies's.[119]

    Love always

       Ben.

Ludwig Wittgenstein to Ben Richards (probably April 14, 1947)[120]

1 Cwmdonkin Terrace
Swansea
Monday

Dear Ben,

Thank you for your letter. As I wrote in my last one, I shall come through London on Friday (18th), arriving at Paddington 1.45 midday. Question: – can you meet the train &

---

118 This letter is undated, but since it replied directly to multiple themes from Wittgenstein's letter of April 10, 1947, it clearly fits here; and the rough date can be derived from the fact that in 1947 Easter fell on April 6th.
119 Variously Wittgenstein's hosts and neighbours in Swansea.
120 Wittgenstein did not date this letter, and Richards has added 'Jan 1947 (?)' by hand. However, as Wittgenstein only lodged at 1 Cwmdonkin Terrace from April 1947, this cannot be right. Given Wittgenstein's references to the contents of his previous letter, it seems certain that this letter fits here; and given that he instructs Richards to send his next communication to Drury's address it's likely just before he left, hence April 14, 1947.

can you spend a considerable portion of the afternoon & evening with me? (I might even take a room in London & stay till Saturday, as I'm not lecturing until Monday.) Please reply by wire so I have your answer on Thursday, at the latest. My address will be c/o Drury, 3 Colleton Crescent, Exeter.[121]

I shan't write more today as I'm hoping to see you.

    With love

        Ludwig

Ludwig Wittgenstein to Ben Richards, April 24, 1947

                                        Trinity College Cambridge

                                                      24.4.46.

                                                        /47/[122]

My dear Ben,

This is to tell you, what you already know, that I loved being with you. I was in time for the train & it wasn't as close a shave as I thought it would be, & as I ought to have had that morning. (Pretty good!)

My lecture on Monday wasn't bad. – This place is lousy as usual, a /kind of/ stronghold of loneliness![123] – I know that I was pretty difficult to get along with on Saturday. As I said to you I sometimes felt as though I had no skin & my nerve-endings were laid bare; but when I looked at you I always felt good again. Please forgive me for being difficult! (Though I have an idea you do. /Don't you?/)

I hope your Gramophone will soon be mended & you'll hear the Schubert,[124] & I want you to think of me when you do.

Tonight at the Moral Science Club Dr Ewing[125] is reading a paper "Is metaphysics impossible?" It's some sort of attack ~~against~~ /on/ me, & I hope I'll survive it.

---

121 A couple of weeks later, after his stay with Drury, Wittgenstein reported to Rhees: "I found Drury perfectly normal. He talked with great intelligence about his illness. He is going to stay in Dublin as Dr Moore's assistant until X-mas. How far he is safe, I mean, how likely it is that his former state will return, that, of course, I don't know, & I don't feel in the least sanguine about it" (Wittgenstein to Rhees, April 30,1947).

122 Wittgenstein mistakenly wrote the year as '46', and Richards corrected it to '47' underneath (the accuracy of this change being confirmed by the reference to Ewing's talk which took place on April 24, 1947).

123 The previous day Wittgenstein had written in his manuscript notebook: "Cambridge is becoming more and more odious to me. The disintegrating & putrifying English civilization. A country where politics vacillates between an evil purpose & no purpose" (MS 134, p. 152; April 23, 1947).

124 As is made clear by Richards' reply, Wittgenstein had in mind Franz Schubert's String Quintet in C Major (op. post. 163, D 956).

125 Alfred Cyril Ewing (1899 –1973), English philosopher, and fellow faculty member at Cambridge, and a long-standing critic of Wittgenstein's. For an expanded and developed version of the paper Ewing presented that evening, see Ewing 1948: 33-38. Notes on the discussion of the original paper can be found in Wittgenstein 2003: 338.

There's a big circus on Midsummer Common[126] now. If you were here I'd go with you. It looks nice from the outside.

God bless you! Don't forget me! I'm thinking of you with love always.

    Ludwig

Give my love & thanks to all.

Ben Richards to Ludwig Wittgenstein, April 29, 1947

GREENOGE
40, SWAKELEYS ROAD
ICKENHAM
UXBRIDGE
RUISLIP 2114
29.4.47

Dear Ludwig,

Thank you very much for the letter. I loved having you here though only for such a short time. It was a great pity about the gramophone; the pick-up has been brought back now and I am about to play the Schubert quintet.

I hope things are going well in Cambridge. I think of you a great deal.

My mother and Angela came back last night. They had a very good time in Paris and the weather was lovely.

Virginia and Tazza[127] go back to school to-morrow.

It is really spring here. The foliage is all an extraordinary bright green and I have heard the cuckoo a lot in the mornings. I saw a pair of cuckoos quite close while waiting for my train at Ickenham on Sunday (I was on duty at the hospital all day Sunday – we were pretty busy Saturday too, operating till half past seven).

I hope to go climbing again, in Skye in a fortnight or so.

If you write to Drury will you please give him my love.

I am looking forward to seeing you again before long either in Cambridge or here.

By the way I hope you have been suitably edified by the Tongue of Mars.[128]

    With love
    always
        Ben

---

126 A large park in Cambridge, northeast of the city center.
127 The middle two of the Ben Richards' four younger sisters.
128 Wittgenstein asks the meaning of this allusion in his next letter (of May 2, 1947), and Richards explains in his reply (of May 8, 1947).

Ludwig Wittgenstein to Ben Richards, May 2, 1947

Trinity College
Cambridge
2.5.47.

My dear Ben, dear O. H.,

Thank you for your letter. I believe that if you'd seen the relief & other feelings with which I saw it in the post, you'd have felt it was <u>worth-while</u> writing me often. For, I'm afraid, I need it badly. – I wish you were here & could look at the new flowers in the window-box. They are yellow Violas (not string instruments) & look nice, & I hope they'll still do so when you come here again. – My lectures (& one at-home) have been all right, so far. – Dr Ewing read a /[I find it saves a lot of time to turn /over/ the leaf like that.]/[129] rotten paper to the Moral Sc. Club last week[130] &, of course, was lousy in discussion. Altogether the M. Sc. Cl. & the whole faculty are extremely depressing. The lecturers, though they disagree a good deal among each other, agree in their hatred of me, which perhaps is natural but not a good state of affairs at all; & I can't do anything about it. – I have a <u>very</u> intelligent & <u>very</u> talented man at present in my classes, Professor von Wright from Finland, but he's here only for a term. He had been here before, in 1938, & impressed me then just as he does now. If we had such a man in our faculty it would transform it entirely, I believe. Because <u>I</u>'m no good at subduing what / in my opinion is/ worst in it, Mr B…t[131] for example. – I hope you'll enjoy your climbing in Skye, but be good & take care of yourself. – I want to make one more remark which is somehow connected with our talk /on the Embankment/ about your work, & I wonder if you'll understand me: – If you make mistakes & do what you shouldn't have done, or neglect things, in your work (as you're bound to do) don't think that it's wrong to be ashamed of yourself. It isn't, & it'll keep you safe (like a disinfectant) in the future. If you <u>won't</u> be ashamed of yourself, you won't learn what's most important. If this sounds foolish, or worse, I can't help it; it's still what I believe. I'm writing it because I feel it somehow applies to you. In case what I sayid <u>is</u> foolish

---

129 Wittgenstein wrote this letter on both sides of a couple of sheets of paper. On the top edge of the reverse side of the first sheet, he added this remark in square brackets, to (playfully) account for the fact that rather than turning the page over along the long edge, he had flipped it over along the short edge (so that the reverse side was written going in the opposite direction to the first side).
130 See the relevant footnote to Wittgenstein's prior letter, of April 24, 1947.
131 This is presumably a reference to Richard B. Braithwaite (1900-1990), one of Wittgenstein's colleagues (with Wittgenstein overlooking the silent 'e' at the end of his name).

you know it isn't said in a bad spirit /& you'll forgive/. – May God always be with you. – I'm thinking with love of you always.

  Ludwig

P. S. Give Angela my good wishes.

P. P. S. What is the 'Tongue of Mars'? Please explain. L. L.

Ben Richards to Ludwig Wittgenstein, May 8, 1947

AVENUE	2849	ST. BARTHOLOMEW'S HOSPITAL,
"	2960	LONDON, E.C.1.
CENTRAL	1101	8/5/47

Dear Ludwig

Thank you very much for writing – I love to hear from you.

I am going to Skye for a fortnight to-morrow, and will be staying at the Glenbrittle Youth Hostel. I hope you will write to me there. We are going on the night train to Inverness and across Scotland from East to West – the same way as I went last summer.

I have played the Schubert quintet[132] three times I like it very much indeed. I like the second movement best of all. I also liked particularly the second tune in the first movement, and the trio; and the end part of the last movement. I went to some Beethoven concerts by Busch quartet;[133] I thought they were very good.

I am very glad you have a really good man in your classes and I hope it makes you feel less as though you were 'giving a performance'.[134]

If I remember right, 'The Tongue of Mars' was the title of a review of "Monty's" book of speeches, etc. in the Times Literary Supplement quoted on the inside of the front cover.[135]

---

132 This is a response to Wittgenstein's remark in his letter of April 24, 1947.

133 The Busch Quartet – founded in Germany in 1913 – was one of the most important and influential quartet associations of the first half of the 20, century. The members emigrated to America in 1939, and the quartet continued until 1952.

134 See Wittgenstein's letter to Richards of October 18, 1946, and the relevant footnote there.

135 On Saturday August 14, 1943 *The Times Literary Supplement* ran an article (p. 391a-b) about the series of messages from General Montogomery to the Eight Army that had been appearing over the previous few months. This article was entitled 'THE TONGUE OF MARS'. The later published book of these messages and speeches to which Richards referred here may have been: Field-Marshal the Viscount Montgomery of Alamein's *Forward to Victory: Messages to His Armies from El Alamein to the Baltic, and His Speeches on The British soldier, and The Army and the Nation*, London, Hutchinson, 1946. Wittgenstein kept a collection of newspaper cuttings and the like which he found particularly ridiculous or absurd, and Montgomery features in it a number of times. In 1948 Wittgenstein wrote to Rhees: "[T]hanks for your letter & for the cutting. Isn't Monty incredible?! If only I could get those <u>marvelous</u> war speeches where he said something like "The thing is very nice, I like it very much", refering to the operations in France, I believe" (Wittgenstein to Rhees, June 23, 1948).

Anyway, it's the overwhelming minority who read Vogue, as they say.[136]
>God bless you
>>love, always
>>>Ben.

Ludwig Wittgenstein to Ben Richards, May 11, 1947

>>>>Trinity College
>>>>Cambridge
>>>>11.5.47.

Dear Ben, o. h.,

Thanks for your letter of May 8th. If the weather where you are is as fine as it's here right now you're very lucky. Somehow I don't find it easy to-day to write to you: There are plenty of things I'd like to say, but then when I think of you in Skye they don't seem to be quite suitable, & I find myself saying "He wouldn't want to read <u>this</u> now". Perhaps that's quite wrong; perhaps it's right. I don't know. I thought that I should be honest about it with you, anyway. – I am thinking of you a very great deal, & it would be wrong to deny that I wish I could see you.

My lectures & at-homes go quite well, but there is a good deal going on in the faculty that's <u>most</u> distasteful to me & makes me wish to quit my job. (Perhaps foolishly, or cowardly.)

I want to say that what I wrote to you in my last letter, about it not being wrong to be ashamed etc. (if you remember what I mean), was very important to me & not /as it might have seemed/ just the outburst of some queer mood of mine; but something I'd thought of a good deal.

May you be lucky & happy, & /yet/ serious at the same time. <u>God bless you always</u>, whatever you do! If you find it in your heart, let me hear from you soon.

>With love
>>Ludwig

P. S. I heard from Drury. He seems to be getting on all right & to like his work. He sends his love.

L., L.

This ↓ is what's called 'paper shortage'.[137]

---

136 The advertising slogan of the American fashion magazine *Vogue* was: "Vogue – for the overwhelming minority".

137 The sheet is torn off at the bottom. There was a significant paper shortage in many European countries for some years after the Second World War.

Ludwig Wittgenstein to Ben Richards, May 17, 1947

Trinity College
Cambridge
17.5.47

Dear Ben,

This is mainly to tell you that I am thinking of you a lot. God bless you. – Last Tuesday I went to Oxford to attend a meeting of the Jowett Society[138] (a kind of Moral Sc. Cl.) on Wednesday night. The J. Society had, until now, been run on different lines from the Mor. Sc. Cl. They had very long papers & a formal reply to each paper & very little discussion. They have now introduced two short-paper meetings a term & there is to be someone in the chair at these meetings who keeps the discussion to the point. The first of these /new/ meetings was last Wednesday, an Undergrad. read a paper & I was in the chair.[139] The paper wasn't at all bad, but there were about 100 people present & it was extremely hard work to keep up even a moderately good discussion. It lasted till 11 p.m., when these meeting <u>have</u> to end at Oxford; & as people seemed to be pretty lively I told them that if anyone wanted to continue the discussion the next day I'd stay in Oxford for that discussion. One of the people offered us his room & we had another 3-hour discussion on Thursday. About 25 people turned up & it was deffinitely good. I returned on Friday (yesterday) afternoon & lectured as usual, feeling <u>very</u> tired indeed, I still do, & my brain feels as though it wanted a longish rest, I'm afraid. I stayed with Smythies & his wife[140] & saw a good deal of M^{iss} Anscombe, too. They were all very kind to me. When I'll see you again I'ld like to tell you more about it all. My dxxx hxxxx, if you still lxxx mx[141] write to me soon.
May you have a <u>pleasant</u> time!
 God bless you.
  With love, always
   Ludwig

---

138 A philosophical discussion society at Oxford, named after Benjamin Jowett (1817-1893).
139 Oscar Wood (an undergraduate at the time, and president of the society), presented a paper discussing the validity of Descartes' 'I think therefore I am', and Wittgenstein – being in the chair – gave an extemporaneous reply afterwards. The meeting attracted almost every member of the Oxford philosophy faculty, and every philosophy graduate student, and many others, so that people were sitting on the floor and on the windowsills. For a more detailed description of the evening see Rowe 2023: 410-11 and Monk 1990: 496-7.
140 Yorick Smythies and his wife, Diana ('Polly') Pollard, who lived at 22 Banbury Road, Oxford.
141 Instead of spelling these words out fully, Wittgenstein has completed them with small x's. Presumably he meant: 'My dear heart, if you still love me'. (In a few of his later letters Wittgenstein spelled words like 'love' entirely with small x's or dots – see for example his letters to Richards of April 19 and 25, 1951; and compare, also, his letters to Richards of March 28 and May 2, 1948).

Ben Richards to Ludwig Wittgenstein (undated, end of May 1947)[142]

GREENOGE
40, SWAKELEYS ROAD
ICKENHAM
UXBRIDGE
RUISLIP 2114

Dear Ludwig,

I have had a jolly good holiday; only two or three wet days in the fortnight, although Skye has the reputation of being very wet generally. And it's baking hot here now. My mother & father have gone to South Wales for a fortnight's holiday and Heshe has gone to my aunt's house at Virginia & Tazza's[143] school in Sussex. So there is no one here but Ann[144] & Angela & me. Angela has her French & German vivas next week for the Higher School Cert.[145]

Thank you for both letters to Skye. You were wrong to be afraid I should not want to hear something serious from you when I am on holiday. ~~One~~ I cannot help feeling serious in the presence of such scenery, and I thought of you a great deal. I am afraid I will do many things to be ashamed of; but I am often more acutely ashamed, or embarrassed, over trivial things and not sufficiently over things I should be more ashamed of. I hope I will develop my sense of proportion. It is hard without examples; I know few of the students I am with very well, none enough to respect very deeply, and I hardly ever have a serious talk – probably because I am usually so reticent & shy myself. I do not suffer much through this; I find a lot of the work very interesting. I like most of my patients, but with them too, as with everybody I often feel awkward. I was very interested in your visit to Oxford and I should like you to tell me more about it. I am longing for the next time we shall see each other. Your term will end before long I expect and you could perhaps come here again, or me to Cambridge when my mother is back to free Ann at the week-end.

I was on night duty at the hospital last night – not very busy. I saw an article (broadcast talk) by Prof. Broad in the Listener, he says "Nearly everyone finds the

---

142 This dating can be inferred from the fact that Richards returns from his holiday to Skye around May 22, 1947 (see his letter of May 8, 1947), and this letter was written shortly upon his return.
143 The middle two of Ben Richards' four younger sisters.
144 Ann Phillips was the Richards family housekeeper.
145 Until 1951 the Higher School Certificate Examination was the standard final Secondary School examination in England and Wales, taken at the age of about 18 (roughly equivalent to the Matura or the Abitur in other European countries).

notion of irreducibly prepresentative precognition very hard to swallow":[146] I do – don't you?

Love always, Ben.

Ludwig Wittgenstein to Ben Richards, May 31, 1947

TRIN. COLL. CAMB.

31.5.47

My dear Ben,

I am thinking of you <u>a great deal</u>. I also wonder why I don't hear from you. I wish you happiness! And I promise that, if it should turn out that I can't <u>give</u> you any, <u>I'll do my best</u> not to take any away from you.

My term ends in 10 days. My last lecture will be either on Monday (June 2nd) or Friday (6th). My lectures went well, on the whole, but I'm rather exhausted now & in need of a change.

On Monday June 9th or Tuesday (10th) I shall have to be in London & It's very important for me to see you. Please let me know as soon as you possibly can which of these two days would suit you best. I'ld have to come to London with an early train, arriving Liverpool St. 10^{36} a.m. &, of course, it would be nice if you could meet the train. If you can't, we could arrange to meet at lunchtime wherever you like, & we could then arrange to see each other in the afternoon.

I am thinking of you with love, & with many good wishes!

Ludwig

P.S. Thank you for your card from Skye. I sent two letters to the Youth Hostel. I hope you got them <u>both</u>. <u>God bless you</u>. L. L.

---

146 C. D. (Charlie Dunbar) Broad (1887-1971) was a colleague of Wittgenstein's at Cambridge, and Professor of Moral Philosophy from 1933 to 1953. *The Listener* was a weekly magazine (from 1929 to 1991) which published in print many of the talks that were broadcast on BBC radio. The May 8, 1947, issue of *The Listener* included an article by Broad entitled, 'Philosophical Implications of Precognition', which included the following remarks: "Suppose, for example, that I knew telepathically that a certain person was intending to poison himself. Then by a perfectly normal process I could form the expectation that he would be found poisoned, and the chances are that my expectation would be fulfilled. Any case that could plausibly be explained on these lines might be described as a case of pre-cognition normally based on supernormal cognition of contemporary or past data. If no explanation even on these lines can be suggested I shall say that we have a case of 'irreducibly pre-presentative precognition'… There is good evidence for the occurrence of irreducibly pre-presentative precognition." Broad recognized, however that "[n]early everyone finds the notion of irreducibly pre-presentative precognition very hard to swallow" (*The Listener*, Vol 37:954, p. 709).

Ben Richards to Ludwig Wittgenstein (undated, probably early June 1947)

AVENUE	2849	ST. BARTHOLOMEW'S HOSPITAL,
"	2960	LONDON, E.C.1.
CENTRAL	1101	

Dear Ludwig

Thanks for your letter. I hope you got my last.

Please come on Monday. We operate late on Tuesdays, and I am changing my evening duty from Monday to Tuesday. Will you be staying the night at Ickenham?

There is a fair preparing itself by Ickenham station to start on Friday – I hope it will be there by Monday.

I am in the courtyard at Barts[147] and there is a ten-inch goldfish in the fountain watching me.

I am afraid I won't be able to meet the morning train from Cambridge, but I will be out in front of Barts at 12.15^{PM} and we can have lunch together and arrange to meet when my work is finished.

If you can come earlier – on Sunday – please do & let me know. I am on duty Saturday night and get off about 9.0 Sunday morning.

        With love – always
            Ben.

Ludwig Wittgenstein to Ben Richards, June 6, 1947

6 Ju 47   Trinity College
Express[148]   Friday

My dear Ben,

Thank you for your letter. I'll come on Monday & will meet you at 12.^{15} in front of Barts. I should love to stay Monday night in Ickenham. It is possible, however, that, after I have talked to you, you will not really want me to stay.

    <u>I love you always</u>.
            Ludwig

---

147 St Bartholomew's Hospital – commonly known as 'Bart's' – was (and is) a teaching hospital in London.

148 The date was added in Richards' hand, as was the word below it. The word is hard to make out, but likely says 'Express'.

Ludwig Wittgenstein to Ben Richards, June 9, 1947

TRIN. COLL. CAMB.

Monday
Morning
9/6/47

Dear Ben,

That I had to let you down couldn't have been more disagreeable to you than it was to me. During last night I suddenly got violent pain in the abdomen, sickness & diarrhoeha. By this morning I was so weak that I could hardly stand up. I hope I haven't caused you great inconvenience, though probably I have. If I get better quickly, as I hope I shall, I'll ring you up in Ickenham on Wednesday evening, & perhaps we could arrange to see each other on Friday.

    God bless you
        with love
            Ludwig

Ludwig Wittgenstein to Ben Richards (undated, probably mid-late June 1947)[149]

---

149 This letter is written on (and refers to) an article by Kate Aitken entitled 'June Bride: Weddings Have an Etiquette and Pattern Which, When Followed, Make for Dignity' (in *The Standard. Comics, Novel, Magazine, Roto, News*, Montreal, June 7, 1947). It's not certain how Wittgenstein came into possession of a page from a Montreal periodical, but one plausible route is that it was sent to him by William Heriot Watson, a friend of his who lived in Montreal, and who sometimes sent Wittgenstein cuttings of articles which he thought Wittgenstein would consider ridiculous or absurd, as Wittgenstein collected these (see, for example, Watson's letter to Wittgenstein of November 12, 1931: "You ask for nonsensical articles, I enclose a gem of a cutting from the Montreal Star"). This was probably one of those articles. Wittgenstein and Richards often exchanged examples of such things as well (see for example Wittgenstein's letter to Richards of March 12-14, 1951, and Richards' letter to Wittgenstein of the end of May 1947). Wittgenstein called his collection of these ridiculous clippings – gathered from Watson, Richards, his brother Paul, and others – his 'Nonsense Collection' (see Wang-Kathrein 2021). The date of this letter is estimated from the date of the article on which it is written, plus the fact that there's a longer than usual gap in the correspondence at this point which this short note may have filled, along with some other contextual clues.

Dear Ben,

Can you imagine that this is a happy marriage? I find it difficult!

W. l., a....s[150]

Ludwig

Ludwig Wittgenstein to Ben Richards, June 18, 1947

TRIN. COLL. CAMB.

Wednesday
18/6/47

Dear Ben,

Dear old h....t,[151]

At Liverpool Street I bought a "Tribune" & in their heading article it they says: "Such opportunities come rarely & they never come twice." What do you think of that? I'm writing to say that I loved being with you & am looking forward to Sat. 27th. I hope we'll be able to arrange it that I can see you for a longer time before long! I want to get away from here as soon as possible &, if possible, into a human surrounding. I gave your good wishes to my sister[152] – I thought you wouldn't mind – & she sends you her's. God bless you!

    With love

        Ludwig

Ludwig Wittgenstein to Ben Richards, June 23, 1947

TRIN. COLL. CAMB.

Monday
23/6/47

Dear Ben,

When I'll see you this week-end it's necessary that I make some sort of plans for the summer. Please think about possibilities a bit. I'll be at Barts on Saturday noon. I'm looking forward to seeing you, as I always do.

    With love

        Ludwig

My dear, <u>God bless you</u>! I have no right to your friendship. Please don't <u>rashly</u> think that you can give it to me. For what I need is a friend in life & action, not only in thoughts & feelings (though that too). You have my love: don't rashly think that you

---

150 Stands for: 'With love, always'.
151 Stands for: 'heart'.
152 Margaret Stonborough-Wittgenstein

can give me yours, for **there is really nothing in me that is lovable**.[153] Please don't think that I'm sentimental /in writing this/. I'm trying hard to be honest with you.

    God bless you, again.

        W. l.

            Ludwig

Ludwig Wittgenstein to Ben Richards, June 30, 1947

Trinity College
Monday
30/6/47

Dear Ben,

Something occurred to me this morning about which I think I ought to write to you straight away. (I wish I didn't have to bother you with it, but it's necessary.) It occurred to me that your parents, foreseeing that you'll be alone in Ickenham in August, might already have invited someone (some relative perhaps) to stay at their house during that time, so to speak, to keep you company. Now if this were so /I feel/ my coming to stay with you would make no sense. You see, under other circumstances we would have spent our holidays together, which would have meant being together alone for a considerable part of each day. If I stay with you, this must be a substitute for such a holiday; i.e., while you're busy I'll work for myself, & in your free time & during week-ends we'ld be together as we would be if we were on holidays /in Swansea/. – If I stayed in your house, with a stranger /(I don't mean the doctor)/, & had to be with you in the company of a stranger /I mean a stranger to me/, it would destroy all that I'm looking forward to completely. – I know that you'll agree with me if you try to imagine the situation; but I thought that you might conceivably not imagine it clearly & then make an arrangement which would prove no good to either of us. – Please don't take what I've written in a presumtuous sense!! I don't want you, or anyone, to make special arrangements to suit my tastes; but I had to tell you what kind of arrangement I know I couldn't go through with.

May it be possible to make arrangements which are good & pleasant for both of us! (If they aren't good for both they'll not be ~~good~~ for either of us.)

---

153 Wittgenstein stressed his statement that "there is really nothing in me that is lovable" by strongly marking the two lines on which these words were written with double vertical lines on either side. We have represented this with bold font.

I enjoyed being with you <u>a lot</u>! Meaning, that I enjoyed <u>a lot</u> being with you the few hours we were together.
<u>Do only what you really want to do!</u>*
    God bless you, always.
        With love
            Ludwig

* I mean, in the matter of inviting me, etc.

P.S. If I give you too much bother I wish you'ld throw me overboard as unnecessary ballast. L. L.

Ben Richards to Ludwig Wittgenstein (undated, probably early July 1947)

AVENUE	2849	ST. BARTHOLOMEW'S HOSPITAL,
"	2960	LONDON, E.C.1.
CENTRAL	1101	

Dear Ludwig,

Thanks for the letter. I understood you wouldn't want to come, with visitors & strangers to you at Ickenham. The family are probably going away round about August 20th.

I shall get off to-morrow by half past four and will wait at the usual place. I work on Saturday morning, but I hope we will have a better week-end this time. I loved your coming last week-end but it was very short.

    Love always
        Ben.

Ludwig Wittgenstein to Ben Richards, July 8, 1947

                      1 Cwmdonkin Terrace
                            Swansea
                              Tuesday
                              9/7/47[154]

Dear old Heart,

I've only just arrived & want to write to you about our talk concerning 'stinginess'. What I said may have seemed, & perhaps was, ill-timed, but I felt strongly about it &

---

154 This date was probably added by Richards. July 9, was a Wednesday in 1947. But since Wittgenstein wrote 'Tuesday' on this letter, it's likely that Richards noted the date he received the letter, and that Wittgenstein had written it the previous day, Tuesday July 8.

thought I should say something, though really there was no time to explain. So I'll do it now. I had borrowed £5 from you & said I was going to give you a cheque, & you replied that I needn't do it as you owed me money for hotel bills etc. – Now you couldn't possibly think that I'd answer: "Yes, you do owe me for those bills, so I shan't pay you back the 5 pounds". You couldn't have expected that meanness of me. (Even though I <u>am</u> mean at times.) So you knew that I certainly wouldn't accept your offer. But then why did you make it? – What I want to say is: Don't ever offer what you know the other man isn't going to accept, & don't make an offer <u>in such a way</u> that he can't accept it. If you <u>really</u> want to give, or to pay, give & pay wholeheartedly. If, e.g. you want to pay, pay briskly, not fumblingly. Fumblers are bad givers, & you <u>oughtn't</u> be a bad giver, you ought to be a good giver. When I mentioned stinginess, you asked me, did I think you were stingy. I said, there wasn't the slightest danger of it. But I wasn't definite enough: The danger is very real, unless you observe yourself more closely. If you <u>don't</u> see that there is the danger of your being stingy, you <u>will</u> become stingy. And even if no one else will tell you that, it's still so. Giving has to be <u>practiced</u>, & owing to various circumstances you've had very little practice, so far. – When you get this I wish you'd write me a line & say if you understand me, & also that you take what I've said in a kind spirit. I don't want you to be a bad giver because I love you so much.

You know that I loved being with you. Thanks for everything! & God bless you always. I'll miss you terribly. Think of me – & be good – & look after yourself!

    With love

        Ludwig

Read this letter once more. I wish I could have expressed what I mean more clearly.
L. L.

Ben Richards to Ludwig Wittgenstein (undated, probably mid-July 1947)

~~AVENUE~~   ~~2849~~   ~~ST. BARTHOLOMEW'S HOSPITAL,~~

     ~~"~~   ~~2960~~   ~~LONDON, E.C.1.~~

~~CENTRAL~~   ~~1101~~

                                                       Hotel Mont Collon

                                                             Arolla

                                                             Valais

                                                             Switzerland

Dear Ludwig

Thank you for coming & thanks for your letter.

I know I am naturally often very stingy, though I am not sure my suggesting we should cancel our mutual debts was an example of my stinginess. It was probably an example of something bad – I often make suggestions in a way which makes it difficult to accept them. Thank you very much indeed for writing about it – I am very glad you did. I understood it – I hope I will learn to be more generous. Please always tell me when I am mean; and my other faults too.

I hope you are well and happy in Swansea – are you?

How is your work going?

Give my regards to the Clements, the Morgans and the Davies's. I hope they are well too.

As you see I have arrived safely on the third day, and the weather is hot & sunny & perfectly clear.

I look forward to seeing you again soon

   Love always

    Ben.

Ludwig Wittgenstein to Ben Richards, July 17, 1947

                  1 Cwmdonkin Terrace

                        Swansea

                        17.7.47

Dear Ben, o. h. !

Thanks for your letter, & please write to me <u>often</u>. If you <u>want</u> me to feel happy & well, & to work decently, do it; God bless you, always. – The weather /here/ is changeable but not too bad & I go out a fair amount & often & often enjoy it (though with you I'd enjoy it more). I also work & not <u>too</u> badly, so far.[155] I like the air here, it's altogether different than in Cambridge.

I wasn't able to get any sailing tickets for Ireland in August, but I booked a passage by plane to Dublin on Aug 6th, & back Aug 19th. These were the only dates I could get tickets for /← <u>bad</u>/. I intend to come to London on Aug. 4th in the afternoon & I've asked M^{iss} Wilkinson*[156] to put me up till Aug. 6th. I didn't want to ask your mother as I thought she might have the house full. I shall also try to stay with M^{iss} W. from

---

155 A few days earlier – on July 12, 1947 – Wittgenstein had begun working in MS 135. At the beginning of that manuscript notebook he noted (presumably once he'd reached the end of the notebook): "In this volume there is no more than one halfway good paragraph in every 10 or 20 pages" (MS 135, p. 1r).

156 Naomi Wilkinson was a radiographer at Guy's Hospital, where Wittgenstein had worked between 1941 and 1943.

Aug 19th to 21st. If that isn't possible I can go to Cambridge for a couple of days. Still, if you're in London I hope /& want/ to see you on Aug 4th &/or 5th. On Sept 12th I shall probably go to Austria; it seems now that they'll give me the permission. I'll stay there for three weeks. Where I'll spend my sabbatical Michaelmas Term[157] I don't yet know. This letter, so far, seems to be full of dates. (I <u>could</u> now make a pun, but I'll suppress it.) I'm sure you were overjoyed at Lizzy's engagement to Phillip.[158] It will, therefore, interest you to see the enclosed photo. Please look at it (& gape)!

The Clements send their good wishes.

Please read <u>the first four lines</u> of this letter carefully again.

I am thinking of you with love, always.

     Ludwig

I'm looking forward to seeing you.

* No relative of Cuthbert's[159]

Attachment affixed to the letter of July 17, 1947:

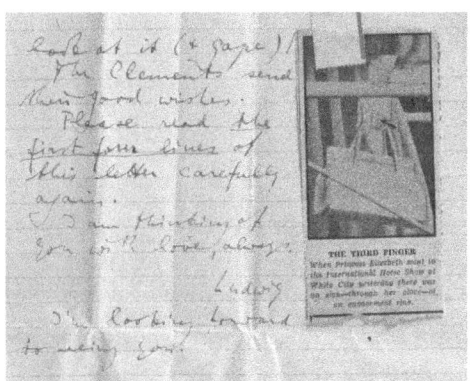

---

157 On June 8, 1947, Wittgenstein had formally applied to the university's General Board for a sabbatical for the Michaelmas Term (October to December) of 1947, and this was granted (see Wittgenstein's letters to J. T. Saunders of June 8 and 18, 1947). Ten days after writing this letter, Wittgenstein wrote to Yorick Smythies: "I don't know where I'll spend my sabbatical Michaelmas Term, nor whether I hadn't better resign my job for good, as that term, in all likelihood, won't be enough for me to get a part of my book ready for publication (if this can be done at all). For this seems to be the thing I want to do" (Wittgenstein to Smythies, July 27, 1947).

158 This refers to the engagement of Queen Elizabeth to Prince Phillip on July 9, 1947.

159 Wittgenstein inserted this footnote at the foot of the first page of this letter (rather close to his mention of 'M[iss] Wilkinson' to which this footnote refers back). It is unclear to who 'Cuthbert' is.

Ludwig Wittgenstein to Ben Richards, July 27, 1947

1, Cwmdonkin Terrace
Swansea
27.7.47.

Dear Ben,

Thanks for your card. <u>It was good to hear from you.</u> I'm coming to London on Aug 4th in the early afternoon; my plane leaves on Aug. 6th in the morning. I shall spend the two nights in London (c/o Mrs Rhees[160] 104 Goldhurst Terrace N.W.6) so I shan't clutter up your house, though I'd like that better. If you can't meet my train at Paddington on the 4th (I'll let you know the time later) <u>wire</u> me what time I can meet you in front of Barts, or at Lyons' between the two counters.

I hope you've had a good time!!

I'm thinking of you a lot & wishing you were with me on walks. I'm out a good deal but the weather is pretty bad most of the time. I am working a fair amount & not too badly. I saw <u>half</u> of a film "Ceasar & Cleopatra" the other day. It was incredibly bloody.[161] I'm looking forward a lot to seeing you. There are lots of things I'd like to talk to you about. God bless you!

   With love

    Ludwig

P.S. The Clements send their kind regards. L. L.

P.P.S. My train on Aug 4th arrives at Paddington at 3$^{.40}$ p.m. L. L.

---

160 Jean Rhees; see the 'Short Biographies of Frequently Mentioned Family and Friends'. Though Jean Rhees was married to Rush Rhees (Wittgenstein's old student and friend), during this period she lived and worked in London while he lived and worked in Swansea.

161 The 1945 feature film – directed by Gabriel Pascal – was based on the 1898 play of the same title by George Bernard Shaw. The film starred Vivien Leigh and Claude Rains.

Enclosure included with the letter of July 27, 1947:

Institute of Contemporary Arts

FOR some months a committee, representative of all the arts (painting, sculpture, architecture, literature, music, the theatre, film, ballet, and broadcasting), has been holding meetings in London to prepare a scheme for an Institute of Contemporary Arts. The need for such an institute will be obvious to all who are aware of the aimless and sporadic character of artistic activities in our capital city. While institutions exist for the purpose of exhibiting contemporary art, there is also needed some centre where artists of all kinds can meet with a co-operative intention, and where their activities can be presented to a public ready to encourage art in those preliminary stages of experiment which are so vital for its development.

The institute will differ from existing institutions in that it will initiate definite projects, and not merely collect and exhibit the chance productions of isolated artists. It will attempt to establish a common ground for a progressive movement in the arts, in which artists of all kinds can come together. A statement of the policy and aims of the proposed institute has been prepared and will be sent to anyone applying to the hon. secretary at 23, Brook Street, London, W.1. The first step is to raise the necessary funds. The committee have estimated that a sum of £50,000 is required, and are asking founder members willing to subscribe a minimum of 100 guineas each to come forward. Already some £15,000 has been promised, but this is far from the total which has to be reached before the scheme can go forward.

Once the institute has been established with the support of the founders, it is intended that it shall be currently financed by the regular support of a body of subscribers. Contributions to the foundation fund should be sent to the acting hon. treasurer, Mr. Roland A. Penrose, care of Barclays Bank, Ltd., 10, Southampton Row, W.C.1.

The organising committee consists of Frederic Ashton, Jack Beddington, J. B. Brunius, Edward Clark, Alex Comfort, M. St. Denis, E. C. Gregory, Geoffrey Grigson, G. M. Hoellering, Robert Melville, E. L. T. Mesens, Roland A. Penrose, Herbert Read, J. M. Richards, Peter Watson, W. E. Williams.

HERBERT READ
Chairman, Organising Committee, Institute of Contemporary Arts.

Ben Richards to Ludwig Wittgenstein, Postcard, July 29, 1947

Ici[162] 29.7.47

I got here yesterday, am staying with friends & off home to-morrow.

Yesterday it was about 106°[163] in the shade – several degrees hotter than the Sahara I gather – it felt it too! I have enjoyed my holiday very much indeed – only 2-3 days when it wasn't very fine altogether.

I hope one or two of the rubies, emeralds etc. reach you intact.[164] On the real thing they shine out for miles around.

Hope to see you very soon

    Love, Ben.

---

162 French: Here.
163 106° Fahrenheit corresponds to about 41° Celsius.
164 The postcard was apparently decorated with imitation gems.

II. In Ireland
(August 1947 – July 1949)

On August 6, 1947, Wittgenstein headed to Dublin for a fortnight to visit his friend and old student, Maurice O'Connor Drury, who had begun working at St. Patrick's Hospital there.[1] Wittgenstein eventually found accommodation that suited him in Ross's Hotel on Parkgate Street,[2] on the opposite side of the Liffey from Drury's hospital. (Indeed, Ross's Hotel turned out to be sufficiently congenial that Wittgenstein returned multiple times, including for more than five months in the winter of 1948/49). That summer of 1947 Wittgenstein resolved to resign his chair at the end of the year and leave Cambridge, to look for a quiet place to devote himself entirely to his writing.[3]

In September 1947 Wittgenstein – with some trepidation – visited his family in Vienna, for the first time since the outbreak of the Second World War in 1939. He was there for three weeks, staying with his niece, Marie Stockert, the eldest daughter of his sister Helene.

Wittgenstein returned to Cambridge in October 1947, and tendered his resignation in accordance with his decision earlier that summer. It was arranged that Michaelmas Term would be counted for him as sabbatical leave – so while his professorship would officially end on December 31, 1947, he was free to leave Cambridge and work on his book from that point onwards. He decided that with his newfound freedom he would

---

1 Wittgenstein reported his plans to Yorick Smythies as follows: "I'm intending to go to Ireland to see Drury on Aug. 6th and to return on Aug. 19th. Between Aug. 19th and Sept. 12th I'll probably be in Ickenham with Richards, and then I hope to go to Austria for 3 weeks. About Oct. 7th I'll be in Cambridge for a few days" (Wittgenstein to Smythies, July 27, 1947).

2 What used to be Ross's Hotel, at 10-13 Parkgate Street, is now called 'The Ashling Hotel'. A plaque next to the entrance of the hotel commemorates Wittgenstein's various stays there.

3 See Wittgenstein's letter to von Wright from August: "I believe that I'll then resign my professorship & go somewhere where I can be alone for a longish time in order to think &, if possible, to finish a part of my book. I thought of going to Norway for that purpose but may go to Ireland instead. I'm not sure. I haven't told the Cambridge authorities anything about it so far, as it's not yet absolutely certain" (Wittgenstein to von Wright, August 27, 1947). Drury notes in his memoirs that it was he who had drawn Wittgenstein's attention to Ireland as a possible place of retreat (Drury 1984: 151-2).

go back to Ireland to write, but he stayed in Cambridge through to the end of November, dictating the best material from his recent manuscript notebooks so as to create a typescript that he could take with him when he left. During this time Richards was completing his medical training at 'Bart's' (St. Bartholomew's Hospital) in London, and he and Wittgenstein met up regularly on weekends.

At the end of November 1947 Wittgenstein left for Ireland, for a stay which was to last – with two breaks – for over a year and a half. After some initially unsuccessful accomodation searching, Wittgenstein – on the recommendation of a colleague of Drury's – moved into Kilpatrick House, just outside the village of Redcross in County Wicklow, about 35miles south of Dublin.[4] Not long after he settled in, Richards and Drury came out to visit him – from London and Dublin respectively – for the days between Christmas and the new year. The remainder of his time at Kilpatrick House – the first few months of 1948 – however, were not very happy ones. At first he was working well, but before long his flow was interrupted by the house becoming noisier (a combination of workers and children). He found it hard to sleep and harder to work, and he worried that perhaps his philosophical capacities were leaving him altogether. And against this background of sleeplessness and fear for his future, he came to fear for his sanity as well, and fell into a depression. In February and March 1948, Wittgenstein tried to move out of Kilpatrick House by arranging to rent a rather run-down – but quieter – nearby cottage. But in the end this plan didn't work out. In April, after hesitating for some time, Wittgenstein eventually decided to move over to the other side of the country, to stay in the Drury family's remote and isolated holiday cottage in Rosroe, Connemara, on Ireland's west coast. On April 15, 1948, Wittgenstein wrote to Rush Rhees:

> "[T]he last 6 or 8 weeks have been a bad time for me. First I suffered much terrible depressions, then I had a bad flu, & all the time I didn't know where to go from here. I am now gradually getting better & I intend leaving here next week & to go to Rosro in the West. This has **great** disadvantages (it's a 10 hours journey from Dublin) but there's nothing else I can do, so far as I can see."

Wittgenstein was already familiar with the Drury's Rosroe cottage from a brief holiday he'd taken there – with Maurice Drury and Francis Skinner – back in the summer of 1934.[5] The cottage was located at the mouth of the Killary Fjord, on the Atlantic coast.

---

4 See Hayes 2017: 33.
5 See Monk 1990: 524-5.

The conditions were spartan, as Rosroe did not yet have any electricity – so heating, cooking, and lighting were all by flame, and there was no running water. But Wittgenstein was helped with supplies and house chores by a local, Tommy Mulkerrins, who was employed by the Drury family.[6] Wittgenstein reported almost daily downpours, but he was fascinated by the surrounding nature. He went on regular walks and described the local flora and fauna in detail to Richards. He was particularly interested in the local birds, which he observed closely and fed daily.

In the second half of May 1948, Richards visited Wittgenstein in Rosroe for a week.[7] Wittgenstein stayed in Rosroe for a further two months, then – at the end of July 1948 – he visited Drury in Dublin, Yorick Smythies (a friend and old student) in Oxford, and then went on to stay with the Richards family in their Ickenham home for a few weeks. Wittgenstein spent most of September 1948 in Vienna with family, as his sister Hermine was seriously ill.[8]

On his return from Vienna, Wittgenstein stopped off for a couple of weeks in Cambridge to do more dictating. And from there he returned to Ireland in mid-October 1948. He had earlier thought that he'd return to Rosroe, but he ended up following the advice of his friends to stay in Dublin for the winter, where he again took up residence at Ross's Hotel until March 1949. While in Dublin that winter, Wittgenstein often worked in the warm Palm House in the Botanic Gardens at Glasnevin – wandering around to think, and sitting on a step to write – especially when the weather was cold and rainy.

These final six months in Dublin were eventful. Richards visited Wittgenstein twice: first in mid-November 1948 and then again in March 1949 (when he and Wittgenstein went on holiday in Howth, on the east coast of Ireland). Elizabeth Anscombe visited Wittgenstein for some urgent advice in early December 1948. And Rush Rhees visited him for Christmas. There were darker events too. From mid-April to mid-May 1949 Wittgenstein visited his family in Vienna again. Hermine was now bedridden and dying of cancer, and he felt that this would be his last opportunity to see her. Then – at the end of May – shortly after his return to Dublin, Wittgenstein was diagnosed with an atypical

---

6   See Monk 1990: 525-6.
7   Contrary what Monk reports (Monk 1990: 526) this visit was not in the summer of 1948, but between May 15 and 23.
8   See Wittgenstein's letter to Norman Malcolm from July 1948: "I intend to stay here another 3-4 weeks & then to go to Dublin to see Drury for a few days, then to Oxford for a week or so, then I want to stay with Richards (whom you haven't met) near London & after that I want to go to Austria for [3-4 weeks] if I can get the permit. From Austria I'll return to this place, God being willing" (Wittgenstein to Malcolm, July 5, 1948).

anaemia by a Dr. Synge, an old teacher of Drury's. Synge thought that the anaemia was likely to have an internal cause, but he couldn't find one.

During the period of his Ireland stay Wittgenstein was largely working in what are now known as manuscripts 137 and 138, while the typescript he dictated was TS 232.

Unfortunately, Richards' letters throughout this period – from October 1947 to July 1949 – have not been preserved.

Ludwig Wittgenstein to Ben Richards, August 7, 1947[9]

At the moment: Silvervale Hotel
Enniskerry
C$^{\underline{o}}$ Wicklow
Eire
Thursday

Dear Ben,

I arrived in Dublin yesterday about 1$^{.30}$ after a <u>very</u> nice journey. I'd have written you immediately but I thought I'd wait until I had settled down in the hotel. The hotel, unfortunately, proved to be a very depressing place, dingy & noisy, but we had to take it because every other place seemed to be full. To-day Drury & I are going to hunt for a better place. I'm not sure that we will be successful. The <u>country</u> round here is <u>very</u> fine. As I hope that the above address will <u>not</u> be ~~our~~ /my/ permanent one for these two weeks, please write to me % Dr Drury,

St. Patrick's Hospital
    James Street Dublin
        Eire

If I find a suitable place I'll let you know. The food here is extremely good & there's lots of it, so that I am in constant danger of overeating.

I feel very stupid just now as I've had a rotten night & this letter is only to tell you where to write to. As soon as I'll feel wide awake again I'll write you a really marvelous letter.

---

9 Richards added '7/8/47' to the letter, which was a Thursday. On most of the letters which Wittgenstein didn't fully date, Richards added a date in pencil to the top left-hand corner of the letter. He usually put the date on which the letter was received – which was sometimes the same day as Wittgenstein sent it, and sometimes a day or two later.

You know how much I enjoyed being with you in London. It was lovely being with you, as always.

God bless you.

Drury sends you his love.

    With love

        Ludwig

I hope your Asthma is better! d. o. h..

Ludwig Wittgenstein to Ben Richards, August 8, 1947[10]

                              Eastwood Hotel

                              Leeson Street

                              Dublin

                              Friday

Dear Ben,

this is a P.S. to the letter I sent you yesterday. I spent about 4 hours hunting for a suitable room with Drury, & we found one which isn't too bad. I shall stay here till Monday (Aug. 11th) & then move to the following address: Ross's Hotel

                              Parkgate Street, Dublin.

That's a nice place,[11] near the gate of a big park, and near Drury's hospital,[12] but it's full up until Monday. So, if you haven't yet written to me when you get this letter, please write to <u>Ross's Hotel</u>. – The weather's nice & the food is far too nice & too much. I slept fine & am feeling ditto. (Have you ever felt ditto??). I'm thinking of you a great deal & looking forward to seeing you before long.

I loved being with you.

    God bless you!

        With love

            Ludwig

---

10 Richards added '8/8/47' to the letter, which was a Friday.
11 Elizabeth Anscombe later recalled: "When Wittgenstein was in Dublin he stayed at a hotel called Ross' Hotel; he liked the woman who was manageress; it was comfortable and quiet" (Anscombe 2025: 171).
12 If you follow Parkgate Street from Ross's Hotel (now the Ashling Hotel) westward for about five minutes, you get to one of the entrances to Phoenix Park. If you leave Ross's Hotel southward for about ten minutes (crossing the Seán Heuston Bridge and then heading down Steeven's Lane, you get to St Patrick's Hospital, which is where Maurice O'Connor Dury worked. Phoenix Park was a large park where Wittgenstein often took walks (sometimes alone, and sometimes with Drury).

Ben Richards to Ludwig Wittgenstein, August 10, 1947

GREENOGE
40, SWAKELEYS ROAD
ICKENHAM
UXBRIDGE
RUISLIP 2114
Sunday
10/8/47

Dear Ludwig,

Thanks for your letter. I hope you find a better hotel.

It was good to see you, in London, and I am looking forward to the next time. The whole family have driven down to Dorset to-day (except me). My father & Angela are coming back again to-morrow, while my mother & all the little girls[13] are staying at a farm near Swanage[14] – some of them camping. They don't know what it will be like, we just wrote to an advertised address and got a nice letter back. How long they stay will depend on how they like it.

Angela is going to stay with friends in North Wales on Tuesday.

I was in bed a couple of days with asthma but I am quite all right now.

The students of my group are all having their holiday now, & as there is nothing much doing at Bart's. I am getting a few days off extra, & going to see some friends – I shall be % Garnett (Mr. or Mrs.) Hilton Hall, Hilton, Hunts.

Please let me know exactly when you are coming back. There will probably be no one else here but my father & Ann[15] & you can then come here straight away.

Give my love to Con Drury. I hope you both have a very good time. Eat well, sleep well & keep well.

    Love always
        Ben

---

13 Angela was the oldest of Richards' four younger sisters; 'all the little girls' were presumably the three youngest, Virginia (18 years old), Isabella (14 years old), and Julia (7 years old). For all four sisters, see the 'Short Biographies of Frequently Mentioned Family and Friends'.

14 A small town on the south coast of England (in the southeast of the county of Dorset).

15 Ann Phillips was the Richards' family housekeeper (see Richards' letter to Wittgenstein of 8th February 1947)..

Ludwig Wittgenstein to Ben Richards, August 12, 1947[16]

COLLEGE GREEN AND BANK OF IRELAND, DUBLIN.
[At the top of the postcard – with an arrow pointing to what was actually a statue of Irish lawyer and politician, Henry Grattan (1746-1820) – Wittgenstein has playfully added:] Prof. Wittgenstein

It wasn't a bit easy to get these columns just right & I still feel exhausted.[17]

WESTMORELAND STREET AND O'CONNELL BRIDGE, DUBLIN.

Ross's Hotel

Parkgate Street

Dublin

Eire

Tuesday

---

16 Richards added '13/6/47 ?' to the postcard. This dating cannot be right, however (and the question mark indicates Richards' own doubts), not least because Wittgenstein mentions Richards' letter of August 10. Given the content, the postcard must have been written on a Tuesday after August 10 and before August 19. It must therefore have been written on Tuesday August 12, 1947. Wittgenstein wrote this letter on the backs of two postcards – treating them simply as blank pages to write across – and he presumably sent the two postcards inside an envelope.

17 This joking remark regarding the columns in the image on the front of the first postcard, was inserted into the space on the top left corner of the back of that card.

Dear Ben, Thanks for your letter of Aug. 10th. This hotel is <u>very</u> respectable, almost too much so. It has a very nice elderly proprietress. We have excellent weather. I'm seeing Drury every other /late/ afternoon & evening, & Saturday from 1 p.m. & the whole of Sunday. I'm looking forward to being with you. I shall leave here on the 19th. My 'plane is supposed to leave the air-port at 3.¹⁵ p.m. &, W.W.P.,[18] will arrive in London /i.e. at the air-port/ about 5.³⁰ p.m., I imagine. Let me know by air-mail, or wire, if I can come to Ickenham[19] straight away. May you think of me with /real/ love as I do of you! or let me know that you don't. – I think of you a great deal. With love

Ludwig.

Drury sends his.

Ludwig Wittgenstein to Ben Richards, September 13, 1947[20]

L. Wittgenstein, bei Frau v. Stockert[21]

I. Opernring 6

Wien Austria

Dear Ben, d. o. h.,

I arrived here yesterday morning after a very agreeable journey.

My travelling companions were all right & I had no end of food. I had Greenoge sandwiches at breakfast to-day & I've still some left which I'll eat to-morrow /& perhaps the day after/. – It's sad to see all the destruction here & the various signs of military occupation.[22] I found my sisters and my friends all in good health. My

---

18 Probably stands for: 'Wind & Weather Permitting'.
19 Namely, to the Richards' family home (where Ben was living with his parents), at 40 Swakeleys Road, Ickenham, Uxbridge.
20 Richards added '13/9/47 ?' to the letter. Despite his uncertainty this must indeed have been the date on which it was written, as Wittgenstein mentioned in the letter that he had arrived in Vienna the day before, and we know that he arrived on September 12, 1947 (see his letter to Rush Rhees of September 21, 1947). The first page of this letter has been stamped, in the top left corner: "Österreichische Zensurstelle 403" [Austrian Censorship Office 403]. At this time Austria was still under Allied occupation, and the Allies set up the 'Austrian Censorship Office' in 1945, which censored the mail until 1953. All Wittgenstein's succeeding letters from Austria are similarly stamped by the censorship office (though the office number sometimes varies).
21 German: 'c/o Mrs. von Stockert'. Marie von Stockert (1900-1948) was Wittgenstein's niece, the eldest daughter of his sister Helene Salzer. Wittgenstein stayed with her during his visit to Vienna from September 12 until October 4, presumably because the palatial family home on Argentinierstrasse (formerly Alleegasse) – where Wittgenstein would usually have stayed – had been badly damaged during the war (see Prokop 2003: 253).
22 This was Wittgenstein's first trip back to Austria after the end of the Second World War. Shortly before his trip Wittgenstein had written to Georg Henrik von Wright: "My mind just now is in <u>great</u> disorder. It's partly due to this, that I dread seeing Vienna again after all that's happened" (Wittgenstein to von Wright, August 27, 1947). A little later into his visit Wittgenstein wrote to Rush Rhees: "As you can imagine Vienna isn't a nice sight at present. In spite of everything the people I meet are in astonishingly good spirits" (Wittgenstein to Rhees, September 21, 1947).

youngest sister, the one you know,²³ is in Austria too, i.e. she is in upper Austria /where she has a house/ in the American zone, but /she/ couldn't get permition to visit Vienna.

Oddly enough, in spite of all the misery, you can still hear good music here. At least so I'm told, & after our experience the other day I can believe it. – I live here vey comfortably in my nieces flat & am treated very kindly.

I think of you <u>ever</u> so often & of the wonderful time I had in Ickenham. God bless you! Pease write to me soon. As you'll gather from the date on this letter even air-mail takes a long time between here & England. – I haven't slept much, lately, I'm having a very busy time, & consequently feel very stupid, so I'll close for now.

Please give my love & my thanks to everybody.

   As always, with love
    Ludwig

Ben Richards to Ludwig Wittgenstein (undated, September 15, 1947)[24]

AVENUE	2849	ST. BARTHOLOMEW'S HOSPITAL,
"	2960	LONDON, E.C.1.
CENTRAL	1101	

Dear Ludwig

I hope the journey was a good one, and that you are not finding things too difficult; and that your relatives and friends in Vienna are well.

After you had gone I met the family at Westminster and we went to Greenwich by boat. The guide with a megaphone gave us information about the buildings we passed on the way; for instance that tower like a lighthouse is used for making lead shot: molten lead is poured from the top & the drops have hardened by the time they reach the bottom.

---

23 Margaret Stonborough-Wittgenstein (1882-1958); apparently she had previously met Richards, presumably on one of her trips to – or through – England from her home in America where she was living at the time.

24 Richards did not date this letter, but in Wittgenstein's letter to Richards of September 23, 1947, he says that he just received Richards' letter of September 15. This was most likely that letter (with Wittgenstein referring to the date on the now lost postmark). This dating is confirmed by the fact that the controversy surrounding the Pastoral Symphony – to which Richards refers in the letter – took place precisely in the days leading up to September 15, 1947.

I thought you might be interested in what happened about the Pastoral Symphony. I don't care for the tone of the letters & don't suppose any good will come of them but isn't it rather surprising the B.B.C. should apologize at all?[25]

I am looking forward very much to seeing you soon and perhaps hearing from you even sooner. I miss you.

>Love always
>
>Ben.

Ludwig Wittgenstein to Ben Richards, September 16, 1947

>From: Prof. L. Wittgenstein
>
>bei Frau v. Stockert[26]
>
>I. Opernring 6
>
>Wien
>
>Austria

16.9.47

Dear Ben,

There isn't much to write. I spend almost every day in seeing various relatives & friends. My eldest sister[27] & a friend of mine[28] play piano duets for me. Her eyes are very bad & unfortunately she dropped & broke the pair of spectacles which she needs for reading music, & it takes a long time to get them repaired here nowadays. Hence she can only play things she knows almost by heart. She has a gramophone & a recording of Bruckners 5th symphony. I didn't know it had been recorded. We played it the other day & enjoyed it hugely in spite of the mediocre performance, I thought of you & wished you could hear it with me. All the people I meet are in astonishingly

---

25 On September 8, 1947, the Vienna Philharmonic Orchestra – under Bruno Walter (a conductor with close connections to the Wittgenstein family in Vienna) – performed in Edinburgh. Their programme concluded with Beethoven's Symphony No. 6 (op. 68), the 'Pastroral Symphony'. The concert was being broadcast on the radio by the B.B.C – but shortly before the end of the symphony, the radio faded the concert out, so as to begin its next broadcast, a game show. This cutting short of the performance prompted indignant letters in various newspapers, and it seems that Richards enclosed some clippings of newspaper letters to the editor about this (though the clippings have not survived so it's unknown which publication they were from). The longest exchange of letters on this subject appeared in *The Scotsman* – between September 12 and 16 – concluding (the day after Richards sent this letter) with an apology from a representative of the B.B.C.

26 German: '% Mrs. von Stockert'.

27 Hermine Wittgenstein (1874-1950); see the 'Short Biographies of Frequently Mentioned Family and Friends'.

28 Rudolf Koder (1902-1977), a close friend of Wittgenstein's, whom he had got to know when they were both teaching at the primary school in Puchberg am Schneeberg in the early 1920s. Koder had then become close with Wittgenstein's sisters as well, and he often played music with them.

good spirits although there isn't much to be in good spirit about. – The weather's fine & <u>very</u> hot. There hasn't been rain for 8 weeks, I think.

I hope I'll hear from you soon.[29] I think of you a very great deal, with all the old feelings & wishes.

Please give your mother & Angela my very best wishes & thanks for all their kindness to me.

    God bless you!

        With love, always

            Ludwig

P.S.

I'm looking forward to seeing you again. I intend to leave here on Oct. 4th. I.e., I'll arrive in London on Oct. 6th. On the 7th I'll go to Cambridge to settle things. L. L. Forgive the bad spelling.

Ben Richards to Ludwig Wittgenstein (undated, September 23, 1947)[30]

    GREENOGE
    40, SWAKELEYS ROAD
    ICKENHAM
    UXBRIDGE
    RUISLIP 2114

Dear Ludwig

Thank you for writing. The air mail is slow. It was quite reasonably quick from Switzerland & shouldn't take so very much longer from Austria. I hope my letter reached you safely. The censors had opened yours but made no deletions.[31]

---

29 Wittgenstein had not yet received Richards' first letter to him in Vienna, which he had only sent the previous day.

30 Richards did not date this letter, but the date can be inferred jointly from his statement that a radio performance of Cosi Fan Tutte by the Vienna State Opera had been broadcast on the radio on the same day that he was writing, and from his statement that had been to see their performance of Don Giovanni the previous Saturday. Since Cosi Fan Tutte was broadcast on both September 18 and 23, and since the Vienna State Opera had not begun their run on the Saturday prior to September 18, Richards must have written this letter on Tuesday September 23, 1947, and been to the Don Govanni performance on Saturday September 20.

31 It seems that when he wrote this letter Richards had received Wittgenstein's second letter (of September 16), but not his first letter (of September 13). This can be inferred from the fact that Richards says that he had only received one letter, and he refers to information included in Wittgenstein's second letter (namely, Wittgenstein's expected return date); and in Wittgenstein's next letter to Richards – of September 23 – he expresses the hope that Richards has finally received his first letter. Regarding censorship, see Wittgenstein's letter to Richards of September 13, 1947, and the relevant footnote there.

Angela, Virginia & Michel[32] came back from Paris and go ~~back~~ to school to-morrow – Angela has started already at St. Paul's.[33]

We managed to get seats for the Vienna State Opera on Saturday & saw Don Giovanni.[34] The music of course was wonderful – I wish I could listen to it with you. The best part of the performance I thought was the orchestra; I was not really struck by any of the singers, the men were better. But I don't think they had all their best singers that night. Cosi Fan Tutte on the wireless to-night sounded better sung.[35]

I hear that the first night there were a lot of musicians with placards, parading outside Covent Garden & protesting against importing foreign orchestras as "we have the best".[36] I also was told that Beecham[37] gave a concert at the Albert Hall and had an audience of about 200 & that he supposed everyone else was going to the Vienna opera which was not to their credit, etc.

I am looking forward to seeing you on October 6th – will you be staying here? Please give my best wishes to your sister when you write to her.

    Love always

    Ben.

---

32 The eldest two of Richards' four younger sisters. Michel has not been identified.
33 St Paul's Girls' School, a private secondary school in Hammersmith, west London.
34 Wolfgang Amadeus Mozart's opera (KV 527). The Vienna State Opera played a three week season at Covent Garden, from September 16 until October 4, 1947. Their performances during this run included Mozart's Don Giovanni, Cosi Fan Tutte, and Figaro, Beethoven's Fidedio, and Strauss' Salome – some of which were also broadcast on the radio around the same time. Richards' likely went on Saturday September 20.
35 Wolfgang Amadeus Mozart's opera (KV 588). This performance was broadcast both on September 18 and 23; Richards likely listened to the latter broadcast.
36 The protests were reported as follows in the press at the time: "The dispute between the Musicians' Union and the Ministry of Labour over the visit of the Vienna Philharmonic Orchestra to play at Covent Garden was carried a stage further on Tuesday when some 300 British musicians demonstrated outside the Opera House. Placards were displayed bearing such slogans as "Stop Importing Orchestras; We Have the Best," and leaflets were distributed. A spokesman of the Union said that they do not object to foreign orchestras as such, but they feel that British orchestras should be engaged to play in theatre-pits when available, or else that a reciprocal arrangement should be made when foreign orchestras are engaged" ('Musicians', in *The Stage*, Thursday September 18, 1947, p. 6c).
37 Sir Thomas Beecham (1879-1961) was a well-known English conductor; he founded, among others, the New Symphony Orchestra, the London Philharmonic Orchestra, and the Royal Philharmonic Orchestra.

Ludwig Wittgenstein to Ben Richards, September 23, 1947

From L. Wittgenstein bei Frau v. Stockert[38]

I. Opernring 6, Wien

23.9.47.

Dear Ben,

Thanks for your letter of Sept 15th, it arrived this morning. I hope the letter I wrote you the day after my arrival has reached you by now.[39] I'm having a very easy & enjoyable time, too much so. I wanted to send you a few picture postcards but I'm not allowed to. We've had the most incredibly dry weather here. It was difficult to imagine that it would ever rain again, but it did, quite unexpectedly, yesterday. To-day is fine & hot again. I'm leaving here on Oct. 4th at 11 p.m. by the Arlberg Express. It arrives in London on the 6th about 4 p.m., I imagine. Could you make sure &, if you can meet me at Victoria?

I'll stay the night in London with Mrs Rhees[40] & go to Cambridge the next day. My plans concerning my resignation haven't changed, which means that I've got to be in Cambridge /right/ at the beginning of term.[41]

It was <u>good</u> to hear from you! I'd been rather nervous yesterday, wondering if I'd soon hear from you, so it felt good when they brought me your letter.

I miss you.

  With love, always

    Ludwig

Thanks for the cuttings.[42] There are <u>many</u> things I'd like to talk to you about. God bless you always.

---

38 German: '% Mrs. von Stockert'.

39 Wittgenstein's letter to Richards of September 13, 1947.

40 Jean Rhees; Wittgenstein used to stay in her flat in London when he was visiting for short periods.

41 Wittgenstein had been tempted to resign his professorship – and thereby his job at Cambridge altogether – for some years, but he had not brought himself to make the decisive move. In August 1947 he finally came to the brink of a decision, which he reported to Norman Malcolm as follows: "My mind is rather in a turmoil these days. I am almost certain that I shall resign my professorship in Autumn. I have not yet told Rollins, & <u>please keep it to yourself</u> as it's not yet certain. I <u>hate</u> to let down Rollins & Lazerovitz but I think I won't be able to help it. I'd like to be alone somewhere & try to write & to make at least one part of my book publishable. I'll never be able to do it while I'm teaching at Cambridge. Also I think that, quite apart from writing, I need a longish spell of thinking <u>alone</u>, without having to talk to anybody. But I haven't yet told the autorities about my plan & I don't intend to do so until October when I'll decide definitely" (Wittgenstein to Malcolm, August 27, 1947; and see also his letter to Georg Henrik von Wright of the same date). The reason he needed to be in Cambridge at the beginning of term in order to enact this plan was presumably so that he could meet with the Vice Chancellor of the university in person so as to tender his resignation (which is indeed what he eventually did; see his letter to Richards of October 10, 1947).

42 These have not been preserved, but regarding their contents see Richards' letter to Wittgenstein of September 15, 1947, and the relevant footnote there.

Ben Richards to Ludwig Wittgenstein, September 30, 1947

[Written in train – please excuse writing][43]

AVENUE	2849	ST. BARTHOLOMEW'S HOSPITAL,
"	2960	LONDON, E.C.1.
CENTRAL	1101	

Dear Ludwig

Thanks a lot for your last letter (23rd) /(arrived to-day, 30th)/. I am glad you got mine – I hope the others including this one reach you in time: - I am going to try to express it.
I have been staying with the Garnett's again over the week-end and helped in panelling the room I told you they are building, with a bay window. The window is in-place; all the brick walls, concrete floor & ~~beams~~ rafters for the ceiling. And we screwed most of the panelling on over the week-end – to wooden plugs between the bricks. When it is finished it will be all home-made except the ceiling & ~~flo~~ wood floor which are being done by professional builders. I think it will make a very nice nursery. The bay window makes the room about half as big again; and, facing south, catches most of the sun. The window is roofed outside with a large sheet of lead.
The New London Opera company are adding Don Giovanni to their repertoire, starting about October 16th. They are about the best English opera company at the moment (!) and I should very much like to hear it with you, if you liked the idea.
I went in the National Gallery yesterday and was very impressed by a portrait by Ingres – I think it was called M. Norvins;[44] do you know it? I also looked at some of the old Dutch pictures. I want to go there with you one day, too.
I begin my new appointment to-morrow surgical outpatients, and will have more to do I hope. I will try to meet you at Victoria at 4.0 on Monday – if you don't see me ring Ruislip 2114; I will tell them at home my plans for meeting you. I am very happy thinking I shall see you again very soon.
Love always, Ben.

---

43 This note was added in the space at the top of the first page (the square brackets being Richards' own).
44 Jean-Auguste-Dominique Ingres' portrait of Monsieur de Norvins (1811), who had recently been appointed Chief of Police in Rome. The National Gallery (in Trafalger Square, London) had bought the painting in 1918.

Ludwig Wittgenstein to Ben Richards, October 10, 1947[45]

Trin. Coll.

Friday

My Dear, how are you?! I hope you're better. It was lovely being with you.

I caught the 5.54 train all right on Tuesday. On Wednesday I saw the Vice Chancellor about my resignation[46] & yesterday wrote to the Master of Trinity[47] & to Prof. Broad[48] that I'd tendered /to the V.C./ my resignation.

I gather that the College will let me stay in my rooms for some weeks.

I take it that you will work at Barts on Saturday 18th till noon. If so, I'll be at the gate about 12.15 p.m.. Let me know if this is all right.

I could stay, & should like to stay /if you let me/, until Monday morning. I very much need you, as always.

With love

Ludwig

P.S.

The other day when I said "chalet" I meant "châtelet".

Ben Richards to Ludwig Wittgenstein, October 12, 1947

GREENOGE

40, SWAKELEYS ROAD

ICKENHAM

UXBRIDGE

RUISLIP 2114

12.10.47

Dear Ludwig,

I expect to find you in front of Bart's at 12.15 on Saturday and I hope you'll find me less of a wreck than last time. Everything is arranged for you to stay here, as before; let there be no mistake this time. I am looking forward very much to seeing you.

As I expect you noticed last week there are some plans for altering the garden. At present the plants in the border under the hedge on the left don't get enough sun &

---

45 Richards added '10/10/47' to the letter, which was a Friday.

46 Charles Earle Raven (1885–1964). See the relevant footnote to Wittgenstein's letter to Richards of September 23, 1947. Wittgenstein tendered his resignation on Wednesday, October 8, but it was arranged that Michaelmas Term would be counted for him as sabbatical leave – so while his professorship would officially end on December 31, 1947, he was free to leave Cambridge and work on his book from this point onwards.

47 George Macaulay Trevelyan (1876–1962).

48 C. D. (Charlie Dunbar) Broad (1887-1971), Knightbridge Professor of Philosophy at Cambridge, was a colleague of Wittgenstein at both the Faculty of Arts and Trinity College.

water because of the hedge, and on the chapel side ash saplings, bindweed etc. come under the fence. The plan is to dig up the "gravel" path, move then borders towards the lawn and have a narrow brick path between them and the hedge /which can then be clipped/ or fence, and expand the lawn a bit. We are not decided what to do this end. The grass cannot be properly cut where it comes right up against the wall or a raised step. A border or slightly sunk path would be all right. I would be very interested indeed to hear your ideas.

As it is (approx.)   As it may be
                          (not very accuarate)

Heshe has been having some horse riding lessons at Ruislip.

I hope you are not finding things too hard. I am very glad they are letting you keep your room for a while.   G. B. Y.

       Love always

       Ben.

Ludwig Wittgenstein to Ben Richards, October 14, 1947[49]

Trin. Coll.
Tuesday

Dear Ben, o. h. –

This is an experiment: I'd like to see if a letter as small as this will reach you.[50] Thanks for your letter. There will be no mistake this time! On Saturday I had your express letter back from Vienna.[51]

I loved reading it. I take it you're better; but even if you weren't I'd enjoy being with you just as much.

I'll look at your garden if you pay me a proper fee.

So long!

God bless you.

With love

Ludwig

P. T. O.

Next time I'll try a still smaller envelope.

L. L.

---

49 Richards added '14/10/47' to the letter, which was a Tuesday.
50 The envelope measures 10 x 6.3cm.
51 This was Richards' letter to Wittgenstein of September 30, 1947, which Richards had sent to Vienna by express mail so that it would catch Wittgenstein before he left. Apparently it did not.

Ludwig Wittgenstein to Ben Richards, October 22, 1947

Trin. Coll. Camb.
22.10.47

Dear Ben, old heart –

If it's O.K. with your parents & also with you, I could come to London on Saturday after next, i.e. on Nov. 1st, or if it suits you better, on Nov. 8th. Please let me know about it. – I'm busy dictating[52] & I'll probably have two typists working for me soon, as the one I have now can't give me enough time. (Does that mean I'm a Mormon[53]?) – I'd like to say that I believe that the remarks you made about my letter to Lazerowitz were most probably true;[54] & anyhow it's good /to think/ that you'll go for me when I deserve it! Bless you! – It was lovely being with you! – Miss Anscombe sends you her best wishes. – I think of you a lot.

With love

Ludwig

I saw Prof. Moore to-day.[55] He isn't too well, I'm sorry to say, but as nice as ever.

L. L.

---

52 A couple of weeks later Wittgenstein wrote to Georg Henrik von Wright: "I have resigned but my professorship ends on December 31st. I shall stay here for another 3 weeks, I'm dictating some of the stuff which I wrote during the last 2-3 years. It's mostly bad but I've got to have it in a handy form, i. e. typewritten, because it may possibly give rise to better thoughts when I read it" (Wittgenstein to von Wright, November 6, 1947). These dictations constitute TS 229 and probably also TSs 244 and 245.

53 This is a joke about Mormon polygamy. Wittgenstein had been interested in the Mormons at least as far back as 1929, having been struck by Charles Dickens' account of them in his essay 'Bound for the Great Salt Lake' (in his *The Uncommercial Traveller*; see Drury 1984: 104-5). Wittgenstein had also read Eduard Meyer's *Ursprung und Geschichte der Mormonen* [*Origin and History of the Mormons*], Halle a S., M. Niemeyer, 1912 (see Wittgenstein's letter to Rush Rhees of November 28, 1944).

54 Morris Lazerowitz (1918-1985) was an American philosopher, and the husband of Alice Ambrose (1906-2001) who had been a close student of Wittgenstein's in the 1930s. Lazerowitz had planned to come to Cambridge to study under Wittgenstein, and Wittgenstein had written to him to say that due to his resignation this would not, in the end, be possible. Lazerowitz apparently responded to Wittgenstein's news with an angry letter, which Wittgenstein answered just as angrily. A few weeks later Wittgenstein described the incident to Norman Malcolm, as follows: "I had an impertinent letter from Lazerovitz reproaching me for not letting him know beforehand about my resignation. He told me that this showed a 'shocking' 'fault of character' & that I was 'a gross person'. I replied & tried to tell him 'where he gets off'. He seems to be an ass" (Wittgenstein to Malcolm, November 16, 1947; and see also Wittgenstein's letter to Malcolm of August 27, 1947). Richards had presumably critiqued the tone of Wittgenstein's response to Lazerowitz.

55 G. E. (George Edward) Moore (1873-1951), a friend and colleague of Wittgenstein's; see the 'Short Biographies of Frequently Mentioned Family and Friends'. A few weeks later Wittgenstein reported to Norman Malcolm: "I'm seeing Moore once a week. I like being with him almost more than ever. Somehow we seem to understand each other better. He is alternately well & a little ill & has to take it easy" (Wittgenstein to Malcolm, November 16, 1947).

Ludwig Wittgenstein to Ben Richards, October 27, 1947

Trinity College
27.10.47.

Dear Ben,

Thank for your letter. I'll come this weekend (Nov. 1ˢᵗ). It's unfortunate for me that you're not having dinner with me, but, please, arrange things in such a way that we can be together leisurely until, as it were the dinner-gong sounds. – One thing would make a great difference to me, viz., if we could travel to Ickenham together _after_ your dinner party. I might go to a flick meanwhile. Still you can tell me what you think about this on Saturday.

If there is any hitch, or _if_ you /should/ think you might not exactly be in the right frame of mind for seeing me on Sunday after the party*, let me know & I'll come on Nov. 15ᵗʰ, instead. – If I don't hear from you I'll be at Barts this Sat. 12.¹⁵.

I'm thinking of you with love; as always

Ludwig

*I don't mean, of course, that you'll have a hang-over; only that it mightn't feel /just/ the right thing for you, & you might, therefore, prefer the later date. L. L.

Ludwig Wittgenstein to Ben Richards, Postcard (undated, probably September or October 1947)⁵⁶

 GOOD LUCK FROM LONDON

Dear Ben, old heart – What I did was this. I rang up the "Dog Sanatorium" of Spratts & there someone recommended me <u>very highly</u> a Vet. Mʳ Fawcus (FAWCUS), Hackbridge Kennels Telephone Walington⁵⁷ 3030. They said he <u>might possibly</u> even come to see the dog. I'm sorry I couldn't lunch with you. Hope to see you in 2 weeks.

   With love
    Ludwig

---

56 Richards added 'Sept. Oct 47?' to the postcard.
57 Presumably: Wallington (in the south of London).

Ludwig Wittgenstein to Ben Richards, November 7, 1947

7.11.47

Dear Ben – old heart,

First I want to say that it was lovely as always; being with you the other day. I enjoyed everything. – I'd have liked to have travelled to town with you Monday morning & was sorry I was too late. – I had to go to London again the day after (Tuesday) because my sister[58] was passing through London on her way to America. She sends you her good wishes. – Dictating my stuff has progressed more quickly than I thought it would. It'll come to an end at the beginning of next week. Can you see me next week-end? i.e. Nov. 15th? If you can't I could go to Oxford from here, stay with Smythies for a few days & see you /the weekend of Nov. 22th/, right before leaving for Ireland. I'd prefer seeing you on Nov. 15th if it's all right with you & your parents. I'd be grateful if you could wire me your reply as I've got to make some arrangements for either case. – It got very cold here the night before last & in the morning the twigs of the trees were encased in ice – believe it or not. That's about all the news. Let me hear from you soon. God bless you!

    With love
    Ludwig

This place is reserved for notes of the recipient:[59]

Ludwig Wittgenstein to Ben Richards, November 16, 1947[60]

Trin. Coll. Camb.
Sunday

Dear Ben,

Thanks for sending the case & for your letter. It was rather a disappointment not to be able to see you this weekend, for I had, perhaps foolishly been longing to see you. But I felt much more disappointed when I didn't get a letter from you.

---

58 Margaret Stonborough-Wittgenstein.
59 Wittgenstein finished his letter with about a quarter of a page to spare. This is a joke about the remaining blank space.
60 Richards added '16/11/47' to the letter, which was a Sunday.

I'm not saying that I had any right at all to feel that way, but I did. Then in my wire[61] I asked you to write to me & that was wrong, for obvious reasons; but I am weak & foolish.

<u>I am afraid of this</u>: – that I shall always ask you for more than is completely natural for you to give me, i.e., for more than quite naturally flows from your feeling for me. Yet when I don't get it I shall be <u>unhappy</u>. I also know that I never shall be able to reduce my demands to what is /perhaps/ sensible; unless I <u>cease</u> making any demands on you. – This is the terrible danger in our peculiar relation. But if anyone can be blamed it's not you, but /only/ me. You've always be kind & good to me. – I wanted ~~you~~ to write you all this before seeing you next Saturday. And if there is anything you can say about it, also if it bears on my coming to Ickenham, please write me a line, not anything kind, but <u>frank</u>.

   God bless you always.
    With love
     Ludwig

My address from Tuesday (day after to-morrow) till Saturday will be:
 ℅ Smythies
 22, Banbury Rd.
 Oxford.

Ludwig Wittgenstein to Ben Richards, November 26, 1947[62]

         ℅ Dr Drury, St Patrick's Hosp.
           James' Street Dublin
              Wednesday

Dear Ben, old heart –

My journey yesterday wasn't quite as pleasant as the one last summer. Our plane started 20 min. late & taxied to the place where it was supposed to take off, but when the engines had run for some minutes we were told that there was an 'operational snag' & that we'd go back to the sheds. There we waited for 1½ hours & in the end went by a different plane. The journey was smooth. Drury met me at the terminal. The weather is fine but <u>very</u> cold & damp, ~~especially~~ Even the water in my jugs was damp this morning! – To day I started reconsidering & I put two 'ads' in the papers. The

---

61 This has not been preserved.
62 Richards added '26/11/47' to the letter, which was a Wednesday.

prospects of finding a suitable place don't seem easy. But I'll just have to try. – I have written a short letter to your mother. I wrote her <u>two</u> longer ones but tore them up. May she understand my letter as it's meant. That's difficult, as our languages (her's & mine) are so different. <u>Please don't postpone</u> having a talk with her. It's difficult but it's got to be. Don't let her spare either you feelings, or me.

It's been <u>wonderful</u> being with you (as usual)!

God bless you, always
With love
Ludwig

I hope I'll be able to settle down soon! I'm thinking of you constantly. I enjoyed eating the chocolate during our long wait at the airport. Drury sends his good wishes.

L. L.

Ludwig Wittgenstein to Ben Richards, December 7, 1947

℅ Mrs Kingston
Kilpatrick House[63]
Red Cross
Wicklow <s>Arklow</s>, Eire
7.12.47.

Dear Ben,

When, 3 days ago, I was given the envelope with your writing it immediately made me feel good, I'd had a depressing time hunting in the icy weather for a place where I could stay /& I longed to hear from you/. Then when I glanced through your letter I felt happy knowing that I'd see you soon. But when I read it again more carefully there was a sentence at the beginning which made me feel very queer. I wondered <u>why</u> your parents should have objected my making a present to you of your flight to Ireland; whether they knew that they were taking away from me a very real pleasure, & to what purpose? /But/ You go on: "<u>& I really should prefer you to give me a different kind of Christmas present</u>". When I read that I just didn't know what to think. – I

---

63 After almost two weeks of looking unsuccessfully for suitable accommodation in Dublin, a colleague of Drury's mentioned a guesthouse – called Kilpatrick House – where he had spent holidays, about an hour's drive south of the city. It was a farmhouse about 2.5m (4km) outside of the village of Redcross, in County Wicklow. As Drury reports: "Wittgenstein said he would travel down and inspect it. On his return he said he thought he could work well in that quiet surrounding... So it was arranged that he would move down to Red Cross" (Drury 1984: 153; see also Monk 1990: 520). Wittgenstein moved into Kilpatrick House on December 9 – a couple of days after writing this letter – but he presumably put that address on this letter preemptively, so that any replies would be sent there.

thought a lot about that sentence (that's why I didn't write /you/ sooner) & I could write a lot about it; but I won't, because I'm afraid I might hurt you. I can't help feeling, & in a way I hope, you were very thoughtless when you wrote those words. Dear Ben, please let nothing & nobody come between us – that is if you still feel as strongly & seriously about us as you ~~used~~/did/. I won't go on, because you know what I want to say. – May God be with you!

I may not be able to meet you at the airport, but, unless I'm ill or have had an accident, I'll wait for you at the Dublin air terminal /on Boxing day at 1.45 p.m/ where you'll be taken by a special bus. From there I'll take you to the above address. –

The other day I saw in a bookshop a kind of biography of Mahler's by Alma Mahler, his wife.[64] I didn't look into it & I'm sure it's bad, but on the dustcover there were about a dozen siluettes of Mahler, conducting.[65] I had seen them before, ages ago & and they are perfect, & I was immensely impressed. Normally, of course, one couldn't from the gestures of a conductor say much about him, but in this particular case, if you look at those wonderful movements you can see what an extraordinary man this was! Please, if you possibly can, go into a likely bookshop & ask if they have Gustav Mahler's biography, & then look closely at those siluettes,! I was so impressed, wanted to buy the dust cover & pay heavily for it, but they wouldn't sell it to me & I didn't want to buy the whole book (18/-) just to have the cover. I even thought of buying the book & selling it straight away, without the cover, second hand; but that wasn't possible either. I will end now.

God bless you, & keep you – your body & your soul. – Please write to me very soon. Letters take a longish time. If there's any alteration /in your plans/ let me know by wire.

    With love

    Ludwig

P.S. Drury sends you his love. & May you never feel or act shallowly! As always L.
P.P.S. Don't forget the flowers & send the little parcel to Miss Anscombe. – I left my hot-water-bottle by accident; I wished I had it now!

---

64 Presumably: Alma Mahler-Werfel, *Gustav Mahler: Memories and Letters*, New York, Viking Press, 1946 (originally published in German in 1940).

65 Wittgenstein is most likely referring here to a series of very animated silhouettes-pictures of Mahler mid-conducting, made by Otto Böhler, and published in his *Dr. Otto Böhler's Schattenbilder*, Vienna, Wilhelm Lechner, 1914, image §13.

Wittgenstein is probably referring to these silhouettes-pictures of Mahler by Otto Böhler, in his letter of December 7, 1947

Ludwig Wittgenstein to Ben Richards, December 16, 1947

c/o Mrs Kingston
Kilpatrick House
Red Cross
Wicklow Eire
16.12.47

Dear Ben, old heart –

Thanks for your letter of Dec. 14th the sight & content of which did me a lot of good. In particular what you wrote about the fare etc made me very happy, (I'd felt pretty bad about it.) – The above address is temporarily permanent. I.e., I'll be here for the next couple of months.[66] When you'll come here – to which I'm looking forward terribly – you'll understand why.

---

[66] On the same day, Wittgenstein wrote to Rush Rhees: "I feel better here now than I did when I arrived. I'm more accustomed to the people & they to me, the weather's warmer & I'm in better health. My work which had stopped completely for a few days – partly because of intestinal trouble, partly because of general dullness – is stirring again a little. May it continue!!" (Wittgenstein to Rhees, December 16, 1947). And a few days later he wrote to Georg Henrik von Wright: "As you see form the above address I'm not solitary. This is a big sort of farm & they take guests in summer but not during the winter, & so I'm alone with the family. They are very quiet, I have my meals in my room & am very little disturbed. Still, I could do with greater loneliness & I intend to exchange this place for a more lonely one later in the year. Red Cross is a village but the farm is about 2 miles outside it & fairly isolated" (Wittgenstein to von Wright, December 22, 1947). Wittgenstein ended up staying in Redcross until mid-April 1948.

I've had a good deal of bad luck since I came here. My luggage, two cases, haven't arrived, owing to the negligence of a rotten travelling agency (Bells in K.P.). Then when I came here I contracted a bad indigestion which made things very difficult all round. But I'm rapidly getting better now, & when you come we'll eat them poor (the Kingstons, I mean).

I'm afraid I've lost your last letter but one (lost it, not destroyed it deliberately) in which you gave me all the various times of your journey, but I do remember that you're due at the terminal in Dublin on Dec. 26th at 1$^{.45}$ p.m.. (If I don't hear to the contrary I'll assume that that's right.) Now if you're in time I should very much like to take you by bus almost immediately to Arklow, 5 miles from here, where we can have a proper meal & from where we'll get by car to Kilpatrick House. ~~I'll have~~ The bus journey from Dublin to Arklow is 2½ hours, the bus leaves Dublin at 2$^{.30}$ p.m. We might just have a snack before we go & I'll have sangwidges with me anyway so you don't starve. There is another bus at 5 p.m., but it's dark then & the journey not nearly as pleasant.[67] That's why I'd rather catch the 2$^{.30}$ bus. I hope that suits you. – On Monday we'd have to travel back to Dublin where we can be together with Con Drury. He is free on Monday from 5 p.m.. He will also be at the terminal when you arrive. Of course we could stay the night of Dec 26th in Dublin, but I confess I'd rather you come with me into the country straight away! the time being so short. –

I have booked ~~a~~ rooms for us in Dublin for Monday night, quite near Drury's hospital & the Zoo.[68] We could come up to Dublin about noon & you could still see a little of the town. Do you think that'll be all right? – I was glad to hear that Angela had done so well, & rather surprised that she should have liked M^{iss} Curtis /the old pug-dog/. To me it only shows that she /Angela/ hasn't much judgment (which doesn't surprise me). Give her (Angela) my good wishes!

I'd be grateful if you could squeeze my hot-water-bottle, & perhaps a shirt & a pair of /warm/ pants /which I've got in Ickenham/, into your rucksack. If you can't it's no great tragedy.

'I had a very nice letter from your mother two days ago & answered it before I had your letter.

---

67 Drury reports that of his very first trip down to Redcross Wittgenstein had said: "On my journey down in the bus I kept remarking to myself what a really beautiful country this is" (Drury 1984: 153).
68 Maurice Drury worked at St Patrick's Hospital on Steeven's Lane (James Street), and the Dublin Zoo was in Phoenix Park – these were about a 20-minute walk from one another.

Please dress <u>very</u> warmly for this place & take good shoes with you, (The 'plane, of course, is well heated.)

<u>God bless you!</u>

I am thinking of you with love always.

Ludwig

P.S. Thanks for the stamps. Please give Angela the enclosed note from the Registry. L. L.

Ludwig Wittgenstein to Ben Richards, January 1, 1948

Red Cross
Wicklow
1.1.48.

Dear Ben, old heart –

I got up rather late yesterday & did my shopping & went to the customs people for my cases. About midday it suddenly became milder & I began to feel better. I caught the $2^{.30}$ bus to Arklow & when I arrived there it rained heavily but was quite warm; & this is how matters stand right now. – I needn't tell you that is was <u>lovely</u> to be with you.[69] Let me hear from you soon. I hope you had a good journey. – I have resumed work, though I'm still a bit wobbly; but I think I'll soon be all right again.[70] While I'm writing this the sun is making an attempt to come out, I hope it may succeed! – It has.

Please don't forget & don't postpone too long seeing the H.M.V. people about the Bruckner.[71] I am very anxious that you should get it, & perhaps they need nudging a bit.

I'm thinking of you constantly with love. Bless you & thanks for everything!

Ludwig

Remember me to your mother. L. L.

---

69 Richards and Maurice Drury came to stay with Wittgenstein in Kilpatrick House between Christmas and the New Year, as Wittgenstein reported to Leonida Malcolm a few days later: "I spent Christmas alone here, but on Boxing Day I saw two friends, one of whom had come over from England to see me & stayed with me here for a few days" (Wittgenstein to Malcolm, January 4, 1948).

70 At this time Wittgenstein was working in MS 136, filling many notebook pages every day (see pp. 37b ff).

71 H.M.V. is a large chain of music shops in the UK, founded in 1921. Wittgenstein was referring to a recording of Anton Bruckner's 8th Symphony in C minor (WAB 108) – in the version of 1887 – which he had ordered to H.M.V for Richards (see Wittgenstein's next letter to Richards, of January 8, 1948, and the following few letters).

Ludwig Wittgenstein to Ben Richards, January 8, 1948

Kilpatrick House
Red Cross
Wicklow
Eire
8.1.48.

Dear Ben, old dear heart –

Thanks for your letter of New Year's Day.[72] It did me good to get it. I'm now entirely well again. Proof: I could eat a butter-scotch today without revulsion.[73] My cases arrived to-day & I had a letter from H.M.V., saying that they had notified you of the arrival of the Bruckner records. Don't delay fetching them & let me know how they sound to you. Especially the 3rd movement which is, & I think is played, 'hinreissend'. (I don't know an English word for it.) Look out for a certain short forte drumm roll which always makes me <u>gape</u> (I think in the development).[74]

Please let me know also if my X-mas card (the one with the cheque in it) has arrived. My work isn't going badly;[75] but I often wish it were still more quiet in this place. But, of course, I could <u>never</u> be as quiet & undisturbed in Cambridge as I'm here!

---

72 This letter has not been preserved.
73 Wittgenstein had been suffering from painful indigestion, as he had written to Leonida Malcolm a few days earlier: "My work's going moderately well & I think it might even go very well if I weren't suffering from some kind of indigestion which I don't seem to be able to shake off. I'll have to come to Ithaca & eat your good cooking. – Actually it's gradually getting better, & my landlady here gives me all I need" (Wittgenstein to Malcolm, January 4, 1948). Wittgenstein's best remedy for the indigestion was to subsist almost entirely on a diet of 'Scragg's' charcoal biscuits, so it was a good sign if he could stomach something else (see Monk 1990: 522).
74 'Hinreissend' (German) could be translated as 'enchanting', 'ravishing', or 'gorgeous'. Wittgenstein was referring to the 3rd movement of Anton Bruckner's 8th Symphony in C minor (WAB 108), in the version of 1887. The 'short forte drumm roll' in that movement to which Wittgenstein was referring is likely the short timpani tremolo at bars 125-128. Thanks to Drs. Inbal and Eran Guter for this and the following details about Bruckner.
75 At this time Wittgenstein was working in MS 136 (see pp. 78a ff).

I've used your dry-shaver every day & I look all right 'in parts', i.e. it works quite well on those parts, e.g. the chin, where the hair sticks ~~up~~ /out/ straight, whereas it hardly touches the cheeks because there the hair lies rather flat. Still I look good enough for <u>this</u> place, & every week, or so I'll have a <u>real</u> shave.

This I wrote 2 days ago. We're having very changeable weather: rain & gale yesterday, & beautiful sunshine to-day. I walked to the sea enjoying it hugely, especially because I was thinking about my work while walking (I take a notebook with me).[76] Whenever I saw something very wonderful I thought of you & wished you could look at it with me. – When I feel low thinking of you gives me strength.

May it be given to you to be serious & happy in your work! God bless you!

  With Love
   Ludwig

P.S. There's another place in the Bruckner I want you to notice. It's in the 2nd movement, a long dreamy passage with a soft drumm-roll accompanying it which stops for a moment & then begins again, & one has the feeling that now he's <u>fast</u> asleep.[77] L. L.

Ludwig Wittgenstein to Ben Richards, January 13, 1948

Kilpatrick House
Red Cross
C^o Wicklow
Eire
13.1.48.

Ben, dearest, you bl . . . old so & so! – I got your lovely parcel to-day & what I felt about it I needn't tell you. Everything in it is <u>marvellous</u>. I am keeping my diet & am feeling very well indeed. I'm working quite well[78] & I walk an hour or two every day &

---

76 Ray Monk writes: "He took his notebook with him on his walks around Red Cross, and would often work outdoors. A neighbour of the Kingstons', who often saw Wittgenstein out on his favourite walk, reports that he once passed him sitting in a ditch, writing furiously, oblivious of anything going on around him" (Monk 1990: 521)

77 Wittgenstein was referring to the 2nd movement of Anton Bruckner's 8th Symphony in C minor (WAB 108), in the version of 1887. The 'dreamy passage' in that movement to which Wittgenstein was referring is likely bars 125-150. In a letter to Felix Weingartner – who was considering performing the symphony in its new version in 1891 – Bruckner wrote concerning this movement: "Scherzo: Main theme — named deutscher Michel [German Michael]. In the second part, the fellow wants to sleep, and in his dreamy state cannot find his tune; finally, he plaintively turns back" (Bruckner to Weingartner, January 27 1891; quoted in Korstvedt 2000: 51).

78 At this time Wittgenstein was working in MS 136 (see pp. 102a ff).

enjoy it <u>very</u> much, especially the <u>colours</u>[79] & the many little birds. I don't think I've ever seen such a lot of them together. The other day I saw a whole – now what's the word – of 20 or 30 chaffinches. I think of you a very great deal whatever I do. – I'm glad you've begun to like the Bruckner. Unless I'm very much mistaken you're going to like it still very much more. Also I'm glad you got my X-mas card. – Getting your letter made me feel <u>very happy</u>. /In fact I seem to get more than my proper share of happiness./ Thanks for everything. God bless you always.

I love to think of the time when you were here. The weather is very erratic just now, constantly changing, a lot of rain, many fields flooded. I enclose an ivy leaf & a gorse blossom to give this letter local colour, & a laurel leaf which comes from the laurel wreath with which I crowned myself the other day, there being no one else /here/ to do it. Dear Ben, please look after yourself. May you be lucky in every way.

        With love

           Ludwig

P.S. Drury sends his best wishes; I had a letter from him a few days ago. L. L.
P.P.S. Please think of me when you listen to the last 8 or 10 bars of the 3rd movement[80] which sounds as though some queer mechanism were playing them e.g. a music box. I think this is peculiarly wonderful.

Ludwig Wittgenstein to Ben Richards, January 22, 1948

                                                                         Red Cross

                                                                         Wicklow

                                                                         22.1.48.

---

79 A few days earlier Wittgenstein had written similarly to his sister, Helene: "The region here wouldn't have much appeal for me if the colours weren't often so wonderful. I think it must be the atmosphere, because not only the grass, but also everything brown, the sky & the sea are magnificent. – I feel much more comfortable than I did in Cambridge" (Wittgenstein to Salzer, January 10, 1948). To Rush Rhees – his friend in Wales – Wittgenstein echoed this sentiment a few weeks later: "There is nothing like the Welsh coast line here, but the colours are most wonderful & make up for everything" (Wittgenstein to Rhees, February 5, 1948).

80 Wittgenstein was referring to bars 317-326 of the 3rd movement of Anton Bruckner's 8th Symphony in C minor (WAB 108), in the version of 1887.

Ben, dear heart,

<u>Thanks</u> for your letter. I hope that by now you have received the one in which I thanked you for your lovely parcel & the letter in it. Thanks for writing to me about your health. I needn't say that I am <u>sorry,</u> you have to use such a nasty cure for your cough – if only it really cures it! I'm sorry about your grandmother's illness. I imagine that you're fond of her. – I'm very well & my work isn't too bad either, though not as good as it was a short time ago; partly because they've had workmen in the house for the last week & there's been a lot of noise; & I'm afraid I'm very sensitive to noise. The weather is as changeable as ever but I go out almost every day & now often take Rex the dooog, with me. He seems to love going out & generally runs about 50 or 100 yards ahead of me; but as soon as he comes to a branching of the way he always stops & waits till I come & decide which way we're going. Also when I stop, which I often do, after a few seconds he comes back to where I'm standing. He comes whenever I call him, except when he is after rabbits, or something, in which case it's difficult to attract his attention. – <u>Of course</u> what you say about the ending of the 3rd movement (Bruckner[81]) isn't final. His 'abruptness' is an essential part of his language. He writes in 'main clauses' (I'm not sure if that's the right grammatical term; I mean the opposite of 'subordinate clause'). He doesn't say "If it rains I shan't go", but "It rains. I don't go." A good example of it the introduction to the first movement which sounds like so many scraps but is a connected whole. People generally, when they first hear Bruckner, & for a <u>long</u> time, can't hear his music '<u>connected</u>'. In the same way that ending of the 3rd movement is <u>not</u> abrupt, but of course it seems so, unless you can listen to his way of telling the story. (By the way, the 3rd movement does not lead into the 4th.)

I <u>hope</u> you'll be better soon! Look after yourself & be good! – I'm thinking of you with love <u>constantly</u>.

 Ludwig

 God bless you!

---

[81] The reference is to Anton Bruckner's 8th Symphony in C minor (WAB 108), in the version of 1887 (see Wittgenstein's remark about the ending of the 3rd movement in his previous letter, and the relevant footnote there).

Ludwig Wittgenstein to Ben Richards, January 29, 1948

Kilpatrick House
Red Cross
Wicklow
29.1.48.

Ben, dear old heart,

My work in the last two weeks hasn't been going quite as well as it did before that time; the reason being partly, perhaps, that there were workmen in the house making a racket for about a week, & now the family is keeping very late hours & I don't get enough sleep. I hope things will get better again. – Con Drury came to see me last Saturday night & stayed till Sunday night. We went for a long walk on the sand dunes which we both enjoyed. I wished I could have taken you to the same spot, but I hadn't discovered it when you were here. It's to the left (facing the sea) of where we walked along the shore, & a <u>little</u> river there flows into the sea (not the one we crossed on going there). It's very lovely along that river & I thought of you. On the whole we're having very wet (though mild) weather, which I don't like. My brain works by far better when the sun shines. – I often wonder if it will be given to me to finish off my work, or whether it will always /have to/ remain a fragment.[82] I wish I had more strength & could bear <u>whatever</u> is decreed. – I <u>hope</u> you're better again! & that your grandmother is, too. I also hope to hear from you soon. – Con sends his best wishes. – I think of you <u>with love</u> constantly.

    Ludwig

I hope that you possess both moral intuition &, above all, the ethics of self-realisation.[83] For, if you don't, – how are you to know who you are? —Take care of yourself, & be good, & God bless you! L. L.

---

82 Wittgenstein was here referring to what was posthumously published as *Philosophical Investigations*. What was eventually published as 'Part I' of *Philosophical Investigations* was already completed at this time (as TS 227), but Wittgenstein was still at work on what ended up being published as 'Part II' (the eventual text of 'Part II' was derived from the later lost TS 234, which drew on remarks which Wittgenstein had been writing between May 1946 and May 1949).

83 This sentence playfully alludes to the prestigious 'Annual Philosophical Lecture' of the British Academy, that was to be given that year – on January 28, 1948 – by Charles Arthur Campbell. The lecture was to be entitled, 'Moral Intuition and the Ethics of Self-Realization' (and it was later published in the *Proceedings of the British Academy* for 1948, pp. 23-56). Wittgenstein had received an invitation to the lecture, and he enclosed the invitation card in his letter to Richards. Wittgenstein had himself been elected by the British Academy to deliver the 'Philosophical Lecture' to the British Academy for 1942, but after initially accepting he later withdrew (see Wittgenstein 1993: 445-458).

Enclosure included with the letter of January 29, 1948:

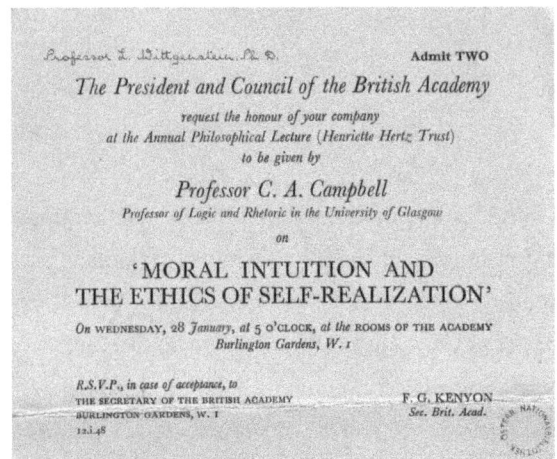

Ludwig Wittgenstein to Ben Richards, January 31, 1948

> Kilpatrick House
> Red Cross
> Wicklow
> 31.1.48.

Dearest Ben,

I wonder what you will think of me for writing so soon again. I want to say: I think you'll never know how good it was to get your letter. I'd felt a bit rotten lately; not bodily, but as though I were in a labile state of mental equilibrium, a feeling I very much dread. And just before your letter came I started writing to you about my queer state, saying among other things (what I still want to say): "Pray that it doesn't happen to my mind".[84] After I had written for a while I felt a bit better, & then the boy brought me your letter. When I read your kind words the nightmare left me & I felt happy & felt that now I wanted to go out & and enjoy the sun, which I did. God bless you! – I went to Red Cross & bought this huge writing pad.[85] – I hope the fact that you don't

---

84 Throughout his adult life Wittgenstein was plagued by periods in which he felt that he was in imminent danger of slipping into madness. A few days after writing this letter, he wrote in his notebook: "I feel unwell. Not physically, but mentally. Fear the outbreak of insanity. God alone knows if I'm in danger" (MS 137, p. 4b; February 3, 1948). And a couple of days later still he wrote to Norman Malcolm: "I am now in very good bodily health & my work isn't going bad either. I have occasional queer states of nervous instability about which I'll only say that they're rotten while they last, & teach one to pray" (Wittgenstein to Malcolm, February 5, 1948).

85 Namely, the notebook now known as MS 137. The first entry in this notebook is dated from two days later: February 2, 1948.

mention your health means that it's better! – I'm glad you saw M^iss Anscombe. I wish you hadn't been so rushed. – I don't know how much a paper, even if it's <u>ever</u> so good, can do in Oxford against a poison like C. S. Lewis.[86] I think it might help someone who is intelligent, & inexperienced, & perhaps doesn't feel quite happy about Lewis in the first place. It might help such a person to see through the fraud.
Bless you, again. I am thinking of you <u>constantly</u>.

   With love
     Ludwig

P.S.

How my 'labile' state came on, I mean what caused it, I don't know. I'm taking Vit. B, which has helped me in the past[87] & I try to get a good deal of sleep, which isn't so easy because the Kingstons go to bed late, as a rule, & rather noisily.

I find my work extremely difficult & can't say if it is it's intrinsic difficulty or my waning powers. This is no complaint, though; just a statement of fact. May it be given to me to look at it in this way always! Thanks for thinking of me a lot. I need it. L. L.

2.2.48[88] I've had some good nights & am feeling much better. Yesterday we had rain & a terrific gale. This morning the wind is still strong but the sun's out at least for the moment G. b. y. It was beautiful out & I thought of you.
Ludwig

---

86 Wittgenstein was referring to a paper that Elizabeth Anscombe was due to present a couple of days later at the Socratic Club in Oxford. Anscombe's paper was entitled 'Miracles: A Reply to Mr. C.S. Lewis', and it was intended to undermine the argument against naturalism which Lewis had put forward in the third chapter of his recent book *Miracles: A Preliminary Study* (London, The Centenary Press, 1947). The 'poison' which Wittgenstein had in mind was likely Lewis' attempts to rationally ground and justify Christian belief in apologetic works such as his book on miracles, which was an approach to religiosity and religious belief to which Wittgenstein was profoundly opposed (see, for example, Wittgenstein's remarks about Father O'Hara in his 1966: 57-59). Anscombe gave a detailed description of the Socratic Club meeting in a letter to Wittgenstein which Wittgenstein enclosed in his next letter to Richards (see the letter from Wittgenstein to Richards of February 11, 1948, and the Anscombe enclosure).

87 The previous day Wittgenstein had written to his sister, Helene: "It's good that you're taking the vitamin B, because it's certain that it works, and not an empty delusion, as with so many medicines" (Wittgenstein to Salzer, January 10, 1948).

88 Wittgenstein squeezed this extra postscript – upside down – into the space on the top left corner of the letter's first page (to the left of his address and the date).

Ludwig Wittgenstein to Ben Richards, February 11, 1948

Kilpatrick House
Red Cross
Wicklow
11.2.48.

My dear Ben,

Thanks for your letter. I was glad to hear that you could get away into the mountains for a short time. We, too, had gales here recently, though nothing like what you describe. – Yes, the painters have left, ages ago, so has the boy George. But Keneth, who for some reason or other hasn't been sent to school lately, now rarely goes to bed much before, & sometimes after, midnight, & there is at that hour talk next door between him & someone, his mother, I imagine. This, I have no doubt, isn't good for him, but there is nothing I can do about it; & if I said anything they'd rightly suspect that I had selfish reasons.[89] – How long I shall stay on I don't yet know. I imagine, for another month. I'll try to be sensible about it. I know that going to Rossroe[90] has it's dangers & I'll bear this in mind. – My work, as far as I can judge, isn't going badly. It <u>seems</u> to me as though in the last few months I had learnt a <u>lot</u> about the questions (philosophy of psychology) which have been bothering me. Whether this is <u>true</u> the future will show. – My states of 'labile equilibrium' still continue, but they haven't been so dreadful of late as they were some time ago /in fact nothing like as bad/. It's almost hopeless to try to describe what it feels like to be in this state, for even I find it almost impossible to imagine when it's over. This I want to say, that while it lasts I feel as if I were in <u>imminent</u> danger of going mad.[91]

---

89 Maurice Drury reports that around this time Wittgenstein despairingly said to him: "It has come... What I have always dreaded: that I would no longer be able to work. I have done no work at all for the past two weeks. And I can't sleep at nights. The people under my room sit up late talking and the continual murmur of voices is driving me crazy" (Drury 1984: 155).

90 Rosroe is a small hamlet in the northwest of County Galway, on the west coast of Ireland. Its Irish Gaelic name was 'An Ros Rua' which now tends to be Anglicized as 'Rosroe' – but Wittgenstein spells it in a number of different ways. Maurice Drury's family had a small holiday cottage on the Killary Harbour in Rosroe, in which Wittgenstein had stayed for a holiday with Francis Skinner and Drury, back in 1934. Drury later recalled that on hearing from Wittgenstein of the noise problem in Kilpatrick House, "I reminded him that the cottage at Rosro in Connemara, where he and Francis had stayed with me, was now empty, and that he would be more than welcome to have the use of it for as long as he wanted. This thought seemed to give him some relief, and he said that that might be the solution to his problem. He then returned to Red Cross to think the matter over, and I prescribed some tablets to help him to sleep. I also wrote off to Rosro to have the cottage made ready in case he decided to go there" (Drury 1984: 155).

91 See Wittgenstein's previous letter to Richards (of January 31, 1948), and the relevant footnote there. Wittgenstein had long been plagued by periods of feeling that he was dangerously close to madness. Compare a remark that he wrote in his notebook of 1946: "I often fear madness. Have I any reason to assume that this fear does not spring from, so to speak, an optical illusion: of seeing something as an abyss that is close by, when it isn't? The only *experience* I know of that speaks for its not being an illusion, is the case of Lenau. For in his 'Faust' there are thoughts of a kind I too am familiar with. Lenau puts them into Faust's mouth, but they are no doubt his own about himself. What is important is what Faust says about his *loneliness* or *isolation*" (MS 132, p. 197; Wittgenstein 1998: 61).

And I can't say to my self that it'll be all right again in a few hours because it feels as though my soul were dying. May it all pass away completely! I could say more about it, but I won't, & you may wonder why I should describe it to you in such detail, anyhow. But the reason is a) that I think I should let you know what happens to me; b) that I feel that this, as it's rather repellant, you ought to know, – I think you'll understand, why. If, on account of it, you feel somewhat uncomfortable about me, or us, you couldn't be blamed. If you don't, & only in this case, I want to say "Ben, please write to me regularly, as hearing from you is the greatest help I have". – On the other hand, you know that I know that what is given can be taken. And if it is taken God will help me. – You know all that I want to say. – One more thing: In my last letter I wrote to you something like "Pray for me that it doesn't happen", meaning: that I don't go insane. That I meant it seriously you know; but I wondered afterwards if you thought it a queer thing to say to you. If you did, I just don't want you to think that it was rott. If you didn't think it queer I'm grateful. – Con Drury advised me in a letter to take a good deal of salt with my food if I ~~took~~ take a bromide every night. This may help me. – I shall ask him about the psychiatry book when I write to him. – I had a letter from M^{iss} Anscombe which I enclose as it may interest you. There is a remark in it about yourself, but as it isn't unkind it doesn't matter. – My you be lucky in your work, & serious & kind, & not mind too much when you're different from many of your surroundings. – I wish I could see the new posters. – What's a figure "compounded of bits of railway tickets & ⊕ signs" like??
God bless you always! With love
   Ludwig

Enclosure included with the letter of February 11, 1948: Letter from Elizabeth Anscombe to Ludwig Wittgenstein, February 3, 1948

            Somerville, Oxford
            February 3rd.

Dear Professor Wittgenstein,
I've had my discussion with Lewis.[92] He was much more decent in discussion than I expected, though he was glib and played all sorts of tricks to obscure the issue – but

---

92 See Wittgenstein's letter to Richards of January 31, 1948, and the relevant footnote there. Anscombe's talk to the Socratic Club took place on February 2, 1948, and it has been published as 'A Reply to Mr. C. S. Lewis' argument that 'Naturalism is Self-Refuting' ' along with notes regarding Lewis' response and the discussion that followed (in Anscombe 1981: 224-32, and see also pp. ix-x). The original minutes of the session (on which Anscombe's published version of the discussion seems to have been based) have been published in Stockton & Lipscomb 2021: 45-6).

he wasn't really objectionable. The club was very pleasant, much more so than the Jowett or the Moral Science Club when a lot of people /are/ there.[93] (It was a colossal lot of people, Lewis is a very popular speaker.) My paper was fairly bad as a treatment of the subject, I think, but it was short and reasonably good as supplying something to discuss, and the discussion on the whole kept to the point. Smythies was there and took a small part, but very good. (He'd helped a lot with the paper, it would have been absolutely rotten without him.) One really funny thing happened. The secretary, who's a friend and obviously an admirer of Lewis',[94] and who when the subject was first raised said to me: "I suppose you agree with Mr. Lewis' book?" & was extremely surprised when I said I didn't – started going for Lewis, who had said something about having written the book "at a fairly popular level" – he reproached him almost in moral terms, that one should not, for the sake of popularizing, put up a bad argument. He was obviously completely convinced by my argument, probably much too easily so.[95] This protest, in these circumstances, seemed to me very effective,[96] and I was extremely glad that I had not gone in for pompous indignation at Lewis which I'd been tempted to do, but Smythies stopped me by writing "Shit!" against my remarks. Lewis oiled out of it, of course.

---

93 The Jowett Society (in Oxford) and the Moral Science Club (in Cambridge) are the chief discussion circles at those two universities respectively where philosophical papers are presented by an invited speaker and then discussed. Wittgenstein was a regular participant in the meetings of the Moral Science Club, and he been an invited speaker at a Jowett Society meeting back in May 1947.

94 The secretary of the Socratic Club at that time was Frank Goodridge, who was a student of Lewis'. Goodridge and Anscombe later became friends. In fact, Goodridge was one of the lodgers in the Anscombe house – at 27 St. John Street – in 1950, when Wittgenstein moved in for almost a year, and he therefore later got to know Wittgenstein too.

95 The minutes – written by Frank Goodridge, the club's secretary – conclude: "From the discussion in general it appeared that Mr. Lewis would have to turn his argument into a rigorous, analytical one, if his notion of ['] validity['] as the effect of causes, were to stand the test of all the questions put to him" (Stockton & Lipscomb 2021: 46).

96 Anscombe's paper seems to have had a fairly powerful effect on Lewis himself (though there is some controversy over the matter). In a letter a couple of years later, Lewis expressed his desire for Anscombe to present a paper to the Socratic Club entitled 'Why I believe in God'. He explained to Stella Aldwinckle – the founder of the Socratic Club – that "I shd. press hard for No. 4 [i.e. the paper from Anscombe]. The lady is quite right to refute what she thinks bad theistic arguments, but does this not almost oblige her as a Christian to find good ones in their place: having obliterated me as an Apologist ought she not to *succeed* me?" (Lewis 2004: 35; Lewis to Aldwinckle, June 12, 1950). On the other hand, Anscombe later recalled: "The fact that Lewis rewrote that chapter [in response to some of the objections in Anscombe's paper]... shows his honesty and seriousness. The meeting of the Socratic Club at which I read my paper has been described by several of his friends as a horrible and shocking experience which upset him very much... My own recollection is that it was an occasion of sober discussion of certain quite definite criticisms, which Lewis' rethinking and rewriting showed he thought were accurate." (Anscombe 1981: x).

I had a letter from von Wright yesterday.[97] He told me that he <u>had</u> just applied to submit himself as a candidate for the chair, though he seems very doubtful and unhappy about it.[98]

Now, to-day, I am having a hellish time trying to get my paper ~~written~~ /finished/ for the Jowett tomorrow, on "calculating in one's head". It's a short paper meeting chairmanned by MacNabb,[99] of whom Smythies has a poor opinion, but I think he may be all right. The paper is sure to be very bad, I've not had the time to think about it properly. Then on Thursday I'm going to a small Socratic Club gathering. – They make a practice of resuming the discussion; rather like your second Jowett meeting.[100] They are certainly keen, which is what makes it pleasant.

There is a physicist here, Max Born, delivering a set of special lectures called "The Natural Philosophy of Cause & Chance".[101] I've tried them, but they are full of mathematics which I can't understand, interspersed with philosophical remarks which <u>seem</u> to me a bit childish.

I saw Ben Richards in London a week or two ago. He told me you may be leaving your present address. Still I suppose this will get to you. I enjoyed being with him, but he was shy & uncommunicative; this was offset by his very great friendliness when we met & parted.

Good luck with everything.

        Yours ever

           Elizabeth Anscombe.

P.S. I find public discussion very difficult indeed. I am in a frightened hurry to reply to what's said to me; if I try to check this and pause to think about it, my mind goes blank. So I say a lot that is no use.

---

97 Georg Henrik von Wright, an old student and friend of Wittgenstein's; see the 'Short Biographies of Frequently Mentioned Family and Friends'.

98 Von Wright had applied for the Cambridge chair of philosophy which Wittgenstein had just vacated. A couple of weeks later Wittgenstein wrote to von Wright: "Miss Anscombe wrote to me a few weeks ago that you had put in for the professorship. I shall write the recommendation in a few days & send it to the Registrary as you suggest. May your decision be the right one! I have <u>no</u> doubt that you will be a better professor than any of the other candidates for the chair. But Cambridge is a dangerous place. Will you become superficial? smooth? If you don't, you will have to suffer terribly" (Wittgenstein to von Wright, February 23, 1948). Von Wright's application was successful.

99 Donald G. C. MacNabb (1905-91), a philosopher at Oxford who worked on David Hume.

100 See Wittgenstein's description in his letter to Richards of May 17, 1947.

101 See Max Born, *Natural Philosophy of Cause and Chance: Being the Waynflete Lectures Delivered in the College of St. Mary Magdalen, Oxford in Hilary Term 1948*, Oxford, Clarendon Press, 1949.

Ludwig Wittgenstein to Ben Richards, February 19, 1948

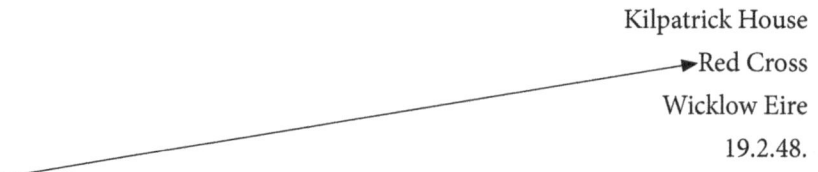

Kilpatrick House
Red Cross
Wicklow Eire
19.2.48.

This is wrong; it ought to be "Redcross", in one word.

Dearest Ben,

It was good to get your letter yesterday. – You were right to be optimistic. I am completely all right again. I think of you a <u>lot</u>, especially when I'm doing anything I like to do, like walking when it's fine. It's suddenly turned cold again & I'm shivering in my room, but it won't be for long. – There is a gate lodge along the road which we drove to the police station; the lodge belongs to a big house about 200 yards off the road.[102] It's just <u>conceivable</u> that I might rent the lodge if the owner of the house, who isn't living here now, will let it. It's in very bad repair & completely unfurnished, but something <u>might</u> be arranged about that. I am making enquiries but I'm <u>not</u> optimistic. It's about 10 minutes walk from here, has three rooms, two tiny ones & a bigger one &, at present, no 'convenience' at all. Drinking water has to be fetched from the house.

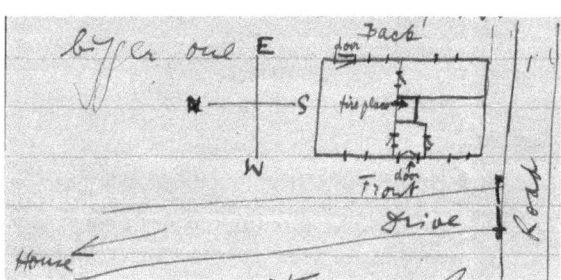

For washing purposes one can use rainwater. I shall let you know the results of my negotiations. – My work isn't going badly but I'm a bit <u>lazy</u>.[103] – May you be lucky in yours! I'm curious what you will think of Ryle's book.[104] I <u>imagine</u> it's a good antidote against a certain prejudice in favour of measuring, ~~as opposed~~ /& neglecting to/ study ~~any~~the <u>physiognomy</u> of an illness with the naked eye etc.

---

102 The big house was called 'Riversdale House' at the time, and is now called 'Spruce Lodge'. It was set back from the principal road that led from Kilpatrick House towards Barndarrig, where there was a police station at the time. The gate lodge and the farm surrounding it was owned by a Dr. Brady, who lived in Dublin, and it was about a 10- or 15-minute walk from Kilpatrick House. Wittgenstein had described the lodge to Maurice Drury as "a ruined cottage near the farm which he thought could be cheaply restored, and that might provide the quiet he needed" (Drury 1984: 155).

103 At this time Wittgenstein was working on MS 137.

104 Wittgenstein was presumably referring to John A. Ryle's booklet: *The Aims and Methods of Medical Science: An Inaugural Lecture*, Cambridge, Cambridge University Press, 1935. In this lecture Ryle argued for the value of an intuitive approach in diagnosis, over an exclusive reliance on measurement and laboratory tests and the like.

God bless you, & thanks for all you say in your letter.
>With Love
>>Ludwig

P.S. Drury hasn't yet written to me about the book on psychiatry. The enclosed daisy is the first flower I've come across on my walks. L. L.

Ludwig Wittgenstein to Ben Richards, February 25, 1948

>>>Kilpatrick House
>>>Redcross
>>>Wicklow Eire
>>>25.2.48.

Dear Ben,

Thanks for your letter & the drawings. I think I can perfectly imagine the originals & they'd give me the creeps.

It seems to me, perhaps quite wrongly, that it needs an extraordinarily <u>dull</u> population for this sort of humor to be possible. I imagine that a good many people find these pictures <u>mildly</u> amusing, & a tiny minority, /only/ nauseating. On the other hand this dullness perhaps makes for a certain strength, or toughness. Maybe that's all rubbish. – Here, too, it's got cold & there was some snow, but it's all gone again.[105] I find the cold easterly wind <u>trying</u>. – My work is going so-so.[106] I find it very difficult indeed. Sometimes I feel a kind of despair when I think that I'll never finish it. ~~Sometimes~~ I tell myself that I ought to take what's given to me, but I find it <u>very difficult</u>. I work frightfully slowly. I mean: every thought is chewed <u>hundreds</u> of times. It's the only way I know. Perhaps I'm too old, /though,/ & shall in the end get lost in that maze of thoughts, instead of making myself a master of it. What I need is more modesty, less conceit. – I hope your Bach performances will be good & I hope you'll enjoy them. The program is enormous! I wonder why they are doing so much. Surely <u>one</u> of the Passions is heaps! Yes, the short choruses! – Dear Ben, I wish I could see you before too, too long – I think of you such a lot! Of course I've <u>plenty</u> of time to do so, & plenty of reason! – Drury is probably coming here next weekend. He'll then tell me about the psychiatry books. The negotiations /& deliberations/ about the lodge

---

105 A few days earlier Wittgenstein had written to Irma Sraffa: "I am very grateful for this mild winter, though just now it's pretty cold & snowing heavily. But we have, so far, not had more than two days snow this whole winter" (Wittgenstein to Sraffa, February 21, 1948).

106 For the most part there are entries in MS 137 almost every day, but there are also a number of longish interruptions, for example between February 20 and March 3, 1948.

haven't yet led to anything. – May all go well with you! & may you think of me with love, as I do of you!

Ludwig P.T.O.

P.S. Nature is awfully backward here, or I'd ~~send y~~/enclose/ some flowers, but so far there's nothing. I'm going out now. I wish you were with me. – God bless you, always – whatever you may think of, or feel about.

Ludwig

Ludwig Wittgenstein to Ben Richards (undated, February 26, 1948)[107]

P.P.S. to the letter I sent off yesterday.

Dear Ben, heart,

When I wrote to you yesterday I was feeling a bit sad (perhaps because I was tired). On the way home from my walk when it was getting dark I began to feel differently; there were birds singing (along the road that leads from here to the main road) which I never hear during the day, I think perhaps they are curliews[108] /it's marshy both sides of the road/; hearing them in the dark felt good. I then felt I'd written to you in a depressed way. I am sorry I complained about my work; I had no earthly right to. Of course it is very difficult for me; that's /only/ natural.

It's true also that I often long to see you, to talk to you, & everything. (That's natural, too.) May God grant me that you continue to l.[109] me; or, if that's not to be, enough understanding to take it /moderately/ decently. G. b. y.! Forgive whatever there is to forgive. I th. o. y. w. l. a.[110] I hope that your work is going well; I know that it's difficult work (for anyone who takes it seriously).

L., a.

      Ludwig

---

107 Richards added '27/2/48' to the letter, and since Wittgenstein wrote that he was following up on the letter he had written "yesterday" (that letter having been dated February 25), Richards was presumably noting the date the letter was received.
108 This should be: 'curlews'.
109 Stands for: 'love'.
110 Stands for: 'I think of you with love always'.

Ludwig Wittgenstein to Ben Richards, March 5, 1948

> Kilpatrick House
> Redcross
> Wicklow Eire
> 5.3.48.

Dear Ben, dear heart –

Thanks for your letter which I loved reading. I found it when I returned from Dublin this evening. I went there yesterday to talk to the sister of the owner of the little lodge. She is not attractive /I mean her personality/, & it wasn't agreeable to negotiate with her, but after we had talked for 40 minutes, or so, I felt that I could put down in writing exactly what I was prepared to pay & <u>for</u> what. So I wrote her a letter /last night/ which she will send to her brother in London & he can decide whether or not he agrees to my conditions. If he doesn't I may have to go to Rossroe, after all, the disadvantage of which would be the great distance from Dublin.

About my remark about 'dullness' – there isn't much in it, anyway, & what truth there is in it, if any, could only come out in a conversation /which might make me see more clearly what I'm talking about/. I might say this: Standing in queues, or riding in buses etc, say in Cambridge, I've often had to listen to humorous conversations around me (I'm <u>not</u> talking of University people now) which never amused me in the least, rather the opposite: but I often on such occasions told myself that this kind of humour might last through an air-raid, say. I believe that in English queues there is less grumbling than in queues in most European countries, & the rather dull, unwitty humour seems to me the lubricant which makes the machine work smoothly & noiselessly. The humour seems to me that of a very <u>patient</u> people, & the patience to prevent, or /greatly/ to postpone, catastrophes. I can't say that I love or admire it, but I believe it makes for steadiness. – A lot of this is probably utter rubbish. Forgive it & forget it. – I should have liked to have seen the Indian exhibition with you.[111] I've seen extremely little of Indian art & none of it ever impressed me: I was just unable to get hold of it. Perhaps it would have been different if I'd been with you. As to "silly chatter" after one has seen or heard great works – don't I know it – by doing it myself! And when you say "It is humiliating . . . . . ." – this is what I've felt thousands of times, though perhaps I've never expressed it so well. –

---

111 This was presumably the exhibition that was being held in London at the Royal Academy of Arts – between November 29, 1947 and February 29, 1948 – entitled 'Exhibition of Indian Art (Chiefly from the Dominions of India and Pakistan)'.

I'm glad you saw M^iss Anscombe; she's good company. I was in good company too, seeing Drury /here/ last weekend & in Dublin last night after my talk with M^iss Brady (whom I wouldn't call good company). – I gave Drury your love & he sends his.
The titles of the psychiatry books are:
1) Physical Methods of Treatment in Psychiatry by Sargent & Slater[112] (Drury says it's good except the introduction.)
2) An Introduction to Psychiatry by Curran & Guttman[113] (Drury says it's sensible.)

I <u>hope</u> your Bach concerts will go satisfactory. I'm sorry to say I don't remember the 'Confiteor',[114] I wish I did, but I don't know the Mass anywhere near well enough. – I can't complain about my work. I have become <u>very</u> much clearer about the problems that baffled me for years. – I must now say something which weighs on my mind: I <u>long</u> to see you & hope you will come to see me sometime this spring.
<u>I pray that nothing may ever come between us! God bless you!</u>

With love always
Ludwig

P.S. I don't like to write what goes without saying – that I can <u>easily</u> pay your fare & that <u>wherever</u> I'll be it'll be wonderful to be with you.

I had a sight several times these days which impressed me very much. People are ploughing their fields now, & you can see a ploughman & behind him a dense swarm of <u>black</u> & <u>white</u> birds, rooks & seagulls, it looks beautiful & phantastic. L. L.

---

112 William Sargant & Eliot Slater, *An Introduction to Physical Methods of Treatment in Psychiatry*, Edinburgh, E. & S. Livingstone, 1945.
113 Desmond Curran & Eric Guttmann, *Psychological Medicine: A Short Introduction to Psychiatry*, Edinburgh, Churchill Livingstone, 1943.
114 Richards had presumably referenced the 'Confiteor' section of Johann Sebastian Bach's Mass in B minor, namely the lines towards the end of the 'Credo' section which read: "I confess one baptism for the remission of sins, and I await the resurrection of the dead and the life of the world to come, Amen".

Ludwig Wittgenstein to Ben Richards, March 12, 1948

Kilpatrick House
Redcross
Wicklow Eire
12.3.48.

Dear Ben – heart!

Thanks for your letter! I suppose by now you've got the one I wrote last week. You write about a 'silly' remark, in your previous letter, which you'd meant to be clever. <u>None</u> of your remarks struck me that way. – I'm in very good health & in better spirits than I deserve (God bless you). My work is going <u>fairly</u> well. It's a long & tortuous job; my thoughts always move something like this: 〰️ .[115] I.e., <u>almost</u> in circles. Which means that I may have to travel many miles in order to progress an inch. This is no complaint, just a statement of fact. – To read with you what I've written would be good only if I could make you see what poor stuff it is. But I wouldn't be able to do that. Because the poorness is <u>not</u> on the surface; & because, in my heart, I'm vain about /the work/ it.

—— I had a letter to-day from M^iss Brady saying that her brother has agreed to let me rent the lodge furnished for £2 at week. The snag is that I can't sign a lease unless they let me see the furniture, they intend to supply me with, first. I wrote this to M^iss B & I don't know if she'll agree. – I've also looked at other places – which were no good at all. – The weather these last 3 days hasn't just been good but marvelous & warm like in summer. May you have good weather, too! Thanks for the blossoms; they repose in my M.S. book. – I've never read a play by Priestley,[116] only once an article & a short story, I think, which were too dull & bl. . .[117] for words. But photographic likeness is, of course, the one thing people can produce nowadays; & if they knew themselves, & didn't try to be what they aren't, I suppose it would be fine. Only <u>I think</u> they do exactly what our photographers do (M^rs <u>Ramsey</u>).[118] – I hope Angela[119] will be lucky,

---

115 Wittgenstein had used the same image to illustrate the nature of his philosophical progress in his notebook from 1931: "My path of thought: ⟲ or 〰️ a lot of movement that makes little progress" (MS 110, p. 82; February 15, 1931). Special thanks to Alois Pichler for this tip.
116 J. B. (John Boynton) Priestley (1894-1984), English playwright and literary critic.
117 'Bloody' (used here as an expletive – in Wittgenstein's idiosyncratic way – rather than an adjective).
118 Lettice Ramsey (1898-1985) was the widow of Wittgenstein's late friend and discussion partner, the important philosopher Frank Plumpton Ramsey (1903-1930), and was herself a friend of Wittgenstein's (see, for example, MS 183, p. 39). She worked as a photographer, running a successful photographic studio in Cambridge with Helen Muspratt.
119 Angela Richards, the oldest of Richards' four younger sisters.

& also that it'll turn out lucky for her to have been lucky. (What a remark!) Give her my good wishes!

Dear Ben, I hope —— But you know all I hope /don't you?/. Bless you, <u>always</u>.
> With love
> Ludwig

There are no primroses yet, the first I'll find you'll get.

Ludwig Wittgenstein to Ben Richards, March 18, 1948

> Kilpatrick House
> Redcross
> Wicklow
> 18.3.48.

Dearest Ben,

Although there isn't much to write to-day, & nothing that's urgent, I still feel I don't want to wait with writing until I get your letter. Perhaps you can understand, <u>why</u>. I haven't been working particularly well these last few days,[120] I often felt <u>very</u> tired & rather sad.

A queer thing is happening to me: I'm sure you know that normally a good deal of music runs through my mind every day, generally expressive, in some way, of what I feel. – For about 2 months /now/ practically no music comes into my head – except the Scherzo from the Midsummer night's Dream![121] Now I admire the scherzo, but it isn't a piece which is very near to my heart & it isn't at all expressive of my present

---

120 The previous day Wittgenstein had written to Georg Henrik von Wright: "My work is progressing very slowly & very painfully. I often believe that I am on the straight road to insanity: It is difficult for me to imagine that my brain should stand the strain very long. That I dread this end I needn't say. You're not the only one who needs more courage. May our fate not be too terrible! & may we be given courage" (Wittgenstein to von Wright, March 17, 1948).

121 Felix Mendelssohn Bartholdy's A Midsummer Night's Dream. The instrumental music – including the Scherzo – was written in 1842 (op. 61). A few days earlier Wittgenstein had also described the situation to his sister Helene: "Something strange has been happening to me for about two months: almost no music goes through my head anymore, except for the Scherzo from A Midsummer Night's Dream! It is, of course, very beautiful, but it is certainly not music that is very close to me; & it doesn't suit my mood. So there must be non-musical reasons why it keeps coming to mind. Freud would perhaps say, and perhaps rightly so, that I always want to say to myself 'I am an ass'; because the part in which the ass cries goes through my head particularly often" (Wittgenstein to Salzer, March 13, 1948). Back in 1937 Wittgenstein had recorded a similar experience in his notebook – that time in relation to the overture to The Merry Wives of Windsor by Otto Nicolai: "This doesn't particularly correspond to my mood, nor am I particularly fond of the piece & yet it keeps coming back to me. I would like to know why" (MS 119, pp 68-9).

mood. I have been rather perturbed by it haunting me & I thought of what Freud says about this phenomenon. I thought he might say that I want constantly to tell myself: that I'm an ass. I wonder if there's something in that. – I'm enclosing the first primula, as I promised. – <u>May you be well, & not unhappy, & still love me! God bless you!</u>
        With love
        Ludwig

P.S. My negotiations about the lodge are still going on. Always remember that I love you. L.

Ludwig Wittgenstein to Ben Richards, March 19, 1948

        Kilpatrick House
        Redcross
        C⁰ Wicklow Eire
        19.3.48.

Dearest Ben,

Thanks for your letter of March 15. I don't know what cembalos are. I imagine the concerto was one of the two concertos for three 'pianos',[122] as I should have called them; &, if so, I wish I could have heard it, too, because they are /both/ <u>terrific</u>. I loved reading all you wrote about the Bach festival /particularly what you wrote about the Evangelists/.

I'm sorry you're losing Ann.[123] I wish I knew more clearly /why, &/ in what <u>spirit</u>, she was leaving.

Your flowers were lovely – <u>but</u>: they made a complete mess of part of ~~the~~ your last page & some of it I can only guess. The primula which, I suppose, was yellow when you enclosed it arrived <u>dark blue</u>! /Bless you/ — Dear Ben, in my last two letters I wrote (<u>very seriously</u>) that I longed to see you, & that I hoped I would, sometime this spring. You didn't reply to this at all; I wonder, why? Am I being a fool? If so, I'm afraid I'll remain that way. Forgive me /please/ if you can! Pray for my old & foolish mind. God bless you always! With love
        Ludwig

---

122 Johan Sebastian Bach, Concerto in D minor for three harpsichords (BWV 1063) and Concerto in C major for three harpsichords (BWV 1064).

123 Ann Phillips, the Richards family's housekeeper. It was perhaps around this time (or shortly thereafter) that she moved to Canada (see Richards' letter to Wittgenstein of December 12, 1950).

Ludwig Wittgenstein to Ben Richards, March 23, 1948

Kilpatrick House
Redcross
Wicklow Eire
23.3.48.

Dearest Ben,

Forgive me for writing to you so soon again. I've got to ask you a great favour. I had a letter from my American sister,[124] the one you know, saying that she is travelling to Europe on a boat, The "Veendam" (VEENDAM) which leaves New York on March 27th. I can't, therefore, write to her at her N.Y. address, but I believe one can send a letter to Southampton where my sister is going to land so that it's handed to her on board, or on the quay. She will probably stay in England for a couple of days, but I don't know <u>where</u>. – What I want to ask you to do for me is this: – a) Find out (perhaps at Cook's) if there is a boat of exactly that name. My sister writes "Veendam", or so I read the name, but please make sure of it. (It's probably a Dutch boat.) b) Find out if it's possible to send a letter to the quay to a landing passenger. c) <u>If</u> that can be done, please address the enclosed letter in whatever way they tell you it ought to be addressed to reach her /Find out the <u>safest</u> way./. If there is no way of sending a letter to a passenger going ashore, just burn the letter. – I know you're busy – but I'd <u>very</u> much like her to get my letter before she leaves for Austria. (I can't write to Austria in the same way, as letters there are opened by the censor.[125]) She is going to have an <u>extremely</u> difficult time. —— My own affairs are roughly where they were when I wrote my last letter. It's <u>less</u> likely now that I'll get the lodge. The owner is <u>too</u> unreliable. I think within the next fortnight I'll know what to do. — God bless you always. I think of you with love, constantly

Ludwig

---

124 Margaret Stonborough-Wittgenstein.

125 Allied censorship of the mail in Austria continued until 1953 (see Wittgenstein's letter to Richards of September 13, 1947, and the relevant footnote there).

Ludwig Wittgenstein to Ben Richards (undated, around March 28/29, 1948)

Easter Greetings

Bright and
   happy Easter,
Springtime
   of the year,
May the season's
   gladness
Fill your heart
   with cheer.

To Ben
From Ludwig
w.l.

Ludwig Wittgenstein to Ben Richards, March 28, 1948[126]

Kilpatrick House
Redcross
Wicklow Eire
Easter Day[127]

Dear Ben, Heart –
Thanks for your tiny musical letter & for your Easter letter; <u>thanks for drawing me an Easter egg!</u> I was very glad to get the photos, too. I shall return them soon. I can

---

126 Richards added '31/3/48' to the letter, which was most likely the day he received the letter.
127 In 1948, Easter Sunday fell on March 28.

understand how the sculptures can greatly impress someone, but the only one that impressed me was the sitting young man with the broken nose. I should very much like to know more about him. Is it a portrait, or a religious figure?? Do you know? — I wrote what I think is the answer to your question about the definition of a millilitre on an Easter card to Angela. I wonder if she thought that I'd gone completely nuts. (If so, she is not far wrong.) —

The nearest thing I know to geriatrics is gerrymandering which means "to manipulate (constituency etc.) unfairly so as to secure disproportionate influence at election for some party." – But why you should study anything like that at a hospital I can't conceive.

– After writing to you that your primula had arrived blue /or rather dark purple/ it struck me that possibly it wasn't yellow to start with. – It lies in my M.S. book[128] & so does the big blossom which has it's right colour, too. –

The question where I'm to go when I leave here is not yet decided! I could, of course, have made up my mind /long ago/ to go to Rossroe & brake off negotiations with M^{iss} Brady.[129] I don't know if it was sensible, or foolish & cowardly, not to do so. – You see, although in Norway, in a sense, I lived exceedingly isolated, I had friends in Skjolden, whom I liked to see & with whom I had something serious in common.[130] Here, or in Rossroe there's no one like that. The people in this house, e.g. are really complete strangers to me & would never become friends. I can't help thinking that they're snobs. I didn't feel this as strongly when I came here as I do now. (Though I immediately suspected it in my landlady.)

---

128 Until a few days earlier Wittgenstein had been working regularly in MS 137. But after a short entry on March 25, 1948, he made no more entries in this notebook until May 28, 1948 (see pp. 37b-38a). Around this time Wittgenstein was also working in MS 167.

129 Rosroe is the small hamlet on the west coast of Ireland where Maurice Drury's family owned a small cottage which they had offered to Wittgenstein to stay in. Miss Brady was the sister of the owner of the gate lodge near Kilpatrick House that Wittgenstein was considering renting (see Wittgenstein's letters to Richards of February 11, 19, and March 5, 1948, and the relevant footnotes there).

130 From Wittgenstein's first stay in Skjolden, Norway – from 1913 to 1914 – he made friends with a number of the locals, including especially the Klingenberg and Drægni families, Arne Bolstad, and Anna Rebni. He often stayed with them when he visited Skjolden for short periods or during the winter, and even when he stayed in his small cabin outside of the village he would often come into the village to meet up with his friends, play music together, and talk. And he stayed in touch by letter when he was away. See Vatne 2016, and Johannessen, Larsen, & Åmås 1994.

– I was going to say that this lack of anyone around me whom I can give as much as a real smile isn't good when one's liable to feel low, as I so often do[131] /May God help me!/, & the comparative nearness of Drury in Dublin is a precious thing which I'm afraid of losing (Rossroe is a 10 hours journey from Dublin). – All this I only say as an explanation, not as an excuse, for my indecision of which I am /rightly/ ashamed. I feel that it is due to a kind of blindness, & I hope that this will be lifted away from me. — Dear Ben, the most important thing for me in your letter was that you gave me the hope to see you before very long. There is something I want to say about it & I wish I knew how to say it. I'll try: You know that your coming to see me is the most wonderful thing that could happen to me. But one can't take for granted that the most wonderful thing will ~~happen~~ be granted to one, & under no circumstances must one counterfeit it. I know you will understand what I mean when I say that I've loaded my side of the scales so very much that it ~~would~~ needs a huge weight on ~~your~~ /the other/ side to balance it. That is, I have made thing very difficult; not out of sheer cussedness, but it just happened like that! I shan't go on, because you know it all. Come only if. . . . . You know that, however foolish I may be, I'm serious about this. – God bless you! May you be lucky in your work. If you come I long to hear about it, & I long to talk to you about no end of things. – Always forgive everything /especially that I express myself badly in a letter/.

    With love always

        Ludwig

I hope your Easter weather is as fine as ours. These violets are a /incontrovertible/ proof that the weather's dry!

P.S. The weather didn't stay fine here after all & I'm afraid that you, like many others who needed a few fine days, didn't get enough sunshine. I hope you got some. – The Mendelssohn Scherzo no longer pesters me.[132] – Wish me luck, please. I need no end of it right now! L. L.

---

131 Wittgenstein had written similarly to Norman Malcolm a couple of months earlier: "I haven't anyone at all to talk to here, & this is good & in a way bad. It would be good to see someone occasionally to whom one could say a really friendly word. I don't need conversations. What I'd like would be someone to smile at occasionally" (Wittgenstein to Malcolm, February 5, 1948).

132 See Wittgenstein's letter to Richards of March 18, 1948, and the relevant footnote there.

Ludwig Wittgenstein to Ben Richards, April 6, 1948[133]

Kilpatrick House
Redcross
Wicklow
Tuesday

Dear Ben, d. h. –

I'm writing this with pencil because I'm in bed with flu. I have had a bad time, lately. First I was so worried about my mind that I could think of nothing else but the imminent danger of becoming insane. Then I contracted this flu which, however, was a blessing because it drove <u>all</u> thoughts out of my head, & now I'm feeling pretty rotten <u>but sane</u>. – Less than an hour after posting my last letter to you I made up my mind <u>not</u> to take the lodge. The reason why I hadn't been able to give up the idea of renting it was that I thought it wasn't as likely that anything should happen to my mind here as in Rosro. But then it suddenly seemed to me quite clear that this was a wrong kind of cautiousness & that my mind could be preserved there too, D. v.;[134] & vice versa. So now I <u>intend</u> to go to Rosro as soon as I'm ~~shall be~~ well enough. I don't know exactly when this will be so, <u>please</u> write to <u>this</u> address. As soon as I know anything definite I'll let you know. – I have often thought of your question whether it might be good /for us/ to read some of my stuff together, & although I don't think it would be I should very much like to explain to you exactly <u>why</u>. But I can't do this in a letter. – Ben, dearest – ~~if~~ /in case/ you still feel /for me/ as you used to I'd like you to p. f. m.[135] But if you don't feel /any more/ exactly as you did I <u>can't possibly blame you</u>. God bless you.

I had your card the other day. I hope the trip did you good! Drury is on a 3 weeks holiday in England. I think of you with love always. Ludwig P.S. I'd like to write more but I don't know how to express myself. May you be lucky & not unhappy in your work. And, if you still l.[136] me, may we meet & talk about no end of things!

L. L.

---

133 Richards added '8/4/48 ?' to the letter, which was a Thursday; and since Wittgenstein wrote 'Tuesday' on the letter, Richards was presumably noting the date the letter was received.
134 Stands for: 'Deo volente' (Latin: God willing).
135 Stands for: 'Pray for me'.
136 Stands for: 'love'.

Ludwig Wittgenstein to Ben Richards, April 13, 1948

Kilpatrick House
Redcross
Wicklow
13.4.48.

My dear Ben, d. h. –

Thanks for two letters.[137] The first is the one you wrote on your sailing trip. I loved getting it. I also admired the painting which must have been produced in a <u>tearing</u> hurry! /I think Raphael produced his stuff that way./ – I'm out of bed since last Wednesday but still very weak. I'd be much stronger if I hadn't had a relapse on Sunday. It came on just when I was writing you a letter. But now I definitely am on the upgrade, D. v.[138] What I want more than anything almost is to be able to work again! & also to <u>enjoy</u> looking around when I'm out of doors (the two hang together).

Your second letter came yesterday. Thanks for <u>everything</u> you say in it. – Only there is <u>nothing</u> courageous about my decision to go to Rosro. What I'm doing I'm doing with <u>funk</u>.[139] And how could you say that it might sound 'presumptuous' if you wish me sufficient strength?! You know that I have no strength at all. I hardly <u>ask</u> for strength because I ~~know I'll never have it~~ /can't imagine my ever having it./ I'm asking for <u>luck</u>. I'll never be even a moderately good rider, all I hope for is that I'll get a tame horse that won't throw me.[140]

But please wish me a <u>little</u> strength & a <u>little</u> courage – Please thank your mother, in my name, for the <u>great</u> trouble she's taken about the letter, & give her my kind regards.

---

137 Richards' letters from this period have not been preserved.
138 Stands for: 'Deo volente' (Latin: God willing).
139 Compare what Wittgenstein wrote about *funk* in his 1940 notebook (the first sentence having been written in English by Wittgenstein): "Not funk but funk conquered is what is worthy of admiration & makes life worth having been lived. Courage, not cleverness; not even inspiration, is the grain of mustard that grows <u>up</u> to be a great tree. To the extent there is courage, there is connection with life & death. (I was thinking of Labor's & Mendelssohn's organ music.) But it is not by recognizing the want of courage in someone else, that you acquire courage yourself" (Wittgenstein 1998: 43-4; MS 117, p. 151). A couple of days after writing this letter to Richards Wittgenstein wrote to Rush Rhees: "It's in no way clear that I'll be able to live in Rosro. In fact I've got grave doubts, but I've got to try" (Wittgenstein to Rhees, April 15, 1948).
140 Wittgenstein often used the image of riding a horse when discussing his relation to life's exigencies. Compare, for example: "One could say 'if you don't sit on the horse, thus completely commit to it, then of course you can never be thrown, but you can also never hope to ride.' And one can only say to that: you have to devote yourself completely to the horse, but still be prepared to be thrown at any time" (MS 183, pp. 26-7; May 9, 1930); and: "I sit on life like the bad rider on the horse. It's only thanks to the horse's good nature that I'm not thrown right now" (MS 162b, p. 56r; Jan/Feb 1939). Wittgenstein had learnt to ride (literal) horses from a young age.

— I wonder if you saw the Easter card I wrote to Angela with my proposed solution of your problem about the millilitre. Do you think it's correct? — I wrote to Tommy Mulkerrin, the caretaker of Rosro, that I'd arrive there on Apr. 23rd.[141] If all goes well I'll leave here on the 20th. But please write your next letter still to Kilpatrick House; for post will be forwarded to me &, somehow, I don't feel so sure of myself ~~that~~ & of developments yet. I feel I don't yet know what's really going to happen. Probably this is just sheer cowardice /which is my chief vice/. – As soon as I arrive anywhere I'll send you a wire. —— Yes, wish me a little strength & a little courage! I'm thinking of you constantly. May I see you before long, & may I then not be too utterly lousy company!

   With love

    Ludwig

P.S. I can hear the curlews calling in day-time now & see them flying; I like it very much. I shall send back your photos in a day or two. Thanks for letting me have them. – God bless you always!

---

141 The Mulkerrins family – which Wittgenstein always spelled incorrectly, leaving off its final 's' – lived in Salrock, about a mile from the Drurys' cottage. If you take the main road inland from Rosroe Pier (at whose tip, the Drurys' cottage sits) – following the road along the north shore of the inlet of Little Killary – you'll find the Mulkerrinses' old cottage on the left near the tip of the inlet, just on the corner of the left-turning that leads from the main road to the Salrock Graveyard. Thomas (Tommy) Mulkerrins took care of the Drurys' cottage in their absence, and he was tasked with looking after Wittgenstein (keeping him supplied with essentials, helping him a little around the house, and the like) while he was staying there. In his letter to Tommy Mulkerrins Wittgenstein wrote: "I intend to come to Rosro to stay there on Friday the week after next, April 23rd. Please have the cottage ready. I don't know yet what time I shall arrive but I shall try to get there about midday if that's possible. I shall stay in Galway for a night & I'll buy some supplies there, but please get me 2 pints milk & some eggs. Dr Drury told me that you would help me & look after me, I hope you will. I am looking forward to seeing Rosro again after so many years" (Wittgenstein to Mulkerrins, April 10, 1948). In the end, Wittgenstein's arrival was delayed until April 28 (see Wittgenstein's letters to Richards of April 19 and 26, 1948).

Ludwig Wittgenstein to Ben Richards, April 15, 1948

Kilpatrick House
Redcross
Wicklow, Eire
15.4.48

Dear Ben, d. h.,

I hope these photos will be all right when they reach you. I'm gradually getting better. Wish me luck!

I'm thinking of you with love

        always

            Ludwig

Ludwig Wittgenstein to Ben Richards, Postcard, April 19, 1948

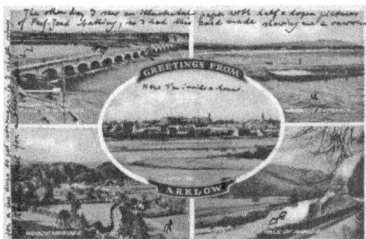

[On the front of the postcard, Wittgenstein has written along the top:]

The other day I saw an illustrated paper with half a dozen pictures of Prof. Joad bathing,[142] so I had this card made showing me in various positions.[143] Here I'm inside a house.[144]

GREETINGS FROM ARKLOW

---

142 C. E. M. (Cyril Edwin Mitchinson) Joad (1891-1953) was a philosopher at Birkbeck College, London, and was well known as a public intellectual and a populariser of philosophy, publishing many popular books and articles on philosophical topics, and being a regular panellist on the BBC's immensely popular radio program 'The Brains Trust'. Wittgenstein considered him a bad philosophical influence and thought his celebrity was absurd (see also Wittgenstein's letter to Richards of May 4, 1948).

143 Wittgenstein has added small stick-figures of himself in the four main pictures on the postcard: swimming in the harbour, swimming up the Vale of Arklow, diving off the Arklow Bridge into the water below, and the like.

144 Wittgenstein wrote this above the central picture of a number of buildings and houses in Arklow, to which he – therefore – did not have to add a stick figure.

[On the back of the postcard:]

Kilpatrick House
19.4.48.

Dearest Ben, To-morrow morning I'm leaving here for Dublin. I intend to leave Dublin the day after /the day after/ to-morrow morning. To-morrow I shall see Dr Moore,[145] Drury's boss, with whom I've made an appointment. I've been feeling more quiet & comfortable during the last days but <u>very</u> weak, bodily, so that I think I'd better see a doctor before going West. I think all it is is the <u>long</u> aftermath of a 'flu. – I wish Drury were in Dublin now. He's in Exeter & coming back next Sunday /25th/. Please write your next letter to me ℅ him, St. Patricks Hosp., James' Street. There are a good many things I've got to do in Dublin; one is to get a permit for paraffin. This I only heard about yesterday. Without it I shall only have candle light in Rosro.[146] – Another thing is to have my hair cut. But it won't look too awful by the time you come here. – That I long to see you, you know; & I know that when you come you'll bring peace with you: God bless you. —If I go to Rosro my address will be: Rosro Cottage, Renvyle P.O. /RENVYLE RENVYLE/ C^o Galway, Eire, Europe N^r.[147] Asia. (In case there's another Europe somewhere.) – Dear Ben, wish me lots of luck. – I wish you the same, – in your work & in every way. I'll let you know where I am as soon as I'm <u>somewhere</u>. I'm thinking of you always. With love Ludwig

P.S. I saw Dr Moore to-day (20th) & he advised me to stay here P.T.O.[148] for a few days to get stronger. So I shall stay at Ross's Hotel for another week. L. L.

---

145 John Norman Parker Moore (1911-1996) was medical director of St. Patrick Hospital, Dublin, from 1946-1979.

146 Most rural areas in Ireland were not connected to the electricity grid at this point. The Rural Electrification Scheme was only passed in 1946, and took decades to bring to completion. All heating and cooking in Rosroe therefore had to be done by flame, and lighting was only by means of candles or – for a stronger and more consistent light – paraffin lamps. The same had been the case in Wittgenstein's cabin in Skjolden.

147 Stands for: 'Near'.

148 Wittgenstein reached the end of the space on the back of the postcard, so he turned over and finished this sentence up the left margin of the postcard's picture side.

Ludwig Wittgenstein to Ben Richards, April 26, 1948
Telephone No 76247

Ross's Hotel,
Kingsbridge,
Dublin.
26.4.48
Monday

Dear Ben, d .h. –
I've been here for 6 days now & am quite all right again ~~my~~ & almost as strong as ever. I'm leaving to-morrow, staying the night in Galway (because I have some shopping to do) & going to Rosro the next day (Wednesday). – I have not heard from you for almost a fortnight. That I'm a bit worried about it I'm sure you can imagine, & I know you wouldn't cause me worry if you could help it. But suspense is almost the worst, & even bad news are better than none. My address will be Rosro Cottage, Renvyle P.O., C⁰ Galway. Post, so Drury tells me, will be delivered there only once or twice a week, so please wire anything /at all/ urgent! – Drury came back from Exeter on Saturday. He had a good holiday. If he knew I was writing to you he'd send his love.
<u>May God bless you & keep you!</u> & may I hear from you <u>soon</u>!
        With love, always
            Ludwig

Ludwig Wittgenstein to Ben Richards, May 2, 1948

Rosro Cottage
Renvyle p P.O.
C⁰ Galway Eire
Sunday 2.5.48.

Dear Ben, old heart –
Thanks for your letter & the photographs. They reached me /in Dublin/ on Tuesday, the day of my departure, 5 minutes before I left the hotel. Drury, in his great kindness, rushed from the hospital to Ross's to bring me my post because he knew that I was worried. Otherwise I'd have a <u>bad</u> journey & arrival here. This may sound like an exaggeration but it's an understatement.
I got here on Wednesday after buying lots of stuff in Galway. I spent the first two days ~~with~~ arranging & cleaning things. I have to do a lot of housework, but that's good for me if it isn't <u>too</u> much. How it will work in the long run I don't yet know. Life is rather

more difficult here that it was in Norway, partly because I'm 11 years older now. Tommy Mulkerrin comes here every day & brings me my milk & helps a little around the house but not much.[149] /He's quite nice./ In a way I've been lucky so far because there's been some sun every day, which makes an enormous difference.

My sleep has improved greatly & I've been working the last three days;[150] not very well & and not ~~very~~ much, but perhaps it's the beginning of a better time. – The cottage is right on the sea-shore, there are mountains all round, quite bare & rather bleak, but I don't mind that. – I've looked at the photos only once, so far. The only one which impressed me was a mother with her child; what impressed me was her head. – I'm glad you enjoyed reading 'Hadshi Murat'.[151] It certainly is 'full of life' & 'not distorted'; but what you said sounded rather as though you thought that it was just very excellent, whereas I think it's very <u>great</u>. The quiet way in which it's told doesn't come from a lack of passion but from a great passion which has been subdued. You wrote that you thought it was as good as anything you've ever read. You wouldn't say of the Jupiter symphony,[152] e.g., that it was as good as anything you'd heard! though I dare say it is. I'd understand it if you said "this is as good a photograph of my mother as I've ever seen". But how can one say this sort of thing of a great work? /As it's almost impossible to compare one great work with another![153]/ — Re: the milliliter: $\underline{1\,l} = 1000\,cm^3$, & the <u>definition</u> of 1g is that it's the ~~weight~~ /mass/ of $1\,cm^3$ of water at 4° C. Now there's a snag here: the gram-<u>mass</u> (which doesn't change from one place to another) is the mass of $1\,cm^3$ of water at 4°C.; the g-<u>weight</u> is probably the weight of that mass in Paris (as the g was introduced in Paris). So the g-weight is slightly different in London (measured by a <u>spring</u> balance). This <u>may</u> have something to do with the queer definition of the millilitre. But this isn't what I wrote to Angela. What I then thought was that the English didn't use "milliliter" to mean exactly $\frac{1}{1000}$ of a continental litre which is the volume of a kg of water at 4° C, but ~~as here~~ to mean the

---

149 See Wittgenstein's letter to Richards of April 13, 1948, and the relevant footnote there.
150 Wittgenstein's entries in MS 137 do not begin again until May 28, 1948, but he was also using MS 167 at this time.
151 Wittgenstein had admired Tolstoy's novella since 1912 (see Wittgenstein's letter to Richards of September 6, 1946, and the relevant footnote there).
152 Wolfgang Amadeus Mozart's Symphony No. 41 in C major (K. 551), nicknamed the 'Jupiter Symphony'.
153 Compare Wittgenstein's remarks in a conversation with Rush Rhees from 1942: "One common source of difficulties in philosophy is that we have certain ideas about *metrics*. We can say that one thing is greater than another. And then we feel that it must always make sense to ask regarding any two things which are compared in that field whether the one is greater than (or equal to or inferior to) the other. Whereas this need not be so in the least. (Beethoven is greater than Schumann. But is Beethoven greater than Bach?) Similarly, we may suppose that if something is greater than another, then it must make sense to speak of something as twice as great as something else. Here we are clinging to ideas about metrics which *are* applicable in particular fields" (Wittgenstein & Rhees 2001: 411)

volume of 1 g of water at 0° C. Supposing I were right in this, I'd like to know whether the expansion of water from 4° to 0° C would account exactly for the number given in your pharmacology book /you might try this/. – Dear Ben, this letter is very lengthy & very bad, but I'm tired & my thoughts are fuzzy. – If you still .... I'll hear from you soon, & God being willing, I'll see you soon!!
Wish me strength & courage.
God bless you, always.
                With love
                    Ludwig
P.S. The postman, Tommy tells me, comes every day. Drury had informed me wrongly. – I'm glad you heard the quartets in G.[154] Do you remember my whistling to you the slow movement in Redcross?

Ludwig Wittgenstein to Ben Richards, May 4, 1948

                                              Rosro Cottage
                                              Renvyle P.O.
                                              Cº Galway Eire
                                                        4.5.48.

Dear Ben, d. h. –
Thank you for your letter of April 30th. You know what your coming means to me! There's one thing, however: could you possibly come a day earlier? You see, if you arrive on Saturday (15th) we <u>have</u> to stay in Dublin till Monday morning as the only train to Galway leaves Dublin at 10·30 a.m. & there's <u>no</u> train on a Sunday. So we'd only have 4 days in Rosro. If you could come on Friday we could leave Saturday morning. Please see if you can do something! (It would also do, of course, to postpone your arrival until Monday, <u>if</u> you can also postpone your departure the same way; but I dare say you won't be able to do that.) Whatever you do is all right, but if we didn't have to stay so long in Dublin it would be a great advantage.
Thanks for the photos. I've kept two: the one of you in profile & mine standing against the wall & <u>not</u> smiling.[155] The smiling one is <u>hellish</u>, the ones of me in the Fellows' Garden are just nasty, & on the full-face ones ~~of you~~ you look like a actor educated at

---

154 Probably either Wolfgang Amadeus Mozart's String Quartet in G major (KV 387), or Franz Schubert's String Quartet No. 15 in G major (D 887).
155 These are most likely the portraits that Richards and Wittgenstein took of one another in Swansea in 1947, standing in front of the back wall of the (now defunct) bus shelter at Brynmill Railway Station (on Mumbles Road). Thanks to Alan Sandry for this information.

King's College. The two decent ones need cutting, perhaps circular, very close to the head. – It's just like the B.B.C. to ban Joad not because he's a /bum philosopher/ but because he defrauds a railway![156] –

Please bring good strong shoes with you & warm things /it's cold here/ & don't forget the Ephedrine.[157] If you can get hold of some invalid bovril & some nescafe /or Café Vieye/ it would help.[158] – I hope your tooth is all right again! I'm longing to see you. God bless you. – Let me know <u>as soon as possible,</u> /in fact/ <u>by wire</u>, whether you can change the day of arrival, /& if is so the hour of your arrival/; for I have to book rooms in Dublin! So long!

With love, always
Ludwig

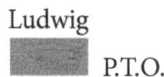 P.T.O.

P.S. I ought to have written about the bad connection between Dublin & Galway sooner, but my head was so <u>choked</u> full of difficulties that I forgot. Bring a book to read together. L. L.

These are most likely the two photos to which Wittgenstein was referring – Richards in profile, and Wittgenstein standing unsmiling against the wall – in his letter of May 4, 1948

---

156 Regarding C.E.M. Joad, see Wittgenstein's letter to Richards of April 19, 1948, and the relevant footnote there. Since 1941 Joad had been one of the regular panellists on the BBC's immensely popular radio program 'The Brains Trust'. But on April 12, 1948, he was convicted – in Tower Bridge Court – of railway fare evasion, and ordered to pay a fine and costs. This scandal was reported widely in the British press at the time – and even discussed in parliament – and as a result the BBC dropped him permanently from the program (see Judge 2016: 180ff).

157 Ephedrine is a stimulant. In 1948 ephedrine sulphate was added to Vicks Vatronol nose drops to increase their capacity for nasal decongestion. It's likely that Wittgenstein wanted ephedrine – or perhaps just Vicks Vatronol – for this reason.

158 Wittgenstein was apparently trying to stock up with cold remedies. 'Bovril' is the brand name of a beef extract paste, which – in addition to being used in cooking – was sometimes used to make a 'beef tea' which was thought to be good for easing colds and for clearing the sinuses. Wittgenstein was also seeking out Nescafé far and wide. A few days later he wrote to Norman Malcolm – in America – "There's one thing I'd be very grateful to you for sending me, i.e., a tin or glass of some powdered coffee extract, like "Nescafe", or one made by a Firm Borden. Lee will know what I mean. But do it only if it's <u>very</u> easy for you" (Wittgenstein to Malcolm, after May 9, 1948).

Ludwig Wittgenstein and Ben Richards to Angela Richards, Postcard (postmarked: May 19, 1948)

Miss Angela Richards
40 Swakeleys Rd
Ickenham
        Uxbridge
        England

Dear Angela,

Are you intelligent enough to guess this riddle?

If you <u>have</u> it you <u>aren</u>'t it, but if you <u>haven</u>'t you may <u>be</u>.[159]

Whatever else there is of any importance Ben will tell you.

Ludwig W.

[160]The sun shines all the time here (except at night). There are many more jelly fish than the photograph overleaf might lead you to suppose.[161] Love from Benedict

Ludwig Wittgenstein to Ben Richards, May 25, 1948[162]

        <u>Tuesday</u>

                      Rosro Cottage
                      Renvyle P.O.
                      C$^{\underline{o}}$ Galway Eire

Dear Ben, d. H. –

After your plane had taxied to the run-way Drury & I kept standing & watching it until it had taken off.[163] I waved my hand at it, just in case. – Then we went back to the

---

159 One solution to the riddle could be: a child.
160 These final sentences of the postcard were added by Richards.
161 Richards is referring to the two jellyfish that he drew onto the photo of the Killary Fjord on the front of the postcard.
162 Richards added '27/5/48' to the letter, which was a Thursday; and since Wittgenstein wrote 'Tuesday' on the letter, Richards was presumably noting the date the letter was received.
163 Richards had stayed with Wittgenstein in his Rosroe cottage from May 15 to 23, when he flew back to England.

lounge & drank some coffee & talked, then we went for a short walk & came back to the lounge for tea & later we took a bus to town & had supper. On Monday morning I left for Galway. The train was crowded & so was the bus to Leenan.[164] Between Galway & Leenan we had heavy showers of rain but when we got to Leenan the weather was fine though very cold. It felt queer & sad to be in the cottage alone & to put away the things that you had been using. I think of you <u>constantly</u> with love & gratitude. To-day I did some work & went for a moderately long walk. I also visited the place where we had seen the two irises. They both ~~have~~ had faded but two new ones were in full bloom & there are lots of buds! I broke off one of the flowers & shall enclose it in this letter. –

Dear Ben, Please look after yourself, <u>don't go to bed too late</u>! God bless you for your love, your kindness & your patience with me! It was all much too good for me.

With love
Ludwig

P.S. I've written to Mrs Barbrooke[165] & asked her to send you some Nescafe for me if she has any.

I find that the iris I've pressed isn't quite dry enough to enclose in this letter. I'll send it next time. Here's an orchid meanwhile.

These holes are for ventilation.[166]   L. L.

Has Angela guessed my riddle?[167]

Ludwig Wittgenstein to Ben Richards, June 1, 1948

Rosro Cottage
Renvyle P.O.
C^{o} Galway Eire
1.6.48.

Dear Ben, dear H. –

Thanks for the letter from the plane. /It crossed mine just at the gate./ It did me good to get it! God bless you. I'm thinking of you constantly. There are lots of things I'd like

---

164 Leenane (or Leenaun) is the nearest village to the cottage on Rosroe Pier where Wittgenstein was staying. It's about an 8 mile walk inland along the southern shore of the Killary Fjord (it's just a little before fjord's tip).

165 Mrs Barbrooke was the owner of the grocery store on East Road in Cambridge, above which Wittgenstein had lived with Francis Skinner in 1938/39. During that time they grew close with the Barbrooke family.

166 Wittgenstein wrote this letter on lined paper with four ring-binder holes punched in the margin. This is a jocular reference to those holes – to which he drew a four-pronged arrow from the word 'holes'.

167 See the joint postcard from Wittgenstein and Ben Richards to Angela Richards, of May 19, 1948.

to talk to you about. I'm living my old routine. I don't work really well but I can just go on.[168] There is of course nothing one can do about it. I must go on till one day I see that I've got to stop doing philosophy for good & and try to get my-self some other kind of job. (Teaching German, if necessary; though this would be the <u>ultima ratio</u>.[169]) So just now I'm mucking about, hoping for better times. The weather is very changeable now; lots of rain but every day some sunshine. I generally walk along the Killary on the old road looking at the birds etc.. Do you remember the big thistle we saw there? It's now about 2 ft high & the /bottom/ circle of leaves 2 ft in diameter. There are lots of buds but they're all closed, I think because of the cold weather; it's hardly ever warm now & there was frost a few days ago not far from here. Once I went on our peninsula to the point where it comes nearest the island with the beacon on it (we past through there in the boat).[170] It's a nice walk & would be much nicer still with you. – I enclose an iris, it's one from /around/ the well.[171]

Please take care of yourself, please be sensible &, as I've said before, don't go to bed late. I hope your work is satisfactory! I'm thinking of you with love always.

      Ludwig

P.S. Before leaving Dublin the other day I bought some fly-paper (or that's what it's called although it hasn't killed a single fly so far, & I'm sure never will.) On the box it says that the flies "disappear with <u>dramatic completeness</u>." Doesn't that remind you of something. It's just pure undi-bl. . .-luted[172] paper.

---

168 See the dated entries in MS 137 on this and the following days (pp. 44a ff).
169 Latin: last resort.
170 The two inlets of Little Killary and the Killary Fjord form a peninsula between them that juts out into the Atlantic Ocean. Wittgenstein's cottage was on Rosroe Pier – which sits about a mile inland from the tip of the peninsula (on the north side). Just off the tip of the peninsula, there is a small island – Inis Bearna (or Inishbarna) – with a beacon on it that was used to guide ships safely into Killary Harbour. If Wittgenstein and Richards had taken a boat from Rosroe Pier, and rowed from the mouth of Killary Fjord, round to the inlet of Little Killary, they would likely have passed between the tip of the peninsula and Inis Bearna.
171 If you exit the back of Wittgenstein's cottage in order to head to the end of the peninsula, you need to climb up and over a small hillock just to the west of the cottage. On that hillock, near the cottage – just overlooking Rosroe Pier – there is a well.
172 That is, 'undi-bloody-luted' (an expletive infixation used for emphasis, using Wittgenstein's favourite expletive 'bloody').

I get very easily upset by trifling things like dirt, insects etc. etc.: I wish I weren't such an old woman!!!¹⁷³ L. L.

Ludwig Wittgenstein to Ben Richards, June 2, 1948¹⁷⁴

Rosro Cottage
Renvyle P.O.
C° Galway Eire
Wednesday

Dear Ben, o.h. –

Thanks for your letter. Simultaneously I had one from my groceress, Mrs Barbrooke,¹⁷⁵ saying that she'd send a big tin of Nescafe to your address. If you succeed in sending it, as I hope you will, the best thing might be to send it to Con & to write a line separately that it's for me. For someone will have to go to the customs people in Dublin (damn them!) & I can't. – I was glad to hear about Aristotles lantern¹⁷⁶ & all that, but I confess I'd rather have heard a little more about yourself /or in addition to the scientific information/. You didn't write, e.g., wether you enjoyed listening to the Bruckner Scherzo or not. Please remember that in many ways I live in a kind of desert. Specially when the weather's gloomy & other things, too. Your letters are food & drink for a whole week /& and that's no exaggeration/.

It's not the same thing at all walking on two legs only, ~~from~~ /as/ walking on four – as any Natural History book can teach you!¹⁷⁷ I, too, miss you! [Of course the sea-urchin with all his stilts must have a soft time /or a cushy job/ – if I may say so.¹⁷⁸] Everything /without exception/ you say about yourself is good to hear; – remember that; I have 5 Robins in the yard now, two old ones & 3 young ones (/still/ without a red breast).

---

173 A few days later, Wittgenstein wrote similarly to Leonida Malcolm: "My health is as fine as can be expected of an old codger, & the things that I'm always inclined to beef about are necessary evils. My work, e.g., is only so-so; but then my talent is only that size & I'm getting a bit shop worn & nothing can help this. I often get exasperated about it but I just must (or ought to) learn to bear it. The solitude here is often a strain, but it's also a blessing; that I have to do all my housework is a great strain, but it's undoubtedly a great blessing, too, because it keeps me sane, it forces me to live a regular life & is in general good for me although I curse it every day. The truth is I oughtn't to be such an old woman & complain such a lot; but then that's also one of the things that can't be changed" (Wittgenstein to Malcolm, June 5, 1948).

174 Richards added '4/6/48' to the letter, which was a Friday; and since Wittgenstein wrote 'Wednesday' on the letter, Richards was presumably noting the date the letter was received.

175 See Wittgenstein's letter to Richards of May 25, 1948, and the relevant footnote there.

176 'Aristotle's Lantern' is the name for the complex and unusual jaw apparatus of sea urchins.

177 Compare Wittgenstein's remark to Rush Rhees a few years earlier: "It is true that the blind can't lead the blind; but two blind men have 4 feet between them and can therefore stabilize each other a bit" (Wittgenstein to Rhees, October 17, 1944).

178 The square brackets are Wittgenstein's own.

Hundreds of irises are out. The weather is <u>very</u> <u>cold</u> & windy & showery. – God bless you! May you always love me as usual, & and as I do you

> Ludwig

P.S.
I have often been thinking that if it weren't for you I couldn't live here at all.

Ludwig Wittgenstein to Ben Richards, June 8, 1948

> Rosro Cottage
> Renvyle P.O. C° Galway
> 8.6.48 Eire

Dear Ben, o. h. –
Thanks for your letter & for sending the Nescafe. The tin arrived battered but otherwise in excellent condition. – It's odd about the Reinecke Kinderlieder:[179] I hummed some of them the evening before your letter came (the ones beginning "Wer hat die schönsten Schäfchen",[180] "Der Schnitzelmann von Nürenberg"[181] & "Eins, zwei, drei"[182]) & I thought: if only I could get hold of a copy I'd give it to you, & that it might be all right for Heshe, too. – But you don't say a word about whether you liked them, or some of them!! & you must have known that I'd want to know. – I'm thinking of you an awful lot. E.g., when I'm on a walk & enjoying anything I see. The other day on the old Killary road I saw the most wonderful rainbow I've ever seen.[183] It was just after a /short &/ <u>very</u> heavy storm, such as we had about a dozen every day for a week, or so. One could see more than half a circle & the colours were incredibly bright. – The big thistle has grown a lot, it's about 2 ½ feet tall. The Foxgloves are out & look wonderful against the gray rocks. (I'm enclosing a specimen /not of a rock, though/.). – Dear Ben, I love to write to you about lots of small things, but I've one big thing on my mind. It is that I felt /a/ coolness in your last letter. (You may, or may not have been aware of it yourself.) This is no complaint, still less a reproach: a letter ~~shouldn't~~ /oughtn't to/

---

179 Carl Reinecke (1824-1910) was a German composer, pianist, and conductor; he wrote over 100 'Kinderlieder' [children's songs].
180 German: 'Who has the prettiest little sheep'; Carl Reinecke, *Acht Kinderlieder* (Op. 37), no. 7 (for voice and piano).
181 German: 'The Schnitzel Man from Nürenberg'; Carl Reinecke, *Zehn Kinderlieder* (Op. 75), no. 3 (for voice and piano).
182 Presumably Wittgenstein meant Carl Reincke, 'Wie es in der Mühle aussieht' ['What it Looks Like in the Mill'], from his *Acht Kinderlieder* (op 91), no. 8 (for two voices and piano). The song begins with the words: "Eins, zwei, drei" [One, two, three].
183 Regarding the old Killary road see Wittgenstein's letter to Richards of June 23, 1948, and the relevant footnote there.

express more feeling than is felt; & it's natural that your's should get cooler, there being so many good conductors around you, whereas I am <u>well</u> isolated (in more senses than one). Please think ~~it over~~ /about it/ & do the <u>right thing</u>. My side of the balance is terribly heavily loaded*, & if it can't be balanced – it can't be balanced. <u>You know all about it</u>. — One thing I said to myself several times these last few days (before your letter arrived) was, that I hoped you'd forgive me if ever I was surly, or mean, or that kind of thing, while you were here, & that you'd know that it was due to /my/ <u>stupidity</u>, not to a lack of love. (This has nothing to do with what I wrote about your letter.) May you be lucky! – God bless you! I'm thinking of you with love, always.

Ludwig

*As things are – I depend so <u>very</u> much on our relation, I let it /I mean the ~~beliefe in~~ {faith in} it/<u>support</u> me /in all my difficulties/, & I'm liable to do so until you tell me not to, frankness is the <u>greatest</u> kindness. To let me deceive myself would be cruel.
P.S. I've had pretty good nights lately & my work wasn't bad either, on the whole. L. L.

Ludwig Wittgenstein to Ben Richards, June 16, 1948

Rosro Cottage
Renvyle P.O.
C^o Galway Eire
16.6.48.

Dear Ben, d. H.,

Thanks for your letter & the lovely rose!! (By the way, did you ever get my letter with the yellow iris? Please let me know.) I am well, & sleeping well, & working /quite/ well <u>sometimes</u>.[184] – There is something /connected with my last letter/ I want to say – if only I succeed in saying it as I want to! You know what your stay at Rosro meant to me, or at any rate you have an idea; &, as I once wrote to you, I'm letting the thought of you <u>support</u> me. Whether this is right, or wrong I won't say, but it would certainly be exceedingly wrong if I were to deceive myself /in fact, nothing would be worse/, ~~as~~ /&/ naturally, I have a tendency to do so. I <u>know</u> that you don't deceive me & never will; but your feeling might gradually diminish, & you might think that it'll still do. And of course it might /diminish/ ~~a great deal~~ & still be <u>more than I deserve</u>; but it would no longer be enough to lift the weight on my side &, therefore, it would be not

---

184 At this time Wittgenstein was working in MS 137. A few days earlier he wrote in his notebook: "Feel quite miserable; stupid, without ideas, and as if I have reached a dead end. In the process, my misery takes on a demonic aspect" (MS 137, p. 50a; June 11, 1948).

~~longer~~ good. Please try to understand what I am, perhaps, expressing very badly. Anything at all, I think, is preferable to a lopsided relation, & I love you & need you (<u>that</u> defines the weight on my side). Of course it seems paradoxical to say: "This thing is <u>enormously</u> important in my life: <u>that's why</u> I've got to get rid of it as soon as it turns out not to be exactly the thing I believed it to be." Yet that's how it really is. Forgive me my stammering. I'm sure in your heart you will understand me. — Your letter which I got yesterday cheered me up quite a lot. Of course it would be wonderful to stay with you, & the middle of August suits me fine. Sometime in September I want to go to Austria & return to Ireland in October. I hope I'll see you soon! God being willing. –

Two chaffinches, man & wife, come in my yard every day now to feed on crumbs, & I love seeing them. I often on my walks see a bird these days & I wonder if you know what it is. I'll describe it. It's size & shape is roughly that of a chaffinch, but the beak is thin and pointed like a Robin's. The colouring is as follows: breast a light yellow or beige, the belly white, the top of the head & the back grayish, the wings dark brown, the tail partly black partly white; if the bird sits the tail looks black, if it flies it spreads the tail & then it looks like this.

The beak is black & there is a black line from it's edges to each eye, so that if you see the bird from the front it has a black line across it's face from eye to eye. It always lands on the top of some stone & there sits quite a long while & makes a noise consisting of peeps & ticks. A "peep" is a short high peep /or seep/.[185] A "tick" sounds /exactly/ like that of a morse key. It sometimes only peeps, sometimes only ticks, & sometimes peeps & ticks which sounds as though it were sending a morse telegram. How it produces the tick I don't quite know. <u>Not</u> by hitting anything with it's beak, as I originally thought. When it peeps it opens it's beak, but when it ticks it doesn't seem to, but I suppose it does, only <u>very</u> quickly. That's about all. I sometimes came as close to it as 12 ft & could observe it for several minutes closely. Perhaps your mother will know what it is. – May your work go satisfactorily! God bless you, always!

I haven't yet got my birthday present for you, but I know what it'll be.[186]

What I wish you <u>you know</u>! Forgive me my stupidity, etc, etc..

        With love

           Ludwig

The rose leaves are from our porch.

---

185 Wittgenstein presumably meant this word onomatopoeically.
186 Richards' birthday was a week later, on June 23.

Ludwig Wittgenstein to Ben Richards, June 18, 1948

Rosro Cottage
Renvyle P.O. C<u>o</u> Galway
18. 6. 48.   Eire

Dear Ben, m. d. h.

Thanks for writing me your letter of June 14th, thanks for <u>everything</u> you say in it! One thing I must correct, though: I never wrote, nor of course thought, that your letters were cool; I thought that <u>one</u> of them was, & I'm sure I was wrong, now you've told me. Please forgive me. And <u>please continue to have patience with me</u>. You need more with me than I'll ever need with you. – God bless you. – Thanks for the rose bud & the honey suckle! I'm glad you could get into the country a little. Seeing the birds here gives me a lot of satisfaction. Chaffinches, Robins & a bird which, I think, is a Hedge Sparrow come into the yard to feed; & there were two Goldfinches in the front garden the other day & 5 tiny young seagulls ~~whi~~ only 3 inches /or so/ long ~~or so~~; they looked wonderful & I couldn't at first imagine what they were until some old ones came, too. – I have rather big plans for improving this kitchen – perhaps I am a fool! You see, I can stick it here all right now, in spite of the bad floor (big gaps), the falling plaster, & no ceiling, all of which makes for dirt & vermin: but in Autumn, or Winter this place will be ever so much more gloomy, & I'm afraid of sitting alone & looking at the dirt /& the wood lice/, which to me is always very depressing. So I thought I might have things altered, the floor made of cement throughout, the walls repaired & white washed, & a ceiling made which would make the place much warmer & lighter. And, if it doesn't cost too much to do it, people after I've gone will profit by these improvements. So, possibly, if you come again – v. D.[187] – the kitchen will be nicer.[188]

God bless you. With love
Ludwig

P.S. I hope your tooth will behave itself! – I could send you a whole Aristotles Lantern & you could have five inserted in the place of one.

Look after yourself, please & keep reasonable hours.

We get about 20 or 30 heavyish showers a day now. 4 days ago I had to empty the big barrel in the yard because the water was so foul, & Tommy cleaned it & made me a lid for it; & this morning it was already overflowing again! L. L.

---

187 Stands for: 'Deo volente' (Latin: God willing).

188 About a month later Wittgenstein returned to the theme of these kitchen renovations in his notebook: "I have decided to make improvements to the kitchen here. These are expensive, and it's madness that I am having them done, since I will almost certainly find it impossible to winter here. But I've decided to try it" (MS 137, p. 73a; July 17, 1948).

P.P.S.: I hope this will arrive exactly on your birthday.[189] <u>Happy</u> returns! Whether many, or few doesn't really matter. L. L.

Ludwig Wittgenstein to Ben Richards, June 23, 1948

> 23.6.48.
> Rosro Cottage
> Renvyle P.O.
> C⁰ Galway, Eire

Dear Ben, H.,

By a hellish concatenation of things the letter in which I thanked you for your letter of June 14th did not leave here till /last/ Saturday &, therefore, didn't leave Renvyle till <u>Monday</u> afternoon, & I suppose you haven't got it yet. I addressed it to Park Hospital & wrote after your name "Medical Student from Barts Hospital", I thought it would reach you quickly that way. – You see the postman comes here only if he <u>brings</u> letters, not just to collect them, & the letter to you I gave to old Mrs Mulkerrin in case the postman had nothing to deliver that day, but he didn't even come as far as Salrock.[190] – I won't repeat what I said in my letter /(for I still hope you may get it)/, except this: thanks for <u>everything</u> you said in your letter, & God bless you. When I feel exasperated & all wrought up, as I often do, & for no sufficient ~~cause~~ reason, I think of you & feel human again.

I wanted to enclose a yellow iris but in the process of pressing it all shriveled up, so I'm enclosing something else that I found on my walks. There are lots of flowers about now, ordinary ones, but they look nice. Do you remember the place where the old Killary road branches off from the main road? There is the house where the children had built a kind of shop with stones, shells, etc.[191] Just there on the edge of the old road ~~there~~ are some plants, a bit like Aloes. One of them has grown a shoot about 6 ft tall with 50 or more buds on it. One of them had opened when I passed it yesterday & the blossom looked something like this:

---

189 Namely, on June 23.
190 The area around the tip of the inlet of Little Killary, on the road that leads to Rosroe Pier (where Wittgenstein's cottage was), about a mile before you get there. Salrock was where the Mulkerrins lived.
191 From the cottage on Rosroe Pier there is a road that heads inland along the north shore of Little Killary. If you follow that about 500ft from the cottage, you arrive at a small house on the left, and just before the house a path leads off to the left that bends quickly round to the southern shore of Killary Fjord and runs along its full length – about 10 miles – inland. This is the path that Wittgenstein refers to as the old Killary road (it is also sometimes known as the 'Famine Road').

a little bigger I think, with a long /dark/ chalice & greenish petals. (I must say, the flower looks a little nicer than my drawing has turned out.)[192]

I'm thinking of you constantly.

With love, always

Ludwig

P.S. Please always be patient with me!

P.P.S. I thought of another one of the Reinecke Lieder which I like very much; it's a kind of Christmas song & begins, I think, "Ein Räppchen zum reiten".[193]

L. L.

Ludwig Wittgenstein to Ben Richards, June 24, 1948[194]

Rosro

Thursday

Dear Ben, d. H.,

This is a P.S. to the letter I wrote you yesterday & is only to thank you for your letter of June 21st which I had to-day. <u>God bless you!</u> If ever I wrote, or should write, anything that hurts you please just think that I'm an old <u>fool</u> & forgive me. You will, won't you? – Drury has O.K.'d the proposed improvements in the kitchen, & so, I suppose, I'll have them done. I don't know yet actually when, because I've got to be away at least when the kitchen floor is done, as then the stove must be moved & one won't be able to cook for a few days. — Thanks for drawing me the hospital. I suppose the tower is meant to look inspiring (not on your drawing I mean, but on the building). — I had <u>6</u> female chaffinches & one cock chaffinch in my yard yesterday /& about 4 to-day/.

---

192 This is, perhaps, a drawing of a fuchsia flower. They are prominent in many of the hedgerows in the area, and there is a particular profusion of them precisely at the point Wittgenstein described, where the path branches left off the road.

193 German: 'A Little Horse to Ride'; Carl Reinecke, *Acht Kinderlieder* (Op. 37), no. 4 (for voice and piano).

194 Richards added '26/6/48' to the letter, which was a Saturday; and since Wittgenstein wrote 'Thursday' on the letter, Richards was presumably noting the date the letter was received.

They come right to the open kitchen door & sometimes /though rarely/ even a little into the kitchen.

I think of you constantly with love.
Ludwig
I'm glad you told me about your dream – may you be well. May I see you before long!

Ludwig Wittgenstein to Ben Richards, July 1, 1948

Rosro Cottage
Renvyle P.O.
C^o Galway Eire
1.7.48.

Dearest Ben,

Thanks for your letter of June 27th. You once wrote to me: "I know that living alone must be very hard". That's true, it sometimes is very difficult, at least, for me when sadness gets hold of me. It's natural that if a man is bad he should tend to be sad, though my sadness is mostly of a wrong kind. But both kinds hurt, & I <u>long</u> to get some light again when I seem to be all wrapped up in darkness. I then think of you & say to myself that I shall soon hear from you again. God bless you for writing to me as you do!! – I remember the play by Hans Sachs you wrote me about. It's German title is, I believe, "Das Käsedrücken".[195] I enjoyed it when I read it a long time ago. – I think the Reinecke-Lied I like best is the one "Ein Räppchen zum Reiten".[196] I'm <u>glad</u> you like them! They do remind a little of Schubert, though ~~of course~~ they haven't, I think, anything like the intensity & depth of Schubert's songs. For when you've heard a Schubert song for years you can one day see a greater depth in it than you'd seen all that time. When I sat in the Salruck graveyard[197] with you I suddenly understood the introduction to "Hark, hark, the lark" as I hadn't understood it before, & recently "Sylvie" became clearer to me, in particular the introduction & the accompaniment.[198] — I'm sure that the bird I wrote to you about is the wheatear or stonechat.[199] But the

---

195 German: 'The Cheese Press'. Hans Sachs (1494-1576) – the German poet and playwright – did not write a play of this title, so it's not clear what exactly Wittgenstein had in mind; perhaps one of Sachs' carnival plays, such as 'Das Kälberbrüten' ('The Calf Breeding').

196 See Wittgenstein's letter to Richards of June 23, 1948, and the relevant footnote there.

197 If you take the main road inland from Wittgenstein's cottage on Rosroe Pier – following the road along the north shore of the inlet of Little Killary – there is a path on the left, near the tip of the inlet, which curves round from the main road to the Salrock Graveyard.

198 These are two songs by Franz Schubert, based on texts by William Shakespeare: D 889 and D 891 respectively.

199 See Wittgenstein's letter to Richards of June 16, 1948.

tail is exactly as I drew it. At least that's <u>exactly</u> what it looks like when it's spread out in flight. The noise isn't "chak-chak", but if anything "tack-tack". You wouldn't describe the click of a Morse-key as "chack-chack"! and there is a story to the effect that Morse got the idea of his telegraph by hearing the bird tick. He said to himself: "If that bird can make himself understood in that way why not I!" – As to the black streak, I'm sure what you say is right. I just <u>assumed</u> that the eyes were at the ends of the streak. – D. o. H., please /if you can/ try to find out, & as soon as possible, about your parents' plans & let me know, ~~as~~ because my own plans depend on them, & it would be a huge help to know more clearly what I'm going to do. – Just now a Robin is in the kitchen, about 4 or 5 feet from where I sit. (It's left again!). The finches too come into the kitchen every day now though not quite so close. – Be patient with me always. I'm thinking of you constantly. Please look after yourself & please don't go to bed very late!
With love
  Ludwig

Ludwig Wittgenstein to Ben Richards, July 2, 1948

Rosro Cottage
Renvyle P.O.
C° Galway, Eire
2.7.48.

Dear Ben, H.,

<u>P.S.</u>: In the letter I sent off yesterday I did not make the point about finding out your parent's plans sound very important. A lot depends for me on when I shall be able to stay with you. Now if your parents have not yet made definite plans it would help me to know, at least, <u>when I may expect to know anything definite</u>. You see, I shall have to book my flight /or passage/ to England, & August is the <u>worst</u> month. Before staying with you I should very much like to stay at Oxford for, say, 10 days seeing Smythies & M[iss] Anscombe; but I can't let them know anything definite before I hear from you. I am <u>not</u> beefing (or grousing) – only I had to explain why this is so important for me. Also, of course, more certainty would be good for my state of mind. Forgive me for pestering you. I know you will. – I saw a young seal a few days ago from fairly close. I was standing on this peninsula where it comes closest to the island with the beacon.[200] He /it/ came up three times in different places stayed with his /its/ head

---

200 See Wittgenstein's letter to Richards of June 1, 1948, and the relevant footnote there.

above the water for 10-15 seconds. – We have very cold weather, but I can't say I suffer from it, though more sunshine would be good. <u>God bless you!</u> With Love

Ludwig

P.P.S. If you can't find out anything let me know that too without delay, & I'll make plans accordingly, or try to. L. L.

Ludwig Wittgenstein to Ben Richards, July 8, 1948

Rosro Cottage
Renvyle P.O.
C° Galway
8.7.48

earest Ben,

Thanks for your diminutive letter which I got in record time. I can't quite see how you did it for it took only 2 days instead of 4 as normal. Did you hand it in at the airport? – I loved getting it. – I was glad to hear about Heshe, I imagine she leads a healthier life now she goes to school. Her half wild, half spoilt life in Ickenham was <u>bad</u>, I can't help thinking. – You don't write anything about the date, or approximate date, of your parent's holidays, but I suppose you'll have had by now my letter & P.S. asking ~~you~~ for information. Among the many points which make it so important I think I haven't mentioned this: I very much want to see Drury before long. But to travel to Dublin & back to Rosro & back again to Dublin when I go to England is too costly. So I have to see Drury on my way to England, i.e. sometime at the end of this month or the beginning of August. But that means telling him well in advance when I'm coming, because Dublin hotels are full /with English tourists/ at the end of July & August & he can't get a room for me unless he books one soon. You see how it all hangs together. If by the time this reaches you you have not yet been able to ~~give~~ /write to/ me anything more definite please <u>wire</u> me: either information, or that you can't get any. – I, too, long to see you. You know it. Not ~~to be able~~ to see you /this summer/, or not to see you for a goodish time, would be a <u>great</u> misfortune for me. But you know this, too. – My work (& my house work) vary, & it's not a case of "variatio delectat".[201] Still, if I could learn a little more <u>patience</u> it would be something! <u>May I learn something!</u> –

---

201 Latin: variety is pleasing.

Sometime you must tell me about the National Health Service.[202] I hope it's not all eye-wash & there isn't too much burocratisme connected with it. How a doctor can look after more than 4000 patients, I can't understand, but I trust there is some explanation for it. – God bless you & keep you! (I'm trying to be good, though not very successfully.) I'm thinking of you with love always.

Ludwig

P.S. This writing paper with genuine Dürer engravings I find very expensive.[203] P.P.S. If you give me very important information please don't send it in the tiny kind of envelope; it might get lost. (Though it's very nice.) L. L.

Ludwig Wittgenstein to Ben Richards, July 13, 1948[204]

Rosro Cottage
Renvyle P.O.
C° Galway Eire
13.7.48.

Dearest Ben,

Thanks for your little /& very kind/ letter! I shall leave here on the 29th, or 30th July & fly to England on the 3rd or 4th (probably 3rd) of August. I will then stay at Oxford till Aug. 15th & after that at Ickenham. I wired to Drury yesterday & asked him to ~~reserve~~ /book/ a flight for Aug. 3rd. As soon as I know (i.e. in about 4 days) exactly what date & ~~when~~ /the time/ I'm flying I shall let you know, because I want, if possible, to meet you in London when I arrive. This is important because we ought to talk over a few things /& also for other obvious reasons/. Of course if you can't get away from your hospital I shall try to see you there; but I hope you can wangle to get a few hours off on that day

---

202 The National Health Service had been launched just over a week earlier, on July 5, 1948, by Health Minister Aneurin Bevan, under the Labour Prime Minister Clement Attlee. The move had sparked controversy among practicing doctors. When the British Medical Association had held a vote of its members in January 1948, 84% of General Practitioners had voted against the introduction of the National Health Service – with fears about pay, workload, and loss of independence. But when the service launched in July, 86% of all General Practitioners joined (and this increased further over the following months).

203 A playful reference to Albrecht Dürer (1471-1528), the German painter and engraver, and to the illuminated 'D' that Wittgenstein had pasted onto the beginning of his letter. Judging by the image, it seems most likely that Wittgenstein cut it out of one of the detective magazines he liked to read.

204 Wittgenstein addressed this letter to Richards at his family's address at 40 Swakeley Road, Ickenham. But Richards had moved, so the envelope was readdressed to his hospital at: St. Andrew's Hospital, Devons Road, Bow, E.3.

(in all likelihood the 3rd). Also it would be a great help if I could stay that night in Ickenham as I ought to see the Permit Officer for my journey to Austria as soon as I get to London & before going to Oxford. Please write to me a) whether there is a chance of my seeing you in London on the 3rd (or 4th) α) at Airways House, or β) at Lyons, or γ) at your hospital

b) whether I can be put up at Ickenham that night. – Please thank your mother/in my name/ for saying I can ~~stay~~ /come/ to Ickenham whenever I like. I hope to God that it won't prove too much of a strain for her, & that she won't dislike it <u>too</u> much. – To think that I shall see you in 3 weeks feels grand. Please think of me always & pray for me![205] – As I said: seeing you ~~when~~ /the day/ I arrive in London is of great importance for me. – Re the wheatear: The bird which I described in detail to you the other day[206] is certainly your fig. <u>3</u>, the one with the black <u>srteak</u>.[207] It's tail, however, is like this

E.g. your fig <u>1</u>. They don't send Morse messages but make a short "peep" at <u>regular</u> intervals (say, once a scond) & go on like that half an hour on end. Is there some Museum in London with stuffed birds? If so I'd like to go there with you & see things.

M. d. H., I long to see you, I <u>hope</u> we shall be able to have a lot of time together & that luck will be with us. I'm always afraid of Luck. – Please write the answer to this letter still to Rosro as I'm not leaving here before the 29th, i.e. the day after tomorrow fortnight. – <u>God bless you always</u>! With love
Ludwig.

P.S. If you ~~have~~ /feel/ <u>any</u> doubts about my accepting your mother's invitation to stay at Ickenham when the family is there, please write to me about it! Let me know what you feel. – I shall <u>wire</u> the day & time of my arrival. – Keep well! G. bl. y. L.

---

205 A few days later Wittgenstein wrote in his notebook: "Don't feel happy in Rosro. Out of good ideas, also working at a snail's pace. But this can't be explained by external circumstances, since I've worked better under worse circumstances. It's probably now a symptom of aging. But I can't draw any conclusions from it now. I believe I still have to wait. I am not wise enough to determine anything under the present circumstances... The man on whom I am entirely dependent here is unreliable! – I pray a lot. But whether in the right spirit, I do not know. – Without the kindness of X and Y, I could not live here" (MS 137, pp. 72b–73a; July 17, 1948).
206 See Wittgenstein's letters to Richards of June 16, and July 1, 1948.
207 Wittgenstein presumably meant 'streak'.

Ludwig Wittgenstein to Ben Richards (postmarked: July 17, 1948)
Dear Ben, <u>Heart</u> –

Thanks for your letter & the lovely book!²⁰⁸ I was glad when I saw your writing on the parcel. I looked up various birds immediately & recognized e.g. the kittiwake.²⁰⁹ The descriptions are of course more reliable than the coloured illustrations which don't agree with the descriptions, nor with the real thing. A Robin, for instance /certainly/ hasn't any <u>blue</u> on his head!²¹⁰ It must be extremely difficult to get hold of good likenesses of birds. What's needed, I imagine, isn't a <u>great</u> artist, but yet an <u>artist</u> who is very truth loving & very humble. There have ~~of course~~ been such people. – I had your letter telling me about your parents' plans, or lack of plans, at the beginning of the week & I replied to it immediately (to Ickenham) saying I want to come /there/ on Aug 15ᵗʰ if it's all right & that I shall fly to London on ~~July~~ Aug. 3ʳᵈ (or 4ᵗʰ) & <u>very</u> much want to see you then if you can possibly arrange it. We must see each other before I go to Ickenham. I also said that it would be a great help if I could stay that night (3ʳᵈ or 4ᵗʰ) in Ickenham. I'm going to Oxford the next day. Write to me about it, please. – The engraving on this letter is a very rare Dürer & was difficult to get hold of.²¹¹ As to my steeple chasing I only jump <u>that</u> kind of hurdle & as they are so rare I rarely jump, – except mentally.²¹² – <u>May we be lucky, & may I see you soon!</u> Please look after yourself. – Your letter was quite legible, except the address!! /You old so & so/ One word of it, between "Devons Rd." & "E.3.", I <u>couldn't</u> make out.²¹³ I hope this'll reach you nevertheless.

---

208 Richards' letters from this period have not been preserved, but from Wittgenstein's next letter to him (of July 21) it becomes clear that Richards' gift was an illustrated book about birds by S. Vere Benson – most likely her: *The Observer's Book of British Birds*, London, Frederick Warne & Co, 1937.
209 See p. 183 of Benson's book.
210 On p. 86 of Benson's book there is a colour drawing of a robin with a blue-grey stripe running along the top of the red area on its breast and head.
211 See Wittgenstein's letter to Richards of July 8, 1948, and the relevant footnote there.
212 A steeple chase is a long-distance horse race in which the competitors must jump over various obstacles, and there is also a purely athletic version with hurdles and ditches. It's not clear exactly what Wittgenstein was referring to here, but the mental hurdles are presumably those related to his philosophical work, in which connection he often spoke of various inner obstacles that had to be overcome (see, for example, MS 111, pp. 63-4; MS 134, p. 76; and MS 135, p. 38v).
213 This was presumably 'Bow' (Richards' hospital was in Bromley-by-Bow).

God bless you, always! I'm leaving here to-day fortnight & my address between July 30th & Aug 3rd will be % Drury.

So long!
With love
Ludwig

To-day looks a fine day, the first we've had for <u>many</u> weeks. We have a new brood of three Robins. One of them picks crumbs off my hand if I have a household glove on, not otherwise.[214]

Important:
P. P. S. I ~~have~~ heard just now that my flight to London is booked for Aug. 3rd, arriving London Airport at 4:30 p.m. L. L.

Ludwig Wittgenstein to Ben Richards, July 21, 1948

Rosro Cottage
Renvyle P.O.
C° Galway
21.7.48.

Dearest Ben,

Tomorrow week, D. v.,[215] I'm off. I long to see you, to talk to you, etc. etc. etc..

Things here are pretty much as usual, except that the weather is even fouler than usual. The day I wrote my last letter to you was the only day without rain we've had for

---

214 Maurice Drury later recalled: "[Wittgenstein] told me he found great interest in observing the very varied bird life in the area: he had tamed some of the birds by putting out food for them, and some even came and ate out of his hand. I was able to send him several illustrated books on birds which helped him to identify the different species." (Drury 1984: 155).

215 Stands for: 'Deo volente' (Latin: God willing).

months & there is a cold wind, almost a gale, blowing into the bargain. Still, the weather doesnt bother me <u>very</u> much. If I could work better I wouldn't mind it. But I'm dull & stupid & my brain tires <u>very</u> /very/ easily. – I go for a walk every day, & almost every day to the west point of our peninsula, leaving by the back gate.[216] About 50 yards from the house in that direction I found the 'giant heather' (I think that's what it's called) which you'll find /enclosed/ in this letter. It looked rather wonderful. The birds are doing fine. The young Robin now eats off my bare hand though still with some hesitation. I often look at your lovely bird book thinking of you![217] I have found that some descriptions as well as pictures are inaccurate. E.g. the Hedge-Sparrow is said to be "striated brown above & sombre slate-grey beneath",[218] but in fact its <u>whole</u> head right down to the neck is grey. I see it every day quite close to me. So I wouldn't swear to M^{iss} Benson's description of the wheatear either.[219] I have reason, by the way, to think that what I used to see /& hear/ here was the Greenland Wheatear /I no longer hear it telegraphing/. I'll tell you my reasons when I see you.[220] May it be <u>soon</u>! I hope you find your work satisfactory at the new hospital.[221]

I'm thinking of you with love <u>constantly</u>. God bless you.
Ludwig

---

216 See Wittgenstein's letter to Richards of June 1, 1948, and the relevant footnote there. The gate behind Wittgenstein's cottage would have led directly out onto the peninsula in the direction of its westerly tip.
217 See Wittgenstein's letter to Richards of July 17, 1948, and the relevant footnote there.
218 See Benson 1937: 94.
219 See Benson 1937: 91.
220 Benson briefly mentions this particular kind of Wheatear at the end of her general entry on Wheatears (see Benson 1937: 91). She points out that it is "only a passage migrant, appearing sometimes in spring and autumn" (ibid.) – which would explain why Wittgenstein had seen them a little earlier in the year, and no longer did. Indeed, their disappearance may have been part of his reason for identifying them as such.
221 Earlier in the month Richards had started working at St Andrew's Hospital, Devons Road, in east London.

Ludwig Wittgenstein to Ben Richards, July 27, 1948

Rosro Cottage
Renvyle P.O.
C° Galway Eire
27.7.48.

Dearest Ben,

Thanks for your letter from St. Andrew's Hospital. I'm glad you like midwifery, I think I can understand it because it combines <u>skill</u> with a human element. – I can hardly believe that I'm to see you to-day week! <u>May fate be kind to us!!</u> – I'm leaving here the day after to-morrow morning.

The weather here has, on the whole, been <u>terrible</u> lately, but yesterday was fine & so is today, but it's very close & we'll have more rain before long. The day before yesterday there was a warmish <u>gale</u> blowing from the East with heavy rain, & I felt in a kind of ~~dread~~ /terror/ the whole day. – I long to see you! I'll wire the exact time of my arrival from Dublin. –The little flower you liked is 'bog pimpernel',[222] I like it too. – Yes, I can hardly believe that I shall see you in a week. May nothing happen to prevent it! <u>God bless you!</u> I'm thinking of you with love constantly.

Ludwig

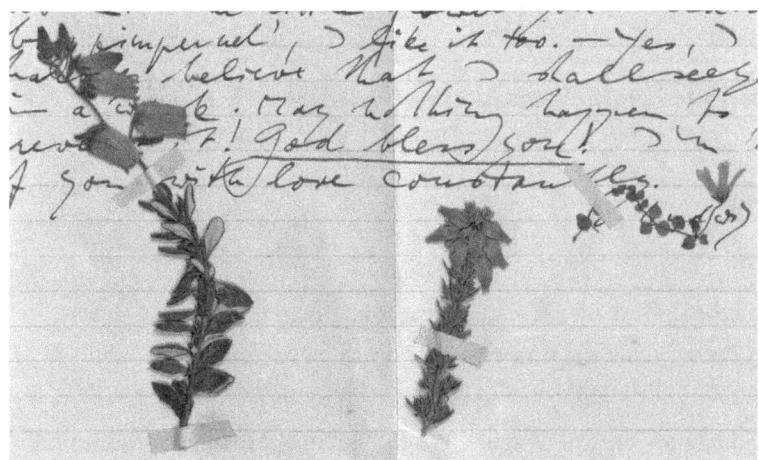

---

222 The common name (in Britain) for the *anagallis tenella*.

Ludwig Wittgenstein to Ben Richards (postmarked: July 30, 1948)

> Ross's Hotel
> Parkgate Street
> Dublin
> Friday

Dear Ben, d. H.,

As you see I'm here. I'm going to town now to find out what time ~~my plane~~ /I/ arrives at ~~Airways House~~/Kensington Air Terminal/. I'll wire you & also put the time in the square below

> Arrival at
> ~~Airport House:~~
> Kensington
> 5.^{25} p.m

The heather comes from Rosro. I had good /hot/ weather there the last two days & it's <u>very</u> hot here now. <u>I'm looking forward to seeing you!</u> God bless you. With love, always

> Ludwig

P.S. Drury sends you his best wishes.
I'm told the Kensington Terminal is 104 High Street Kensington
> L. L.

Ludwig Wittgenstein to Ben Richards (postmarked: August 9, 1948)

> ℅ Smythies 22, Banbury Rd.
> Oxford
> Monday

Dear Ben, <u>d. H.</u> –

This is chiefly to say that I think of you a <u>great</u> deal & am longing to see you. It was good to see you on Tuesday; but the time was <u>so</u> short that I don't feel as though I'd really been with you. It is as though you had been shown to me from a distance /only/. Almost as though I had only dreamt of you. – When I got out of the bus at Kensington you seemed to be under a strain &, therefore, for some time I didn't look into your face, for I didn't want to elicit an expression from you which might not have come completely naturally. And later it was dark & we weren't alone, either. I'm longing to see you. God bless you always. And you know that I mean this whatever your feelings are. – I told you that I'd come to London (Ickenham) on Sunday 15th but I <u>could</u> come on the <u>evening</u> of Saturday 14th if (a) there were room in Ickenham & (b) you were free. Both are unlikely; the latter even more so than the former. If you can, please wire me, or write me a line about it. If I know by Friday, or even Saturday <u>morning</u>, it's soon enough. – I am well, except that, so far, my nights aren't good. Everybody is very nice to me, but it's not exactly the right kind of life. I've had a few good conversations with Smythies & M[iss] Anscombe. Today the Smythies left for their holiday & I shall live alone in their flat. I'll see M[iss] A. every day, though. Whether I'll do any work apart from discussing I don't know. My nights will probably be better now because I'll have a quieter room. – May I see you, & <u>really</u> see you, soon! <u>I am thinking of you with love, always.</u> Forgive me whatever there is to forgive.

     Ludwig

Forgive the pencil. I hope you can read it.

     L. L.

Ludwig Wittgenstein to Ben Richards, September 9, 1948

TEL. U 40 402   WIEN, 9.9.48.

                    IV, ARGENTINIERSTRASSE 16[223]

Dearest Ben,

I wanted to write to you on the plane & send you a letter straight back by giving it to the attendant (there was no 'hostess'). But he told me that letters must go through the ordinary mail & that he wasn't allowed to take them. So heaven knows when this will reach you. – Thank you for getting up yesterday & having breakfast with me & seeing me off. It meant a great deal to me. That it was wonderful for me being with you, you know. – I had a very calm journey. The food was good but they didn't give me enough coffee. When we landed in Frankfurt I hoped I'd be able to buy some at the air-port, but they don't give you anything for English money there, you must have American money, & of course I hadn't any. – I found everybody here in fairly good health. The sudden death of my niece[224] has been a great shock to them, of course. My American

---

223 This was the palatial Wittgenstein family home on Argentinierstrasse (formerly Alleegasse), in Vienna's 4th district, which had been acquired by Ludwig's father – Karl Wittgenstein – in 1891. It was the principal home in which Ludwig grew up, and at this time it was the home of Ludwig's sister – Hermine Wittgenstein – who lived there until her death in 1950. It had been seriously damaged during the war, but by this time was repaired. On this and the following letters Wittgenstein used a pre-printed letterhead with the mansion's address and telephone number. The mansion no longer exists today.

224 This was Marie von Stockert (1900-1948), the eldest daughter of Ludwig's sister, Helene Salzer (with whom Wittgenstein had stayed during his visit to Vienna a year earlier (from September 12 to October 4, 1947). She had died just a few weeks prior to Wittgenstein's arrival – on August 14, 1948 – at the age of just 48.

sister,[225] the one you've met, is coming here next Monday from Upper Austria & will stay here for a few days. I'll give her your good wishes. Please give mine to everybody at Ickenham. – <u>God bless you! With love, always</u>

       Ludwig

I think of you a lot.

Ludwig Wittgenstein to Ben Richards, September 16, 1948

TEL. U 40 402   WIEN, 16.9.48.

                     IV, ARGENTINIERSTRASSE 16

Dearest Ben,

It was good to get your letter this morning. I think of you a great deal as usual. I hope you're having a good holiday. It's very warm here, too warm for the town, but not for a sailing trip. – I'm seeing a good many people here & leading a rather useless life. The other day I heard a suite by Bach on the gramophone, played by Busch & his orchestra,[226] also two Walzes by Strauß played by the Philharmonic orchestra conducted by Karajan of whom I told you.[227] I didn't like either of the performances. On the other hand I heard again the old recording of the Brahms C minor string quartett by Catterall & was greatly impressed.[228] I wish you could hear it.

Dear Ben, I shan't write much today because I'm feeling very stupid. I'm coming back on the 29th & I should very much like to stay a night in Ickenham, if I may, before going to Cambridge. Perhaps we could travel to Dublin together. I'm glad you got such good service at the Strand Palace. I suppose M^{iss} Parker is the original M^{iss} Parker.[229]

---

225 Margaret Stonborough-Wittgenstein.
226 Adolf Busch (1891-1952) was a German violinist, conductor, and composer. He led a conductorless orchestra – the Busch Chamber Players – which recorded Johann Sebastian Bach's four orchestral suites (BWV 1066-1069) in 1937, released by H.M.V.
227 Herbert von Karajan (1908-1989) was an Austrian conductor. It's not clear exactly what recording Wittgenstein was referring to here, but it could have been the Vienna Philharmonic Orchestra – conducted by von Karajan – playing Johann Strauss Jr.'s Künstlerleben Walzer [Artist's Life-Waltz] (op. 316), which was released by Columbia in 1947.
228 This was presumably the Catterall Quartet's recording of Johannes Brahms' Quartet No. 1 in C minor (Op. 51, No. 1), which was released by H.M.V. in 1923.
229 Miss Parker was apparently an employee known to Wittgenstein in the travel agency at the Strand Palace Hotel in London (see Wittgenstein's letter to Richards of October 3, 1948). Richards was looking to book passage to Ireland, as he was planning on spending some time with Wittgenstein in Dublin.

I'm sending you a view of Vienna & if you keep it I'll show you where I live when I get back. I shall let you know the exact time of my arrival later, in case you can meet me either at Airways House or at Northolt.[230] I'm leaving here about 2 p.m, which means I'll probably arrive in London round about 9 p.m. They could tell you the exact time at Cooks. – I hope to hear from you soon anyway.

Please give my good wishes & my thanks to your parents. I'm looking forward very much to seeing you. God bless you!

                With love, always

                    Ludwig

Ludwig Wittgenstein to Ben Richards, September 20, 1948

TEL. U 40 402   WIEN, 20.9.48.
                                                                 IV, ARGENTINIERSTRASSE 16

Dear Ben,

This is chiefly to say that I think of you a great deal. I've just had a letter from M^{iss} Anscombe, written the day before she went sailing with you, in which she writes about her illness & her poisoned finger. I hope it didn't spoil the trip & that things went well in general. I imagine it can't be easy to make a success of a trip in which so many very different people take part. – My stay here isn't quite as cheerful & easy as last year's. Partly because of recent events in my family,[231] partly, I think, because I myself am less sanguine now. I feel more strongly that perhaps I'm seeing these people for the last time.[232]

I hope you've got the letter I wrote you less than a week ago.[233]

---

230 There was a Royal Airforce military airport in Northolt in west London, but it was also used for civil aviation.
231 Such as the recent sudden death of Wittgenstein's niece, Marie von Stockert, at the age of just 48 (see Wittgenstein's letter to Richards of September 9, 1948, and the relevant footnote there).
232 As had been the case at various points in his life, Wittgenstein could not quite shake the feeling that his death was imminent – as he wrote to Rudolf Koder at around this time: "As you know, I feel much closer to my end than is probably the case. Because I'm physically pretty healthy and will perhaps still live a long time. My thoughts and feelings may come from the fact that at a relatively advanced age I still have to change my way of life from the ground up, which brings with it serious problems" (Wittgenstein to Koder, end of September 1948).
233 Wittgenstein's letter to Richards of September 16, 1948.

Just in case you haven't, I repeat that I'm coming back on Wednesday 29th evening by a plane which leaves here about 2 or 3 p.m. & that it would be wonderful if you could meet me either at Northolt, or at the London terminal. I'd like to stay at Ickenham for a night if I may. You may have a shock when you see me because I'm going to have my hair cut to-day & it'll look pretty queer still when I get back.

Please give my good wishes to everybody. I long to see you again. God bless you.

With love
Ludwig

Ludwig Wittgenstein to Ben Richards (postmarked: October 3, 1948)

49 Chesterton Rd.
Cambridge
Sunday

Dear Ben, d. H.,

This afternoon I moved to the above address. I wish I could have stayed with Miss A. but the house was by far too noisy.[234] I couldn't have stood it, not even for a few more days. This place isn't bad, apparently quiet & cleanly, but also pretty expensive; & I can only get breakfast here & have to go out for all other meal. – As I told you over the phone I've found a typist.[235] – I also told you over the phone: I wish you'd been more frank with me at the station the other day. Whichever way you feel about it I <u>will</u> be

---

234 Elizabeth Anscombe lived mainly in Oxford during term time, but she spent the university vacations in Cambridge – at 19 Fitzwilliam Street – where her husband, Peter Geach (1916-2013), and their children lived. The house was noisy both with the children and also with bed and breakfast guests, whom Geach hosted to make ends meet.

235 This was Gitta Deutsch Arnold, who later described their sessions as follows: "In October 1948 a friend asked me if I would 'type for Wittgenstein'. I knew nothing of philosophy and little of typing, but he needed someone who knew German. He arrived at my home one Monday morning and said: 'I am Wittgenstein. I hope you will be able to put up with me.' On Tuesday and the following six days he brought me a selection of vitamin tablets which he considered essential if I were to stand his pace of work. I learned after a few hours that I had to listen with my ears alone: to attempt to listen with my mind was fascinating, puzzling, and quite distracting. He would dictate slowly and clearly (laying great emphasis on certain words) and announce every stop and comma. He would pause frequently, cancel one paragraph and replace it with another. He would walk up and down for a while and then sit down and mutter: 'No, no, no. Forgive me . . . just a moment . . . yes, I am a fool.' On one occasion he started up violently, striking his forehead with the back of his hand, and then – suddenly very calm – he said quietly: '*Ich bin ein Esel*' ['I am an ass'] and continued to dictate his short, very precise and carefully punctuated sentences" (Deutsch Arnold 2016: 755-6). When he returned to Ireland Wittgenstein himself described these sessions to Maurice Drury, who recalled them as follows: "[Wittgenstein] told me that he had dictated from his manuscript to a typist in Cambridge. [He said:] What I was dictating to her must have seemed completely incomprehensible; yet she never asked me to explain what it was all about. An excellent trait" (Drury 1984: 160).

frank & explain <u>why</u> I made the suggestion that we might share a cabin for two.[236]
(I thought on Friday my reasons were obvious but suppose the weren't.)
a) M^iss Parker had told me that she wouldn't be able to get me a cabin for one ~~person~~.
b) I should prefer sharing a cabin with you to sharing it with a stranger.
c) I thought (stupidly) that you too might not mind sharing it if it was with <u>me</u>.
d) M^iss Parker said ~~she thought~~ she might be able to get a cabin for two for us.
Only when I mentioned the matter to you at the station did I notice that I'd been thoughtless in assuming <u>c</u>; but had you told me straightforwardly that you didn't like the idea of sharing a cabin with me <u>I think</u> I'd have had sense enough to understand it & to drop that idea. As it was, your tone put me off & I didn't know where I stood. For I <u>hate</u> to have to ~~read~~ /guess/ a friend's meaning from his tone. That's all right in a drawing room /where one mustn't say things outright/ but not between you & me: I wish you understood that.
It made me feel better when you said on the phone that you ~~were~~ are coming Saturday next. Please wire exactly when you're arriving, so I can meet the train.
        God bless you!
        I am thinking of you with love,
            as always.
                Ludwig

Ludwig Wittgenstein to Ben Richards (undated, mid-November 1948)[237]

                                                            Tuesday

Dearest Ben,
I'm writing you this letter because in talking to you about certain subjects I often find it difficult to speak the truth plainly & simply & am tempted to be influenced by your attitude either to exaggerate or to minimize things.[238]

---

236 The cabin was for their crossing – by boat – to Ireland, as Richards was planning on returning to Ireland with Wittgenstein so that they could spend some time there together (see Wittgenstein's letter to Richards of September 16, 1948).
237 Wittgenstein left this letter undated, and Richards – somewhat unusually – did not add a date. But we can infer from the letter's contents that it must have been written some time in mid-November 1948, because it was written at a time when Richards was visiting Wittgenstein in Dublin and Wittgenstein was staying at Ross's Hotel. Richards made a few trips to visit Wittgenstein in Ireland – but only in his mid-November 1948 trip were they in Dublin with Wittgenstein staying at Ross's Hotel during the trip.
238 Wittgenstein had said something similar in a letter to his friend Rudolf Koder, during his stay in Vienna in September, just a month and a half earlier: "Please resolve to read this letter with seriousness and patience. It naturally concerns the subject of our conversation yesterday. I'm not writing it out of the joy of writing, for writing is difficult for me, – but because it's easier for me to write the truth than to tell it to you in conversation. Because when I speak, I'm easily confused by your somewhat dull, cloudy, and unwilling manner, or carried away by exaggerations or unfriendliness. When writing, it's easier for me to tell the naked truth" (Wittgenstein to Koder, end of September 1948).

You know that we have had lovely times together, but this present time is difficult. The difficulty lies in me. Or perhaps there are several difficulties which come together. One certainly is that my work worries & doesn't satisfy me. I feel after it tiredness without contentment. Again I don't know how much of this is due simply to the nature of my task & how much to my present state of mind. Anyhow, after some hours of work my nerves are all taught & /highly/ irritable & if I succede in suppressing my irritability (which I do rarely enough) I just feel dull & sad. Hence, when I come to you I'm in a way more like a sick than like a healthy man: I say & do all sorts of silly things &, having done them, feel bad about it, which doesn't improve the situation; etc, etc.. (This of course I say, not to complain ~~about it~~ but just to describe the state of affairs.) I also am now in an irreligious frame of mind & I don't do anything about it. I can't blame my bad frame of mind on having to live at Ross's[239] for I have a warm room now & it's quiet, too. I have a kind of feeling of guilt because I feel that I don't make the right use of your being in Dublin now, & when you're gone I know I'll feel bad about it. But knowing this doesn't help me now. It's just as though I hadn't just a cold in my head (as I have) but a cold in my soul; it feels all numb, dull, & not quite there. Now what follows from this for us I don't quite know. This state of mine may last a long, long time, or a short time; I don't know. I know you're kind & you try not to make me feel bad about it, & your kindness improves things but it can't make a new man out of me. I know, all this is exceedingly difficult for both you & me.

  May God bless you!
  With love
  Ludwig

Ludwig Wittgenstein to Ben Richards, November 17, 1948

Ross's Hotel
Parkgate Street
Dublin
17.11.48.

Dearest Ben,

When I had left you at the North Wall I walked back to town,[240] but I didn't want to go back to Ross's as I couldn't have worked & was afraid I'd just mope. So I went to the

---

239 Ross's Hotel, Parkgate Street – where Wittgenstein usually stayed when he was in Dublin.
240 The North Wall Quay – on Dublin's River Liffey – is right by the Dublin Port, from which Richards presumably left for his return trip to England.

Corinthian;[241] but there the show didn't start for another hour, so I went to one of the Cafolas & asked for a cup of cocoa. They said there was no cocoa, but would I have some hot chocolate? So that's what I had, & it was the oddest 'chocolate' I'd ever seen or tasted in my life. It was paler than the palest cocoa & tasted of dishwater. After that I saw two rather stupid but not too bad Gangster films.

While I waited in the queue I constantly listened if by any chance I could hear a boat's whistle blowing, but I didn't hear anything.

I'm thinking of you all the time. Thanks for having been here!

I had three answers to my advertisement in the Evening Mail.[242] I havent yet seen the places. Two answers are obviously by very uneducated people, one of them is almost completely illegible, even the address.

I fetched the second copy of our photo to-day.[243] I'll cut myself away & keep you. The picture shows what an unsuitable companion I am for you, though you've always been an <u>wonderful</u> companion to me, against all reason.

God bless you. Please look after yourself. Don't go to bed late & dont bolt your breakfast.

You are in my loving thoughts always

        Ludwig

I hope your journey wasn't too bad! L. L.

---

241 The walk from North Wall back to Ross's Hotel would have been about an hour, directly west along the River Liffey. Wittgenstein stopped off a little less than half way back, at the Corinthian Cinema which used to be on East Quay.

242 The 'classifieds' in Dublin's *Evening Mail* were anonymous, but – judging by the details of its requests – the following advertisement, placed two days earlier, is most likely to have been Wittgenstein's: "MIDDLE-AGED gent requires Apartment, furnished [o]r unfurnished, short distance from Phoenix Park; quiet, warm room essential. Box G663 L16" (*Evening Mail*, Dublin, November 15, 1948, No. 32,191, 'Apartments Wanted', p. 1, column h). Phoenix Park was a five-minute walk from Ross's Hotel, where Wittgenstein often walked – and it was also near Maurice Drury's work, so that they could meet up there easily and often. Around this time Wittgenstein wrote to Rudolf Koder: "I will most likely not go to Rosro in the winter, but am looking for an apartment near here. I think I can now work without complete solitude, perhaps even better without it" (Wittgenstein to Koder, October 1948).

243 This is likely the photo described in slightly more detail in Wittgenstein's letter to Richards of March 21, 1949 (see the reproduction of it there).

Ludwig Wittgenstein to Ben Richards, November 24, 1948

Ross's Hotel
Parkgate Street
Dublin
24.11.48.

Dearest Ben,

Thanks for your card (Showing the boat) & your letter. You can't miss me more than I miss you. From your letter it appears that you didn't get mine which I wrote to you a week ago. Perhaps it has got lost in the 'chaos' of your house. Please enquire! – Nothing much has happened here. I had 4 replies to my advertisement. All four places were impossible, in particular: the landladies. Two of the rooms would have been /quite/ pleasant otherwise; right near the river. The landladies impressed Con even more strongly than they did me. – So I'm still at Ross's; I will advertize again, though. – One piece of sad news is that they're no longer making the proper meringues at Sherry's.[244] They've changed the recipe & the meringues are soft, sticky & synthetically stained red! I sometimes go to the Botanical Gardens after lunch & take my notebook with me & and walk in the glass-houses.[245] I'm still working fairly well. Yesterday I learned two things: a) I noticed that the begonia has two kinds of flowers, male & female. The male with four petals like this ⚘, the female with five like this: ⚘.
And b) the gardener showed me that as aspidistra has a flower! I enclose one in this letter. – I'm glad you saw M^{iss} Anscombe & Smythies, & that you liked him. – I'm afraid I haven't written to her yet about the typescript.[246] But I'm not in a terrible hurry about it. – I see the Bank of Ireland is still open; though why – with their principal customer gone – I don't know. – Last Sunday I went to the Zoo, alone.[247]

---

244 Sheries Café Bar, 3 Lower Abbey Street, Dublin; established in 1947.
245 The National Botanic Gardens of Ireland, in Glasnevin – about an hour's walk northeast of Ross's Hotel. As Maurice Drury recalled: "I introduced him to the Botanical Gardens at Glasnevin, and he often went there alone. He found the heated Palm House very congenial to work in during the winter, and would often sit on a step there with his small notebook for long periods" (Drury 1984: 157).
246 Wittgenstein had given a copy of TS 227 – the final version of the first part of the *Philosophical Investigations* (one of only three in existence) – to Elizabeth Anscombe (see Wittgenstein's letter to Norman Malcolm of November 6, 1948). It seems that Wittgenstein had been intending to write to Anscombe to ask her to add a clause to her will stipulating that in the event of her death the typescript should be returned to Wittgenstein or to his executors if he was no longer alive. G. E. Moore had a further copy of part of the same typescript, and Wittgenstein wrote to him with a similar request in a few weeks later, saying that by making the change to his will Moore would thereby "avert a <u>great</u> deal of distress" (Wittgenstein to Moore, December 16, 1948).
247 The Dublin Zoo was in Phoenix Park – just a few minutes' walk from Ross's Hotel – and Wittgenstein enjoyed visiting (partly to see the animals, but also to spend time in the gardens and to eat at the restaurant (see Wittgenstein's next letter to Richards – of December 6, 1948 – and the relevant footnote there).

The animals weren't anything like as lively as when we were there together, & neither was I.

I'd give anything to have you with me. I'm thinking of you with love <u>constantly</u>.

      Ludwig

Please let me know to what address to write when you're at St. Albans.[248] Look after yourself & God bless you!

Ludwig Wittgenstein to Ben Richards, December 1, 1948

Ross's Hotel
Parkgate Street
Dublin
1.12.48.

Dearest Ben,

Thank you for your letter. I was glad that mine reached you in the end. – The aspidistra flower (when it's not squashed) looks like a tiny flattened rose, something like this. ⟨sketch⟩. The petals are dark green & the stamina blue & white. It grows quite close to the ground, hidden by the leaves. Con sais it's fertilized by slugs, or snails. – I'm still working pretty well on the whole.[249] Trouble is: I get rather exhausted, & I haven't got such a wonderful tonic like seeing you to straighten out my mind again. – I still go to Sheries for supper, but to Bewleys for lunch because it's more restful & quiet.[250] (I get meringues there, too.) — When I read in your letter that

---

248 Between December 1948 and the summer of 1949 Richards worked at Hill End Hospital, St. Albans (Hertfordshire, England).

249 At this time Wittgenstein was still working in MS 137. Maurice Drury recalled of that autumn: "I was now able to see Wittgenstein nearly every day, and when I had a day off I spent longer with him. He seemed to me to be writing copiously; when I went up to his room he was nearly always working and would continue to do so for some time before we went out. Indeed I remember on one occasion when we had planned to have lunch together he said to me, 'Just wait a minute until I finish this', and then continued to write for two hours without saying a word. When he did finish he seemed quite unaware that it was now long-past our lunch time" (Drury 1984: 156-7).

250 Regarding Sheries (and their meringue) see Wittgenstein's letter to Richards of November 24, 1948, and the relevant footnote there. Bewley's Café is a beautiful and storied café at 78-79, Grafton Street, Dublin. It was opened in 1927 and was a popular haunt of many of Dublin's literary giants (including James Joyce, Samuel Beckett, W.B. Yeats, and others). Drury recalled: "On other occasions he would go to Bewley's Cafe, in Grafton Street, for his midday meal - always the same: an omelette and a cup of coffee. What pleased him was that when he became well known there the waitress would bring him his omelette and coffee without a word and without his having to order it. 'An excellent shop: there must be very good management behind this organization' " (Drury 1984: 156).

you'd be in St. Albans for 4 months I thought of the long separation.[251] Don't be annoyed at this; you can't have certain feelings without certain others (at least, not if you're just an ordinary ~~person~~ /creature/ like me). – I go to the cinema a lot. I wish I could cut down on it. I know it's not the right thing. But I feel so tired in the evenings that I can't think, or read anything serious. And my room, though it's all right as long as I can work, is depressing when I'm tired, & I want to get out. This doesn't make things right, but it's an explanation. At Redcross, or Rosro I didn't miss the cinema. I'm not complaining about circumstances, only about myself.
You're in my thoughts constantly & you keep me going. God bless you, & think of me! I hope your work will be satisfactory to you at the new place.
Please write how you are.

    With love, always
      Ludwig

I enclose a male & a female begonia flower.

Ludwig Wittgenstein to Ben Richards, December 6, 1948

            Ross's Hotel
            Parkgate Street
              Dublin
              6.12.48.

Dearest Ben,
Thanks for your letter. It rather sounded as though, when you wrote it, you hadn't got the letter I wrote you last week. I sent it to Ickenham. – My health is all right & I'm

---

251 See the relevant footnote to Wittgenstein's previous letter to Richards of November 24, 1948. Richards ended up being there for more like six or seven months.

still working pretty well, except when I'm too d.[252] tired. I always miss you & wish I could refresh my soul by seeing you. – I often go to the garraithe naisiúnta na lus – I'm sorry, I forgot you don't know Irish, – it means our botanical garden. It's pleasant to work there walking about in the glass houses (& one doesn't have to pay to get in). Con is trying to get me a membership of the Zoological Society /as a Christmas present/. If I become a member I can go to the Zoo free,[253] & for an extra 2/–[254] I'm allowed to beard the lion in his den. – À propos Christmas presents – I got an advertisement the other day from which I enclose a cutting. Although <u>three</u> <u>great</u> men agree in recommending book tokens, I don't think I'll give you one. – This →

is primula which I stole from the botanical garden. –
I sometimes talk to the gardeners, but on the whole, they're rather dull/apparently/ not keenly interested in their job, & not too friendly. – I can easily imagine that it's good for you to be away from home. I mean, it'll be easier for you to be <u>serious</u> about your work. (Though perhaps I'm wrong there.) Look at every patient of yours as a human being who is having a /rotten/ time in this world.[255] Think of me <u>often</u>, please. God bless you & keep you! I'm thinking of you <u>with love always</u>.

Ludwig

P.S. Drury sends you his love.

---

252 Stands for: 'damn'.
253 Maurice Drury later recalled: "The hotel where Wittgenstein was now staying was only a short distance from Phoenix Park and the Zoological Gardens. I was a member of the Royal Zoological Society and was able to propose him as a member. This enabled him to have free access to the gardens and to have his meals in the members' room. He liked this; and we had many walks and meals together there" (Drury 1984: 156).
254 Two shillings (i.e. a tenth of a pound).
255 More than a decade earlier he had given similar advice to Maurice Drury when he was having doubts about his medical vocation: "Look at your patients more closely as human beings in trouble and enjoy more the opportunity you have to say 'good night' to so many people. This alone is a gift from heaven which many people would envy you. And this sort of thing ought to heal your frayed soul, I believe. It won't rest it; but when you are healthily tired you can just take a rest" (Drury 1984: 96).

Enclosure included with the letter of December 6, 1948:

> J. B. PRIESTLEY says that BOOK TOKENS "remove the one great drawback to giving books as presents."
> ALDOUS HUXLEY describes them as an "indispensable convenience."
> SIR NORMAN ANGELL says that "they throw the burden of choice upon the givee—a really great idea."

Ludwig Wittgenstein to Ben Richards, December 14, 1948

Ross's Hotel
Parkgate Street
Dublin
14.12.48.

Dearest Ben, d. H.,

Thanks for your letter. Don't <u>ovedo</u>[256] things: cycling like hell, then operating. – Until yesterday I was still working a lot & very intensely.[257] I know of course that this period will be followed by one of exhaustion & depression; but I want to make hay while the sun shines, & that's what I'm doing now, or <u>was</u> until yesterday. For this morning M^{iss} Anscombe arrived & in rather a bad frame of mind, & I spent the whole day with her, I had to[258]. What this will do to my work I don't know & I can't say that it doesn't worry me, but she is in need, & it's <u>fate</u>.[259] (Please don't talk to anyone ~~else~~ about this.) Drury is going to see her /tonight/ & I hope he may give her some good advice. He, by the way, sends you his love. – I still go to the garraithe naisiúnta na lus[260] & work

---

256 Presumably: 'overdo'.
257 See the fairly long daily entries in MS 137 from the days preceding this date (e.g. from p. 120b until 126a).
258 Ancombe later wrote: "I visited [Wittgenstein] in Dublin in 1948 in need of some help and advice because of a matter that was troubling me... I had certainly got into a queer state of mind, partly assisted by having employed a hypnotist to help me to give up smoking; this had been partly successful, as I had succeeded with efforts of will power but I was beset by a troublesome obsession and by insomnia" (Anscombe 2025: 171–2). The obsession in question may possibly have been the brief flaring of romantic feelings between Iris Murdoch and Anscombe (Murdoch had fallen in love with Anscombe, and it's not clear to what degree her feelings were reciprocated), which shook Anscombe sufficiently to prompt her to leave Oxford with haste and seek out Wittgenstein for advice (see Conradi 2001: 283-5, and Lipscomb 2022: 121-4).
259 Anscombe later recalled how she felt this from her side. She recounted how when she visited Dublin "[Wittgenstein] was at peak form working at the time, and reflection shewed me that this must be an interruption; but he responded to a request for help, booked a room at the hotel, and never shewed that I was disturbing him. This was the only time I made demands on him and he turned up trumps" (Anscombe 2025: 171–2).
260 Irish: 'National Botanic Gardens' (see Wittgenstein's letter to Richards of November 24, 1948, and the relevant footnote there).

while walking in the glass houses. I enjoy it very much. They have <u>lots</u> of Geraniums there which on the whole are pretty dull plants; but there is <u>one</u> called "Miss Vera Dillon" which is <u>very</u> beautiful. The petals are purple with a scarlet center. I wish I could steal a flower to send it to you. – I've seen some quite good, mostly old, films. A very nice one was called "The mating of Milly".[261] I have to stay ever so often to hear that d. . . .. Irish national anthem. And, believe it, or not, I have not yet been able to learn it by heart! But every time I hear it it seems to get more vulgar & asinine. – My next letter to you will be a Christmas letter & I'll send you a kind of token, for, the present which I bought for you I have, as yet, no means to transport to England! But my <u>loving</u> thoughts are always with you. <u>Please</u> don't overwork, take care of yourself, & let us hope that we'll see each other before very long!

    God bless you. With Love

        Ludwig

Ludwig Wittgenstein to Ben Richards, December 20, 1948

Ross's Hotel
Parkgate Street
Dublin
20.12.48.

My dearest Ben,

Thanks for your letter. Yes, Miss Anscombe arrived here last Tuesday & she was in a bad state. She is leaving to-day & she is <u>better</u> now; <u>not</u> thanks to any thing that I could do for her, & Drury, too, could only give her some sleeping-capsules; but the change of mental atmosphere & sleep have done her good; though she is not back to normal yet.[262] That her coming at this <u>particular</u> moment greatly upset my work & me I will not deny; but her health is more important than my work. (All this, of course, is between you & me.) I have, in spite of everything /been able to/ do some work every day, though without the peace & joy I felt before. Perhaps some of it will come back. If it doesn't, it doesn't.

---

261 'The Mating of Milly' was an American romantic comedy released in 1948 (directed by Henry Levin, and starring Evelyn Keyes and Glenn Ford).

262 Anscombe later recalled: "Wittgenstein got Con Drury to advise me, who first got me into good nights' sleeps, and reassured me by his good sense and friendliness… Sometimes when [Wittgenstein and I] were talking my mind would wander and become fixed on one of the troubling images that were disturbing me; he observed this and recalled me, saying 'I can see you are not in your usual state'. But after a few days of good sleep and reassuring friendliness and having resumed smoking, I was quite cheered up and returned to England" (Anscombe 2025: 172 & 175).

I've never thought more of you, or longed more for your company than in these last days, for, as you know, you have a way of bringing peace to my mind. – D. H., as I told you in my last letter, I have no way of sending you my X-mas present so as to reach you on Christmas Day. So, right now, I'll send you a drawing of it from which you may guess what it is. I hope to let you have the thing /in/ itself (Kant) sometime in January. This is it's <u>appearance</u>: (¼ natural size)

closed:  colour: dark blue
material: leather

open: 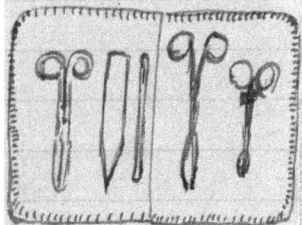 This is not <u>very</u> exact.

God bless you & keep you. May I see you before long! With love, always
        Ludwig

Ludwig Wittgenstein to Ben Richards, Christmas Card (postmarked: December 22, 1948)

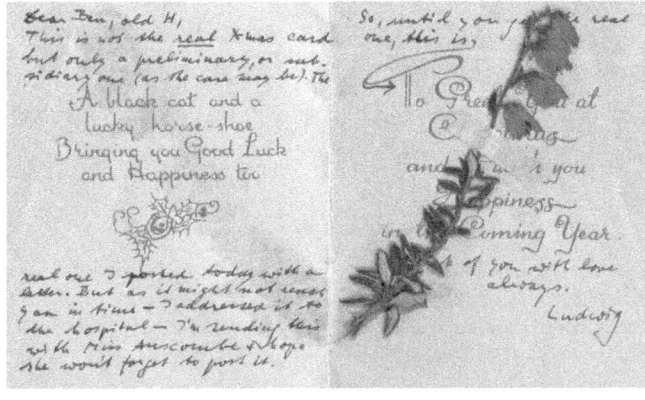

Good Luck
with the
Best of Good Wishes
Dear Ben , old H,
This is not the real X-mas card but only a preliminary, or subsidiary one (as the case may be). The
A black cat and a
lucky horse-shoe
Bringing you Good Luck
and Happiness too

real one I posted to-day with a letter. But as it might not reach you in time – I addressed it to the hospital – I'm sending this with M^{iss} Anscombe & hope she won't forget to post it.

So, until you get the real one, this is ↓

To Greet You at
Christmas
and wish You
Happiness
in the Coming Year

I think of you with love always.
Ludwig

Ludwig Wittgenstein to Ben Richards, December 27, 1948

Ross's Hotel
Parkgate Street
Dublin
27.12.48.

Dear Ben, dear H.,
Thank you for the lovely handkerchiefs, & the card, & your letter. I was glad that it arrived on Christmas-eve, for if it hadn't I would have felt sad & depressed all through the weekend. – Your letter I couldn't quite understand & I wish you'd write to me a ~~kind~~ /nice sort of/ commentary to it. a) You didn't write whether you could guess what the drawing in my letter meant. b) you write: "I sent you off a big tin box. If its not what you want for your papers, please sell it." What's that mean?? Is the tin box (it

hasn't yet arrived) a present from you? If it is, how can you suggest that I sell it? Would you like me to treat your presents that way? – Or is it all a misunderstanding? – Please explain. My work's no longer /going/ very well, though I can still work a fair amount. But I tire quickly with queer feeling of tension in my head & stomac.

At this very moment the deed-box has arrived! & with it a lovely card from you. So it was a present. And could you <u>really</u> imagine that I'd sell it? – I think you must have been a little nuts when you wrote that! – The box is wonderful & and most useful; but it wouldn't have given me <u>anything like</u> the joy it did without the card. – I had been <u>very</u> worried these last days for a reason which a) has nothing to do with you, b) I'd like to talk to you about, but not in a letter.[263] When your present & card arrived it did me good; I feel much more cheerful now than I did before.

May I see you before long! God bless you! Thinking of you keeps me going.

I'm thinking of you with love, constantly.

Ludwig.

Ludwig Wittgenstein to Ben Richards, January 1, 1949

Ross's Hotel
Parkgate Street
Dublin
1.1.<u>49</u>
A Happy New Year!

Dearest Ben,

This afternoon Rhees[264] left Dublin & took <u>that object</u> with him which my drawings represented. I hope you'll get it within the next week & in good condition. Thanks for your letter which arrived to-day. I'm glad you had a good time & that you like looking at my cards.

I didn't work much in the last two days of which I partly spent with Rhees, partly with other non-philosophical business, but otherwise my work hasn't gone too bad.[265] I have seen <u>very</u> little of Drury lately, & that worries me because he is overworking & so <u>obsessed</u> with his work now that he doesn't get the right kind of pleasure out of his spare time which is terribly meager. Christmas, e.g., has /been/ nothing but a hectic & exhausting

---

263 Wittgenstein was probably referring to his worries for Maurice Drury's wellbeing given the immense stresses of his job (see Wittgenstein's next letter to Richards, of January 1, 1949, and the relevant footnote there).
264 Rush Rhees; see the 'Short Biographies of Frequently Mentioned Family and Friends'.
265 The previous day Wittgenstein had written to G. E. Moore: "Rhees leaves me tomorrow . . . I can still work fairly well though not as I did a month ago" (Wittgenstein to Moore, December 31, 1948).

time for him, I believe. This is a <u>bad</u> business. – I feel that I am quite powerless.[266] – The weather has been rather trying lately: very cold, very windy & damp. I dislike to go out, of course I do every day; e.g. to the 'National Botanical Garden' to work. They have lovely smelling orchids there now. – Your 'hankies' are <u>lovely</u>.[267] I wish I had a better laundry to wash them. Mine tears them to shreds <u>& starches</u> them, into the bargain.

D. H., may you still think of me & l.[268] me a little. – I need you a lot! I think of you constantly.

Always with love

Ludwig

P.S. I don't know which of Tolstoy's stories the 'prisoner in the Caucasus' is.[269] Is it the one in which two Russians are captured & one of them makes dolls for children, or the one in which a man is sentenced to prison for a murder he hasn't committed?[270] Or is it neither of these? I remember that the 'Prisoner in the Caucasus' was one of the <u>two</u> stories of Tolstoy /in his book 'What is Art?'/ of which he himself approved, condemning all ~~the~~ /his/ others.[271] L. L.

Ludwig Wittgenstein to Ben Richards (postmarked: January 10, 1949)

Ross's Hotel

Parkgate Street

Dublin

Dear Ben, d. o. H.,

I am slightly worried because I haven't heard from you. I know this may have <u>many</u> causes. I hope you are not ill. But please remember that even <u>bad</u> news is better than <u>no</u> news. So let me hear from you without delay in <u>some</u> form or other.

---

266 Wittgenstein did, in the end, find something to do – for about a week later he went to speak with Drury's boss (Dr John Norman Parker Moore, 1911-96); as Wittgenstein reported to Rush Rhees: "Last Friday I had my talk with Drury's boss. I made things <u>very</u> clear, & he seemed to listen & took it in a kind spirit, but I very much doubt if it's done any good. I don't like the look of things at all" (Wittgenstein to Rhees, January 13, 1949).

267 See Wittgenstein previous letter to Richards, of December 27, 1948.

268 Stands for: 'love'.

269 Leo Tolstoy's short story 'The Prisoner of the Caucasus', written in 1872.

270 The first of these options is the correct one.

271 In his short book *What is Art?* Tolstoy wrote that "the Christian art of our time can be and is of two kinds: (1) art transmitting feelings flowing from a religious perception of man's position in the world in relation to God and to his neighbour – religious art in the limited meaning of the term; and (2) art transmitting the simplest feelings of common life, but such, always, as are accessible to all men in the whole world – the art of common life – the art of a people – universal art. Only these two kinds of art can be considered good art in our time" (Tolstoy 1904: 166). In a footnote he then noted: "I must, moreover, mention that I consign my own artistic productions to the category of bad art, excepting the story *God Sees the Truth*, which seeks a place in the first class, and *The Prisoner of the Caucasus*, which belongs to the second" (Tolstoy 1904: 170, fn. 1).

I've been well & working quite well until recently, when I contracted a slight gastric upset. It's nothing bad at all but, ~~it~~ of course, it interfers with my work.[272] – There is one thing I wanted to ask you for some time: A good many weeks ago you wrote me that you had received a parcel containing Nescaffé from Cambridge, & that your mother was going to send it to me. It has not arrived yet. Please, if you can, make enquiries about it. Has it really been sent off & can it be traced. – Rhees took your X-mas present to England a week ago & he wrote me that he posted it to you. I <u>hope</u> you got it. There was another, posthumous, New Year card in it, too.

Dear Ben, I shan't write more to-day because I don't feel very bright. Please, if you've been ill, or anything else has happened, let me know. God bless you! <u>I am thinking of you with love always</u>.

Ludwig

Ludwig Wittgenstein to Ben Richards, January 16, 1949

16.1.49   Ross's Hotel
Parkgate Street
Dublin

Dear Ben, d. o. H. –

Thanks for your letter which I received the day after I wrote /you/ mine.[273] I sent it to Ickenham, for I had an idea you might be ill, & if you were, you'd either be at home, or your people would be in contact with you wherever you were. Perhaps you were a bit angry with me for imagining such things so easily, but that can't be helped, any more than my nose or my eyes can. And perhaps I imagined illness the more easily as I was getting ill myself. I had to go to bed with a /mild/ gastric flu on Tuesday.[274] But I've been up for two days now & /am/ rapidly getting better & stronger. – It's wonderful to think that I may see you again soon. But luck is treacherous, & I'll only <u>hope</u>, & not <u>believe</u> until I see

---

272 Wittgenstein wrote to Rush Rhees a few days later: "Last Sunday I, too, fell ill with a mild gastric flue & I've heard since that there are lots of other cases about. I'm out of bed today, at least <u>so far</u>. I still worked on Sunday but not after that, & I may not be able to work for quite a time" (Wittgenstein to Rhees, January 13, 1949).

273 Richards' letters from this period have not survived, but – because Wittgenstein had sent his present for Richards via Rhees – Wittgenstein mentions this letter from Richards in a letter to Rush Rhees: "I had a letter from Richards two days ago, saying that he had received my present: Thanks!" (Wittgenstein to Rhees, January 13, 1949).

274 The previous day Wittgenstein had started a new manuscript notebook – MS 138 – and his first entry was the rather despondent note: "Was sick this week. Stomach flu. Even now still can't work, & who knows if I'll be able to work again" (MS 138, p. 1a).

you. <u>Any</u> time suits me equally well. The one consideration I can think of (& it's not a very important one) is this that in March the days are a bit longer & we <u>might</u> be out in the open air a bit more. But whenever you come it'll be lovely. You know that. Please decide <u>as soon as you can</u> & let me know. – I'm surprised at your not knowing that the flower I sent you /which looks like an umbrella/ was Malvaviscus Molle[275] which, as every school boy knows, grows in South America. — I haven't been to our National Botanical Garden for a whole week but perhaps I'll go to-morrow. My work stopped completely for some days. It's beginning again now but only in a <u>very</u> weak sort of way. Just before I fell ill it had picked up again & I was working very well. – One <u>never</u> knows! – My dear, look after yourself. I know that there's flu about. (It's pretty mild here for the moment – the flu is & the weather, too.) Take care of yourself, & think of me if you have time.

  With love, always

    Ludwig

I'm <u>glad</u> you liked the case & the instruments.[276] I thought that you might gradually fill it yourself. The peculiar forceps <u>might</u> be good for handling very small, thin things, – Drury, when I showed it to him, thought – for removing stitches. – About him I'll tell you more when I see you.

May I see you soon & in good health & spirits!

    L. L.

This spa<u>ce to be u</u>sed for Notes:[277]

Ludwig Wittgenstein to Ben Richards, January 19, 1949

      Ross's Hotel
      Parkgate Street
      Dublin
      19.1.49.

Dearest Ben,

Thanks for your letter of Jan 18th. What I shall write in this letter I'm afraid <u>you won't like</u>. ~~to hear.~~ But I've got to write it. Please believe that what I shall say is just the pure

---

275 'Malvaviscus mollis' and 'malvaviscus arboreus' are the scientific names of a plant in the hibiscus family, more commonly called 'wax mallow' or 'turk's cap'. MS 167 begins with the words: "Malvaviscus Molle / South America" (MS 167, p. FCv), which was presumably a note that Wittgenstein made of this information around the time of writing this letter – so he was apparently using two notebooks simultaneously.
276 See Wittgenstein's letter to Richards of December 20, 1948.
277 With the word 'spirits!' Wittgenstein had to dip over onto the back side of the paper, which he then signed with his initials, leaving the vast majority of the page blank – hence his joke about the remaining space.

& unexaggerated truth; & I'm only writing it because you must <u>know</u> the truth. – I've often said to you that your letters 'keep me going', & that wasn't just a façon de parler.²⁷⁸ I need them; & if they keep me waiting /for some days/ after the week's past, I spend these days in constant anxiety, feeling wretched, mentally & physically. – <u>That's the truth.</u>

Now what follows from it? I think, simply this, that if you care for me <u>as I do for you</u>, you won't make me miserable <u>if you can avoid it</u>. (For your power to do so is only due to the way I feel for you.) If you're ill, or so terribly busy that you <u>can't</u> write, then I've just got to take it /& I will/ – If you feel that I'm being a nuisance & troublesome draw the write²⁷⁹ consequences from it. (And you know what I think these are.) I dare say I <u>am</u> a nuisance; but I can't help it. I can't give myself a new nervous system. – Imagine you had bought a dog. For a time you give him his food regularly, & you enjoy his pleasure & gratitude. Then, may be, it gets monotonous, & you're busy & feed him at odd times when it suits you. You make the animal wretched & ill. – Now there is no reason why you should keep such a delicate animal (on the other hand, it's not the animal's fault that it is like that). If you feel that you haven't bargained for all that regularity in feeding him, you must get rid of him without delay.

Dear Ben, all this doesn't contain an <u>element</u> of reproach. I <u>know</u> you're trying to be kind to me, & you're ever so kind & good. But those are the facts & you must know them & decide accordingly. If you feel disgusted with me I'll understand it perfectly, but <u>don</u>'t think that ~~that~~ I'm not serious.

Also, don't think that I'm now writing in some queer mood. I was indeed feeling bad until your letter came (an hour ago), & it's true that now, being weakened /by/ flu, I'm still more susceptible to worry than I am normally, – but I'm feeling fine just now with your letter before me. And, therefore, what I wrote wasn't written in some sort of nasty spirit, but you ha~~ve~~d to know the facts.

About your coming I feel just what you do: in a way I feel "the sooner the better" & in a way I'm afraid of the long time of separation after you're gone. So, decide whatever you feel /is/ wisest – if, that is, you want to have anything more to do with me after what I've told you.

<u>I love you always.</u> God bless you & keep you.

Ludwig

---

278 French: 'manner of speaking'.
279 Wittgenstein meant: 'right'.

P.S. I hope the Mozart Requiem will sound good & that you'll get a great deal out of it.[280] I wish I could hear it, too.

The Nescaffe arrived to-day with an odd little note from your mother. I've written to thank her.

I'm gradually getting stronger. It always takes a long time with me. – <u>Please look after yourself</u>. L. L.

If you have no time to write a letter
P.T.O.[281]
write <u>two</u> words on a bit of paper & post it to me. If you're ill let some one else do it. L. L.

Ludwig Wittgenstein to Ben Richards, January 25, 1949

25.1.49.　　Ross's Hotel
Parkgate Street
Dublin

Dear Ben, d. o. H. –

Thanks for your letter. It <u>wasn't</u> a lack of faith in you that made me write what I did; only a great fear, almost kind of certainty, that something untoward has happened to you /which sometimes possesses me/. And I felt that, on the one hand, I couldn't drive away the fear, & on the other, that you had every right to be disgusted with me because of it. I am afraid, that d. . .[282] flu, or rather its aftermath, hasn't yet left me, & that's what makes me still more foolish than I normally am. Please be patient with me! – It always takes a long time for me to get rid of an infection. – It didn't matter at all that the Nescaffe arrived late, – but there was <u>no</u> note with it from the Cambridge sender. I suppose it got lost somehow. I shall write to Mrs Barbrooke[283] & ask her what it contained. I <u>imagine</u> it was a Christmas card. – I go out a little every day, but the weather is changeable & , on the whole, chilly & it's no fun being out. I <u>hope</u> there'll be sunshine when you're here! But it'll be wonderful, sunshine or rain. – Will your concert be broadcasted? for, if so, I'd like to hear it. I know that choral works don't come through the radio well but I still want to hear it. Drury is going to listen, too, if it's all possible. <u>Think</u> of me when you sing "confutatis maledictis" & "recordare" & "et

---

280　Wolfgang Amadeus Mozart's Requiem in D minor (K. 626), composed in 1791. Richards was a member of a choir that was going to perform it.
281　The final lines were written on the back of the page.
282　Stands for: 'damn'.
283　See Wittgenstein's letter to Richards of May 25, 1948, and the relevant footnote there.

lux perpetua luceat eis"[284] with the drums. And listen to that introduction at the beginning, with bass clarinetts, or whatever it is, that isn't serious but terrible. /It has a kind of dance rhythm./

– My work is rather slow & painful now, but that's natural in my condition.[285] I'm taking a tonic "Neurophosphates". Perhaps it'll help. – Con Drury is in good health & not in bad spirits, on the whole. He works too much & that's bad; but just now nothing can be done about it because he is reading for that d. . .[286] exam in February. (A very ~~difficult thing~~ /great strain/ at his age.) I hope when thats over things will get better. – Dear Ben, I think of you constantly & long to see you. Please be patient with me. God bless you.

With love always
Ludwig

P.S. Drive slowly.[287] Look after yourself.

I append an advertisement I want you to perpend:[288]

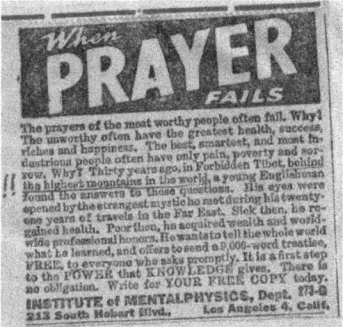

L. L.[289]

---

284 Latin: 'When the accused are confounded', 'Remember', and 'And let perpetual light shine upon them'. These are all lines from Mozart's Requiem, which Richards was going to perform with his choir (see Wittgenstein's previous letter to Richards, of January 19, 1949, and the relevant footnote there).

285 At this time Wittgenstein was working in MS 138 (see pp. 9b ff). A few days later he wrote to Norman Malcolm: "I had a pretty good run of work in the last 3 months, or so, but I fell ill with some sort of infection of the intestines about 3 weeks ago & it hasn't yet cleared up. If it goes on for another week I shall consult a specialist. Of course it hasn't done my work any good. I had to interrupt it completely for a week & after that it just crawled along, as I do when I take a walk, these days" (Wittgenstein to Malcolm, January 28, 1949). A few days later Wittgenstein finally booked an appointment with a specialist – but he was very despondent, and wrote in his notebook: "Still very ill. See a specialist the day after tomorrow. I wonder if this is my last illness" (MS 138, p. 11b; January 29, 1949).

286 Stands for 'damn'.

287 Richards was learning to drive (see the reference to his eventual driving test, in his letter to Wittgenstein of the beginning of July 1949).

288 Wittgenstein uses the word 'perpend' and the dramatic phrase 'perpend this' a few times in his correspondence with Richards, and it seems to have been a joke between them. For the possible allusion see Wittgenstein's letter to Richards of February 2, 1947, and the relevant footnote there.

289 Wittgenstein taped the advert to the letter just under his 'P.S.', and then signed-off again under the advert. Within the advert Wittgenstein has underlined the words "behind the highest mountains in the world" and added two exclamation points to the phrase in the margin.

Ludwig Wittgenstein to Ben Richards, February 1, 1949

Ross's Hotel
Parkgate Street
Dublin
1.2.49.

Dearest Ben, d. H.,

Thanks for your letter. Yesterday I saw a specialist about my gastric trouble. He thinks it's just gastritis & I'm sure he's right.[290] He gave me medicin & it seems to help me, for I'm certainly feeling better to-day, in fact a good deal better.[291] So let's hope that this is the beginning of the golden age of philosophy! – I saw Drury this evening & I told him ~~about your~~ /I had a/ letter from you, but I can't remember whether I gave him your love & good wishes. I'll make sure next time I see him. I don't see him very often these days; partly because he's busy, partly, I think, because he finds my company rather a strain.[292] – My work, oddly enough, hasn't been going too badly, but I tire very quickly. – I <u>long</u> to see you. May you really come before long & nothing intervene! – The 'dance Rhythm' I talked about is the very beginning of the Requiem. I think it's played by bass clarinets &/or basset horns. Look it up. – That they should play a modern English composer along with the Mozart Requiem is most characteristic! Even if the former isn't muck (a most unlikely hypothesis) it's still damnable to combine them. It's like hanging a portrait of Augustus John next to one by Rembrandt.[293] (Though this may be a rotten simile.) – You didn't write whether you liked the advertisement I sent you.[294] There are several of this kind in my magazines & I enjoy them enormously. – Dear Ben, I hope you still love me, although there is <u>nothing</u> in me that could justify such an attitude. – Drive slowly & look after yourself. (Don't try to drive on your hind-wheels only, with the front wheels in the air & waving

---

290 The specialist in question was Dr. Victor Millington Synge (1893–1976), about whom see Wittgenstein's letter to Richards of February 14, 1949, and the relevant footnote there. On the previous day Wittgenstein had written in his notebook: "Went to the doctor, who says I have nothing serious wrong, just gastritis. I think he's right, but I don't trust his treatment" (MS 138, p. 12b).
291 The next day Wittgenstein wrote in his notebook: "I'm well again, or almost well." (MS 138, p. 14a).
292 A few days earlier Wittgenstein had written in his notebook: "I think Drury is gradually becoming unfaithful to me. He has found friends with whom is it easier to live" (MS 138, p. 11b; January 29, 1949).
293 Augustus Edwin John (1878-1961) was a well-known contemporary Welsh Post-Impressionist painter, as contrasted with Rembrandt van Rijn (1606-1669) who was a Dutch Golden Age painter.
294 Wittgenstein is presumably referring to the small cutting entitled 'When Prayer Fails' which he enclosed with his letter to Richards of January 25, 1949.

at the pedestrians. It looks nice, but it's a bit dangerous.) – Think of me & God bless you! I'm thinking of you with love, always.

Ludwig

P.S. I wish I could see your dear face.

Ludwig Wittgenstein to Ben Richards, February 7, 1949

7.2.49.   Ross's Hotel
Parkgate Street
Dublin

Dearest Ben,
Thanks for your letter. I'm ever so sorry to hear you have a cold. <u>Please</u> take care of yourself! Don't do anything foolish. – I still feel a bit lousy at times & /on the whole/ rather run down[295]. I think I'll soon need a kind of holiday, & if you come here I'll really get one. I'm not just 'looking forward' to seeing you, but longing to see you. I had a letter from Mrs Barbrooke[296]. She says she sent a little diary with the Nescaffe. I imagine it was in the letter you ~~said you~~ mentioned. If it's still in Ickenham I'd like to have it. I don't <u>need</u> it, & it isn't anything precious, but it's a present. Please ask your mother about it if you see her – it's not <u>terribly</u> important /though/. – The leaf I sent you was oxalis[297]. It grew in a pot of begonias where it had no business to be. Today's flower fell off a cypripedium[298] & I stole it. – Drury's exam is in about 3 weeks, it's the one you thought it was. – Dear Ben, I hope to God that you'll soon be well; & also that, when you come, I'll be in better shape, so as not to make a <u>completely</u> unsuitable companion for you. – I go to the Botanical Gardens almost every day to walk about in the glass-houses, or outside if it's not too cold or raw. I'm afraid it mostly is. May we both be lucky. <u>God bless you</u>!

With love always
Ludwig

---

295 The previous day Wittgenstein had written in his notebook: "Am sickly again. My nerves are in a bad state" (MS 138, p. 15b)
296 See Wittgenstein's letter to Richards of May 25, 1948, and the relevant footnote there.
297 A kind of plant in the wood-sorrel family.
298 A kind of orchid, commonly known as a slipper orchid or a lady's slipper orchid.

Ludwig Wittgenstein to Ben Richards, February 14, 1949

Ross's Hotel
Parkgate Street
Dublin
14.2.49.

Dearest Ben, dear Heart –

Thanks for your letter. Thank God your cold has gone. I, too, feel very, very much better. I saw Dr Synge[299] again last Thursday /when I still felt lousy/ & he gave me something that helps digesting starchy food, & after two days there was a great improvement. I'm not quite strong yet but have no pain & no discomfort /& am getting stronger every day/. – I liked Dr Synge <u>very</u> much. He was Con Drury's teacher & Drury talked ~~very~~ /exceedingly/ highly of him &, I'm sure, rightly so. He is conscientious, <u>human</u>, without any affectation, or heartiness /& he has a decent dry humor/. When I left him, I wished you could work under him /& that was before he'd cured me/. I <u>believe</u> you could learn something from him which it would be difficult to learn in England[300]. – When you're here I want you to tell me about your difficulty to concentrate. Has it special reasons, like noise, e.g.? – I wonder whether you're right about E. M. Forster[301]. I read bits of Howard's End once & I <u>liked</u> bits, but the <u>oak</u> is lacking, the hard wood, of which (I imagine) great novelists must be carved /it seems to me fluffy/. Some good aperçus /e. g. about music/ don't make a novel. Now, maybe, all this is <u>rubbish</u>, but that's what I'm inclined to think. – My work's going slowly but it's /always/ moving. The greatest help is thinking of you, & your letters. – I informed you wrongly about the date of Drury's exam. It is to-day week. I'm <u>certain</u> that he's got nothing at all to worry about, but it's difficult to give the examinee that

---

299 Victor Millington Synge (1893–1976), an Irish physician and professor of medicine at Trinity College, Dublin. Maurice Drury later recalled: "[Wittgenstein] complained of a recurrent pain in his right arm and a general feeling of exhaustion. I advised him to let me make an appointment for him to see the Professor of Medicine in Trinity College. I had at one time been taught by this doctor and had a high opinion of his diagnostic ability. Wittgenstein agreed to let me make this appointment. WITTGENSTEIN: Yes, I will go and see this man; only I want you to tell him I am a man of intelligence who likes to be told exactly what is found wrong – to have things explained to me frankly" (Drury 1984: 167).

300 Maurice Drury recalled the following observation that Wittgenstein made about what he admired about Dr Synge's way of practicing: "What does please me is that when I go to have my blood test the doctor first examines the colour of my conjunctiva, before taking a specimen for the biochemical test. Nowadays doctors are so afraid of not being scientific that they neglect such simple procedures" (Drury 1984: 168). Wittgenstein had made related remarks to Richards a year earlier, when commenting on John Ryle's book (see Wittgenstein's letter to Richards of February 19, 1948).

301 E.M. (Edward Morgan) Forster (1879-1970), a well-known English author and a member of the Bloomsbury Group. He became known for social novels such as *A Room with a View* (1908), *Howards End* (1910) and *A Passage to India* (1924).

certitude.– I hope your mother will recover soon from her flu. – I enclose a leaf. Guess what it is. You've heard of the tree. Dearest Ben, may I see you soon!!! God bless you.

    With love <u>always</u> Ludwig

[302]P.S. There are no end of things I want to talk to you about! God bless you, always!

P.P.S. In this letter you must chiefly read <u>between</u> the lines[303].

    L. L.

Ludwig Wittgenstein to Ben Richards (postmarked: February 23, 1949)

Ross's Hotel
Parkgate Street
Dublin

Dearest Ben,

Thanks for your letter from Ickenham. I'm still on the upgrade & my work is going all right. As to Foster, I know much to little about him, but I have an impression. I should say (I hope this isn't nonsense) that a real novelist must look at the whole world out of a very ~~stedy~~ <u>steady</u> eye, – if you know what that means. His head must stand there, quite quietly, & look at the world. He mustn't wriggle about.. . . . I /think/ he must have <u>power</u>, not just <u>sensitiveness</u>. And my impression is that all that Foster has is sensitiveness. If you're sensitive you can sometimes find <u>the right word</u> /& thereby give a vivid idea/, which, of course, is necessary for a novelist, but not sufficient. – (As I said, I hope this isn't <u>all</u> rubbish.) – I haven't read Ivan the Fool & was rather, but without any good reason, afraid it might be something philosophical, & I get most /out/ of Tolstoy when his Weltanschauung is all <u>latent</u> in the story/like in Hadshi Murad/ & ~~never~~ /not/ abstractly expressed[304].

---

302 Wittgenstein completely filled both sides of the page, so this 'P.S.' was added – upside down – in the small space to the left of the address, on the top left corner of the first side.

303 This was a pun based on the fact that in this letter Wittgenstein had made so many insertions, which he squeezed between the main lines of the letter (as indicated by all the words and phrases sitting between slashes in the above transcription).

304 Wittgenstein had admired Tolstoy's novella *Hadshi Murad* since 1912 (see Wittgenstein's letter to Richards of September 6, 1946, and the relevant footnote there), and 'The Story of Ivan the Fool' was a short fairy tale that Tolstoy had published in 1886. In a letter to Norman Malcolm – back in 1945 – Wittgenstein had expressed a similar judgment about Tolstoy's different approaches: "I once tried to read 'Resurection' but couldn't. You see, when Tolstoy just tells a story he impresses me infinitely more than when he addresses the reader. When he turns his back to the reader then he seems to me <u>most</u> impressive. Perhaps one day we can talk about this. It seems to me his philosophy is most true when its <u>latent</u> in the story" (Wittgenstein to Malcolm, September 20, 1945). Indeed, as far back as 1917 he had expressed a similar thought in connection with a poem by Ludwig Uhland ('Count Eberhard's Hawthorne'): "The Uhland poem is truly magnificent. And it is like this: if you do not make an effort to express the inexpressible, nothing is lost. Rather, the inexpressible is – inexpressibly – contained in what is expressed!" (Wittgenstein to Engelmann, July 4, 1917).

— Dear Ben, to say, I think of you constantly & long to see you, is an understatement. May we really see each other! Please make your stay as long as possible; & let me know as soon as possible the day & hour of your arrival! – Drury is now having his exam. It started on Monday & ends on Friday. I believe Monday was the hardest day /of the lot/ & all went well; I saw him on Monday evening. – The leaf in my last letter was (of course) a leaf of cinamonum camphora, the camphor tree /Tsk, tsk!/. – Please, /if &/ when you come, bring a couple of books for us to read. You might bring Grimm[305], among other things, if you like, & if there is a little empty space in your bag bring the ball.

Be good, & hope, & try!

    With love, always

      Ludwig

Ludwig Wittgenstein to Ben Richards (postmarked: February 28, 1949)

            Ross's Hotel

            Parkgate Street

              Dublin

Dear Ben, o. H. –

I am writing this letter with a heavy heart. I've had many bad breaks lately[306]. At present I have very sad news from home[307]. I need you more than ever, if that's possible, & I'm wondering whether you'll really come, & come for as long as you said you would (which is terrible short, anyhow). Please don't disappoint me. This is assuming that you're well, & I hope to God you are.

---

305 Jacob and Wilhelm Grimm's *Children's and Household Tales* (1812ff) was a book that Wittgenstein returned to again and again. He left his copy to Richards in his will.

306 On the same day, Wittgenstein wrote in his notebook: "It seems that I can no longer work, and it gives me the impression that I am not just suffering from a temporary fatigue. I think that the strain, the work & the worries & illness have made me unable to work for a long time. I am in the terrible situation of having no means to recover" (MS 138, p. 29a).

307 A few days earlier Wittgenstein had learned that his eldest sister, Hermine, was dying: "Telephone conversation with Gretl (in England). She has heard over the telephone in Vienna that Mining is dying, no longer recognizes anyone, is sleeping peacefully. – All around, the roots on which my own life depends are being cut. My soul is full of pain. She had many talents and a clever mind. But not bare for all to see, rather veiled; as the human qualities should be." (MS 138, p. 27a; February 25, 1949). On the same day as writing that note, Wittgenstein relayed the gist of his conversation with Gretl to his friend Rudolf Koder, in Vienna – and added: "I do not know what condition Gretl will be in when she reaches Vienna. I hope it won't be a bad one. But I fear the hasty measures she might then suggest. May I be seeing things too darkly! Gretl also said that Helene has the flu, and that is bad, especially now. I know you will be able to cheer her up, if anyone can. Please, when you give me news, tell me the complete truth. Let no one come between us in this matter, or influence you!" (Wittgenstein to Koder, February 25, 1949). In his letters to Koder from this period, Wittgenstein repeatedly asked for updates on Hermine's health.

– My work, for the last few days, has just been crawling along, because I'm /feeling/ tired /& worn out/, mind & soul. Try to give me a break! – Drury got through his exam on Saturday but hasn't yet heard the results; not that there is the slightest doubt that he passed it. Among other things he ~~roa~~ /had/ to write a paper on ~~academic~~ 'psychology'. He showed me the questions. They were incredibly stupid. I wouldn't have known how to answer a single one. – There are so many things I'd like to talk to you about that they'll probably choke me when I see you. – I'm very sorry your concert isn't being broadcast[308]. –

>God bless you & keep you!
>With love, as always
>Ludwig

Ludwig Wittgenstein to Ben Richards, Telegram, March 1, 1949

POST OFFICE
TELEGRAM

Prefix. Time handed in. Office of Origin and Service Instructions.   Words.
248 3·14 DUBLIN CTO 18
B RICHARDS MEDICAL STUDENT HILL END HOSPITAL STALBANS HERTS =
YOUR WIRE MADE ME FEEL BETTER[309] WRITING LOVE LUDWIG + LUDWIG +

Ludwig Wittgenstein to Ben Richards, March 1, 1949

>1.3.49.   Ross's Hotel
>Parkgate Street
>Dublin

P.S.
Dear Ben, o. H. –
Your wire arrived this morning, & when I'd read it I felt more cheerful & hopeful[310]. God bless you. – I'll meet the boat at the North Wall[311], but should anything prevent

---

308 Richards was a member of a choir that was going to perform Mozart's Requiem (see Wittgenstein's letters to Richards of January 19 and 25, 1949, and the relevant footnotes there).
309 As can be inferred from the letter with which Wittgenstein followed this telegram (March 1, 1949), Richards' telegram confirmed that he would be visiting Wittgenstein in Ireland, and provided details of his arrival. Richards visited him from March 5 to March 14, 1949.
310 See Wittgenstein's telegram to Richards of March 1, 1949, and the relevant footnote there.
311 The North Wall Quay – on Dublin's River Liffey – is right by the Dublin Port, where Richards would be arriving.

me you can get a taxi there, if you don't disembark too late (as we did in October). – Take care of yourself! You know how I long to see you. May we be lucky!

With love, always

Ludwig

Ludwig Wittgenstein to Ben Richards, March 15, 1949

15.3.49.　　Ross's Hotel
Parkgate Street
Dublin

Dearest Ben, d. H. –

I hope you had a good journey & that you're not in bad health. You know how wonderful it all was for me[312]. – I want to tell you something I ought to have said yesterday but forgot about. This, that what I said to you, about what I believe to be your mother's attitude & feelings towards me, is not a secret, & that you can make any use of anything I said, that[313] /might/ seems to you wise, or useful. I mean, that, as far as I am concerned, you can quote anything I said to you when /you/ talking to your mother, if quoting me seems to you the right thing. Sorry I'm expressing myself so clumsily. I'm feeling rather stupid to-day.

Nothing much has happened here since yesterday. I miss you, – that's all. (Kitty[314] said to me this morning, how nice you were & what a lot of money you'd left in the room for her though she hadn't done anything for you.)

I shall make enquiries about the price of a ticket to New York to-day but I haven't the slightest idea whether I'll go, & if so, when?[315].

312　During Richards' stay – from March 5 to 14 – he and Wittgenstein stayed at the St. Lawrence Hotel in Howth, a small village just outside Dublin, on Ireland's east coast (see Wittgenstein's letter to Rudolf Koder of March 9, 1949). The day after writing this letter Wittgenstein wrote to Rush Rhees: "Ten days ago Richards came here for a week & we went to Ho[w]th together & spent the week there. It was very enjoyable, but the weather was mostly foul 'e.g. cold East wind & damp & windy' Richards left yesterday" (Wittgenstein to Rhees, March 16, 1949). In his notebook Wittgenstein wrote: "Was with Ben for ten days. Beautiful time. Always loving … Wasn't healthy, slept badly. – Don't know how it will go on" (MS 138, p. 30a).

313　Wittgenstein initially crossed out the word 'that', but then put dots underneath it, indicating – by standard copyediting conventions – that the word should remain as it was, undeleted.

314　Probably a maid at Ross's Hotel.

315　Norman and Lee Malcolm had been inviting Wittgenstein to stay with them for a while in Ithaca, New York, since as far back as 1947 (see Wittgenstein's letter to Norman Malcolm of December 9, 1947), and Wittgenstein was now finally actually considering it – but he was still very unsure. The next day Wittgenstein wrote to Rush Rhees: "I don't know at all what my movements in the near or far future will be. I may go to Vienna, or I may stay here, or I may for a time go to England & in that case I hope to see you, but I don't know anything at present. – The Malcolms invited me over to America (Ithaca N. Y.). Perhaps one day I'll go, but I'm unable just now to decide anything" (Wittgenstein to Rhees, March 16, 1949).

I don't feel a bit like working. In fact, if I look at my notes it is like seeing a dish you've had /much/ too much of already. But maybe that'll change, though I don't think it will soon[316]. – God bless you! I'm thinking of you with love <u>always</u>. Ludwig

Ludwig Wittgenstein to Ben Richards, Telegram, March 17, 1949

POST OFFICE

TELEGRAM

Prefix.   Time handed in. Office of Origin and Service Instructions.   Words.

TS C 6376 9 PM DUBLIN CTO 33

BENEDICT RICHARDS MEDICA STUDENT HILLEND HOSPITAL STALBANS HERTS =

MAY COME LONDON WITHIN NEXT FEW DAYS TO AWAIT PERMIT[317] OUGHT I ASK YOUR MOTHER TO PUT ME UP WIRE IF POSSIBLE TOMORROW LOVE = LUDWIG +

LUDWIG +

Ludwig Wittgenstein to Ben Richards, March 21, 1949

21.3.49.   Ross's Hotel

Parkgate Street

Dublin

Dearest Ben, d. H.,

Thanks for your letter. I sent you a wire on Thursday[318] because I had an idea that my sisters might want me to come to Vienna. I was wrong[319], & I had a /friendly/ letter from

---

316 The next day Wittgenstein wrote to Rush Rhees: "[A]bout a fortnight ago I almost suddenly became exhausted, my ideas petered out, & now I'm completely incapable of thinking about philosophy. This doesn't necessarily mean that I couldn't discuss philosophy, but I can't write. God knows if I'll ever be able to work again, but I feel that I'll <u>certainly</u> not be able to work soon. <u>Perhaps</u> a holiday of a couple of months would make me fit again" (Wittgenstein to Rhees, March 16, 1949).

317 Wittgenstein was thinking of travelling to Vienna to see his ailing sister, Hermine, for which he would need an entry permit (Austria being occupied by the Allies at this time). The previous day he had written to Rush Rhees: "I had the news that my eldest sister had suddenly to be operated on cancer. The operation was successful & the doctors said that she might live 2 or 3 years, but a few weeks after the operation she had a slight stroke & a worse one after that, & now she is dieing. She has no pain but she is getting weaker & weaker, & is sleeping most of the time. My two other sisters who are with her think that my coming would only upset her. I told them, of course, that if there were the slightest chance of my eldest sister wishing to see me they should send me a medical certificate & I could be in Vienna within a week. It would be no sacrifice for me to go" (Wittgenstein to Rhees, March 16, 1949).

318 See Wittgenstein's telegram to Richards of March 17, 1949.

319 On the same day Wittgenstein wrote to his sister, Helene: "I have understood the content of your telegram & you may be right that it is not advisable for me to come now. You <u>see</u> Mining & must judge the matter. But please beware of trying to play fate. And if you discuss these matters with Gretl, as I expect you will, this warning also applies to her" (Wittgenstein to Helene Salzer, March 21, 1949; see also the footnote to Wittgenstein's telegram to Richards of March 17, 1949).

your mother on Friday, or Saturday, saying that I ~~should come to~~ could stay /at/ Ickenham if I come to London. – This, of course, has nothing to do with staying in the summer, so you'll have still to find out about that. I hope you'll do it well, – or maybe you've already done it. – As to going to America, things are difficult & complicated, but the gist of it is that all 3rd class passages are booked out until the middle of July[320]. I intend to book a passage for July 18th to-day, or tomorrow. I was told that I could <u>cancel</u> it & have my money refunded, all but <u>10 shillings</u>. I'm doing it now before anything is settled, as the bookings are going on all the time, & if I wait another month I may not be able to get a birth until much later in the year. I sent a letter to the Malcolms, explaining all the uncertainties & difficulties, & I'm waiting for a ~~letter~~ /reply/ from them[321]. I'm only booking now on the <u>off chance</u> of ~~everything~~ circumstances making it possible & advisable for me to go. – In making my arrangements I was constantly thinking of you, for nothing is more important for me than to see you before long & for as long as possible. There are, <u>as far as I can see</u>, two possibilities. 1) I come to St. Albans before your exam 2) I come to Ickenham immediately after your exam, or anyhow, after your exam[322]. In case 1 I <u>promise</u> to see to it that you work. For case N° 2 I ought to know roughly when your exam takes place. I took it for granted that it would be about the middle of June & that you'd be free after it & we could have <u>at least</u> 3 weeks together before July 18th (supposing that I sail on July 18th). Please tell me if I'm wrong in my assumption. Further please let me know <u>absolutely frankly</u> whether you'd like me to stay at St. Albans. If you'd rather I didn't & told me so I wouldn't take that to mean that things weren't as they should be between us. On the other hand, <u>if</u> you should like the idea you

---

320 The following notes in MS 169 relate to this, and must be form this time:
"To Ithaca
3rd booked till July
2nd booked till end April
From N.Y.
3rd class min. £40
2nd class min. £55" (MS 169, p. 79r).

321 Two days earlier Wittgenstein had sent a long and involved letter to Lee and Norman Malcolm setting out the various complications of a trip and the various hurdles to making a plan to travel – ranging from uncertainty over whether he'd need to go to Vienna to see his sister, to financial difficulties, to a concern that he'd be a burden on the Malcolms without being able to give them anything in return. This is a small part of the letter: "I could afford the trip only by staying with you for <u>2, or 3 months</u> & sponging on you! - Now the prospect of staying with you for that length of time is very pleasant as far as I'm concerned, but there is the snag that I am an elderly man & aging pretty rappidly. I mean, physically, not, as far as I can see, mentally. Now this means that you couldn't take me on any <u>tours</u>. I'm all right for strolling about but I can't do <u>very</u> much more than I did at Cambridge. – For the same reason I wouldn't be any good at gardening. – If it weren't for all these difficulties I'd come <u>like a shot</u>, for I'd love to stay with you, have discussions with one of you & make myself a general nuisance to the other" (Wittgenstein to the Malcolms, March 19, 1949).

322 St. Albans was where Richards was working at the time, and Ickenham was where his family's home was.

should make some enquiries as to where I could stay, in a quiet & not too expensive place. In a way, if I can make you work, it would be a wonderful thing for me. – I think of you <u>constantly</u> & am feeling very <u>lonely</u> for you. – Yesterday I went to the Zoo & you can imagine of what I thought, particularly when I looked at the Emu & at the little bear; he made just the same noise as always. – On Friday I fetched the photo of you & me on O'Connell bridge[323]. If one cuts away most of you & all of me one gets a rather nice picture of your b. o. face. I had two copies made & I pruned one of them & it looks nice; if you want the other one treated in the same way I'll send it to you. <u>I</u> look awful & when I showed Drury the original picture he said that we looked like two gangsters, I like the gangster boss & you like my tough body guard. – Dearest Ben, I miss you, – your old face, our talks, & <u>every</u> thing. Look after yourself, be good, & think of me!

Thanks for the <u>wonderful</u> time you gave me. God bless you.

<u>With love</u> always

Ludwig

P.S. For two days after you left I didn't work at all. ~~Then~~ After that I began again, but I don't work much & not very ~~good~~ well.

I'm enclosing a leaf of a mahagoni tree which I stole for you.

L. L.

P.P.S. This letter is lengthy & /very/ muddled because I'm very stupid these days. I thought of another possibility, viz., I could stay with you for a short time in St. Albans, then go to Cambridge to dictate things while you're having your exams, & then come to Ickenham, or wherever you want to. Think it over, there is no hurry.

L. L.

This is probably the photo of Wittgenstein and Richards on O'Connell Bridge, that Wittgenstein was referring to in his letter of March 21, 1949

---

323 See also Wittgenstein's letter to Richards of November 17, 1948.

Ludwig Wittgenstein to Ben Richards, March 27, 1949

                              27.3.49.   Ross's Hotel

                                                        Parkgate Street

                                                                      Dublin

<u>Dearest</u> Ben,

Thanks for your letter of March 20th. I'm glad you talked to your mother & that the result was what it was, & it certainly means that I can stay in Ickenham again, if you like me to. The question about 'liking & disliking' is not quite so simple. I know you won't think that I don't <u>want</u> to admit having been wrong when I see that I am (either out of vanity, or out of stubbornness). (That would be so in other cases, but not in this one.) Also I don't doubt that your mother <u>meant</u> what she said to you when she said it. But such things are complicated. There isn't just <u>one</u> force pulling but several forces in different directions, & as theyir strength fluctuates the <u>direction</u> of the resultant changes. <u>E.g.</u>: when you come home from a holiday with me, obviously happy, & ask your mother "Do you dislike Ludwig?", I can easily imagine her answering quite frankly "Of course not! Why should I?" – because then you're near & <u>I</u> am far away, & what's dislikable in me is almost forgotten. – Now I don't want to go on with this dissertation, for <u>all</u> I want to say is that this thing isn't /quite/ as simple as you seem to have thought when you wrote that I'd been "quite wrong". But I'll like <u>nothing</u> better than finding that I <u>was</u> quite wrong, & so let's hope that's what I'll find. – I still have no definite news from home & that's very trying. I find it exceedingly difficult to work, & most of the time I think in circles & then get tired & depressed. I go for a walk every day in the Botanical Garden, or in the Zoo. I'm quite well but still ever so stiff & walking with difficulty. I miss you <u>terribly</u> & feel homesick for you. May I see you before long! God bless you & keep you. I think of you all the time with love.

                  Ludwig

P.S. I booked a passage to New York on the "Queen Mary", leaving Southampton on July <u>21</u>st[324]. – Con sends his love. – The leaf I had sent specially all the way from <u>Australia</u>! & the petal from Japan.

              Love

                  Ludwig

---

324 See Wittgenstein's letter to Malcolm dated April 1, 1949: "I have booked a passage to New York on the Queen Mary for July 21st, & if my health & other circumstances permit it I will come & be a d. . . . nuisance to you & Lee for 2 or 3 months. May everything go well."

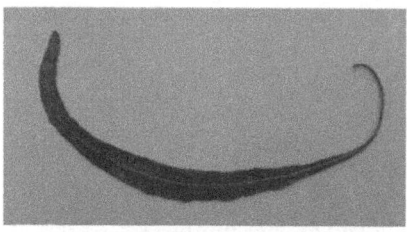
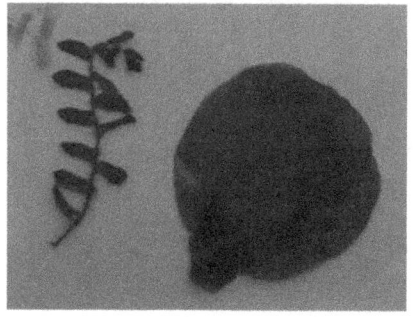

Ludwig Wittgenstein to Ben Richards, March 30, 1949

          30.3.49   Ross's Hotel
                 Parkgate Street
                     Dublin

Dearest Ben,

Thanks for your letter. About St. Albans I don't know what to say. You sound discouraging. When we talked about it at Hoth[325] you didn't say there was no privacy at all at the hospital. Is there less than at the Rotunda[326]? We had some privacy there. At Hoth you said that if I came I'd have to make you work, & I took that seriously & liked it, for I thought it would be good for us to be together when you worked. Perhaps it may seem queer my saying all this when you already said that you'd rather not see me at St. A.[327], but if you really feel just as you did (at Hoth, (e.g.) then there's no harm in my writing what I did. Anyhow, I feel like writing exactly what I feel. I'm in grave trouble all round & have no one to cheer me up even in the slightest, & that makes me long to see you even more than usual. – You say you don't know when your exams will be. Can't you enquire? Aren't these exams roughly the same time every

---

325 This was Wittgenstein's regular misspelling of 'Howth' – the village just outside of Dublin where Wittgenstein and Richards had spent ten days together earlier in the month (see Wittgenstein's letter to Richards of March 15, 1949, and the relevant footnote there).
326 It's not clear what this is a reference to, but perhaps the Rotunda Hospital in Dublin, Parnell Square East.
327 Stands for: 'St Albans'.

year? I have booked a passage for New York on July 21ˢᵗ. If your exam were in July that would mean that we could hardly see each other at all at Ickenham!!
I'm writing all this because I ~~assume~~ /believe/ that what you said at the end of your last letter was the literal truth.
— My work has come to a complete stand-still. I don't know <u>why</u>, ~~unless it is that I'm~~ /except that I'm feeling tired generally./ I think I could still <u>discuss</u> philosophy with someone, but I can't write, or even properly think about it by myself.³²⁸ – Con seems to me to be in a bad state, & there is nothing that I can do to help him³²⁹. Someone by far more easy going than I am (or even was) could /at least/ cheer him up (perhaps not deeply). – I don't like the idea of sending you that 'gangster' photo, unless you promise to destroy it /after looking at it/, or to return it to me for cutting. This isn't vanity; but I don't like nasty photos. One can have fun with them for a moment, but I wouldn't want to possess a nasty photo of my friend! (His face is too serious a matter for me.) And whether friend or not, I wouldn't like to possess a nasty photo /anyhow/ & don't like the idea of you're having one. – May you be <u>good & deep</u> & not unhappy. God bless you & keep you. Of course, <u>if</u> you're serious you're bound to suffer /& if you aren't, you won't be any good whatever/. I think of you with love <u>always</u>.

Ludwig

Ludwig Wittgenstein to Ben Richards, April 2, 1949

2.4.49.   Ross's Hotel
Parkgate Street
Dublin

Dearest Ben,
I had a letter from one of my sisters to-day, saying that ~~they~~ she had now taken the necessary steps to get a medical certificate for me & would send it to Ickenham as soon as she got it³³⁰. (A medical certificate, in order to be valid, has to be stamped by

---

328 A couple of days later Wittgenstein wrote similarly to Norman Malcolm: "I haven't been doing any work at all for the last 2-3 weeks. My mind is tired & stale, partly, I think because I'm a bit exhausted, partly because lots of things worry me terribly just now. I think I could still discuss philosophy if I had someone here to discuss it with, but alone I can't concentrate on it. I suppose it'll all change some day. The sooner the better" (Wittgenstein to Malcolm, April 1, 1949).
329 See Wittgenstein's letter to Richards of January 1, 1949, and the relevant footnote there.
330 The letter from Wittgenstein's sister has not been preserved. Apparently, Wittgenstein needed a medical report attesting to the seriousness of his sister Hermine's illness in Vienna in order to obtain the relevant permit to enter Austria (see Wittgenstein's letters: to Rush Rhees from March 16, 1949; to his sister Helene Salzer from March 21, 1949; and to Rudolf Koder from March 28, 1949).

some Allied Commissioner, or something, & that takes time.) However, I think that the certificate will be sent off by the beginning of next week & as soon as it's sent off my sister will wire me & I shall fly, or sail, to London. I shall have to wait there for a few days (perhaps 3, or 4 /possibly for a week, but not <u>more</u>/) until I get my military permit.

I should <u>very much</u> want to see you during that time (& /of course/ the more, the better). The question is: would it be intelligent for me to take a room at a hotel at St. Albans? I <u>know</u> that your mother doesn't mind putting me up, but if I had more chance to see you /by/ staying at St. Albans, & <u>if</u> you like the idea, I'd come to St. A.. I would in this case stay at least one night at Ickenham, fetch my certificate, see the permit officer & find out how long (roughly) I'll have to wait for the permit. They <u>may</u> in this case give it to me very quickly. It never took them more than 6 days. – When you get this letter, please phone to Ickenham & tell them a) to be sure & <u>keep</u> the med. certif. for me when it arrives, b) to expect me soon after it does arrive. /Of course I'll wire your mother./ When I get there we can talk things over on the phone, but I'd very much like to find a note from you also, telling me what you think best. If this letter reaches you before you've sent off your next letter to me, please don't let it keep you from writing to me <u>here</u>, for I may have to wait here longer than I think, & I <u>need</u> your letters. May you still 'like me a little' when this reaches you, & also when I come to London. I know it's a bad business that I need you so much, but there it is! God bless you, <u>always</u>! With love Ludwig

P.S. Keep this fern. I'll tell you something about it. L. L.

Ludwig Wittgenstein to Ben Richards, Telegram, April 5, 1949

POST OFFICE

TELEGRAM

Prefix. Time handed in. Office of Origin and Service Instructions.   Words.

TS D 6409 9.18 DUBLIN CTO 17 =

BENEDICT RICHARDS MEDICAL STUDENT STALBANS HILLEND HOSPITAL HERTS =

ARRIVING TOMORROW WEDNESDAY 6.30 PM AT NORTHOLT LOVE =

LUDWIG + CT 6.30 + +

Ludwig Wittgenstein to Ben Richards, Telegram, April 8, 1949
POST OFFICE

TELEGRAM

Prefix. Time handed in. Office of Origin and Service Instructions.   Words.
29   12.35   LONDON Z 21
BENEDICT RICHARDS MEDICAL STUDENT HILLEND HOSPITAL ST ALBANSHERTS =
CANT REACH 3.22 TRAIN HOPE REACH 3.51 OR THE NEXT PLEASE WAIT LOVE = LUDWIG +++
CT   3.22   3.51   ++

Ludwig Wittgenstein to Ben Richards, April 12, 1949

4. Argentinierstr. 16

Wien

Austria

12.4.49.

Dearest Ben,

I arrived here last night after a very smooth flight. I had a detective story lying in front of me, but I didn't read because I had too much to think about – chiefly you & the two lovely days we spent together. Thanks for having been so kind & good to me all the time! – I do believe that things went better between your mother & me this time. I hope I'm right in feeling this. Please give her & your father my thanks & kind regards. – I'm afraid I did a very foolish thing. I left my /brown/ leather jerkin behind. It must be either in your room at Ickenham, or on one of the hooks in the hall. Unless, of course, we left it at the caffé at Uxbridge; but I don't believe that. I <u>know</u> I had it at the cinema & also when we left there. Please look for it at Ickenham, etc. & ask your mother to keep it for me. I'm sorry I forgot it, but you can imagine the rush & unrest of the last morning. – I saw my sick sister this morning for a short time[331]. She talked very quietly, & though she didn't mention death, it was clear that she knew she is dieing. The doctors don't know quite what is happening & are inclined now to think that she may live for some weeks, or even for months[332]. Her body is <u>extremely</u> week but her mind at times surprisingly clear & lively. I think she was

---

331 Hermine Wittgenstein had already been seriously ill with cancer for several months, and seeing her was the reason for Wittgenstein's visit (see Wittgenstein's letter to Georg Henrik von Wright of April 29, 1949).
332 Hermine Wittgenstein died, in the end, on February 11, 1950.

exceedingly glad to see me. – Dear Ben, I want you to think of me often & with the old feelings.

God bless you!
With love always
Ludwig

P.S. I hope your cold is better. – I wish I had been able to send you an Easter egg, or at least a card, but there was no time!

Ludwig Wittgenstein to Ben Richards, Easter Card (around April 17, 1949)[333]

Frohe Ostern![334]

<u>With love</u>

<u>always</u>

from Ludwig

Ludwig Wittgenstein to Ben Richards, April 19, 1949

IV. Argentinierstr. 16
Wien
Austria
19.4.49.

Dearest Ben,

I wish I could begin this letter with "Thanks for your letter", but none has arrived so far. A most extraordinary thing happened a few days ago. The medical certificate,

---

333 The card is undated, but its rough date can be inferred from the fact that it must have been sent in 1949, and the fact that Easter that year was April 17. The card must have been sent in 1949, because (i) it was addressed to Richards at Hill End Hospital, and he only worked there in 1949; and because (ii) it was sent from Vienna, and during the years of his correspondence with Richards, Wittgenstein was only in Vienna at Eastertime in 1949.

334 German: Happy Easter!

which, as you know, I waited for at Ickenham was returned to my sister who sent it from Uxbridge. It was addressed to "Dr Ludwig Wittgenstein % Richards, etc" & someone wrote on the envelope with block letters "Unknown at this address". When my sister showed it to me I had a shock. I couldn't imagine that anyone at your house could have done this & yet couldn't see how else it could have happened. Finally I thought of this possibility: that the postman, instead of going to 40 Swakeleys Road, as the envelope clearly said, went to that shop, called Richards, on the other side of the road, & that there they told him there wasn't a D^r. Wittgenstein in Ickenham. In this particular case the muddle was harmless but it might have had terrible consequences. The postman should be told that a man of my name stays at your house.

My sister is apparently somewhat better now than she was when I arrived a week ago. Her mind is completely clear & often very lively, & the worst of it is that she reproaches herself for not doing enough to speed up her recovery. It's sometimes <u>very</u> difficult to know what one should tell her.

My rheumatism is much better now, thanks to the warm weather we've had, & I'm not anywhere near as stiff as I was when you last saw me; but my head feels sad & stupid. I wish I could see you, it would make all the difference. I miss you. I hope I shall hear from you soon. Please forgive my rotten writing. Somehow I find it very difficult now to write.

<u>God bless you & keep you! I think of you with love always.</u>

Ludwig

Ludwig Wittgenstein to Ben Richards, April 25, 1949

IV. Argentinierstr. 16
Wien
Austria
25.4.49.

Dearest Ben,

Thanks for your note of April 14th. I think of you a great deal & I hope you'll write to me regularly! My life here is very sad, & exhausting in a queer way. I shall apply for an extension of my military permit for a week or a fortnight; I believe my sister needs me. I shall let you know if I get the extension & for how long. I long to see you. Seeing you would give me new strength. I find writing terribly difficult just now. Please forgive me for writing such a stupid letter. I know it sounds as though a child had written it but it's as good as I can do it right now[335].

God bless you & keep you!
With love always
Ludwig

P.S. Please write a line to Miss Anscombe & tell her that I'm in Vienna, & why. She should tell Smythies & v. Wright about it.
I wish I could see you & you'd tell me one of the words that help me.

Ludwig Wittgenstein to Ben Richards, May 4, 1949

IV. Argentinierstr 16
Wien
Austria
4.5.49.

Dearest Ben,

Thanks for your letter. It arrived later than it should have done because you didn't put enough stamps on it, as also on the one before. I intend to leave here on Friday next week (May 13th). When I know for certain I'll wire. I may come by an American plane &, if so, I shan't land at Northolt, so you'll probably not be able to meet me at the air port. I'll wire all the details. I think of you a lot & <u>long</u> to see you. I've no end of things to tell you but I don't want to write about them as I hope to see you very soon.

God bless you!
With love, always
Ludwig

Ludwig Wittgenstein to Ben Richards, Telegram, May 7, 1949

POST OFFICE
TELEGRAM

Prefix.   Time handed in.   Office of Origin and Service Instructions.   Words.
115 C CW L 1819 WIEN 20 6 0840 =
= ELT = BENEDICT RICHARDS HILLEND HOSPITAL MEDICAL STUDENT STALBANSHERTS =

---

335 A few weeks later – after his return to England – Wittgenstein described to Norman Malcolm the state he'd been in while in Vienna: "While I was in Vienna I was hardly able to write at all. I felt so rotten myself. I haven't done any work since the beginning of March & I haven't had the strength of even <u>trying</u> to do any. God knows how things will go on now" (Wittgenstein to Malcolm, May 17, 1949).

EXPECT ARRIVE LONDON AIRPORT FRIDAY 13 SHALL WIRE AGAIN LOVE =
LUWDIG WITTGENSTEIN +
13 LUDWIG WITTGENSTEIN +

Ludwig Wittgenstein to Ben Richards, Telegram, May 10, 1949
TELEGRAM
Prefix.   Time handed in.   Office of Origin and Service Instructions.   Words.
80 C CW L 1227 WIEN 19 10 1240
= ELT BENEDICT RICHARDS HILLEND HOSPITAL MEDICAL STUDENT
STALBANSHERTS =
ARRIVING AIRWAYS HOUSE VICTORIA FRIDAY 5.30 P M LOVE = LUDWIG
WITTGENSTEIN + 5.30 P M ++

Ludwig Wittgenstein to Ben Richards, May 17, 1949

17.5.   Ross's Hotel
Parkgate Street
Dublin

Dearest Ben,
I saw M^iss Anscombe for about 2 hours yesterday morning. We drank coffee together at a Corner House in a Help Yourself place, & there behind the counter I saw a notice as large as life saying "Welsh Rabbit". I had a momentary feeling of triumph.[336]
– You know how lovely being with you was for me. Life feels so much easier & sweeter when I am with you. (I mean my life does.) – I had lunch at Ickenham. When at lunch the conversation /seemed to me/ dullish & empty I missed you, for in such a moment looking at you does me good /though it always does/. I thought of our talk about chatting & again I couldn't help wishing that you'd never learn it. (Though if you don't you'll have more unpleasant moments.)
– On the whole your mother & I understood each other better this time than perviously. At least it seemed so. Right at the end there was an incident that didn't seem so good, but perhaps it meant nothing. – Your father was so kind as to take me to Northolt in his car. We put my stick into the luggage compartment of the car[337] &

---

336 The old British (perhaps originally Welsh) dish of a piece of warm or toasted bread covered with a hot savoury cheddar cheese sauce (which is usually mixed with Worcestershire sauce, mustard, and either beer or ale), has been known both as 'Welsh rarebit' and as 'Welsh rabbit' since at least the 18th century (though it contains no rabbit).
337 Wittgenstein had been using a walking stick – at least some of the time – for decades (see, for example: Hans Klingenberg's letter to Wittgenstein of December 30, 1920; see Hausmann & Hargrove 2016: 381-2; and see MS 119, p. 119v).

when I said good-bye to him we forgot it there. I'd like it to be kept at Ickenham until I come again.

– Do you remember that, 5 weeks ago, when I left for Vienna I left my leather jerkin at Ickenham? I think I wrote to you about it from Vienna. Well, I forgot to ask about it this time. If you come to Ickenham, please ask them to keep my jerkin & my stick for me. – I <u>hope</u> that you'll be able to work well & steadily. God bless you! I wish I had you here!! Please don't forget to give both your parents my thanks for their kindness to me. If I find that I can write something sincere & suitable I shall write a line thanking your mother.

I think of you with love <u>always</u>.

Ludwig

P.S. I'll see Dr Synge[338] tomorrow & hope he'll give me some good advice. – God bless you! L. L.

P.P.S. Your father lent me £10 yesterday & told me to pay them back to <u>you</u>. I enclose a cheque for the amount. Please tell your father that I sent it.

Write soon!
Love.

Enclosure included with the letter of May 17, 1949:

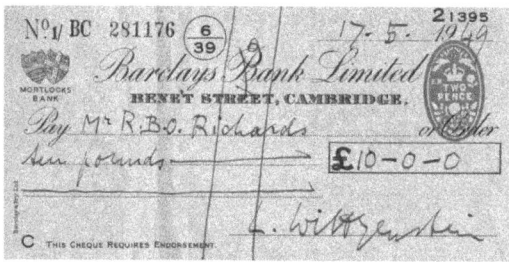

Ludwig Wittgenstein to Ben Richards, May 18, 1949

18.5.49.   Ross's Hotel
Parkgate Street
Dublin

Dearest Ben,

P.P.P.S. Last night I discovered that I'd left my shaving brush in the bathroom at Ickenham! It's the one you gave me. Please send it to me as soon as & as safely as

---

338 See Wittgenstein's letter to Richards of February 14, 1949, and the relevant footnote there.

possible. I'm awfully sorry to cause you all this trouble when you're busy, but I really need the brush.

God bless you!

Think of me if you can.

    Love always

        Ludwig

Enclosure included with the letter of May 18, 1949:

Ludwig Wittgenstein to Ben Richards, May 24, 1949

        24.5.49.   Ross's Hotel

                                Parkgate Street

                                        Dublin

Dearest Ben, D. H.,

Thanks for your letter & the brush & also for the last letter you sent to Vienna. – Dr Synge had my blood examined & they found a severe anaemia. Syng doesn't think it likely that it's a primary anaemia (I only just lernt this term) but believes that it has some inner cause. I'm going to hospital today /for 4 days/ to have a barium meal etc. etc. – You know what all this points to[339]. Will I be able to go to America? Or even to come to Ickenham? I will let you know as soon as I know anything, i.e. in about 4 days. If things go really bad you could ~~co~~ fly to Dublin for a few days after your exams /The journey would be on me/. Please write to me to the hotel, they'll forward it in case I should be in hospital. – <u>I love you</u> & think of you constantly. God bless you! Let me hear from you often! Think of me!

                              Ludwig

P. S. I hope your work goes well. G. bl. you. L. L.

---

339 The doctor suspected that Wittgenstein's anaemia was being caused by a growth in his stomach (see Wittgenstein's next letter to Richards, of May 28, 1949, and Wittgenstein's letter to Georg Henrik von Wright of June 4, 1949).

Ludwig Wittgenstein to Ben Richards (undated, around May 28, 1949)[340]

Ross's Hotel
Saturday

Dearest Ben,

This is only to say that I left the hospital yesterday. I was X-rayed & had a test meal. The X-ray showed that there is no groth in my stomack, the result of the testmeal I don't yet know. I'm very weak, much weaker than I was in Ickenham. I'm taking iron. Next week I shall see Synge again. He told me yesterday, he didn't /yet/ know the cause of my anaemia. I can't work, & any kind of thinking is difficult. I'll have to be patient, perhaps the iron will gradually help me! I'm very impatient & tend to lose hope, but I'll try to be sensible.

I think of you a <u>great</u> deal. God bless you.

May I see you before too long!

With love
always
Ludwig

You mustn't mind if my letters are pretty bloody these days.

Ludwig Wittgenstein to Ben Richards, June 1, 1949

1.6.49.   Ross's Hotel
Parkgate Street
Dublin

Dearest ben, dear H.,

Thanks for your letter. I saw Synge again yesterday & he told me the following. a) The result of my test-meal is normal. b) The report of the pathologist shows that my anaemeia is what Synge calls an a-typical hypochromic anaemia, that it shows certain traits of pernicious anaemia.[341]

He gave me a liver-injection /yesterday/ & I'm taking iron & liver regularly. c) He thinks that, if I respond well, I shall feel an improvement in a fortnight, & that I <u>might</u> be all right again in about two months. – I asked him about going to Cambridge in the middle

---

340 This letter is undated, but the date can be inferred from the fact that he says he had left the hospital the previous day. In Wittgenstein's previous letter to Richards – of May 24 – he says that he's going into hospital that day, for four days, i.e. until May 27. And the next day – May 28 – was indeed a Saturday in 1949.

341 Maurice Drury recalled: "Wittgenstein was admitted to hospital for a full investigation.... The only findings made, as a result of the investigation in hospital, were that he had an unexplained anaemia. He was started on the necessary treatment for this, and from time to time had to go back to the laboratory for tests of improvement" (Drury 1984: 167-8).

of June, & he said that depended on how I'd feel by then[342]. I hope things will go well!! – I wish the weather was a bit steadier. While I'm writing this there's a violent hail shower on. I thought for a moment of enclosing a few of the hailstones but they might brake if the letter were handled roughly in the post. I haven't got any flowers to enclose either, because I don't get into the Botanical Garden these days. Perhaps I'll soon feel energetic enough to go. – You didn't mention the B concert in your letter[343]. Why? I hope it went well. God bless you! Please write to me how you've been getting on. I'm thinking of you constantly.

    With love always
      Ludwig

Ludwig Wittgenstein to Ben Richards, June 7, 1949

          7.6.49   Ross's Hotel
                  Parkgate Street
                  Dublin

Dearest Ben,

Thanks for your letter. I didn't confuse hypo with hyper. Mine is hypocromic anaemia but, as I wrote to you, Synge calls it 'a-typical' because it has certain traits of a pernicious a. One is the percentage of white cells; I don't know what it is, nor do I know what is abnormal about it. Synge told me /the percentage/ but I've forgotten. Also he said that I had a certain brownish pigmentation which normally is characteristic for pernicious a. I only remember that my haemoglobin was, when the test was made, 60% & that the number of corpuscles was a good deal below normal. – I'm taking both liver & iron. – I can't say that I feel any improvement so far, but then it's a bit difficult to say as there are ups & downs in the way one feels[344]. I'm exceedingly weak & have a good deal of pain in my muscles. I'm seeing Synge next week & I shall probably have another test done. I'm not too downhearted. – Now I'm afraid I shall have to write to you about a problem of mine. I don't like to do it as

---

342 His plan was to go to Cambridge to dictate the best material from his latest manuscripts to a typist, so as to produce a typescript of his most valuable thoughts. He did this periodically, and tended to do it in Cambridge – where he could find typists who could type in German. He was intending to stay with Georg Henrik von Wright and his family (see his letters to von Wright and to Norman Malcolm, of June 1 and 4, 1949, respectively).

343 See Wittgenstein's letters to Richards of January 25 and February 1, 1949.

344 A few days earlier Wittgenstein had written a little more positively to Rudolf Koder: "My blood test has shown that I suffer from a rather severe and somewhat unusual type of anemia, which the doctor believes explains all my ailments. I am taking iron and liver extract and already feel a slight improvement, but of course it's slow going. In about 14 days, another blood test will probably be taken and it will show how much progress I've made" (Wittgenstein to Koder, June 4, 1949).

you're reading for your exam like hell. I <u>intend</u> to fly to England (Northolt) on Saturday June 18th. I want to go to Cambridge & stay there until the beginning of July. I have however something to do /on Monday 20th/ at the American Embassy in London[345]. If you are at Ickenham that weekend (18th & 19th) I should <u>very</u> much like to be put up over the weekend. If you aren't I could perhaps change my flight ticket & fly on Monday 20th, as the Embassy won't be open on Saturday. In that case I could perhaps go on to Cambridge the same day /& wouldn't need to be put up./. <u>Please wire</u> me the reply. Of course all my plans depend upon what's going to happen to me, but I certainly don't want to stay here if I can help it. I lie on my bed a good deal, but I also go for short & very slow walks. To-day I went to the Botanical Garden. I stole for you the enclosed leaf & blossom. The leaf comes from Ficus Sycomorus, the sycomore tree of the Bible[346]. The blossom is Arthropodium. (What do you think of me now!) Dearest Ben,

I'm <u>sure</u> you'll do well in your exam. Good luck & be confident!
    I hope to see you soon! God bless you.
        With love always
           Ludwig

<u>P.T.O.</u>

P.S. v. Wright wrote to me that he would put me up at Cambridge[347]. I'd stay with him for about 10, or 12 days & in that time it's bound to come out whether I'll be able to go to America in July I <u>hope</u> to see you soon & I <u>hope</u> that I shall be able to be with you at Ickenham in July.
      Love

---

345 In order to get the requisite visa to visit Norman and Lee Malcolm – in Ithaca, NY – for a few months, the Malcolms had to provide an affidavit stating that they were willing and able to cover all of Wittgenstein's expenses for the duration of his stay. Wittgenstein received this from the Malcolms in May. He tried to take it to the American consulate in Dublin, but they told him that – as he had not lived in Ireland for long enough – he would need to take it to the consulate in London instead. This was the appointment he had on Monday June 20 at the American Embassy in London (see Wittgenstein's letters to Norman and Lee Malcolm of: March 19, April 1, May 17, and June 4, 1949).

346 The sycamore fig or the fig-mulberry – a member of the fig family – is mentioned multiple times in the Bible (see, for example, Amos 7:14 and Luke 19:4).

347 A week earlier Wittgenstein had written to Georg Henrik von Wright: "It's very kind of you to say that you'll let me have two rooms, but one room is <u>ample</u>. There is one thing that I'm afraid of: I may not be able to discuss philosophy. Of course it's possible that things will have changed by then, but at present I'm quite incapable of even thinking of philosophical problems. My head is <u>completely</u> dull" (Wittgenstein to von Wright, June 1, 1949).

L.

P.P.S.

Please <u>wire</u> if you're in Ickenham on June 18th-19th.

L. L.

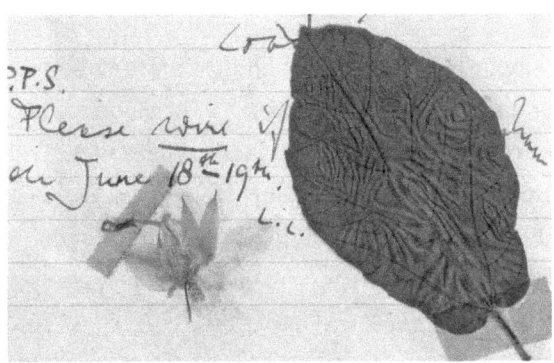

Ludwig Wittgenstein to Ben Richards, Leporello Postcard (postmarked: June 9, 1949)

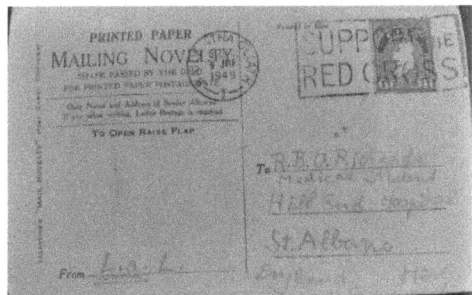 

THREE FOR LUCK!
from Dublin

PRINTED PAPER
MAILING NOVELTY
SHAPE PASSED BY THE G. P. O.
FOR PRINTED PAPER POSTAGE RATE.
Only Name and Address of Sender Allowed
If any other writing, Letter Postage is required

TO OPEN RAISE FLAP[348]
From L. a. L.

Ludwig Wittgenstein to Ben Richards, June 15, 1949

15.6. Ross's Hotel

Dearest Ben,

/Thanks for your letter!/ I sent you a wire on Saturday /to Hill End/, saying that I was much better. I've made very definite progress the last 5 days, or so[349]. The blood count, too, is better 72% haemoglobin instead of 66%, & 4 million read cells instead of 3 million. As you see I was wrong in writing that I had 60% haemoglobin. It was due to a misunderstanding on the 'phone. – I'm glad things are going well with you. Not that I ever doubted they would. – I'm looking forward to seeing you on Saturday. There are such a lot of things I want to talk to you about. I hope we'll have time!

Good luck! & G. bl. y..
With love, always
Ludwig

Hope with me that things will go well at Ickenham!

L. a L.

Ludwig Wittgenstein to Ben Richards, June 25, 1949

25.6. ℅ von Wright[350]
"Strathaird"
Lady Mgt. Rd.
Cambridge

Dear Ben,

I'm extremely tired & so can't write much. I think of you constantly. <u>May God protect you!</u>

---

348 This was a Leporello postcard, namely one that had a flap on the front which could be lifted to reveal a 'concertina' of 11 attached photographs – each of different sites in Dublin – which could be unfolded.

349 The previous day Wittgenstein had written to Norman Malcolm: "I've got good news: I've improved greatly during the last few days. So, obviously, the iron & liverextract do work" (Wittgenstein to Malcolm, June 14, 1949).

350 Wittgenstein likely arrived in Cambridge around June 20 or 21, and stayed for about 10 to 12 days with Georg Henrik von Wright and his family (see Wittgenstein's letter to Rush Rhees of June 11, 1949).

You know how much I want to ~~meet~~ be with you in July & how much I need it, & what it would mean to me if it turned out to be impossible. So hope with me & help me when I come to Ickenham.[351]

I love you <u>always</u>
Ludwig

P.T.O.

I'm sorry I didn't send you a birthday card sooner.[352] Please forgive me.

L. L.

Enclosure included with the letter of June 25, 1949:

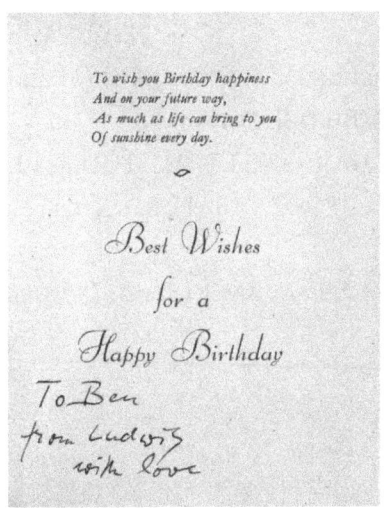

Greetings

To wish you Birthday happiness
And on your future way,
As much as life can bring to you
Of sunshine every day.

---

351 Wittgenstein was nervous about spending time in the Richards family home – his relationship with Ben Richards' parents was sometimes sensitive, and he found the small-talk of family life difficult to tolerate. And this was to be a rather long visit, as he was planning to arrive in Ickenham near the beginning of July and to stay through till he left for America on July 21. A couple of weeks earlier he had written to Rush Rhees about his plans, also expressing his concern: "then to Uxbridge (Richards) until July 21st when I sail on the Queen Mary ... whether I'll be able to stand the life at Uxbridge <u>I don't know</u>" (Wittgenstein to Rhees, June 11, 1949).

352 Richards' birthday had been two days earlier, on June 23.

Best Wishes
for a
Happy Birthday

To Ben
from Ludwig
with love

Ludwig Wittgenstein to Ben Richards, Telegram, June 30, 1949
POST OFFICE
TELEGRAM

Prefix.　Time handed in.　Office of Origin and Service Instructions.　Words.
159 11.50 CAMBRIDGE D 15 *
BENEDICT RICHARDS MEDICAL STUDENT HILLEND HOSPITAL STALBANS =
ARRIVING LIVERPOOL ST SATURDAY 2.40 PM LOVE = LUDWIG ++ 2.40 +

Ludwig Wittgenstein to Ben Richards (postmarked: July 8, 1949)

Strathaird[353]
Lady Mgt Rd.
Cambr.
Friday

Dearest Ben,

I shall arrive at Liverpool Street at 6.43p.m. on Tuesday. I'm not quite shure if it's 6.43 or 6.45, but it doesn't matter. I'm looking forward to seeing you, & I wish you lots of luck & as little worry as possible.

God bless you.
With love, as
always,
Ludwig

P.S. If you can't meet me at the station & know it beforehand, send me a wire. If you ~~can come~~ /don't/ wire I'll assume you'll come & wait for you in the waiting room for a bit. I think of you constantly. L. L.

---

[353] This was the von Wright house (see Wittgenstein's letter to Richards of June 25, 1949, and the relevant footnote there). It's not clear what Wittgenstein was doing back at the von Wrights in Cambridge, since he had moved into the Richards house in Ickenham, five or six days prior to this date. Perhaps this was a brief visit back to Cambridge.

Ben Richards to Ludwig Wittgenstein (undated, mid-July 1949)[354]

King's College[355]
Cambridge

Dear Ludwig

I shall be here until Saturday, so don't write to Hill End[356]. I am taking my driving test on Wednesday week and shall have to practice driving during week-end. My grandmother is coming next Monday and so there will be plenty of room for you until Monday. Jinny & Tazza will be home but they will go to bed quite early.

I hope you are much better. Let me know how you are, and if you are coming. I am looking forward to seeing you.

My papers were to-day, not too bad. I did the surgery worse than the midwifery. The vivas end on Saturday. The conjoint starts about the 28th[357] – I haven't heard the details yet.

Love always
Ben

P.S. Thanks for the lovely card[358].

---

[354] Richards did not date this letter, but a rough date can be tentatively inferred from the content. The fact that Richards mentions Hill End (where he worked from December 1948 until the summer of 1949), and the upcoming conjoint exam (which generally took place in the summer), places this in the summer of 1949. As to the specific date, in Richards' letter to Wittgenstein of July 26, 1949, he says that his driving test is the next day – which would have been Wednesday July 27. Assuming that he is referring to that test in this letter, that would place this letter (given the phrase 'Wednesday week', and not 'tomorrow week') between Thursday July 14 and Monday July 18.

[355] This had been Richards' Cambridge college, and seems to have been where he took his Final M.B. exams in the ensuing years (see also, for example, Richards' letter to Wittgenstein of December 12, 1950).

[356] Namely, the hospital Richards was working at, in St. Albans.

[357] The 'Conjoint' exam was the basic qualification for medical students in the United Kingdom at the time, consisting of a series of sub-examinations on anatomy, physiology, pharmacology, pathology, and the like.

[358] This may have been a 'Good Luck' card which Wittgenstein sent Richards for his exams, which has not been preserved.

III. With the Malcolms in Ithaca, NY
(July – October 1949)

In May 1949, despite his poor health, Wittgenstein decided to accept the long-standing invitation from his friend and old student Norman Malcolm to stay with him and his family in their home in Ithaca, in upstate New York.[1] So, on July 20, 1949, Wittgenstein boarded the *Queen Mary* in Southampton, with the intention of staying for a few months. Norman Malcolm was a member of the philosophy faculty at Cornell University, and Wittgenstein spent much of his time during his stay in philosophical discussion with Malcolm and various of his colleagues and students, including Oets K. Bouwsma (who was at Cornell as a visiting lecturer that semester, especially so as to meet Wittgenstein), Max Black, Stuart Brown, Willis Doney, John Nelson, and Wolfgang Fuchs (sometimes individually, and sometimes in groups). With Bouwsma in particular, he also took long walks in nature while discussing all manner of philosophical, ethical, religious, and cultural matters.[2] Indeed, Wittgenstein was as fascinated by the local flora and fauna as by the philosophical conversation, and also by the various manifestations of American popular culture.

The first month and half of Wittgenstein's stay in Ithaca coincided with Richards' summer holiday with his family, in Ventimiglia, Italy. This caused significant delay in the arrival of some of his letters – and the long periods with no word from Richards worried Wittgenstein greatly.

Once the fall semester began, Wittgenstein even took part in some of Cornell's regular philosophical meetings. He attended a meeting of the graduate and faculty Philosophy Club, where he responded to a paper by Gregory Vlastos. Indeed, Wittgenstein's appearance caused something of a sensation, as John Nelson – one of graduate students who was present – recalled:

---

1 For a detailed account of Wittgenstein's trip to America – and for general background to the events of this chapter – see Pinch & Swedberg 2013.
2 Bouwsma jotted down notes of these conversations (see Bouwsma 1986: 3–42).

> "Vlastos was introduced and gave his paper and finished. Black, who was conducting this particular meeting, stood up and turned to his right and it became clear to everyone's surprise (I mean, the graduate students' surprise) that he was about to address the shabby older man Malcolm had brought to the meeting. Then came the startling words; said Black, 'I wonder if you would be so kind, Professor Wittgenstein' [...] Well, when Black said 'Wittgenstein' a loud and instantaneous gasp went up from the assembled students. You must remember: 'Wittgenstein' was a mysterious and awesome name in the philosophy world of 1949, at Cornell in particular. The gasp that went up was just the gasp that would have gone up if Black had said, 'I wonder if you would be so kind, Plato.'"[3]

Over the following weeks Wittgenstein also led two further discussions with the Cornell philosophy graduate students (running them rather like his 'at homes' at Cambridge: waiting for one of the assembled students to suggest a topic or a question, and then running with it).[4] Towards the end of August 1949, however, Wittgenstein's health had started to deteriorate. In particular, he suffered from pain in his right shoulder. Then, in September he caught the flu, and from that point on he started to feel very weak, and got progressively weaker as the weeks passed. As a result of all this, Wittgenstein went to see a Dr. Louise C. Mooney, whose examination of him impressed him very positively. She sent him for various tests, and it was discovered that his thyroid wasn't working as it should, so she instructed him to take liver, iron, and thyroid extract. But – as with Dr Synge in Dublin before her – she could not find the cause of Wittgenstein's persistent anaemia. In retrospect, Wittgenstein considered it to be a blessing that she had not found the cause of the problem while he was in America. Malcolm recalled:

> "On the day before he went to the hospital he was not only ill, but also frightened. He had told me previously that his father died of cancer and, in addition, his favourite sister was gradually dying of the same disease, despite several operations. Wittgenstein's fear was not that he would be found to have cancer (he was quite prepared for that) but that he might be kept at the hospital for surgery. His fear of surgery came near to panic. It was not the operation itself he dreaded, but to become a useless and bed-ridden invalid whose death had only been deferred for a little. He was also very afraid that the doctors might prevent him from making the return passage to England in October, which was already booked. 'I don't want to die in America. I am a European – I want

---

3 John Nelson, quoted in Pinch & Swedberg 2013: 11.
4 See Pinch & Swedberg 2013: 9–14.

to die in Europe,' he murmured to me in a frenzy. And he exclaimed: 'What a fool I was to come.' He returned from the hospital in quite a cheerful frame of mind. The examination had not found anything seriously wrong with him"⁵

Towards the end of September 1949 Wittgenstein considered bringing forward his trip back to England, which he had booked for October 21, but his doctor advised him against it. He was likely too weak to travel at that point. Indeed, it wasn't even clear that he'd be strong enough to travel by the end of October, as Malcolm recalled:

> "I did not see how he could make the trip since he was so extremely weak: but in the two weeks before he sailed he recovered strength in a surprising way."⁶

Those last couple of weeks before his departure were eventful ones. Most significantly, it was in these weeks that Wittgenstein's and Richards' friendship came closest to coming to an end, as a result of Wittgenstein's overbearing reaction to Richards' announcement that he had been growing a beard. In Wittgenstein's final letter to Richards from America he expressed the hope that Richards will come to meet his boat or his train, but Wittgenstein was unsure whether or not – at that point – their friendship had broken irreparably.⁷

On his way from Ithaca to his port of departure in New York, Wittgenstein visited Bouwsma for a couple of days in Northampton, Massachusetts (Bouwsma was then at Smith College). Then in New York he met up with his sister, Margaret Stonborough-Wittgenstein, who was living there at the time.⁸ He departed New York on the *Queen Elizabeth* on October 21, 1949, and arrived in Southampton on October 27 – unsure whether Richards would be there to meet him, and indeed, unsure whether he would ever see Richards again.

---

5   Malcolm 1984: 76–7
6   Malcolm 1984: 77
7   See the Introduction for a fuller discussion of this incident.
8   See Prokop 2003: 256.

Ludwig Wittgenstein to Ben Richards, July 20, 1949[9]

Queen Mary
Southampton
Wednesday

Dearest Ben, O. H. –

I'm on the Queen Mary now in my 'outside' cabin. It has a porthole which is <u>permanently</u> shut. I've been up & down innumerable times innumerable stairs & am very tired now /& incredibly stupid/. I haven't yet seen my cabin-mate. There is a cinema for the 3rd class. The dinner was very good. That's about all the news. Thanks for the wonderful time you gave me.[10] You know how I enjoyed every hour of it. I shall miss you terribly & right now I wish I could see your b. o. f.! I'm thinking of you constantly!

With love always
Ludwig

Ludwig Wittgenstein to Ben Richards (undated, July 25 1949)[11]

Monday
Cunard White Star
R.M.S. "Queen Mary"

Dearest Ben,

We're due in New York to-morrow 6.30 a.m. The journey has been extremely smooth & would have been wonderful if you'd been with me. As it is it was medium. I sent Malcolm a radiogram,[12] saying when I'd arrive & he sent me one, saying that he'd be at

---

9   Richards added '21/7/49' to the letter, which was a Thursday; and since Wittgenstein wrote 'Wednesday' on the letter, Richards was presumably noting the date the letter was received.

10 Wittgenstein had stayed with Richards and his family, in Uxbridge, for the first few weeks of July, until his departure for America (see Wittgenstein's letter to Helene Salzer, July 3, 1949). He had been worried how day-to-day life with Richards' family would go, as he had written to Rush Rhees from Dublin in June: "I intend to leave here on Saturday 18th & fly to London for a few days, then to Cambridge for 10 or 12 days & then to Uxbridge (Richards) until July 21, when I sail on the Queen Mary. Whether I'll be able to dictate at Cambridge & whether I'll be able to stand the life at Uxbridge <u>I don't know</u>" (Wittgenstein to Rhees, June 11, 1949).

11 The date can be derived from the (corrected) date of Wittgenstein's next letter and his comment about having arrived the previous day; and this date is confirmed by the fact that July 25, was a Monday in 1949.

12 A telegram sent via radio.

the dock to meet me. I'm glad because I'd be pretty lost alone in New York:[13] I think I can't get a train to Ithaca[14] before to-morrow midnight. – I met a lady in the train to Southampton who was rather nice & helped me pass the time by walking up & down with me on deck. – I'm thinking of you all the time & I feel good whenever I remember how wonderful you've been with me. I hope you will have a good time in Italy & that you'll be well & happy. God bless you. I shall miss you a great, great deal! Please think of me. With love, <u>always</u>

Ludwig

P.S.: Please tell Dr Lake to send me the report & perhaps some advice about my right shoulder. – The Mozart Adagio & Fuge[15] is constantly in my minds ear. I hope you had a good talk with Miss Anscombe. Give my good wishes to everyone who might like to get them. –

L. L.

Ben Richards to Ludwig Wittgenstein, July 26, 1949

Greenoge
40 Swakeleys Road
Ickenham
Uxbridge.
July 26th 1949

Dear Ludwig

As you know I had a wonderful time when you were here. Thanks for coming! And thanks for your note from Southampton.[16] I am glad there is a cinema for you. Do they show a different film every day? I hope you had a good crossing and weren't ill, and had a nice cabin mate.

---

13 Wittgenstein had written to Norman Malcolm in early June: "I'm getting a ticket from New York to Ithaca here, so it isn't necessary that one of you should come & fetch me, but if it could be done without difficulty I'd be very glad if you, or Lee did come to meet me at New York as I'm such a complete stranger & exceedingly clumsy these days" (Wittgenstein to Malcolm, June 4, 1949). A few days later he sent a follow-up letter adding that he hadn't realized how long the trip was from Ithaca to New York City, and that he was now feeling a lot better, so that there would be no need to come to meet him (Wittgenstein to Malcolm, June 14, 1949). In the end, Malcolm was waiting for him directly at the dock in New York City (see Malcom 2001: 68).
14 This was Wittgenstein's destination, where Norman Malcolm lived.
15 Wolfgang Amadeus Mozart's Adagio and Fugue in C minor (KV 546). Shortly before his departure for America Wittgenstein had sent two packages of gramophone records of music by Haydn and Mozart to his sister Helene. Of the Mozart he wrote: "I wanted to send you the Mozart Adagio & Fugue of which there was a very fine performance under Busch. But it is no longer in print; instead there is a performance by Karajan with all the characteristic abominable mistakes" (Wittgenstein to Salzer, July 17, 1949). Clearly he had been listening to – or at least contemplating – the recordings that he had bought for Helene.
16 Wittgenstein's letter of July 20, 1949.

On Monday we start our holiday, and my address will be

> Villa Olivier
> la Mortola
> Ventimiglia
> ITALY,

I had my anti-typhoid injection on Friday and that night was the worst. I stayed in bed all Saturday and got up on Sunday. My arm was tender for three days, but is all right now. My mother gave herself an injection on Saturday evening and had recovered by Monday. I drove up to town again to-day and my driving test is to-morrow. It has been extremely hot here the last few days.

After you had gone I met Miss Anscombe and we talked until she had to go back, which I enjoyed very much.

> I miss you.
> love always, Ben.

Ludwig Wittgenstein to Ben Richards, July 27, 1949

> 1107 Hanshaw Rd.
> Ithaca N.Y.
> U.S.A.
> Wednesday 25th? 7.49.[17]

Dearest Ben, d. H. –

We got to New York yesterday at 6.30 a.m. The customs examination took a long time. At 11 a.m. I was through & found Malcolm[18] waiting for me at the dock. We travelled back partly by train; first (in an <u>excellent</u> train) 6 hours to a place called Syracuse, & there a friend of Malcolm's[19] waited for us in a car & drove us 50 miles back to this

---

17 Given the content, Wittgenstein must have written this letter two days after his previous one, so 'Wednesday' must be correct. But July 25 was not a Wednesday in 1949. The closest Wednesday was July 27 – which was presumably the date that this was written.

18 Malcom later recalled: "I went to New York to meet Wittgenstein at the ship. When I first saw him I was surprised at his apparent physical vigour. He was striding down the ramp with a pack on his back, a heavy suitcase in one hand, cane in the other. He was in very good spirits and not at all exhausted and he would not allow me to help him with his luggage. My chief recollection of the long train ride home is that we talked about music and that he whistled for me, with striking accuracy and expressiveness, some parts of Beethoven's 7th Symphony" (Malcolm (1984: 68).

19 The friend of Malcolm's was Oets K. Bouwsma (1898–1978), who wrote in his diary a few days later: "On Tuesday of this week we drove to Syracuse to meet Norman Malcolm and Wittgenstein who had just arrived from Europe. After all the stories about him he struck me as a very attractive man with an easy and a friendly manner" (Bouwsma 1986: 3). Bouwsma and Wittgenstein were to become close friends over the course of Wittgenstein's stay in Ithaca and to stay in touch for the rest of Wittgenstein's life.

place. It was & is incredibly hot. I have an electric fan blowing at me in my room the whole time. Without that I don't think I could stand the temperature. But it quite obviously does my shoulders good, as you may notice from my hand writing. The shoulder hurts much less & is less stiff. – The people are enormously kind to me & the atmosphere most friendly. – I think of you constantly & wish I could have you here! I posted a letter to you yesterday[20] which I'd written on the boat. I wonder whether it'll reach you, because I posted it in a queer kind of machine at Grand Central Station just before leaving. The machine is supposed to stamp the letters & it almost tore it out of my hand, & I wonder what it did with the letter. – I hope to have discussions here & to start working again even if it's only in a mediocre way. – I miss you. Thanks for having been so <u>wonderful</u> to me at Ickenham & Witering.[21] God bless you!

    Always with love

        Ludwig

Ludwig Wittgenstein to Ben Richards, August 2, 1949

1107 Hanshaw Rd.
Ithaca, N.Y.
2.8.49.

Dearest Ben,

I'm afraid it'll take a long time for this to reach you. I think of you & miss you an awful lot. Nothing I do, or look at, is as enjoyable as when you're with me. I'm doing some philosophy again, but I'm not working really well & sometimes I feel disgusted with my work /& with philosophy/ altogether. I sometimes talk philosophy with Malcolm,[22] but our talks, so far, aren't really deep enough. The weather's very queer: fearfully hot during the day & cold at night. We had <u>98° F</u>[23] the other day. – I've been reading a newish book by T. S. Eliot "Notes towards the Definition of Culture"[24] which I find weak & bad, though of course it contains some good remarks. Do you know

---

20 Wittgenstein's letter dated Monday July 2, 1949.
21 Wittgenstein meant 'Wittering' (a town near Peterborough, about 90 miles – or 150 km – north of Ickenham).
22 Over the course of his stay Wittgenstein had many philosophical discussions with Malcolm and with Bouwsma (and sometimes larger discussions involving others as well – such as Max Black, Willis Doney, John Nelson, and Stuart Brown). For accounts of the content of many of these conversations see Malcolm 2001: 70–5; Bouwsma 1986: 3–51, and Monk 1990: 552–58.
23 Fahrenheit, approximately 35.5° C.
24 T.S. Eliot, *Notes towards the Definition of Culture*, London, Faber and Faber, 1948.

it? – I hope you're having a good time & finding something worth while to do. I wish I could see you! G. bl. y..

With love, always
Ludwig

P.S. Thanks for your letter of 26th. All the films on the boat were bad & I didn't go to a single one. L. L.

P.P.S. Did you pass the driving test? If I'd been your examiner you would have.

Ben Richards to Ludwig Wittgenstein, August 5, 1949

Villa Olivier
la Mortola
near Ventimiglia
Italy
Friday August 5th

Dear Ludwig

Thank you very much for your letters: they both arrived safely including the one you put into a machine.[25] I am glad your shoulder is better. My father said that the x-ray report said there was no evidence of arthritis;[26] and that therefore the shoulder would probably be benefitted by treatment: "physiotherapy" & exercises under the supervision or instructions of someone trained in it. He said he was writing to you.

We arrived last night – my father, Angela, Tazza[27] & I – in the car. My mother, Virginia and Heshe[28] had arrived the day before by train. We started on Monday and crossed by the night ferry boat from Dover to Dunkerque, and spent three nights on the way at Troyes, Macon & Avignon. It poured with heavy rain all Tuesday and we stayed at a very nice hotel in Troyes, /Hotel Paris/ where the proprietress was very friendly. The other hotels were not so friendly, but still had a much pleasanter atmosphere than most English hotels. Wednesday was mainly fine and yesterday (Thursday) was very hot. Avignon was very full, including a lot of tourists and we only got into the third hotel we tried. It is an extraordinary place. I should have liked it

---

25 See Wittgenstein's letter to Richards of July 27, 1949.
26 Richards' father – William Arthur Richards (1895–1962) – was a general practitioner.
27 The oldest and the second youngest of Richards' four younger sisters.
28 The second oldest and the youngest of Richards' four younger sisters.

better if it had been less like an exhibit. The Palais des Papes was floodlit! The customs were all very easy – the only time we had to take any bags off the car was at the Italian customs, and then they were not opened.

It is v<u>er</u>y hot here of course, but I have a quiet room, not too hot, which gets only the morning sun. I have brought some books on medicine and think I shall be able to work all right.

I hope you are able to work too. I think of you constantly and hope to hear from you again.

Love, Ben.

Ludwig Wittgenstein to Ben Richards, August 9, 1949

1107 Hanshaw Rd.
Ithaca N.Y. U.S.A.
9.8.49

Dearest Ben,

The heat here is still <u>terrible</u>. The best place in the house is the cellar. We had a discussion there yesterday & we couldn't possibly have had it anywhere else. I can only sleep if I have the fan playing on me all the night. However in the morning the temperature is <u>tolerable</u> (pronounce terrible) & I can work in my room. So far I work very little. I saw a hummingbird the other day & a 'praying mantis' yesterday in the garden & there are all sorts of birds here that I haven't seen in Europe, but nobody in the house seems to know them either.

Dear Ben, I think of you a <u>lot</u> & I long to see you again. Please write me regularly! I need it. I <u>hope</u> you're well & in good spirits. G. bl. y!

With <u>love</u>
Ludwig

P.S: I enclose a spruce twig but I wonder if it'll reach you in moderately good condition. I hope to enclose something nicer the next time. L. <u>a.</u> L.

P.P.S. When I wanted to enclose the spruce twig all the needles came off! So all is left is the good intention. L. L.

Ben Richards to Ludwig Wittgenstein (undated, presumably August 14, 1949)[29]

Villa Olivier
la Mortola
near Ventimiglia
Italy

Dear Ludwig

Thanks for your letter. I hope your work will go better, and the temperature improves. It is not too hot here. My room is on the south-east corner of the house. In the day I close the shutters on the south window, which keeps out the sun but lets in the air, and open them on the east window letting in the light, and I can work well. It is very quiet & I have been reading medicine. After dusk the mosquitoes are very troublesome and if any windows are open they come into the lighted rooms. Most of the windows have a layer of fine wire netting which can be closed and ~~lets~~ keeps them out. There is a little gecko who lives above one of the dining-room windows and in the evening catches the moths as they flutter against the outside of the wire gauze. It is like a greyish lizard /with a pale belly/ 5 or 6 inches long with squarish head and suckers on all its toes and, I think, a long sticky tongue. A few evenings ago we were at a restaurant a little way up the main road on a sort of lighted open balcony looking over the sea, and there were over a dozen of these gecki /or geckos/ on the ceiling upside down.

The blue flowers, of which I enclose one, like convolvulus are a wonderful colour early in the morning – like gentians up in the alps, but by midday they have withered to a palish pink, and a new lot come out next day.

I also enclose a leaf from a eucalyptus tree and one from a lemon tree. The lemons are just about ripe now. If you crush the leaves, they smell very nice. I wonder if they will still do so when they reach you.

We are all very well and mostly getting pretty brown. I am enjoying my holiday, but I miss you a lot.

---

29 This letter took more than two weeks to arrive because Richards had not used the right postage. We know from Wittgenstein's response – in his letter to Richards of September 3, 1949 – that it was postmarked August 14, 1949, so it was likely written that day too.

I have heard of that book of Eliott's but I don't know it. Did I forget to tell you I just passed the driving test this time, though the examiner wasn't very enthusiastic, and I took turns with my father driving through France.

My mother sends you her good wishes

I am looking forward to your next letter.

    Love always,

        Ben.

Ludwig Wittgenstein to Ben Richards, August 15, 1949

1107 Hanshaw Rd.

Ithaca N.Y.

15.8.49

Dear Ben, d. o. H. –

I was glad when I saw the envelope with Italian stamps which was pushed under my door this morning. Your letter took a frightfully long time, <u>10</u> days by air mail. Perhaps it would be better to write "Par Avion" instead of "Per Via Aerea".[30] The Ventimiglia post stamp said "8. 8. 49". – I'm sure Avignion would be interesting if it weren't for the tourists. – My mind seems to be improving. I can think much better now than in the last 5 months though not nearly as well as between last October & March.[31] Still I can work again if the heat isn't <u>too</u> awful. It reached 96°[32] again a few days ago. – A few nights ago I woke up about 3 a.m. with a hiccup as violently as I've never had it before in my life & only once heard it in someone who had an abdominal operation. It shook me every time & made such a noise that Malcolm, who sleeps on the floor below me, woke up (the doors into the hall were open) & came up to see what was the matter. He told me to hold my breath & drink some cold water while doing so. That stopped it. – There are nice woods a few minutes walk from the house & a great variety of trees.[33] A large part of one of the woods consists of sumach trees

---

30 French and then Italian: 'By Air'.

31 This was roughly the period in which he had been living in Kilpatrick House, in Ireland. In December Wittgenstein had reported excitedly to Drury that "Sometimes my ideas come so quickly that I feel as if my pen was being guided" (Drury 1984: 153). And at the end of January he wrote to Norman Malcolm, saying: "I had a pretty good run of work in the last 3 months" (Wittgenstein to Malcolm, January 28, 1949).

32 Fahrenheit, approximately 35.5° C.

33 Malcolm later recalled Wittgenstein's walks in these woods: "He loved to go for walks in some nearby woods, with either my wife or myself. His stamina was surprising. On those walks he took a great interest in identifying the kinds of trees" (Malcolm 1984: 68).

(I enclose a leaf) I'd only seen a few specimens before in England & didn't know that there were whole woods of them. – I hope you have a very pleasant time & that you'll be able to work quietly. G. bl. y. I think of you <u>always.</u> With <u>love</u>. Ludwig

P.S. The leaf I enclose comes from a tulip tree.[34] – L. y. t. . . . bly.[35]

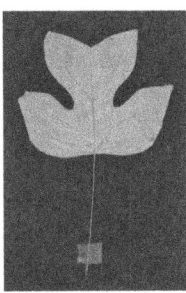

Ben Richards to Ludwig Wittgenstein, August 21, 1949

Villa Olivier
La Mortola
near Ventimiglia
Italy
21st August 1949

Dear Ludwig,

thanks for the letter with the spruce needles. I am sorry the heat is terrible – I hope it is improving now. Here it is much cooler than when we first came. There have been a couple of storms here – quite mild by English standards but apparently severe here for the time of year – and they have altered our little beach below the railway rather. ~~When~~ It is stony with a layer of dead flakes of seaweed along the top of the stones, and when we came there was sand underwater to within about 6 yards of the shore; now it is about 20 yards out and a lot more dead seaweed has been washed up into a sort of little cliff at the edge of the water and near the edge the water is now full of these little brown flakes (I enclose one) which tend to stick to one. The water is always warm enough to bathe without feeling any discomfort on first going in, and one can stay in as long as one likes without getting chilly although there is less sunshine now. There have only been a few drops of rain since we came, and there is ~~quite~~ a drought.

---

34 O.K. Bouwsma wrote about Wittgenstein's particular interest in the tulip trees just a couple of days later in his diary: "This afternoon W. and I rode out to Taughannock and took the path down the gorge to the falls. W. noticed the leaves again of the tulip tree. He had noticed them before with Norman on Tuesday, and sought out the tree after finding a leaf" (Bouwsma 1986: 25–6).

35 Stands for: 'Love you terribly'.

Practically no-one comes to the beach except three Italian families who live here and with whom we have made friends. There was an American and an Australian on holiday from Heidelberg who were very nice but have now gone away. This is not a very popular place for visitors, in fact as soon as one crosses the frontier from Mentone to Grimaldi it is noticeably very much more quiet and peaceful, though of course the main road is very busy.

We live on a steep hillside which goes straight down to the sea and is very intensely cultivated high up into the hills in little terraces growing vines, vegetables & flowers. Where not cultivated the hillside is covered mainly by dry grass and olive trees (I enclose /two/ leafs).

My work is going quite well. My mother has had a bit of a cold and an anti-typhoid injection: otherwise we are all very well.

Love always, Ben

P.S. I also enclose a bougainvillea from beside our front door.

Ludwig Wittgenstein to Ben Richards, August 25, 1949

1107 Hanshaw Rd.
Ithaca N.Y.
25.8.49

Dearest Ben,

I haven't heard from you for a long, long time. I <u>hope</u> the reason isn't one that will alarm me, or make me sad when I hear it. I <u>hope</u> you're well, that you've had a good holiday, that you still think of me just as before, & that I'll hear from you <u>very</u> soon. – I think a little better now than a week or two ago, & <u>perhaps</u> I could work still better if I slept better & felt better. My arms are as painful as they were, in fact I think they're getting gradually worse. I don't know what to do about them.[36] (By the way, I haven't heard from your father.) – The weather here is nice now, not quite so hot, & sometimes in the mornings even <u>cold</u>! It's a queer climate.

I'm going for nice walks in the woods around here. Please write to me soon & regularly /if there isn't a very strong reason for not doing/! I think of you a terrible lot as always. God bless you!

With love a. a.
Ludwig

---

36 Two days earlier Wittgenstein had written to his friend Rudolf Koder: "I'm not feeling very well, either physically or mentally. A doctor here, whom I consulted, believes that the pain in my arms is nerve pain & may be due to an infection from a festering tooth. For various reasons, however, it is not easy for me to have the matter thoroughly examined & treated here. I will have to be patient for a while yet" (Wittgenstein to Koder, August 23, 1949).

Ludwig Wittgenstein to Ben Richards, August 27, 1949

1107 Hanshaw Rd.
Ithaca N.Y.
27.8.49

Dear Ben, o. h.,

I wrote to you 2–3 days ago to Ickenham, complaining about your long silence. To-day I had your letter from Italy of Aug. 25.[37] I liked to hear about your life, & I liked bougainvillea & the leaves, & I'm glad that you're well & that your not writing apparently had no serious cause. Yet it makes me sad to think that you didn't write to me for more than a fortnight. If it is the beginning of a change, please remember what I've <u>often</u> told you about that!

Here, after a few cooler days, it's again terribly hot. I feel pretty lousy now, on the whole, though sometimes I feel o.k..

I don't want to write more to-day because I'm not in the right state of mind.

I think of you & love you as always Ludwig

P.S. There are no nice flowers around here. If there were any I'd enclose them.

L. L.

Ben Richards to Ludwig Wittgenstein (postmarked: August 29, 1949)

Dear Ludwig,

Thanks for your letter and the tulip tree leaf. Did we see one in the Dublin botanical gardens? I remember trying to draw you one once. The leaf you sent me is a lovely colour: a delicate green with deep golden red/-dish-brown/-veins.

I am very sorry you had such bad hiccups: it must have been extremely unpleasant. I hope you don't get them any more.

Last night we all went to see a firework displayed in Ventimiglia. We watched them from the road on the hill going down into Ventimiglia and had a very good view.

They were mostly rockets of different kinds and some sort of catherine wheels which went up in the air. I enjoyed it. It must be a long time since I saw /good/ fireworks in England.

I have been working every day and have been through most of the diseases of the abdomen. My room is quiet and I am not disturbed and I can work very well. It is not

---

37 Wittgenstein seems to be referring to Richards' letter of August 21 (rather than 25), 1949.

at all too hot now, though this morning was the hottest for quite a time (two weeks or so). There has been a little rain lately, but there is still quite a drought and we are rather short of water: our rainwater tank is getting low and we have to use it carefully.
        Love, Ben.
P.S. The oleander flower enclosed grew opposite our front door.

Ben Richards to Ludwig Wittgenstein, September 2, 1949

Villa Olivier
la Mortola
near Ventimiglia
Italy
Friday September 2nd
1949

Dear Ludwig
Thanks for your letter. I am sorry you did not hear from me for a fortnight. I have written regularly every week, so one of my letters must have got held up in the post. I hope it reaches you safely in the end. I wonder if it was the one with lemon & eucalyptus leaves – you never mentioned getting them. I am well. I had the other anti typhoid injection on Sunday which gave me a fever for about a day and a painful arm for several days. I cut myself on a sharp rock bathing.
My work is going very well. I hope yours is possible.
How are the Malcolms? I hope they and you are very well.
Virginia[38] has gone for a few days with her cousin Lois to Padua & Venice. Lois's brother Laurence is staying here, and ~~last night~~ /yesterday evening/ two more cousins: Andy, Phillip and his wife arrived. Angela's friend Tiggy is here and we have had a lot of passing visitors & cousins.
I hope to go for a sail this afternoon.
I hope you got my last letter with an oleander flower. I put "par avion" etc. on it to make sure.[39]
I enclose another bouganvillea in flower. The purple things are only modified leaves called "bracts".
I long to hear from you again.
Love <u>always</u>, Ben

---

38 The second oldest of Richards' four younger sisters.
39 See Wittgenstein's letter of August 15, 1949.

Ludwig Wittgenstein to Ben Richards, September 3, 1949

1107 Hanshaw Rd.
Ithaca N.Y.
3.9.49

Dearest Ben,

To-day I received a long & lovely letter from you with several nice enclosures /Thanks!/. The letter wasn't dated but the postmark on the envelope read 14.8.49 & there was a stamp saying "Affrancature insufficienta per Via Aerea",[40] which explains the <u>terrible</u> delay! I wasn't only glad to get your letter but also that you hadn't neglected writing to me as I was afraid you had. Please forgive me for worrying you! The lemon leaf had lost it's aroma when it reached me, it was completely dry; the big flower looked purple, the eucalyptus leaf seemed to have a very slight medicinal smell, but that may be only my imagination. – I've had a rather bad time lately, my arm hurt day & night & I felt lousy. Yesterday I decided to go to a different doctor[41] who had been greatly recommended to me. I saw her (the doctor) this morning & feel a bit more hopeful now. She gave me an excellent impression. She examined my arm carefully (far more carefully than Dr Lake) & told me that what I had was a bursitis of the shoulder joint. She wants me to take X-ray treatment & gave me tablets for the pain. What makes me trust her is that, after I had told her some things, she immediately very correctly guessed other symptoms, also the businesslike way she

---

40 Italian: 'Insufficient postage for airmail'.
41 This was Louise C. Mooney who had been appointed resident physician at the Cornell University Infirmary and Clinic in 1942 (see *Cornell Alumni News* 1942: 64a). Wittgenstein came to like her so much that in a letter to Malcolm – from the end of 1949, by which time he was back in England – he included her in the group of friends to whom he asked Malcom to send regards: "Give my love to Lee & to Dr Mooney & to Doney & Bouwsma" (Wittgenstein to Malcolm, December 11, 1949).

examined my shoulder. E.g. she moved my arm in various painful positions & guessed precisely at which points the pain was. So I feel more hopeful now than I did the last fortnight, or so when I felt very low indeed.[42] I'm afraid there are no flowers which I can send you. I don't think I've ever been anywhere where there were so few flowers as here, but there are lots of beautiful trees, but these I can't enclose. Instead I enclose something[43] which I want you to read very carefully.

I hope you're still well, & still think of me as always! G. bl. y.

I miss you!

With love always

   Ludwig

P.S. I'm working when I don't feel too bad but my work isn't really any good. I wonder if it ever again will be. I was glad to hear you could work well. I can very clearly imagine one of those nice corner rooms in Italy & also in some parts of Austria, with shutters which are such a blessing. I wish I had them here /I know that one can work well in such rooms/.

Give my kind regards to your parents.

   L. a. L.

Ludwig Wittgenstein to Ben Richards, September 12, 1949

   1107 Hanshaw Rd

   12.9.49.

Dearest Ben, d. h. –

I had your letter with the bougainvillea yesterday.[44] The letter you mention with an oleander flower hasn't yet come. Probably you didn't put enough stamps on it. I wrote you my last letter to Ickenham because I thought that you'd certainly returned by

---

42 Wittgenstein's depressed moods were prompted jointly by his physical condition, his worries for his mental health, and his worries about his life more broadly. He seemed so down at points that Malcolm (perhaps with some over-reaction) worried for Wittgenstein's safety: "More than once Wittgenstein said to me that it was a problem for him as to what to do with the remainder of his life. 'When a person has only one thing in the world – namely, a certain talent what is he to do when he begins to lose that talent?' he asked. Wittgenstein spoke so earnestly and sombrely that I, knowing that three of his brothers had committed suicide, feared that he might attempt the same" (Malcolm 1984: 76).

43 Whatever Wittgenstein enclosed has not survived with the letter.

44 Richards' letter of September 2, 1949.

now. – I'm afraid I am a bit ill with some kind of flu which I contracted 2–3 days ago. I'm very weak[45] & so I only want to say that I think of you constantly with love. Thanks for writing to me!!! God bless you.

  With love, always
     Ludwig

Ben Richards to Ludwig Wittgenstein (postmarked: September 13, 1949)

                Villa Olivier
                 la Mortola
                near Ventimiglia
                   Italy

Dear Ludwig

I haven't heard from you this week. I hope you are well and the weather is cooler. It was extremely hot here at the beginning of the month, about 38°C, I believe a record for September weather in Italy. Now it is cooler; still fine, but windy.

We are ~~going~~ /leaving for/ home in three days, so write next time to Ickenham. I have enjoyed myself very much, but I missed you terribly.

I enclose some wild thyme I picked on a walk up to the top of a hill yesterday; and also a leaf and some berries of what I am told is a pepper tree (I don't ~~know~~ think this is what table pepper is /usually/ made of).

We have made friends with several Italian people, who have been very kind and friendly; and I have learnt a little Italian and had some slow & laborious conversations; but most of our Italian friends can speak English and so I have not had a lot of practice.

I think of you constantly,

with love, Ben.

P. S. I hope my letters have been arriving safely. I hope to get one from you soon.
         l. a. B.

---

45 The day before Wittgenstein wrote this letter, Malcolm had described Wittgenstein's condition in a letter to G. E. Moore: "I regret to say that Wittgenstein's health is very bad. When he came he was pretty vigorous, although he had severe pain in his shoulders. As the weeks passed that pain seemed to increase and he grew weaker. He has been to one doctor and then another. During the past week he became really ill and was in bed most of the time. He suffered from dreadful chills and from extreme weakness and dizziness. Today he is stronger, and he even sat outdoors for a few minutes. He has confidence in the second doctor, who is female. She has sent him to a radiologist to have his shoulders treated by X-rays" (Moore & Malcolm 2001/2: 272–3).

Ludwig Wittgenstein to Ben Richards, September 16, 1949

1107 Hanshaw Rd.
Ithaca
16.9.49

Dearest Ben, d. h.,

This will again be a very short letter, because I'm still very weak, but I'm much better. I've got a ~~pretty~~ /very/ good doctor. 2–3 days ago I got your letter with the oleander blossom.[46] You see, the post is much more particular about <u>how much</u> you post on the letter than on how you arrange the stamps. They're necessary & have no aesthetic sense! Please, o. h., put the right stamps on your letter or they'll go by ordinary mail instead of by air. Thanks for the letter & the flower. I think of you constantly & I hope I'll soon be able to write you better letters. Please write when you plan to go back to England. I was very glad to hear that you can work well. It's so terribly important. Thinking of you is the only thing that makes me feel really good. God bless you.

       With love always
       Ludwig

I l. y. <u>a.</u>![47]

P.S. The other day I read in a story "I'll be a cross-eyed monkey's uncle", which is good.[48]

L. L.

---

46 Richards' letter of August 29, 1949.
47 Stands for: 'I love you <u>always!</u>'
48 An augmentation of the more standard expression of amazement or disbelief: '(Well,) I'll be a monkey's uncle!' – a slang phrase that seems to have originated in America in the early 1900s – which Wittgenstein probably found in one of the detective story magazines he read. He had a particular fondness for American slang.

Ben Richards to Ludwig Wittgenstein, September 20, 1949

GREENOGE
40, SWAKELEYS ROAD
ICKENHAM
UXBRIDGE
RUISLIP 2114
20/9/49

Dear Ludwig

We arrived here safely late last night, after a very smooth crossing from Boulogne to Dover, during which I sat on deck reading "Murder on the Nile"[49] which I am enjoying. We had driven right cross France in four days – I took turns with my father to drive – and I am quite exhausted after the journey.

Angela and Tazza and Heshe arrived here three days before having travelled by train. Since getting back I have got a bit wheezy and developed a cold which I hope will soon pass.

How are you? I do hope you are not so hot. Here in England it sems quite chilly and damp after Italy. It was a lovely holiday.

On our way back we visited an exhibition in a museum at Antibes of a few paintings and some drawings, china & pottery by Picasso some of which I liked very much: almost everything he does is full of life.

We stopped a night at Arles where there is a beautiful /little/ church, besides some remarkable Roman remains.

I miss you. Please write soon. Thanks for your last letter, which arrived just before I left.

Love always, Ben.

---

49 Agatha Christie, *Death on the Nile (A Poirot Story)*, London, Collins Crime Club, 1937. Wittgenstein had long appreciated Christie's detective writing, as Maurice Drury reported from a conversation in 1936: "Today at lunch the conversation turned to discussing 'detective stories'. Wittgenstein said how much he enjoyed the stories of Agatha Christie. Not only were the plots ingenious but the characters were so well drawn that they were real people. He thought it was a particularly English talent to be able to write books like this" (Drury 1984: 133). See also the continued discussion of the book in Richards' letter to Wittgenstein of September 27, 1949, and in Wittgenstein's reply of October 6, 1949.

Ludwig Wittgenstein to Ben Richards, September 21, 1949

> 1107 Hanshaw Rd
> Ithaca
> 21.9.49

Dearest Ben, d. H.,

Thanks for your letter with the pepper tree twig & the thyme![50] I'm sorry you didn't get my letters regularly. I wrote every week. My last two letters were short & bad & so will this be because I still feel pretty rotten & very, very weak. I can't work, nor even read a detective story with pleasure. Some days I go for short walks, crawling about for half an hour or so. The trees have beautiful colours now & once I found a lovely flower. It ~~was~~ seemed to be a kind of sedum /?/ growing 3 or 4 inches high with small fat leaves & with a blossom the size of a small poppy & exactly the same colour. I picked it & Mrs Malcolm who was with me brought it home, but it was all withered when it got there. If I see another one I'll try to press it for you.

Dearest Ben, if it weren't for your letters I'd be very gloomy now! When I think of you I feel good. Only I wish I could see you. – I have a ticket for the Queen Elisabeth, sailing on October 21st. I wish now I could leave here sooner & I thought of exchanging my ticket for an earlier boat, but my doctor wants me to be patient. She sais I'll soon be well.[51]

I think of you constantly. I love you always.

> Ludwig

Ludwig Wittgenstein to Ben Richards, September 26, 1949

> 1107 Hanshaw Rd
> Ithaca
> 26.9.49

Dearest Ben, d. o. H. –

Thanks for your letter from Ickenham. I hope that this letter finds you in better health! It was wonderful of you to write to me in spite of your asthma. I still feel very weak & my doctor wants me to go to the hospital for a few days to examine me thoroughly. I have no pains only can't sleep & am getting weaker. I think she knows her business &

---

50 Richards' letter of September 13, 1949
51 The next day Wittgenstein wrote to his friend Rudolf Koder: "I feel pretty bad all the time. I don't know what will come of it yet. I have a not bad doctor now & what is possible is happening, so I have hope" (Wittgenstein to Koder, September 22, 1949).

is <u>really</u> interested in getting me well so I trust her. I think you'd like her. I go out for tiny walks & I've pressed the flower I talked to you about & enclose it.

You don't mention the 2 or 3 letters I wrote to you to Ickenham while you were in Italy. Please enquire after them. Have they by any chance been sent to Italy now? One of them contains a beautiful advertisement.[52]

To-day the weather is beautiful not too hot notr too cold, which is rare. I <u>hope</u> you can read this letter. Please get better soon!

I think of you and love you always. G. bl. y.

Love always
Ludwig

Take care of yourself please! L. L.

Ben Richards to Ludwig Wittgenstein, September 27, 1949

St Bart's Hospital
27.9.49

Dear Ludwig

Thank you very much for your two letters, one forwarded from Italy. I am very sorry indeed you have 'flu', and hope it is better. You are having terribly bad luck with your health. I am very glad you have a good doctor. How is your arm now? Have you had an electrical treatment?

The cold I had is better, and I am working at Bart's again now. I am trying to get some coaching for the exam in December, which I think will help me to divide my time in the best way.

It has cheered me up a lot to hear you are coming back at last and I shall see you again. It has been a very long time and it still will be ages before the end of October. I look forward to your letters meanwhile.

I enjoyed "Death on the Nile"[53] but I didn't guess the murderer which I ought to have done.

The family are all well, and Tazza has gone back to school. Virginia goes every day from home still.

Get better quickly and write again.

Love always,
Ben.

---

52 The advert has not been preserved. It was most likely beautiful in the sense of being a perfect specimen of absurdity.

53 See Richards' letter to Wittgenstein of September 20, 1949, and Wittgenstein's reply of October 6, 1949.

Ludwig Wittgenstein to Ben Richards, October 1, 1949

1107 Hanshaw Rd
Ithaca N.Y.
1.10.49.

Dearest Ben, d. o. H,

Thanks for your letter of Sept. 27th. I went to a hospital the beginning of this week for two days to have various disagreeable tests made. I don't know yet all the results but they showed that my blood was rather low again (both red & white cells) & that my thyroid doesn't seem to work sufficiently. So I'm again taking liver & iron & also thyroid extract. The doctor (I think she's very good) can't make out where the anaemia comes from; she says that the lack of Thyroid stuff explains my <u>very</u> great weakness. When I left the hospital I felt pretty awful but to-day I'm much better & I hope I'll get stronger again.[54]

I have a ticket for the Queen Elisabeth sailing on Oct. 21st. I hope to God I'll be strong enough by then to travel. If I'm still <u>very</u> weak then, it would be an enormous help if you could meet me at Southampton. I don't yet know of course whether it'll be necessary, nor whether it is possible for you, nor whether anybody is allowed on the boat-train except passengers. – I'm <u>longing</u> to see you! –

I am taking very short walks & now the trees are beautiful. I'm afraid I can't enclose one in this letter. – I am reading some chapters of "Moby Dick".[55] I don't know if you know it. I like bits of it but not <u>very</u> much.[56] You don't mention the two letters I wrote you to Ickenham when you were in Italy. Didn't you get them? One had a beautiful advertisement in it.[57] –

I think of you <u>constantly</u>! With love always

Ludwig

P.S. Everybody treated me <u>very</u> kindly in the hospital. – G. bl. y! L. L.

---

54 Malcolm later recalled: "He returned from the hospital in quite a cheerful frame of mind. The examination had not found anything seriously wrong with him (although later that autumn he was discovered to have cancer); and there was no longer any threat of his being detained in the hospital or of his departure for England being postponed. I did not see how he could make the trip since he was so extremely weak" (Malcolm 1984: 77).
55 Herman Melville, *Moby-Dick; or, The Whale*, New York, Harper & Brothers, 1851.
56 Wittgenstein read the book again a little over a year later – in February 1951 – and judged it rather more favourably (see his letter to Richards of February 21, 1951).
57 The advert has not been preserved. (Wittgenstein had enquired about this once already, in his letter to Richards of 26, September 1949).

Ludwig Wittgenstein to Ben Richards, October 6, 1949

1107 Hanshaw Rd
Ithaca N.Y.
6.10.49.

Dearest Ben, d. o. H.:

This is a supererogatory letter. I want to tell you that I'm a good deal better. My nights are much better & I try to reduce the amount of sedatives, & I'm getting slowly stronger. I imagine that it's the Thyroid extract that does it. – The weather's cool but not yet cold. I take a walk of about 40 minutes every day. I go along the road, which is quite nice. At one place it mounts a bit & that's hard, but when you've reached the top there is a hedge & part of it consists of <u>grapes</u>, real grapes. They are very sweet & when we pass there we usually steal ~~some~~ /a few/. First I only took one berry & now 3. They are surprisingly good & make me think of our eating them in the conservatory. As you know I plan to sail with the Queen Elizabeth on the 21st. I don't know when it arrives in Southampton. In London I shall probably stay with Mrs. Rhees[58] (104 Goldhurst Terrace). You remember the place. There we could see each other & I could go with you to Ickenham etc. <u>I long to see you & be with you</u>! please let me know if, by any chance, you can come to Southampton. Please find out at the Cunard[59] place when my boat arrives.

I think of you <u>constantly</u> with love.

Ludwig

P.S. If you're much too busy to meet the boat or even the train, I shall understand <u>entirely</u>! Just let me know. I think I'll be strong enough by then to manage my things. Always L.

P.P.S. I too have now read "Death on the Nile" & I liked part of it very much; but I didn't like the ending, it seemed to me completely artificial, & how you, or anyone could have guessed it, & why you say you ought to have guessed it, I can't conceive. I

---

58 Wittgenstein had already written to Jean Rhees – on September 10, 1949 – as follows: "Dear Mrs Rhees, I am sailing on Oct. 21, from New York to Southampton on the Queen Elizabeth. I don't know exactly when she arrives at Southampton but I imagine somewhere about the 27th. I should be very grateful to you if you could put me up then for a few days. – I've been ill, or illish most of the time I spent here & I'm still exceedingly weak. So I'll be rather a nuisance. If you can't put me up, please send me a wire to Southampton. I'm travelling 3rd class. I hope to see you soon. So long!"

59 Cunard was (and is) a major British-American shipping company which owned both the 'Queen Mary' and the 'Queen Elizabeth' on which Wittgenstein made his crossings to and from America, respectively.

know, she tried in the last 2 or 3 pages to make the ending more palatable. Still, a good deal of it is very nice. You see I am a very severe critic.[60]
L. a. L.

I hope you're well!

Ben Richards to Ludwig Wittgenstein, October 9, 1949

Greenoge
40 Swakeleys Road
Ickenham
Uxbridge
9/10/49

Dear Ludwig

Thank you for your letter. I am not sure whether I shall be able to come to Southampton – it depends on the day and time of arrival of the Q.E.[61] – but I hope so. I will make enquiries about that and whether I should be allowed on the boat train. I'm pretty sure I should be.

I am extremely glad you were well looked after in the hospital, and I hope the thyroid will be more effective than the liver & iron alone were, and that you will be quite fit enough to travel.

Angela returned to Oxford on Friday, and Tazza is at school. The rest of the family have gone to Wittering for the week-end to collect some fruit from the garden. I am on my own here at the moment. I am up and about and much better, though I still have a residual cough.

The rest of the family are well.

       Love, always

          Ben.

---

60 In 1947 Wittgenstein had jotted in his notebook what he considered to be the principles of a good ending for a detective story. Total unpredictability counted as a significant flaw: "There must at the dénouement be surprise, and yet the surprise must not be complete. Hence the criminal must not be an outsider of whom we've hardly heard. Nor the detective, unless the detective was made out the sort of man, one might have suspected. Nor the nice young man, or nice young woman to whom during the whole course of the story we wish happiness: On the other hand he must not be the one obvious suspect. These rules are very stringent and leave only a very narrow margin for the writer, as it were a tiny dance floor on which to perform" (MS 167, pp. 8v-9r).

61 Stands for: 'Queen Elizabeth' (the Cunard ship).

Ludwig Wittgenstein to Ben Richards, October 10, 1949

1107 Hanshaw Rd.
Ithaca
10.9.49.[62]

Dearest Ben,

I'm <u>sorry</u> that you have again been wheezy! My health is very slowly improving but I'm still <u>exceedingly</u> weak. You don't write about coming to Southampton; I suppose that means you can't come. – Your P.S. about letting your beard grow was a <u>shock</u> for me, & it's difficult for me to write about it. The best I can say is this: If one <u>loves</u> someone that person's face becomes a <u>symbol</u> which one can't arbitrarily change without hurting the person who has come to love it. If you had an accident which changed your face this would be different, I could then always see your old face in your mutilated one. Or if you had a skin disease that made it impossible for you to shave, again it wouldn't matter. But to let your beard grow <u>without serious reason</u> is a <u>wanton</u> way of playing about with something which, if you love /somebody/, is not quite yours/own/. – As I said, it's difficult for me to write about this because I feel so strongly about it. This is <u>not</u> an aesthetic matter for me. – You know that I have always looked at your face with delight. When I felt bad, & depressed I looked forward to seeing it, & when I saw it I felt good again. I say again: if your face were mutilated by sickness or accident, it wouldn't matter in the slightest. But your face is something <u>sacred</u> to the person who loves you & if you play about with it you <u>play</u> with something that's sacred to me. – I mean every word of this.[63]

---

62 Given that Wittgenstein mentions his imminent arrival in Southampton – and given how this letter fits with the following ones – it is almost certain that the correct date of this letter is *October* 10, and that Wittgenstein mistakenly wrote '9' instead of '10'.

63 Wittgenstein's shock and disapproval seems to be partly a matter of Richards' choice to make a major change to his face of any sort, and partly a matter of Wittgenstein's disapproval of beards specifically. Regarding the former aspect, compare Wittgenstein's letter to his friend and old student, Rowland Hutt, back in 1941: "I wonder what the surprise is you mention in your letter. Is it by any chance a mustache or beard that you've been growing? I hope it isn't. For I don't like people to change their faces; par[t]icularly when they are liable to change their souls!" (Wittgenstein to Hutt, August 20, 1941). This seems related to some of Wittgenstein's philosophical remarks, such as: "The human body is the best picture of the human soul" (Wittgenstein 2009: 187 [PPF:iv:25]), and "The face is the soul of the body" (MS 156a, p. 49r). Indeed, Wittgenstein had already mentioned to Richards how seriously he took friends' faces, in a letter form earlier this same year: "I wouldn't want to possess a nasty photo of my friend! (His face is too serious a matter for me.)" (Wittgenstein to Richards, March 30, 1949). As to Wittgenstein's inherent disapproval of beards (independently of the issue of the change), he mentions this – in a far more playful context and manner – in one of his notes to Richards, written under the pseudonym of the attorney 'John Smith': "Professor Wittgenstein, with Schopenhauer, considers it wrong to have his face surrounded, & partly hidden, by dead matter" (the first 'John Smith' letter from Wittgenstein to Richards in chapter VII, and see the relevant footnote there for references to Schopenhauer's position).

I'm leaving here on Monday, or Wednesday next week & sailing on Thursday.
May God be with you. I love you as always.

Ludwig

This letter is lengthy & not as clear as it ought to be, but I think you can understand it if you read it more than once.

I love you always. L.

Ludwig Wittgenstein to Ben Richards, October 13, 1949

1107 Hanshaw Rd.
Ithaca N.Y.
13.9.49[64]

Dearest Ben,

Thank you for your letter of the 9th. I'm <u>glad</u> you're better again. – My last letter was the expression of the shock I had received. It was a sickening shock, particularly because once, some weeks ago, in a very gloomy moment I <u>imagined</u> that you might have done just what, apparently, you did. I /then/ drove the thought away from me; & when I received your letter the nightmare suddenly seemed to have come true, the nightmare that, though I'd get to Europe, I'd still not see your face as it always was & as I <u>longed</u> to see it.

You've always been good & kind, & if you did it you must either have had /a/ very serious reasons, or else you just were thoughtless. Your face isn't an article of fashion like a hat, or a tie which one changes if one's tired of them. But if it changes by <u>necessity</u>, with age, sickness, etc, this in a way is <u>no change at all</u>.

I won't say more. If anything I said hurt you, please forgive me. I <u>never</u> want to hurt you! I know you wouldn't willfully rob me of that which is my <u>greatest</u> joy.

I love you always.

Ludwig

G. bl. y.

May I see you once again as I have always hoped to see you!

L. L.

P.S. This letter I wrote yesterday but couldn't post it. This morning your cable arrived "Don't come back for me. Writing. Ben." I imagine, this means that you are braking with me. Why? I take it, because of my last letter. But that letter, though it was the

---

64 Given how this letter and the previous one relate so closely to the following letter dated '20.10.49', it seems almost certain that this whole exchange took place in October rather than in September, and that – as with the previous letter – Wittgenstein mistakenly wrote '9' instead of '10' for the month.

reaction to something that felt like a nightmare, had nothing in it that could suddenly make you throw our friendship overboard; for at the worst, it seems to me, I might have been <u>unjust</u>, & that couldn't have been anything very new to you. I suppose your letter will explain it. (Though perhaps it won't reach me here.)

What ever you do, God bless you & help you. If /really/ a letter of mine could destroy your love for me then I suppose it was right that it should be destroyed. That this makes me terribly unhappy, you know. (But <u>I</u> am <u>not</u> braking with you.)

I am, of course, sailing on the 21st, & I wish I could once more see you!! May you be well & good & happy.

    With love, <u>as always</u>
      Ludwig

P.P.S. I have an idea that there is an enormous & terrible misunderstanding working between us now, – but perhaps I'm all wrong.

Ludwig Wittgenstein to Ben Richards, October 20, 1949

                Queen Elizabeth
                20.10.49.

Dear Ben,

I had your letter[65] to-day. I <u>understand</u> what you say & I <u>believe</u> it. – I don't think there is anything for me to forgive. I think I understand how you could have been maneuvered by me into a false position. I can't feel the slightest resentment.

I don't think that it is right for us to break with each other, I feel it's wrong, unless you can't any more see me without some bad feelings.

If that is so, please bring, or send, my stuff to Mrs Rhees 104 Goldhurst Terrace[66] (where we once were together).

If it isn't, i.e., if you still can see me with good feelings, please meet my boat or my train.

   God bless you.
      As always
        Ludwig

---

65 This was Richards' promised follow-up to the telegram that he had sent (which Wittgenstein quoted in his letter to Richards of October 13, 1949). Richards' letter has not survived.

66 Wittgenstein often stayed with Jean Rhees during his stays in London, but it's not clear when he and Richards had been there together.

IV. With the von Wrights in Cambridge, & in Vienna

(November 1949 – April 1950)

Wittgenstein arrived back in London on October 27, 1949. Despite the crisis that had erupted between them at the end of Wittgenstein's stay in America – over Richards' growing a beard and Wittgenstein's reaction to it – Richards' and Wittgenstein's friendship remained strong, and they spent time together in London on Wittgenstein's return.

On November 11, Wittgenstein wrote to Norman and Lee Malcolm (who had hosted him for the previous three months in America):

"Unfortunately I fell ill when I arrived here 10 days ago (some kind of flu). I'm better now, but still far from well. So, please forgive me if I don't write more than a few lines today. Thanks for all your great kindness! I wish I could have been a better guest.
I am staying with Mrs Rhees, who is very kind to me, until Wednesday. Then I'll probably go to Cambridge for a few days & after that to Dublin."

A few days later Wittgenstein went to stay with Georg Henrik von Wright and his family, in Cambridge. But he was not, in the end, to head to Dublin a few days later. Indeed, Wittgenstein was never to return to Ireland. He was still ill when he arrived at the von Wrights, so he was examined by Dr. Edward Bevan, a friend of both Maurice Drury's and of the von Wright family. Wittgenstein took a number of tests, and within a couple of weeks Dr. Bevan had diagnosed him with cancer of the prostate, which had already metastasized into his spine.[1] Wittgenstein was started on a hormone therapy to slow the growth and spread of the cancer. At the end of November he wrote to Norman Malcolm to update him on his condition:

---

1 See Rhees 1984: 225, fn. 49.

"The doctors have now made their diagnosis. I have cancer of the prostate. But this sounds, in a way, much worse than it is, for there is a drug (actually some hormones) which can, as I'm told, aleviate the symptoms of the disease, so that I can live on for years. The doctor even tells me that I may be able to work again, but I can't imagine that. I was in no way shocked when I heard I had cancer, but I was when I heard that one could do something about it, because I had no wish to live on. But I cou[l]dn't have my wish. I am treated with great kindness by every one & I have an immensely kind doctor who isn't a fool either."[2]

On December 24, 1949, Wittgenstein flew to Vienna to see his eldest sister Hermine, who had been extremely ill and bedridden for some time, and who was expected to die soon. While there, Wittgenstein visited her every day, until her death on February 11, 1950. His own health improved considerably during his time in Vienna – presumably due to the hormone therapy beginning to take effect.

At the end of January, about a month into Wittgenstein's time in Vienna, Elizabeth Anscombe arrived for a five month stay intended to improve her German – largely for the purpose of making herself better prepared to eventually translate Wittgenstein's as-yet unfinished *Philosophical Investigations* into English, whenever it would eventually be published. Wittgenstein arranged for her to stay with Ludwig Hänsel and his family (the two Ludwigs having been close friends since their time as prisoners of war together in 1919). During the overlap of their visits Wittgenstein and Anscombe met two to three times a week for philosophical discussion and discussions of German.

One of the themes of Wittgenstein's correspondence with Richards during Wittgenstein's time in Vienna is whether Richards should continue his medical training at St Bartholomew's Hospital in London, or instead move to Addenbrooke's Hospital in Cambridge. Wittgenstein pushed for the latter. Towards the end of February, however, Richards decided that he would stay in London, but that he would move out of the family home. In April he eventually found and moved into a student flat in Glenmore Road, Belsize Park (in the inner northwest of London).

On March 23, 1950, Wittgenstein returned to England, moving back in with the von Wrights in Cambridge for another month or so. During this time Wittgenstein and Richards met up regularly in London on the weekends. For these visits Wittgenstein was usually put up by Jean Rhees – the wife of Wittgenstein's friend, Rush Rhees – in her London flat.

---

2 Wittgenstein to Malcolm, end of November 1949.

During April 1949, however, the noise made by the von Wright children came more and more to disturb Wittgenstein, so that he felt he could not stay there any longer. He therefore made plans to move into Elizabeth Anscombe's house – at 27 St. John Street, in Oxford – where she already had a number of lodgers. He made the move from Cambridge to Oxford on April 27, 1950 – the day after turning 61.

Ludwig Wittgenstein to Ben Richards, November 15 and 16, 1949[3]

%% Prof. v. Wright
"Strathaird"
Lady Margaret Rd
Cambridge
Tuesday
& Wednesday

Dear Ben, o. H.

I arrived ~~in Cambridge~~ here in a pretty exhausted state & went to bed straight. Dr Bevan[4] was called & told me to stay there. He took a blood sample which showed the old anaemia. He thinks the cause must be a growth or an infection. I think it's the latter. He's trying to find it. My nights were bad ~~for~~ until last night. I've been up & out a little the last two days. On Monday next another blood count will be made & a sedimentation rate test. I don't know at all if I'm not a fool to submit to all this. It means that I shall stay here certainly for another week, I think.

I feel pretty depressed. – You have been in my thoughts a very great deal. I think, of your kindness to me & of how lovely it was to be with you.[5] – Once, in London, I said a very wrong thing. You had said that you thought it was right that we

---

3 Richards wrote '16/11/49' at the top of the letter, which was a Wednesday, so – given that Wittgenstein wrote 'Tuesday & Wednesday' – this letter was written on that day and the preceding one.

4 Edward Bevan (1907–1988) was a general practitioner in Cambridge; see the 'Short Biographies of Frequently Mentioned Family and Friends'. It seems that he was recommended to Wittgenstein, independently, by both Maurice Drury and Georg Henrik von Wright. Drury had served in the same unit as Bevan during the Second World War (see Drury 1984: 168–69), and the von Wrights were friends and patients of Bevan's. It was G. H. von Wright who called for Bevan when Wittgenstein arrived (see Joan Bevan's letter to Georg Henrik and Elizabeth von Wright, of 25, May 1990, National Library of Finland, call mark: COLL 714.22).

5 On Wittgenstein's return from America he stayed in London – at Jean Rhees' flat – for about two weeks, and was therefore presumably able to spend a fair amount of time with Richards (see Wittgenstein's letter to Norman Malcolm of November 7, 1949).

had stuck together⁶ (those were not your words) & I answered I was sure that it had been the only natural thing to do. I ought not to have said that, because I can't decide what is really natural for you.

That's as far as I got yesterday. This morning I had your letter. Thanks! It did me good to read it. May your studies go well! To-day the doctor said that puss cells had been found in my urine. He thinks they come from the prostate & that he is now on the track of my anaemia.

I won't write any more because I'm very tired.

> May you care for me so deeply as to justify <u>every</u> affectionate word & action!
> May God be with you
> With love
>   Ludwig

Thanks for writing to me.
I <u>need</u> it.
    L. a. L.

*Ludwig Wittgenstein to Ben Richards, November 26, 1949*⁷

Strathaird
Lady Margaret Rd
Cambridge
Friday

Dear Ben,

I postponed writing until to-day because I have been feeling <u>very</u> gloomy & was afraid of writing something unjust, or unreasonable. – Remember how often in the past I told & wrote you that when I felt wretched I thought of you & this made me feel better? I didn't write this to anyone else at the same time, & you know why! But now, when I feel wretched, as I mostly do, my thoughts turn to you, & then I must think of what you wrote to me /to America/.⁸ – I then think of how kind & loving you had

---

6 See Wittgenstein's letters to Richards of October 10, 13, and 20, 1949 – just before Wittgenstein's return to England – in which it looked like there may be a break between them (and see the discussion of the episode in the Introduction).

7 Richards added '26/11/49' at the top of the letter, which was indeed a Friday.

8 This most likely refers to the last letter Richards sent to Wittgenstein in America, in response to Wittgenstein's fierce reaction to Richards' news that he was growing a beard. Richards' letter has not survived, but its contents can be inferred – at least in part – from Wittgenstein's initial reply on October 20, 1949, from this letter, and from a later mention in Wittgenstein's letter to Richards of January 19, 1950 (see also the discussion of the episode in the Introduction).

been in London & try to reassure myself. I feel ashamed of having to write this. – One thing I know /now/ in my illness /is this/: I need a loving friend & nothing else will do. And if I want to lean on you & and take refuge in our friendship I must know that I have a right to do so. For untruth is the worst of all, however sad the truth may be. In my last letter I said something & underlined it twice.[9] Did you see it & understand what I meant? You didn't refer to it in your letter.[10]

All I want to say now is: I feel for you as I always did.

    With love

        Ludwig

P.S. I sometimes think of the outburst of rage you had the other day /in the kitchen/. You said you weren't angry with <u>me</u>. Were you angry with yourself <u>for having come to me</u>? That would have been <u>bad</u>, but I hope it wasn't so. Anyway, I forgive you, as you know. The doctor was here just now. He said the "Gutmann" test[11] seems to show that I have either cancer /of the prostate/ or a disease of the blood. He doesn't know which. He will bring another doctor /a specialist/ with him to-day or to-morrow. But I'm not gloomy about my illness. I wish I could either see you & be with you as always; or /else/ <u>know</u> that I must forget you. If I am a fool, forgive me. As always L.

God bless you, always.

P.P.S.[12]

I wish I could write a better & clearer letter but just now I can't. Please try to understand me & help me <u>truthfully</u>! L. L.

---

9 Wittgenstein is presumably referring to the sentence towards the end of his letter of November 16, 1949: "May you care for me so deeply as to justify every affectionate word & action!" Within this sentence, the word 'every' is double-underlined, but the sentence as a whole was also highlighted by Wittgenstein with a double-line in the margin.

10 Richards' letter has not survived.

11 This was a test of the acid phosphate levels in the blood which was used to detect the presence of prostate cancer. It had been developed by Alexander and Ethel Gutman in 1938.

12 For lack of room at the end of the letter, this conclusion is squeezed in at the top of the letter's first page, in the space to the left of Wittgenstein's address.

Ludwig Wittgenstein to Ben Richards, November 29, 1949[13]

Strathaird
Lady Margaret Rd
Cambridge
Tuesday

My dear Ben,

A few days ago a specialist saw me & confirmed the diagnosis of cancer of the prostate. He also told me that there were pills, containing female hormones, which can cheque the growth & knock out the secondary growths in the bone marow that produce the anaemia.[14] I am taking the pills but can't, of course, notice any effect so far. I am <u>not in the slightest</u> glad that there are these pills, but as they exist I can't help taking them.[15] Not out of any wish to prolong my life, but out of a kind of weakness, I now vegetate without a spark of happiness, or hope in my mind. If I could see you, that could give me some strength; for in many years my only happy hours were connected /in some way/ with you. If you think me a fool for writing you this perhaps you are right. I don't know.

    May you be lucky!
        God bless you.
        With love
            Ludwig

---

13 Richards added '29/11/49' to the letter, which was a Tuesday.

14 Rhees recalled: "Wittgenstein had written that the cancer was inoperable. Drury told me later that this was because secondary cancerous growths had developed and had entered his spine" (Rhees 1984: 225, fn. 49)

15 A few days later Wittgenstein wrote similarly to Rush Rhees: "I am getting slowly better & the doctor tells me that after some months I may be well enough to work. (Though <u>I</u> can't imagine that I'll ever work again.) I am sorry that my life should be prolonged in this way. It was a great shock to me to hear of this possibility. But I dare say I'll get accustomed to the idea. Just now I'm incapable of making a plan, or thinking an intelligent thought; that's the worst" (Wittgenstein to Rhees, December 2, 1949); and see also his letter to Norman Malcolm of the end of November 1949.

Ludwig Wittgenstein to Ben Richards (undated, December 7 or 14, 1949)[16]

> Strathaird
> Lady Margaret Rd
> Cambridge
> Wednesday

Dear Ben, d. H.,

Thanks for your letter. I shall be in Cambridge this week-end, & I needn't say more. – I still feel a bit wretched & can't make any plans. I hope my brain will work again soon; enough at least for me to make plans. I'm treated with great kindness here, but there is a great deal of noise from the children which is very difficult for me to bear.[17] G. b. y.!

> With love
> Ludwig

Ludwig Wittgenstein to Ben Richards, December 20, 1949[18]

> Strathaird
> Lady Mgt. Rd
> Cambr.
> Tuesday

Dearest Ben,

I opened your parcel because I felt a little Christmassy & saw the lovely present! Thanks d. o. H.. I am using it now as a bed-jacket although it's really much too beautiful for that; but I wanted one & that's ideal. I shall leave here on $11^{.50}$ a.m. on Friday & arrive roughly $12.^{40}$ p.m. at Liverpool Street. From there I'll go straight to the Strand Palace Hotel. As you know I'll need my bags there, one of which is at Mrs Rhees.[19]

I'd like to ask you one more thing but it's of no importance. The grocer opposite your house at Ickenham sometimes had a particularly good mild cheese off the ration. It came in smallish round flat loaves, about 9 inches, or so, in diameter & 2 to 3 inches high. Inside it is a very light yellow ~~or~~ with small holes, or no holes at all. /Not cheese in segments/. If he has it still, I'd like to have a whole loaf, or as ~~much~~ /big a part of

---

16 Richards added '12/49' to the letter, and Wittgenstein identified it as 'Wednesday' – so this letter must have been written on one of the four Wednesdays of that December. On the last Wednesday of the month Wittgenstein was in Vienna, and the third Wednesday seems ruled out by the much more upbeat letter he had written dated just the day before (Tuesday December 20). This letter was therefore most likely written on either Wednesday December 7 or 14, 1949.
17 The two von Wright children, Anita (b. 1943) and Benedict (b. 1945).
18 Richards added '20/12/49' to the letter, which was a Tuesday.
19 Wittgenstein often stayed at Jean Rhees' London flat (104 Goldhurst Terrace), when he was in London.

one/ as he will let you have. If he hasn't it doesn't matter a d . . . . [20] – I feel a good deal stronger & am looking better but I'm <u>extremely</u> tired now because I've done a good deal of Christmas shopping. Tomorrow I'll rest up.

Please <u>don't</u> come to see me if you're <u>too tired out</u>. I mean this seriously.

I know exactly what you feel about me & won't doubt it if you can't see me.

With love always
  Ludwig

I have a Christmas present for you too but whether it's any good I don't know.

                        L. L.

I have also a <u>very</u> important message from Dr Bevan for you.[21]

                        L. L.

Ludwig Wittgenstein to Ben Richards, December 25, 1949

                IV. Argentinierstr 16[22]
                      Wien
                      Austria
                     25.12.49.

Dearest Ben,

I arrived in Vienna yesterday about 9.30 p.m. in good health but with my nerves all in.[23] So, to-day, I'll have to take it <u>very</u> easy. I spent the Christmas Eve with one of my friends & his wife.[24] I hope my nerves will soon calm down. I've seen two of my sisters so far. My eldest sister is now much worse & did not recognize me.[25] Perhaps she will one of these days, for her state varies a good deal. I think of you constantly & I miss

---

20 Stands for: 'damn'.

21 See Richards' letter to Wittgenstein of January 21, 1950, and Wittgenstein's letter to Richards of January 24, 1950.

22 This was the palatial Wittgenstein family home on Argentinierstrasse (formerly Alleegasse), in Vienna's 4th district. It was the principal home in which Ludwig grew up, and at this time it was the home of Ludwig's sister – Hermine Wittgenstein – who lived there until her death in 1950.

23 There had been some problems with the flight, and a significant delay – as Wittgenstein mentioned in a letter to Rush Rhees the next week: "When, after that 24 hours delay, we started from the airfield my nerves were pretty much shot. I hope they'll calm down now for good" (Wittgenstein to Rhees, January 3, 1950).

24 This was most likely Ludwig Hänsel and his wife Anna (and their children), who lived in Vienna, and with whom Wittgenstein had been close since he and Ludwig Hänsel were prisoners of war together in Italy after the First World War.

25 Wittgenstein's eldest sister, Hermine, was seriously ill with cancer. A few days later Wittgenstein wrote to Norman Malcolm: "I found my eldest sister so weak that I can't imagine that she will live for many more weeks. She is being taken care of extremely well & has everything she needs" (Wittgenstein to Malcolm, December 29, 1949). She died on February 11, 1950.

you. I hope you had a good Christmas! Good luck & God bless you. I[26] was wonderful to see you.

    With love
     Ludwig

Ludwig Wittgenstein to Ben Richards, Telegram, December 26, 1949
     POST OFFICE
     TELEGRAM

Prefix. Time handed in. Office of Origin and Service Instructions. Words.
XWC 6003 L 2356 OC WIEN 17 25 1700
ELT BENEDICT RICHARDS 40 SWAKELEYS RD ICKENHAM
UXBRIDGEMIDDLESEX =
ARRIVED VIENNA EXCELLENT HEALTH AND SPIRITS LOVE
= LUDWIG WITTGENSTEIN +
40

Ben Richards to Ludwig Wittgenstein, December 26, 1949
     GREENOGE
    40, SWAKELEYS ROAD
     ICKENHAM
     UXBRIDGE
    RUISLIP 2114
     26/12/49

Dear Ludwig

Thank you very much indeed for the records, and for the lovely handkerchiefs. I'll mark them so as to always know them for the ones you gave me, and I'll know them by the patterns. I played the Bruckner this morning – first the scherzo, and then the whole symphony from the beginning. I liked the scherzo particularly – and much more the second time I played it; and also the fourth movement. I understood very little of the first and second movements. The first seems to be very rich and rather complicated and I had no landmarks except the opening theme which you had taught me.

---

26 Presumably this was meant to say: 'It'.

I was very glad to get your telegram /this morning/ and particularly to hear that your health and spirits were good. Here it seemed to be pretty foggy on Saturday morning. I rung up the airport in the evening, and they said the flight had taken place and reached Vienna safely at about 6.30 in the evening.

I hope all goes well with your sisters, and that you & they had a happy Christmas. I needn't tell you what it meant to me to be able to see you those few days. A happy New Year to you and your family.

> Love always,
>
> Ben.

Ludwig Wittgenstein to Ben Richards, December 31, 1949

TEL. U 40 402   WIEN, 31.12.49
IV, ARGENTINIERSTRASSE 16

Dearest Ben,

This is only to say that I think of you constantly, as always.

A day or two after my arrival here I caught a cold, owing to the very sudden change of climate. It's not too bad & getting better slowly.[27] – On the journey I read a nicely written American detective story & was, as always, charmed by the tricks of the American language. Yesterday I started to read a story by Peter Cheyney, written in sham American! The <u>story</u> isn't too bad but I can't read it with real pleasure.[28]

I hope you're having a goodish time & that you're well! & I hope that I'll soon hear from you. – I see my oldest sister every day for a little while. She is mostly half asleep but she recognizes me & is pleased to see me when she opens her eyes.

My good wishes are with you <u>always</u>! I miss you.

> With love
>
> Ludwig

P.S. I've heard hardly any music so far.

---

[27] The next day Wittgenstein wrote to Georg Henrik von Wright: "I'd like to say that my health isn't too bad at all. Unfortunately I caught a cold some days ago, but it's gradually getting better" (Wittgenstein to von Wright January 1, 1950).

[28] Peter Cheyney (1896–1951) was a popular British author of hardboiled crime novels. In Wittgenstein's letter to Richards of January 16, 1950 he identifies the story he'd read as Cheyney's 'Ladies Can Kill', by which he presumably meant Cheyney's novel: *Can Ladies Kill?* (London, William Collins, 1938). The protagonist is the FBI agent Lemmy Caution, and it opens as follows: "I am standin' lookin' at this house and I think that if ever I get any dough I will settle down an' get myself a dump like this".

Ben Richards to Ludwig Wittgenstein, January 5, 1950

GREENOGE
40, SWAKELEYS ROAD
ICKENHAM
UXBRIDGE
RUISLIP 2114
5.1.50

Dear Ludwig,

I am very sorry you have a cold. Please keep warm. I was very glad to get your letter – ~~the~~ I have had two from you now. I was surprised the censor was still opening letters.[29] I hope you got my letter and the Christmas card.

I am glad your sister knows you now, and I'm not surprised she is pleased to see you. I hope your other sisters are well.

It is not at all cold here and we are all well.

I quite enjoyed the Peter Cheyney story I read, but I do not know American well enough to detect sham, or for it to really spoil my enjoyment. What was the story you read on the journey?

I miss you a lot, and am looking forward to your next letter.

Love always,
Ben.

Ludwig Wittgenstein to Ben Richards, January 7, 1950

TEL. U 40 402   WIEN, 7.1.50
                                  IV, ARGENTINIERSTRASSE 16

Dearest Ben,

Thanks for your letter of Dec. 26th. The Christmas card you had posted on the 23rd arrived this morning! I was extremely glad to get it. I'm glad you enjoyed the Bruckner partly. Perhaps you'll enjoy more later. I think of you a lot. I hope you're well, & that you can work well!

My cold is practically gone & I'm <u>much</u> stronger than I was when I arrived here. I'm tempted to eat too much; that's the only trouble. – I haven't been to a concert yet but

---

29 Allied censorship of the mail in Austria continued until 1953 (see Wittgenstein's letter to Richards of September 13, 1947, and the relevant footnote there).

my friend of whom I've often told you plays the piano for me & sometimes for me and my eldest sister in her room.[30] He plays <u>beautifully</u> & some times <u>heavenly</u>, e.g. Schuman.[31] I wish you could hear him. – My sister is half asleep a great deal of the time but some days she understands everything one says & she still listens to music with great intensity.

I gave my youngest sister,[32] the one you met, your good wishes & she sends you her's. Give Angela[33] mine too.

   Good luck & God bless you.
        With love always
         Ludwig

P.S. If you can, please send me a largish bottle of Genasprin.[34] L. L.

Ludwig Wittgenstein to Ben Richards, January 16, 1950

TEL. U 40 402   WIEN, 16.1.50
                      IV, ARGENTINIERSTRASSE 16

Dearest Ben,

Thanks for your letter which I got about 5 days ago & for the aspirin which arrived this morning, it was <u>beautifully</u> packed. I hope I'll hear from you soon. I think of you a <u>lot</u>. I wish you lots of luck, particularly for your exam; but <u>if</u> luck should fail you I wish you <u>courage</u> & good sense!! – I'm very well. My cold has gone & I've got acclimatized again; also my nerves are <u>much</u> better & I have good nights. –

My eldest sister seems to be getting gradually weaker, though very slowly. I sit with her every day for some time & very occasionally we say a few words.[35] – I'm reading a

---

30 This was Rudolf Koder (1902–1977), a close friend of Wittgenstein's, whom he had got to know when they were both teaching at the primary school in Puchberg am Schneeberg in the early 1920s. Koder had then become close with Wittgenstein's sisters as well, and he often played music with them. A few days earlier Wittgenstein had written to Rhees: "I see my eldest sister every day for a short time. It's very difficult for her to talk & for me (or anyone) to understand what she is trying to say, but sometimes it's possible. When she isn't too sleepy she loves to hear my friend Koder play the piano & she listens with <u>great</u> intensity. He sometimes plays <u>heavenly</u> & always beautifully. I wish you, too, could hear him" (Wittgenstein to Rhees, January 3, 1950).
31 Robert Schumann (1818–1856).
32 Margaret Stonborough-Wittgenstein.
33 The oldest of Richards' younger sisters.
34 Genasprin was a popular brand of aspirin in the 1950s with analgesic, antipyretic, and antirheumatic effects.
35 As Wittgenstein reported to Rhees just under a week later: "My sister is rarely more than half awake though occasionally she says astoundingly clear & deep things" (Wittgenstein to Rhees, January 22, 1950).

good deal in a book which both attracts & repels me, Goehthe's Theory of Colours.[36] The title of the story of Peter Cheyney's I wrote to you about is "Can Ladies Kill".[37] It's trying to be frightfully tough, more so than an American story.
Dear Ben, think of me occasionally & don't mind if I'm a fool! –
    God bless you.
        With love always
            Ludwig
I wish I could see you!

Ludwig Wittgenstein to Ben Richards, January 19, 1950
TEL. U 40 402   WIEN, 19.1.50
                                                      IV, ARGENTINIERSTRASSE 16

Dearest Ben,

I wrote to you /only/ on Monday, but I've been thinking of you such a lot that I feel the urge to write to you again. One thing I now see clearly is how very hard & difficult it must have been for you to write to me that last letter you sent to America,[38] & and how wonderful it was that you had the strength to do it. Thank God. –
Not only had I nothing to forgive you but you have to forgive me all the many occasions on which – without fully realizing it – I ~~have~~ exerted pressure on you & your feelings. I wish that I now could make amends for all this, & I can only say that I will never again want you to see me, or write to me, more often than you feel is good

---

36 Johann Wolfgang von Goethe, *Zur Farbenlehre*, published in 1810 (and translated as: *Theory of Colours*, trans. Charles Lock Eastlake, London, John Murray, 1840). On the same day Wittgenstein wrote to Norman Malcolm: "My brain works very sluggishly these days but I can't say I mind. I'm reading various odds & ends, e.g. Goethes Theory of colour which, with all its absurdities, has very interesting points & stimulates me to think" (Wittgenstein to Malcolm, January 16, 1950; and see also his letter to Georg Henrik von Wright of January 19, 1950). In a letter to Rush Rhees the next week he reported that "I have been reading again parts of Goethes "Farbenlehre" which attracts & repels me. It's certainly philosophically interesting, & I've been thinking about it & even written down some <u>weak</u> remarks" (Wittgenstein to Rhees, January 22, 1950). He continued writing remarks on the grammar of colour concepts (and on Goethe's *Farbenlehre*) intermittently until his death, in MSS 172, 173, and 176. These remarks were later gathered together and published by Elizabeth Anscombe as Wittgenstein 1977.
37 Wittgenstein meant Cheyney's novel: *Can Ladies Kill?* (London, William Collins, 1938). See his letter to Richards of December 31, 1949 and the relevant footnote there.
38 As with the reference in his earlier letter to Richards of November 26, 1949, this most likely refers to the letter Richards sent in response to Wittgenstein's fierce reaction to Richards' news that he was growing a beard. Richards' letter has not survived, but its contents can be inferred – at least in part – from Wittgenstein's initial reply on October 20, 1949, from his letter of November 26, 1949, and from this letter (see also the discussion in the Introduction).

for you; & if you feel that you'd rather not see me, or write to me, that, too, is perfectly all right. (Not that my feeling for you is less strong /now/! On the contrary.) – I'm always in your debt! – I hope that things are going fairly well with you & also that you'll have lots of courage & sense if you have bad luck![39] Though you need both those things with good luck, too. — Thanks for your letter of Jan. 12th. It's not terribly cold here. To-day we have -7°C & a good deal of snow. – When I last read Wodehouse[40] I thought he wrote very well & I laughed a lot. I don't know if I could read him to-day. – One of my sisters (the middle one)[41] sometimes plays duets with my friend Koder.[42] The other day they played two string quartets of Schumann's & a sonata ~~written~~ for piano duet by Mozart. I enjoyed them very much.

Please look after yourself! God bless you & protect you. (From me, too, if necessary.)

    With love, always

        Ludwig

P.S. If you have the "Davidsbündler Tänze"[43] handy, please read the motto. I once wrote it down for you.[44] L. L.

---

39 This likely refers to Richards' upcoming 'conjoint' exam (see his letter to Wittgenstein of January 21, 1950).

40 Sir Pelham Grenville (P. G.) Wodehouse (1881–1975) – one of the great English literary humourists – published more than 90 novels, 40 plays, and 200 short stories and essays. In a conversation in 1936 Wittgenstein had told Maurice Drury that Wodehouse's short story 'Honeysuckle Cottage' was "one of the funniest things he had ever read" (Drury 1984: 133).

41 Helene Salzer (née Wittgenstein; 1879–1956), the middle of Ludwig's three sisters; see the 'Short Biographies of Frequently Mentioned Family and Friends'. She was an excellent pianist and singer.

42 Rudolf Koder (1902–1977); see the relevant footnote to Wittgenstein's letter to Richards of January 7, 1950.

43 The motto with which Robert Schumann prefaced the first edition of his 'Davidsbündlertänze' ['Dances of the League of David'] (op. 6) is: 'Alter Spruch: / In all und jeder Zeit / Verknüpft sich Lust und Leid / Bleibt fromm in Lust und seyd / Dem Leid mit Mut bereit' ('Old saying: / In each and every age / pleasure and suffering are intertwined / Remain pious in pleasure and be / ready for suffering with courage'). Wittgenstein had already mentioned this motto in his letter to Richards of December 28, 1946, and he mentions it again in his letter to Richards of February 13, 1951.

44 Wittgenstein had written (a very slightly misremembered version of) the motto on a small piece of paper and given it to Richards. The motto as he wrote it read: "In all & jeder Zeit / Verknüpft sich Lust & Leid. / Bleibt fromm in Lust & seyd / Beim Leid mit Mut bereit" (a facsimile of this note has been reproduced in Nedo 2012: 407).

Ben Richards to Ludwig Wittgenstein, January 21, 1950

HILTON HALL, HILTON, HUNTINGTON.
PAPWORTH ST, AGNES 23
21.1.49[45]

Dear Ludwig

I am very glad you are better. Thanks for the letter.

I have taken the Conjoint Examination,[46] passing in pathology and failing in medicine (separate parts). Thus I have only medicine to take in Conjoint before I qualify.

I am staying a few days with the Garnetts and have come into Cambridge yesterday and to-day.

I have seen four people –

① John Wedgwood (Dorothy Wedgwood's son) who is an assistant to Dr. Cole a physician at Addenbrookes.[47] He qualified on Conjoint and after returning from the forces tried to get Cambridge M.B. and failed being weak in pathology – he came to Addenbrookes and got a good coach in pathology and passed the M.B.[48] He has since also passed the M.R.C.P.[49] He could give me coaching in medicine, but thinks that Bart's[50] might be reluctant to give me a job if I left them for six months. I shall of course ask the authorities there before deciding to come here.

② Dr Bevan who was very kind and made more enquiries from a friend of his at Addenbrookes

③ Mr. Withycombe (his friend) a surgical registrar. He said there were several people who would do coaching and that I could come on his ward rounds provided I saw the secretary of the Cambridge University Medical School and that he said I could register as a student at Addenbrookes

④ I saw this secretary, Mr. Moss, who said that Addenbrookes was not yet a students' teaching hospital, but that they do run a postgraduate course for general practitioners consisting of ward rounds, outpatients etc. He said that a few months ago a

---

45 Given the ways in which Wittgenstein's letter to Richards of January 24, 1950 responds to this one, it's clear that it fits here, and that Richards made the common January mistake of dating to the previous year.
46 The 'Conjoint' exam was the basic qualification for medical students in the United Kingdom at the time, consisting of a series of sub-examinations on anatomy, physiology, pharmacology, pathology, and the like.
47 Addenbrooke's Hospital was (and is) one of the central teaching hospitals in Cambridge, with close connections to the university.
48 Bachelor of Medicine.
49 Membership of the Royal Colleges of Physicians.
50 St Bartholomew's Hospital, London.

/unqualified/ student had registered as a student having failed the MB and wanting to revise, but after coming ~~to~~ a few times stopped, as the consultants who gave rounds were too busy to do much teaching. He said that, if I decided to, I would be able to register.

I am a bit muddled now and don't know what is the best thing to do. Perhaps if I could get digs near Barts it would be better, but I don't know if that would be possible. If so I might stay at Barts until the Conjoint exam in April and then come to Cambridge for the last two months.

I am going to have another talk with John Wedgwood this afternoon.

I miss you very much. Please look after yourself.

      Love always

         Ben.

Ludwig Wittgenstein to Ben Richards, January 24, 1950

TEL. U 40 402   WIEN, 24.1.50

                                                                                 IV, ARGENTINIERSTRASSE 16

Dearest Ben,

I had your letter of Jan 21st this morning. I'm <u>glad</u> you passed /one/ part of the exam & that you talked to people about your future. But what about that Dr Benett about whom Dr Bevan talked to me? Doesn't he exist any more – for you didn't mention him. I <u>hope</u> Bevan was helpful![51]

I can quite understand that you find it difficult to make a decision.[52] What seems to me to speak in favor of Cambridge is a) that you're away from home, really away, & b) that you can get into the open air so much more easily, which I think would do your health good. – I know that Cambridge society is pretty disgusting[53] but you have choice. Also there is Dr Bevan who might be helpful. – Is it essential that <u>Barts</u>[54] should give you a job?–

---

51 Two weeks earlier, Wittgenstein had written to Bevan: "I hope that Ben Richards will make use of the opportunity" (Wittgenstein to Bevan, January 10, 1950). This was presumably a reference to Bevan's offer to advise Richards.

52 Richards had to decide where to complete his medical training, and he was choosing between St. Bartholomew's Hospital in London and Addenbrooke's Hospital in Cambridge. Richards ultimately chose London – against Wittgenstein's advice.

53 See Wittgenstein's letter to Richards of October 6, 1946 and the relevant footnote there.

54 St Bartholomew's Hospital, London.

In a way I wonder if London life is good for you. But I don't <u>know</u> that it isn't. It's just a suspicion & possibly an unfounded one.[55] – I'm glad you went to Huntington /for a rest/; I hope you had decent weather & could get into the fresh air. God bless you! & good luck. – It's cold here (-10°C) but fine. I'm very well indeed. – –

M[iss] Anscombe has arrived & is staying with a friend of mine, the one who's son is at Cambridge.[56] I think she's getting on very well in every way. – I miss you & <u>long</u> to see you again.

With love, as always

        Ludwig

P.S. In case you should go to Cambridge before I return (sometime in March, I imagine), please look up the v. Wrights & give them my kind regards. They are nice & ~~good~~ /kind/ people, & I have an idea you'll like them. L. L.

Ludwig Wittgenstein to Ben Richards, February 2, 1950

TEL. U 40 402   WIEN, 2.2.50

                                                               IV, ARGENTINIERSTRASSE 16

Dearest Ben,

Thanks for your letter of Jan. 28th.[57] It did me good to read it. –

My eldest sister is declining rapidly. I can't imagine that she will last many more days. She no longer speaks or opens her eyes. It's sad for me to watch her though there is nothing unexpected about it. – M[iss] Anscombe is staying with the Hänsels & getting along very well there. She can make herself understood pretty well with her German & is making good progress. Her great difficulty in talking is the order of words & the genders. I see her occasionally & read with her. – I seem to have caught some kind of

---

55 A couple of weeks later Wittgenstein wrote to Dr. Bevan: "Thanks for writing to me about Ben Richards. He wrote to me how very kind you'd been. (As always!) He isn't so much afraid as very shy & very repressed, particularly before he knows someone well. – I wish I knew how important it really is that he should get a job at Barts. He seems to regard it as important. But I wish he could get out of London! I have an idea Barts isn't good for him. I don't mean by this that he is in any danger of becoming superficial, or snobbish, or anything like that. There is no danger there. But I wish he could be with more simple & more kindly people with whom he could open up, or he will get more & more withdrawn" (Wittgenstein to Bevan, February 7, 1950).

56 Elizabeth Anscombe stayed in Vienna – from the end of January 1950 – for a few months, partly so as to improve her German with the intention of eventually translating Wittgenstein's *Philosophische Untersuchungen* [*Philosophical Investigations*]. She stayed with Ludwig Hänsel and his family, who were close friends of Wittgenstein's (see the following letter). Hänsel's son, Hermann (1918–2005) held a scholarship to study at the University of Cambridge in the 1949/50 academic year.

57 Richards' letter has not been preserved.

infection & there is something wrong with my inside. I hope & believe that it'll pass off soon.⁵⁸ I mustn't fall ill here! (Unfortunately Fate doesn't ask me whether I want to fall ill or not.). If you have time, please get me some more Genasprin. I'm afraid I used it up rather quickly. – – It's pretty cold here. The other day we had -13°C. I think of you <u>a lot</u>. I hope you're well! God bless you. I miss you very much.

> With love always
> Ludwig

Ludwig Wittgenstein to Ben Richards, February 7, 1950

TEL. U 40 402   WIEN, 7.2.50

IV, ARGENTINIERSTRASSE 16

Dearest Ben,

This is chiefly to say that I'm very much better. My cold is gone & intestinal trouble is rapidly getting better. – My eldest sister in unchanged. – – I had a letter from Malcolm the other day. He wrote about a book by Prof R̶ Gilbert Ryle, something about the mind – I forget the title.⁵⁹ He said it was partly based on my ideas, of course without mentioning me, & was very /bad &/ disagreeable to read. I heard the same from Miss Anscombe & Smythies.⁶⁰ If you come across it somewhere have a look at it & tell me how it strikes you. Perhaps it won't strike you one way, or another. – The other day I tried hard to read Goethes novel "Wilhlem Meister",⁶¹ it's very famous. It bored me so much, I had to give up. Then I found in a cupboard a book for boys about tobacco plantations in New Guinea,⁶² & that suited me perfectly. – I'm doing a little philosophy when I feel like it – not very much & not very well, but I'm glad I can do it

---

58 On the same day Wittgenstein wrote to Bevan: "I had a rather nasty cold lately, accompanied by stomach trouble; I'm afraid I was on the verge of seeing a doctor & very worried about <u>that</u>, but it cleared up by itself & I'm almost as good as new again. I am, of course, <u>slightly</u> liable to get infections these days, what with my blood not entirely up to scratch & the chageable wintery weather." (Wittgenstein to Bevan, February 7, 1950).
59 Gilbert Ryle (1900–1976) was Waynflete Professor of Metaphysical Philosophy at the University of Oxford from 1945. The book in question was Ryle's major work *The Concept of Mind*, published in 1949, in which he takes up many of Wittgenstein's ideas.
60 Wittgenstein already had this impression of Ryle, as can be seen from the conversation which Wittgenstein had with Bouwsma in October 1949: "He spoke of Gilbert Ryle. Ryle had been good when he was young. Now he just borrowed other men's thoughts. I suggested that this was due to the burden of administrative duties. But W. said it was much worse" (Bouwsma 1986: 50). A few days later Wittgenstein replied to Norman Malcolm: "I can't say that Ryle's book worries me. Perhaps it ought to, but it doesn't. I was interested, however, in what you wrote about it. It tallied with what Smythies & Miss Anscombe told me" (Wittgenstein to Malcolm, February 12, 1950).
61 It is not clear whether Wittgenstein is referring here to Goethe's *Wilhelm Meisters Lehrjahre* (1795–6) or to *Wilhelm Meisters Wanderjahre* (1821/1829).
62 This was perhaps: Christian Keysser's *Nalumotte: Buben- und Mädchengeschichten aus Neuguinea [Nalumott: Boys' and Girls' Stories from New Guinea]* (Neuendettelsau, Buchh. der Diakonissen-Anstalt, 1931).

at all. – I think of you a lot, as always. I wonder what result your last talk /had/ with your friend who had failed his exam & had subsequently studied at Addenbrookes.[63] You didn't mention it in your last letter. I hope sincerely a) you were firm & b) you had no trouble at home. –

I'm seeing my youngest sister[64] to-day & will give her your good wishes &, I'm sure, receive her's for you. – May you be firm & cheerful, God bless you!

My loving thoughts are with you always.

      Ludwig

P.S. I hope your work goes well. Tell me something about it if you have time. L. L.

Ludwig Wittgenstein to Ben Richards, February 9, 1950

TEL. U 40 402   WIEN, 9.2.50

                 IV, ARGENTINIERSTRASSE 16

Dearest Ben,

This is merely a P.S. to the letter that I wrote to you yesterday & that was posted early this morning before your letter of Feb. 4th had arrived.[65] You may be right in what you say about Addenbrooks & Barts. I can't judge. – But there has now been ample proof (in spite of the fact that you're intelligent & grasp things easily & that you are surrounded at home by medical people): that the conditions for studying are not favorable at Ickenham. This fact seems to me to shout louder in your case than anything else & ought to attract your attention. I thought of Cambridge, chiefly because you could live alone & could at the same time take easy walks to rest yourself. Of course I don't know a thing about the merits or demerits of Addenbrooks. – May you be firm & yet cheerful; may you find a good & a not a weak solution of this problem. You must once get to grips with ~~this~~ /it/. /You know/ I'm not trying to get your wind up, on the contrary. I'd like you to be awake & courageous. – – I'm sounding like a parson, /!/ but I mean every word I say. Perhaps you're awake anyway & are doing all that's possible; then I just hope you'll stay that way.

    With love, always

       Ludwig

P.S. Don't hesitate to write to Dr Bevan for advice, for he is experienced & kind & serious. He wrote to me very kindly about your visit to him & said he'd like to see you again. – Thanks for the flowers! Was it forsythia?

---

63 Namely, John Wedgwood (see Richards' letter to Wittgenstein of January 21, 1950).
64 Margaret Stonborough-Wittgenstein.
65 Richards' letter has not been preserved.

Ludwig Wittgenstein to Ben Richards, February 16, 1950

TEL. U 40 402   WIEN, 16.2.50
                                                                         IV, ARGENTINIERSTRASSE 16

Dear Ben,

My eldest sister died last Saturday evening.[66] She had a peaceful end. It did not come as a shock to me, as I had been expecting it hourly for almost 3 days.

I am thinking of you constantly. I have been wondering & worrying whether it was right of me to send you the P.S. to my last letter.[67] For, though it was true that I wish you to be 'firm & cheerful', it may at present not be <u>given</u> to you to be so.[68] Please forgive me if I was rash. – May you be led the right way, whatever the right way is. And don't lose hope.

I am in good health. – I hope to hear from you soon.

        I think of you with love always
                Ludwig

Ben Richards to Ludwig Wittgenstein (undated, around February 23, 1950)[69]

                          GREENOGE
                  40, SWAKELEYS ROAD
                            ICKENHAM
                             UXBRIDGE
                           RUISLIP 2114

Dear Ludwig,

I am very sorry to hear your sister died.

It has been given me so far to be neither firm nor cheerful. I hope it will be.

In the letter before your last you said that the fact that conditions for studying are not favorable at Ickenham ought to "attract my attention".[70] I am very aware that they are not. I have been enquiring for a room in London without success so far.

---

66 Hermine Wittgenstein – the eldest of the Wittgenstein siblings – died of cancer on Saturday February 11, 1950, at the age of 75.

67 Wittgenstein is referring here to his letter of February 9, 1950, which he described as "a P.S." to his previous letter of February 7, 1950.

68 Wittgenstein often reminded himself of the degree to which virtue and cheerfulness depend on grace. For example, in 1937 he wrote in his diary: "I believe . . . that I should be cheerful in a good way if it is given to me, but if not, that I should then bear the gloom with patience & steadfastness" (MS 183, pp. 192–3).

69 The date of this letter can be estimated because Richards is responding to Wittgenstein's letter of February 16, 1950; because there was a general election in the United Kingdom on February 23, 1950; and because Richards had apparently not yet received Wittgenstein's letter of February 24, 1950.

70 See Wittgenstein's letter to Richards of February 9, 1950.

I voted for the Liberal, but I am hopelessly confused about politics. I thought the Liberal party was slightly less dishonest than the other two but there is not much in it and I may be quite wrong. I only heard the Liberal man give one speech and he sounded moderately decent but I may be wrong about that too.
How are you and your sisters?

    Love always,
      Ben

Ludwig Wittgenstein to Ben Richards, February 24, 1950
TEL. U 40 402   WIEN, 24.2.50
                                                            IV, ARGENTINIERSTRASSE 16

Dearest Ben,
Thank you for your letters of Feb. 12th & 19th.[71] It's difficult for me to-day to write to you in such a way as not to hurt your feelings & at the same time to be frank, as I must be if I'm your friend. On Wednesday the week before last I sent you a postscript to a letter which I had written the day before.[72] It concerned your decision not to leave London & to stay at home as before. I wrote the P.S. because I was terribly concerned not only about your future but also about the <u>tone</u> of the short letter to which my P.S. was the answer. That tone had – rightly or wrongly – seemed to me flat & hopeless, particularly compared to the tone of your previous letter (from Hilton) which seemed active & hopeful. Now my impression <u>may</u> have been wrong; & you <u>may</u> have had good & sufficient reasons for deciding as you did; but at any rate my P.S. deserved a <u>reply</u>. Perhaps not necessarily an argument, for you <u>may</u> have felt that you couldn't <u>write</u> about this subject; but then you should have written that this was what you felt! Your mere silence about the subject was <u>no</u> sufficient answer. (In good society perhaps one just changes the subject if someone makes a remark about things that aren't his business, but one doesn't do it to a friend.)
If I could cease to be /deeply/ concerned for your work, your future & and your state of mind I would cease to be your friend. Your life interests me by far more than the

---

71 These letters have not been preserved. When writing this letter, Wittgenstein had apparently not yet received Richards' previous (undated) letter of around February 23, 1950.
72 Namely, Wittgenstein's letter to Richards of February 9, 1950, which he described as "a P.S." to his previous letter of February 7, 1950.

election;[73] & there is very little you can do about politics but a lot you can do about yourself.[74] – Please read this letter carefully – I hope you don't think it's some kind of retoric! – & answer me at least in such a way that I know that you've read & understood it. – I can't imagine that you shouldn't know how <u>much</u> I think of you, how concerned I am about your work <u>etc. etc.</u>, & don't you feel queer when you write to me as though all this were of no interest to me at all? –

You know that I write this only out of love – may you not feel it as a burden!

I wish I could talk to you instead of writing. I hope to see you before long. God bless you. Write soon! I miss you.

<u>With love always</u>
Ludwig

P.S. Please think of me – not as of someone who <u>criticises</u> your actions (though I do this too sometimes) – but of one who accompanies them with his good wishes & /who/ hopes you go the right & and not just easiest way.

L. L.

Ludwig Wittgenstein to Ben Richards, March 2, 1950

TEL. U 40 402　　　　　　　　　　　　　　　　　　　　　　　　WIEN, 2.3.50
　　　　　　　　　　　　　　　　　　　　　　　　　　IV, ARGENTINIERSTRASSE 16

Dearest Ben,

Thanks for your letter without date which I received the day before yesterday. Please don't lose hope! – There is a <u>great</u> deal I'd like to say, but I can't write it. I am leaving here in about three weeks & want to stay in London for a bit. Mrs Rhees will put me up.[75] I long to see you, & to be with you & talk to you, if it's all right with you. I think of you constantly /& wish you luck/. – I am very well indeed & doing some philosophy – as good as can be expected. I see a fair amount of M^{iss} Anscombe (who sends you her love)

73　Since Wittgenstein had apparently not yet received Richards' (undated) letter of around February 23, 1950, Richards must have discussed the upcoming elections in his previous unpreserved letters.

74　This had long been a central tenet of Wittgenstein's moral outlook, as exemplified by a conversation between Wittgenstein and his student, Heinrich Postl, in the early 1920s: "[W]hen Postl once remarked that he wished to improve the world, Wittgenstein replied: 'Just improve yourself; that is the only thing you *can* do to better the world.'" (Monk 1990: 213).

75　A few weeks earlier Wittgenstein had written to Jean Rhees from Vienna, saying: "I intend to stay here for another month, or so & should very much like to stay with you for a short time when I come back, if you can put me up. I hope I shan't be as much trouble then as the last time. I'm in very good health now, even my nerves are in good shape. May it stay that way for a little while longer" (Wittgenstein to Rhees, February 12, 1950).

& sometimes do German with her & sometimes philosophy.[76] My youngest sister is pretty ill with heart trouble,[77] the other one[78] is very well. – The weather is unbelievably mild; the snowdrops are out, though I haven't yet found any. If I do you'll get one. I wish you could be here with me! God bless you.

With love, always

Ludwig

P.S. I haven't yet thanked you for the Genasprin. It came ~~at least~~ /over/ a week ago. Thanks. I hope to see you soon.

Ben Richards to Ludwig Wittgenstein, March 4, 1950

GREENOGE
40, SWAKELEYS ROAD
ICKENHAM
UXBRIDGE
RUISLIP 2114

4/3/50

Dear Ludwig,

Thanks for your letter. I have written a letter about what you said in your "postscript" letter which I hope has reached you.[79] I certainly do not think that what happens to me is none of your business. I hope you will always tell me what you think about it. I am sorry my political letter[80] made you think I was ignoring what you had said.

I have written to the Medical Correspondence College to enquire about a revision course for the M.B. John Wedgwood, the registrar I saw at Addenbrookes, had taken it and recommended it as covering the ground for the exam more thoroughly than a private coach. He recommended private coaching for clinical Medicine & surgery; to examine a lot of patients and be questioned on them. The coaching I had before was

---

76 A few weeks earlier Wittgenstein had written to Georg Henrik von Wright, saying: "I see Miss Anscombe 2–3 times a week, & we even had a discussion the other day which wasn't too bad." (Wittgenstein to von Wright, February 12th 1950); and to Malcolm, on the same day, he wrote saying: "I'm in very good health. So much so that I even had a fairly good discussion with Miss Anscombe a few days ago. I'd be more use to you now than I was last summer in Ithaca" (Wittgenstein to Malcolm, February 12, 1950). A few days before that he had reported to Bevan "that Miss Anscombe is staying with very nice people & learning German rapidly" (Wittgenstein to Bevan, February 7, 1950).
77 Margaret Stonborough-Wittgenstein.
78 Helene Salzer.
79 Richards is referring to Wittgenstein's letter of February 9, 1949, and to his own (undated) reply of around February 23, 1950.
80 Richards' (undated) letter of around February 23, 1950 mentioned politics, but it's likely that he had discussed the upcoming election in his previous one or two unpreserved letters as well.

mainly theoretical and in the theory only covered a small amount of ground. I examined one patient for the surgical coach and none for the medical one. I am going to ward rounds and outpatient departments at Barts ~~but~~ and see and am taught about the patients, but I do not examine many and am not intensively questioned about it. I will let you know of any arrangement I make. Still no luck yet about a room in London. I hope you are feeling well.

 Love always, Ben.

Ludwig Wittgenstein to Ben Richards, March 10, 1950[81]

Wien I. Josefsplatz
Wien, Nationalbibliothek.
Ein Hauptwerk des deutschen Barock.
Von J. B. Fischer entworfen und begonnen,
von seinem Sohn Emanuel 1726 vollendet[82]

Wien I. Kohlmarkt
Im Hintergrund: Michaelertrakt der Hofburg [83]

---

81 Richards added '11/3/50' to the letter, which was a Saturday; and since Wittgenstein wrote 'Friday' on the letter, Richards was presumably noting the date the letter was received. Wittgenstein wrote this letter on the backs of two postcards – treating them simply as blank pages to write across – and he presumably sent the two postcards inside an envelope.

82 German: Vienna 1[st district]. Josef's Square. Vienna, National Library. A masterpiece of German Baroque. Designed and begun by J. B. Fischer, completed by his son Emanuel in 1726.

83 German: Vienna 1[st district], Cabbage Market. In the background: Michael's wing of the Hofburg.

IV, Argentinierstr. 16
Wien
Friday

Dear Ben

Thanks for your letter of Feb. 4th. I'm flying to London on Thursday, March 23rd, with a Dutch plane, arriving at Northolt about 9 p.m. I think. If you ring up Northolt & ask what time the Dutch plane from Vienna via Amsterdam arrives they'll know. Perhaps you could meet me there. I shall stay with Mrs Rhees.

If you can't meet the plane I shall go on to the terminal in Kensington. In this case, please let me have a message at Northolt. – I've been very well for quite a time. Just at present my inside is a bit upset, but it'll soon be all right again. I should like to stay in London for about a week but I won't try to see you if it interferes with your work.

    I long to see you again.
        With love, always
            Ludwig

Ben Richards to Ludwig Wittgenstein, March 14, 1950

Bart's
March 14th 1950

Dear Ludwig,

Thanks for your letter. I am going to a choir rehearsal on Thursday 23rd so I will meet you at the Kensington terminal. It is very good to be going to see you again soon! Give my love to your sister and Miss Anscombe.

A lady doctor, who was once an assistant of my father's, has offered to put me up for a week or two while I look round for a room; and she has several ideas for finding one which I haven't followed up yet. She is very nice and has offered me a very good room. I am going there on Thursday – her name is Dr. Joyce Marshall and the address is:

<u>22 Huntsworth Mews</u>, <u>Ivor Place</u>, <u>N.W.1.</u>

I am starting a correspondence revision course in medicine & Surgery, I hope it will help me to work more methodically through the subjects.

I hope you are feeling well and have a good journey next week. G. b. y. –

        love always
           Ben

Ludwig Wittgenstein to Ben Richards, March 15, 1950

TEL. U 40 402   WIEN, 15.3.50
IV, ARGENTINIERSTRASSE 16

Dearest Ben,

I informed you wrongly in my last letter: my plane /on Thursday 23rd/ is due at the London Airport (<u>not</u> Northolt) at 8$^{.35}$ p.m.. I arrive on a plane that comes from Amsterdam. If you don't meet me at the airport I shall go on by bus to the terminal which, <u>I suppose</u>, is Airways House, Victoria. If I don't find you there I hope I'll find a message from you. – I'm quite well again & have been for a longish walk yesterday in some woods near the Danube. I was hoping to find snowdrops or violets but didn't find any, only some little blue flowers one of which I enclose in this letter. – – I hope you're well & not overworking & not too depressed! I long to see you again. – Please check up on the time & place of my arrival. I'm travelling with a Dutch plane & I'm not sure where they take you from the airport.
I think of you with love,
                      as <u>always</u>.
                            Ludwig

I hope to hear from you once more before I leave. – The London office of the Dutch company is at 202 Sloane Street S.W.1 & has the phone Sloane N^r 9656. I hope they aren't as vague & unreliable there as they are at their Vienna office.
                              L. L.

Ben Richards to Ludwig Wittgenstein, March 19, 1950

Telephone   22 Huntsworth Mews.
PADdington 4833   Ivor Place, N.W.1.
                                                                                    19/3/50

Dear Ludwig,
I have a nice room where I can work well.
I am looking forward to seeing you on Thursday – I will come to the Kensington terminal, and come to Mrs. Rhees's house with you. I have missed you very much.
I moved here on Thursday and since then I have done a good deal more work than at home in a similar period. I can get to Bart's quite quickly too.
On Friday evening I am singing in the St John Passion[84] and on Sunday in the St Matthew Passion.[85]

---

84 Johann Sebastian Bach, Johannespassion (BWV 245), written for a four-part choir, soloists, and orchestra.
85 Johann Sebastian Bach, Matthäuspassion (BWV 244), written for a double choir, soloists, and a double orchestra.

I am very glad you have been able to do some philosophy. I hope you will feel well for the flight and that there will be no hitches or delays this time.[86]

Your friend Professor John Ryle[87] has died.

Give my love to Miss Anscombe – I suppose she is staying in Vienna for some time yet.

  G. b. y. –
    <u>love alwa</u>ys
      Ben.

Ludwig Wittgenstein to Ben Richards, Telegram, March 21, 1950
CABLE & WIRELESS LTD
VIA IMPERIAL
The first line of this Telegram contains the following particulars in the order named: Prefix Letters and Number of Message, Office of Origin, Number of Words, Date, Time handed in and Official Instructions, if any.
L1310 WIEN 19 21 1445 =
/ELT/ BENEDICT RICHARDS 22 HUNTSWORTH MEWS IVOR PLACE LONDON NW 1 =
PLEASE LAKE[88] SURE OF AIR TERMINAL = LUDWIG WITTGENSTEIN +
L1310 22 NW 1 +

Ludwig Wittgenstein to Ben Richards, April 5, 1950

            %̸ v. Wright
            Strathaird
          5.4.50 Lady Margaret Rd
            Cambridge

Dearest Ben,

I'm sending this letter to Ickenham because I've forgotten the name of your street![89]
I never memorized it properly because it was so easy to find from Belsize Park

---

86 Wittgenstein flew back from Vienna to London on March 23, 1950. His flight out to Vienna back in December 1949 had been significantly delayed (see Wittgenstein's letter to Richards of December 25, 1949, and the relevant footnote there).

87 John Ryle (1889–1950), a professor of medicine at Cambridge. He and Wittgenstein had got to know each other during the Second World War, when both did war work at Guy's Hospital in London (see Monk 1990: 431ff).

88 Presumably a typo for: MAKE.

89 Richards had moved out of his parents' house in Uxbridge, and moved into his own student flat at 63 Glenmore Road, in Belsize Park (the inner northwest of London).

station. – This is chiefly to wish you a happy Easter. It was lovely being with you.[90] I wish you were here! I shall come to London on the 13th by the train that leaves here 11.5 a.m. & I'll stay until Monday or Tuesday the following week. I had a letter to-day from Con who writes that he is coming to London (on his way to Woolacombe)[91] on the 15th early in the morning & that he'd like to spend the weekend in London if I'm there, too. So I wrote to him that I would be in London & that I hope he'll spend the weekend with us. I'm looking forward to seeing you! I suppose you won't have time to meet my train on the 13th. <u>If</u> you could & <u>if</u> we could have some lunch together it would be <u>grand</u>. I know that your work comes first. –
So long! Look after yourself, with love
 always
  Ludwig

Ben Richards to Ludwig Wittgenstein, April 8, 1950

63 Glenmore Road
N.W.3.
8/4/50

Dear Ludwig

Thank you very much for the letter and the Easter card.[92]

I will meet your train – I suppose it gets in about 12.30 and we should have time for a quick lunch. I want to be at Bart's at 1.45. We'll fix up then where to meet in the evening. I want very much to see Con, and Smythies.

I am working better this week, but I miss seeing you.

I hope you have a happy Easter. Give my regards to Dr. Bevan.

 Love always,
  Ben.

---

90 After his return to England on March 2, 1950, Wittgenstein had stayed in London for a few days, spending time with Richards. He stayed – as he often did – with Jean Rhees, at 104 Goldhurst Terrace (see his letter to Georg Henrik von Wright of March 15, 1950). The day after his return, Wittgenstein began a new manuscript notebook – MS 173 – by writing: "Back from Vienna yesterday. After that, London seems gloomy to me. The order itself is disgusting here. People are killed by the needs themselves. All momentum is completely drained, as if by a tremendous friction" (MS 173, p. FCv).

91 A seaside resort with a long sandy beach on the north coast of the English county of Devon.

92 This was probably one of the undated Easter cards from Wittgenstein to Richards, included in Chapter VII.

Ben Richards to Ludwig Wittgenstein (undated, probably April 10, 1950)[93]

63 Glenmore Road
N.W.3.
Monday

Dear Ludwig

I forgot when I wrote yesterday[94] to say what you must know already – that I want extremely to see you this next week-end. Please let me know when your train is arriving and I will try to meet it. Are you staying at Mrs. Rhees's house?

I have been feeling a bit low spirited the last few days. I hope to hear from you soon and that will cheer me up.

It has poured with rain all day long.

Angela went back to Oxford to-day. I hope you'll see her.

   Love always
      Ben.

Ludwig Wittgenstein to Ben Richards, April 21, 1950[95]

Strathaird
Lady Margaret's Rd
Cambridge

Friday . ~~28~~ 21.4.

Dear Ben, <u>dear o. H.</u>,

I'm still in Cambridge at the old address. I <u>intend</u> going to Oxford – at least to see what the room there is like – at the beginning of next week. I'm pretty well & I'm working, but the house is noisy because the two children are <u>very</u> noisy[96] it would be good so good being with you & I'm looking forward to Saturday next week, but only <u>conditionally</u>, as it were, because your work comes <u>first</u>. I know you don't like to give

---

93 The dating of this letter is not certain. Given the address, it must have been from Richards' period in Belsize Park (from April to November of 1950), and it seems to naturally fit here, as a follow-up to Richards' letter to Wittgenstein of April 8, 1950. The Monday after that letter was sent, was just two days later – April 10 – which also fits with its nature as a follow-up.
94 If the placement of this letter here is correct, Richards is referring to his letter of April 8, two days earlier – but it's possible that he didn't send the letter until the next day, and Sunday April 9.
95 Richards added '22/4/50' to the letter (a Saturday, the day he received the letter), thereby identifying the year.
96 The von Wright children, Anita and Benedict, who were about 7 and 5 years old, respectively. A few days earlier Wittgenstein had written to Malcolm: "My health at present is pretty good. I'm doing some work but I get stuck over simple things & almost all I write is pretty dull. - I may go to Oxford soon & try to live in Miss Anscombe's house. I <u>like</u> to stay with the von Wrights but the two children are noisy & I need quiet. I wish I weren't so sensitive!" (April 17, 1950).

up things – <u>singing</u> e.g. – & you know me & know how I feel about being with you, but sacrifices have to be made. You must work like <u>hell</u>, & you must give up things that interfere with your work, & I'll ~~only~~ come on the 29th /only/ if you feel you need that recreation & that it will do your work <u>more</u> good than harm. Please be frank to yourself about this matter! – & to me, too.

I heard the Bruckner 7 yesterday, conducted by van Beynum. It was <u>badly</u> played, all bits & pieces.[97] You asked me the other day, was Bruckner difficult to play. He is. <u>Very</u>. Because he leaves out all the <u>conjunctions</u> & you have to understand him to know whether two phrases are joined up by an "and", or a "but" or a "therefore" etc. etc.. The 4th under Kubelik was much better.[98] The Scherzo again[99] is the easiest & I enjoyed it <u>enormously</u>.

Dearest Ben, look after yourself. I hope my friendship will <u>help</u> you, not hinder you in your work. Be good + God bless you.

I love you <u>always</u>
    Ludwig

I'll let you know my Oxford address if & when I go.
    L. L.

Ben Richards to Ludwig Wittgenstein (undated, between April 22 and 24, 1950)[100]

                  63 Glenmore Rd. N.W.3.

Dear Ludwig

Thanks for your letter. I am looking forward to seeing you on Saturday. Please let me know when you are arriving. I shall be at Bart's in the morning till about 12.30.

---

97 Eduard Alexander van Beinum (1901–1959) was a well-known Dutch conductor, second conductor of the Concertgebouw Orchestra Amsterdam from 1931. Van Beinum recorded Anton Bruckner's Symphony No. 7 in E major (WAB 107) for Decca in 1947. In a letter to Rudolf Koder from the following day Wittgenstein described his reaction in more detail: "The evening before yesterday I heard Bruckner's 7th here on the radio, <u>very</u> badly performed, strangely enough by a Dutch conductor, van Beynum, who once performed the same symphony quite well; I heard a gramophone recording of it! But in the performance the day before yesterday, the whole piece was torn into tiny pieces, played without any melodic coherence. Loud, soft, fast, slow, without meaning or context. That is the enormous danger when Bruckner is performed now, that each movement sounds like a series of small ideas. – The Scherzo, which is the simplest, nonetheless sounded wonderful. Something that was completely missing, & also in the gramophone recording, is the <u>sweetness</u> that Bruckner always has & without which everything else would be empty" (Wittgenstein to Koder, April 22, 1950).

98 Rafael Kubelik (1914–1996), a Czech-Swiss conductor and composer

99 This word is very hard to read; 'again' seems to be the best fit both with regards to the context and the look of the word, but it is far from certain.

100 Richards did not date this letter. But given that he is clearly responding to Wittgenstein's letter of April 21, 1950, and since Wittgenstein's letter to Richards of April 25 is clearly replying to this one, the date parameters can be fixed fairly precisely.

I am sorry the house is noisy. You must find somewhere quiet to live. I hope the room at Oxford is satisfactory.

I have been working well until I developed a nasty cold yesterday which makes me dull.

It is a little better already, and I hope it will go soon.

The weather is foul today. There has apparently been rain, hail, snow and sleet; but there was a bit of sun too.

It was wonderful to see you last week-end, and I think it will help me work to see you again. I am following Con Drury's advice & working at medicine.

    Love always
    Ben.

Ludwig Wittgenstein to Ben Richards, April 25, 1950[101]

            Strathaird
            Lady Mgt. Rd
            Camb
            Tuesday

Dearest Ben,

Thanks for your letter. I'm <u>ever</u> so sorry you've got a cold. Please treat it very intelligently!! You can't afford a cold now. (Also you mustn't give me one on Saturday.) If, that is, the people in this house haven't given me one by then. For they have colds too.) The weather is foul!!

To-morrow I intend going to Oxford. <u>If</u> you should want to communicate with me, please use the address: ℅ Smythies 22 Banbury Rd. Oxford.

If things go according to plan I shall arrive at Paddington on Saturday at <u>12</u>.25. As you probably won't be able to meet me there before 1 p.m. I shall wait for you in front of, or just inside, the dining room. If you don't see me there, look into the waiting room. I <u>hope</u> you'll be all right by then & that things will go well with you /all round/ – & with me, too. I long to see you!

    With love, as always
      Ludwig

I don't feel at all like travelling /& moving/ these days!

      God bless you

---

101 Richards added '26/4/50' to the letter, which was a Wednesday; and since Wittgenstein wrote 'Tuesday' on the letter, Richards was presumably noting the date the letter was received.

V. With Elizabeth Anscombe in Oxford

(May 1950 – February 1951)

At the end of April 1950, Wittgenstein moved from the von Wright's home in Cambridge, to Elizabeth Anscombe's house at 27 St. John Street in Oxford. Anscombe was a friend and old student of Wittgenstein's, who was then a research fellow at Somerville College. She leased the house from St John's College – living in one of the rooms herself, while renting out the other rooms to various lodgers to help make ends meet. Wittgenstein took up one of the unfilled rooms and lived there for just under a year, until mid-February 1951 – interrupted only by a long trip to Norway with Richards in October and November of 1950.

Shortly after his move, Wittgenstein wrote to Georg Henrik von Wright:

"I don't yet feel acclimatized at all. The house isn't very noisy but not very quiet, either. I don't know yet how I shall get on. The lodgers seem all to be rather nice, & one of them even very nice."[1]

The lodgers at the time were: Peter Daniel, the recently married Frank and Gillian Goodridge, and Barry Pink with his young son Yorick. Peter Daniel and Frank Goodridge had recently completed undergraduate degrees at Oxford (having previously fought in the war), and Barry Pink was an art student at Ruskin College. And all of them were close with Yorick Smythies, another friend and old student of Wittgenstein's who lived in Oxford, where he worked as a librarian. When Wittgenstein moved into the house in April, Anscombe was still in Vienna, but she returned to England – and moved back into the house – at the end of May 1950. During those years Anscombe's husband – Peter Geach – lived in Cambridge with their children, and she would do a great deal of travelling back and forth between Oxford and Cambridge.[2]

---

1 Wittgenstein to von Wright, April 28, 1950.
2 For a detailed account of the house on St. John Street and its various inhabitants, see Berkman 2025: 70ff.

Angela Richards – the eldest of Ben's sisters, who at that time was 21 – was studying at Oxford in 1950, so Wittgenstein saw her periodically over the course of the year, and wrote her a few letters too (which are included here).

Not long before Wittgenstein moved to Oxford, Richards had moved from his family's home in Ickenham into a student flat at 63 Glenmore Road, in Belsize Park (in the inner northwest of London). Richards was busy both working at Bart's Hospital and also studying for two different sets of upcoming medical exams: the Conjoint exams which he would sit in London, and the Final M.B. exams which he would sit at King's College in Cambridge – both of which would be taking place in the early summer of 1950. The Conjoint exam was the basic state qualification for medical students in the United Kingdom at the time, and the Final M.B. was the last set of exams he needed to pass in order to receive his Cambridge medical qualification (in addition to the Bachelor's degree which he already had).

Wittgenstein and Richards planned to go on an extended trip to Norway after Richards' exams, to stay in the mountainside cabin Wittgenstein had had built in 1914, just outside the village of Skjolden. But Richards failed a number of his papers, so he had to return to his studies in order to prepare for re-sits which would take place at the end of September and the beginning of October 1950. So, much to Wittgenstein's disappointment, their planned trip had to be postponed. Fortunately, they were finally able to make the trip after the re-sits, and they set off on October 15, 1950, for about a month. They stayed briefly in Wittgenstein's cabin, but ended up spending most of the month in Anna Rebni's guesthouse, closer to the village. The move was at least in part because Richards had fallen ill. Indeed, he fell ill twice in the course of the visit – with bronchitis and asthma – and at one point he had to receive treatment in a local hospital. Many years later, Richards described their Skjolden trip to Georg Henrik von Wright, as follows (including a sketch of the floor plan and location of Wittgenstein's cabin):

"Dear Georg Henrik,

Yes. Wittgenstein and I did stay rather briefly in the hut near Skjolden probably in late September 1950. My memory is not reliable about dates, spelling and other facts but I'll tell you what I can about it, some of which you'll already know. I have sketched rough plans of the hut and its situation which was practically inaccessible except across the little lake either by boat or in Winter across the ice when it was strong enough. The first bridge across the river above the lake was some miles up the valley towards Fortun. The path was steep from the lake up to the hut which was timber on a stone basement. It was roughly (or perhaps exactly) square and the windows I think were also square. The entrance to the main floor was at the back and the hillside continued up behind. We did not use the attic room.

We stayed briefly in Bergen after crossing from Newcastle and went by overnight boat to the Sogne Fjord and Skjolden where we may have stayed a night in the village.

Wittgenstein had years before made a gift of the hut to Arne Bolstad who was I think a market gardener. After rowing and climbing to the hut the first thing we did was to remove the various pictures, flags etc. that Bolstad had hung on the unpainted wooden walls and sweep and clean the place. We brought some provisions but I cannot remember what we did for water. There was a pulley to raise buckets from the lake. There <u>might</u> also have been a tank in the hut but probably not. Bringing up water was of course easier with two people – one to fill the buckets and one to wind them up and down – than with one. We would row across the lake for walks and visits. Wittgenstein has several friends in Skjolden. I had brought Austin's recently published translation of Frege's Foundations of Arithmetic (Grundlagen) with German text, and we used to read and discuss this.

After a few days – less than a week – I became ill with bronchitis and a local doctor took me into a small hospital a few miles down the fjord for two or three nights, where I was very well and kindly treated. The weather which had been quite good then turned very cold in early October and the rest of our stay in Norway was in Frøken Anna Rebni's beautiful farmhouse, Eide. . . .

I don't remember just how long we were in Norway altogether in 1950, perhaps three or four weeks, but you may have independent evidence of the dates."[3]

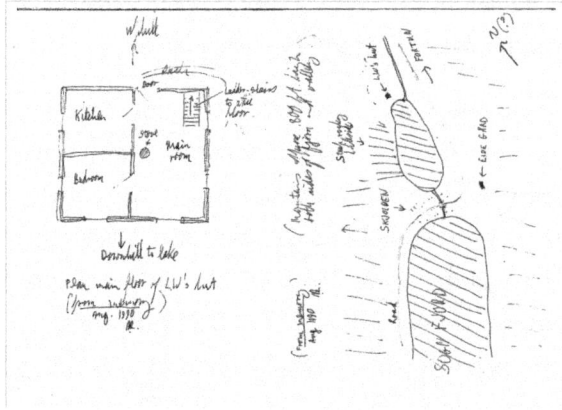

---

[3] Richards' letter to von Wright of August 15, 1990 (Von Wright Archives of the National Library of Finland in Helsinki, call mark: COLL. 714.202); see also Johannessen, Larsen, & Åmås 1994: 55–7.

Once back in Oxford in mid-November 1950, Wittgenstein determined to return to Skjolden around the end of the year, as he wrote to Norman Malcolm:

"I was away 5 weeks & before that I was illish for about a month. In Norway the <u>friend</u> who went with me fell ill with bronchitis <u>twice</u>. So there was no end of trouble & I postponed writing to my friends from one day to the other. This doesn't mean that we didn't enjoy our journey, for we <u>did</u>, & we had wonderful weather. I had intended to do some work but I didn't do any. I may possibly go back to Norway before long & try to work; it's the only place I know where I can have real quiet. Of course it's possible that I'm no longer able to do any decent research, but it's certainly worth while finding out if I am or not."[4]

And so Wittgenstein booked a steamer ticket to Bergen (the first leg of the trip) for December 30, 1950. He didn't feel capable of living in his isolated cabin in the middle of the winter, as the physical work involved in doing so (chopping wood, hauling water, and walking across the ice into town) was now too much for him – but Anna Rebni initially said that she could put him up in her guesthouse again. Unfortunately, just before Christmas, Rebni was in touch to say that on second thoughts it would be too difficult for her to host him in mid-winter. Since Wittgenstein couldn't find any alternative lodging options – and since his health had taken a turn for the worse in any case – he had to abandon his travel plans.

As the year turned, Wittgenstein's health continued to worsen, and he got weaker and weaker, until it became clear that he was dying. His doctor – Edward Bevan – had said that when the time came, Wittgenstein could spend his last weeks or months in his home in Cambridge, with him and his family. So on February 8, 1951, Anscombe accompanied Wittgenstein on his final trip to Cambridge. She later recalled:

"At first when he came to my house he lived on the first floor, i.e. the middle floor; but he could hear the couple below[5] – my family hadn't yet moved to Oxford – and 'she bickers soprano'. So he moved upstairs to the smallest room in the house. I remember when he left for the Bevans at one point he seemed almost apologetic and said: I feel a bit as if I were in a grave in this room. His room at Joan Bevan's was painted pink and much more cheerful. It is possible that if I had not been pregnant I should have felt hurt at his departure, but it seemed wholly reasonable as things were; and in any case it was quite excellent for him to be at the Bevans."[6]

---

4   Wittgenstein to Malcolm, December 1, 1950.
5   This was Frank and Gillian Goodridge.
6   Anscombe 2025: 181–2.

Shortly before he left Oxford – on January 29, 1951 – Wittgenstein updated his will and appointed Elizabeth Anscombe, Rush Rhees, and Georg Henrik von Wright, as the administrators of his philosophical estate.

During his year in Oxford Wittgenstein was mainly working in what are now known as manuscripts 174 and 175, though he did not feel that his work was going well at all.

Ludwig Wittgenstein to Ben Richards, May 6, 1950[7]

27 St. John Street[8]
Oxford
Saturday

Dear Ben,

It was wonderful for me to be with you last weekend, as it always is. You know how intensely I enjoyed being with you.

I'm afraid I acted very foolishly when once, on walking to Mrs. Rhees's place[9] with you, I gave vent to my anxiety about what would happen if one day you felt I was no longer a satisfying companion for you. It was foolish of me to talk as I did, but it wasn't in my power /at the time/ to shut off these thoughts & fears, – I was /then/ overpowered by them. Some kind words of yours made me stop & brought me to my senses. I may have such lapses every now & again, but what I really <u>ought</u> to say, & what I <u>mean</u>, is: "When ever you're ready to leave me – leave me!" Please take this seriously. I am foolish, but I don't <u>like</u> to be foolish; & if you can, please help me not to be, even if it means telling me something that hurts.

I saw Angela[10] yesterday. She doesn't seem to have changed, except that she seems to be a good deal happier than at Ickenham, & that she wears her hair shorter. We had a

---

7 Richards added '6/5/50' to the letter, which was a Saturday.
8 This was the address of the house that Elizabeth Anscombe leased from St John's College, Oxford, and in which she rented out rooms to various lodgers. Wittgenstein became an extra lodger in the house for about ten months from this period.
9 Wittgenstein seems to have spent the previous weekend – of April 29–30, 1950 – in London, and seen Richards. When he did so he usually stayed with Jean Rhees (see Wittgenstein's letter to Jean Rhees of the end of April 1950).
10 The oldest of Richards' younger sisters. She had started studying at St Hugh's College, Oxford, and Wittgenstein made a point of seeing her periodically now that he was living in Oxford too.

longish & quite nice talk in my room. On Tuesday we're going to have tea together. – I'm moderately well but not working well. I'm stupid.[11]

– If I don't hear from you to the contrary I shall arrive at Paddington on Saturday next at 12.^{25} & again proceed to the dining-room entrance.

    I think of you constantly! & love you as always.

                Ludwig

Enclosure included with the letter of May 6, 1950:

Sweet memory is
  the fragrance
True friendship are
  the flowers
Whose precious gifts
  of beauty
Enrich the passing hours.

---

11 Wittgenstein wrote to Rush Rhees the next day, about both his wellness and his work: "As you see I'm in Oxford. My room isn't very quiet & I'm going into another room in the same house where it's supposed to be more quiet. I'm working a bit but my work's no good, & I can't say that it is because of the noise. I'm just not in the right frame of mind; my work only mildly interests me; & you can imagine what under these circumstances the stuff is like I'm writing down. – I'm moderately well. Dr Bevan in Cambridge wrote to a London specialist about me, giving him the history of my case up to the present time & the expert replied that I might easily live for five more years. Nice prospect! Another year of this half-life would have been ample" (Wittgenstein to Rhees, May 7, 1950).

Wishing you all
the things you would wish
for yourself

Ben Richards to Ludwig Wittgenstein, May 9, 1950

63 Glenmore Road
N.W.3.
9/5/50

Dear Ludwig,

Thank you very much for the letter and the card. I am looking forward to seeing you on Saturday in the same place. I long to see you again.

I am very glad you saw Angela and hope you will go on seeing her if you feel like it. I am glad to hear she seems happier than at Ickenham. Do you think she looks w<u>el</u>l? My work is going on but not well this week. My cough which I thought I had got rid of came back, and I didn't feel very good. I saw a doctor at Bart's and am starting a short course of penicillin injections to-day. I hope I'll be well enough to be decent company for you when you come. It will probably do me good to see you.

  Love always,
    Ben.

Ludwig Wittgenstein to Ben Richards, May 10, 1950

27 St. John Street
Oxford
190.5.50.

Dearest Ben,

Thanks for your letter. Please don't come to the station on Saturday unless you feel <u>really fit</u>. I'll be at the old place in front of the dining-room; if you don't show up I'll come straight to your digs.[12] I <u>hope</u> you're better! I saw Angela yesterday; we had tea & went for a walk. She looks pretty well I think. But it's not easy for me to tell, for if one's cheerful one nearly always looks fairly well. – I, too, haven't been feeling very well the last few days & ~~my~~ I didn't get on at all with my work. I'm just completely dull. But in my case it doesn't matter so much.

---

12 Namely, Richards' student flat at 63 Glenmore Road, Belsize Park.

Good luck! I'm looking forward to Saturday. You'll be good company for me in <u>whatever</u> state you are.

   With love, always
     Ludwig

Ludwig Wittgenstein to Ben Richards, May 17, 1950

              27 St. John Street
                   Oxford
                   17.5.50.

Dearest Ben,

When I got to Paddington the other day I asked at a booking office on what platform the train was leaving & exactly what time. The man said "In <u>one</u> minute." So I rushed like. . . . & just caught it. – I asked Smythies about a place to stay in London the Sunday after next. He said, the place <u>he</u> stayed at was <u>quite</u> unsuitable, <u>very</u> noisy. He'd only stayed in one place, not in two. But he's going to write to a friend of his who <u>might</u> have a spare room. Please make enquiries too, so we have several fish to fry. That is, if you still want me to come.

It's been <u>wonderful</u> being with you! but there is your work to consider & of course also what you feel like. – I hope your health is good & you work well!

I'm a bit less stupid than I was last week. Seeing you has done me good. – Yesterday I saw an incredible thing in ~~the~~ a shop window: a duck, made of plastic, with a hollow in its back serving as chamber. An advertisement was stuck into it saying: "<u>Ducky</u>. The practical answer to every parents' problem. Supercedes the old-style chamber. Makes childish duties <u>fun</u>."[13] I couldn't trust my eyes. – I'm pretty well, except for the little trouble I told you about, & if my room was quieter I'd be happy. – Look after yourself. I think of you <u>constantly</u> with love.

        Ludwig

P.S. I had a letter from Con who sends you his love. I'll give him your's automatically when I write him,

   <u>G. bl. y.</u>
       L.

Write soon if you've found something, etc..

---

13 See the accompanying illustration; source: https://www.gracesguide.co.uk/File:Im1949BIF-Ducky.jpg

This is the advert that Wittgenstein was referring to in his letter of May 17, 1950

Ludwig Wittgenstein to Angela Richards (postmarked: May 21, 1950)[14]

27 St John Street

Oxford

Sunday

Dear Angela,

Sorry I couldn't talk to you to-day in the interval. I was in a <u>great</u> hurry trying to get into the hall illegally, & I succeeded. I heard the first part sitting on the doorstep behind the orchestra. – Whenever you feel inclined to & have <u>nothing</u> better to do come & see me.

I hope you know you don't have to.

        Yours

        Ludwig Wittgenstein

---

14 The original letter is in the possession of Gabriel Citron.

Ludwig Wittgenstein to Ben Richards, May 24, 1950

27 St John Street
Oxford
24.5.50[15]

Dearest Ben,

One of Smythies' friends can put me up over the weekend. The address is 38 Brunswick Gdns. W.8, i.e, rather far from you; so <u>if</u> you got something nearer to Belsize Park I wouldn't go to Brunswick Gdns. If I don't hear from you to the contrary, I'll arrive ~~at~~ on Saturday at 1$\underline{^{43}}$ by <u>bus</u> at <u>Victoria bus station</u>. I took a bus ticket because it's cheaper; on the other hand the journey is twice as long, & so, maybe, I was a fool.

It would be nice if you could meet my bus. (In fact I think it's called a <u>coach</u>).—

I haven't seen Angela, at least not to speak to.

I think of you with love <u>always</u>.

Ludwig

Thanks for your letter.[16] G. b. y.!

Ludwig Wittgenstein to Ben Richards, May 29, 1950[17]

27 St. John Street
Oxford
Monday

Dearest Ben,

I've just arrived. The journey wasn't too bad, & I saw the golden ball at High Wycombe.[18] It needs polishing.

I loved being with you more than I can say.

Please forgive me for being foolish & for having spells of a dark & hopeless mood. I shall probably be like that as long as I live. Thanks for having been so kind & wonderful to me, & particularly for coming with me to the bus terminal.

---

15 The '50' was added in pencil, presumably by Richards.

16 Richards' letter has not been preserved.

17 Richards added '30/5/50' to the letter, which was a Tuesday; and since Wittgenstein wrote 'Monday' on the letter, Richards was presumably noting the date the letter was received.

18 The large golden sphere that sits atop the tower of the St Lawrence Church, in West Wycombe. It can be seen from many miles away.

G. b. y.! – I found a letter from Con here in which he mentions your exam & sends you his love. – I think of you <u>constantly</u>, holding my thumbs for you.[19] (Which, by the way, prevents me from twiddling them.)
Please think of me with kind thoughts always.

<u>With love, always</u>

Ludwig

Ludwig Wittgenstein to Ben Richards, June 1, 1950[20]

27 St John Street

Oxford

Thursday

Dear Ben, o. H.,
This is only to say that I'm going to Cambridge (Strathaird Lady Margret Rd.) tomorrow & staying probably until about the middle of next week.[21] I've got to see my dentist & also other things to do. So <u>if</u> you write to me over the weekend write to Strathaird. – I wish I had more quiet here!!! – – I'll write to you from Cambridge. – I hope your work goes well. G. bl. y.! <u>I think of you with love always</u>.

Ludwig

---

19 Wittgenstein directly translated the German idiom "[ich] drücke dir die Daumen" into English, creating an awkward Germanism – perhaps consciously. The nearest English equivalent would be: 'crossing my fingers for you' (i.e. wishing you luck) – but that wouldn't so easily have allowed for the joke about thumb twiddling that followed.
20 Richards added '1/6/50' to the letter, which was a Thursday.
21 That is, Wittgenstein would be staying with the von Wright family, where he had been living before he moved to Oxford. Georg Henrik von Wright later recalled this particular trip as follows: "During these years Wittgenstein came to Cambridge on several occasions. Then he usually stayed with us in the big house we had rented in Lady Margaret Road ... His last stay was in June 1950. When Wittgenstein was with us, he and I had daily talks, sometimes on things he was working on then, sometimes on the logical topics which were mine at the time, but most often on literature and music, on religion, and on what could perhaps best be termed the philosophy of history and civilization. Wittgenstein sometimes read to me from his favorite authors, for example, from Grimm's *Marchen* or Gottfried Keller's *Züricher Novellen*. The recollection of his voice and facial expression when, seated in a chair in his sickroom, he read aloud Goethe's *Hermann und Dorothea* is for me unforgettable" (von Wright 2016: 1029).

Ludwig Wittgenstein to Ben Richards, June 4, 1950[22]

Strathaird
Lady Margret Rd
Cambridge
Sunday

Dearest Ben, o. H.,

I came here on Friday evening & went to the dentist on Saturday. I also talked with Erik Tranöy,[23] the Norwegian, about our trip.[24] He has written to his sister[25] but hasn't yet had a reply, he is also writing to a cousin of his who lives in Hardanger Fjord. He is sure he'll find us something but told me I must book a passage <u>without delay</u> or it'll be too late. I will therefore return to Oxford via London & try to book a passage /with Cook's at the Strand Palace/. It would be very good if I could see you, for an hour, say, before doing so to get the dates right. I shall leave here either on Wednesday or on Thursday & arrive at Liverpool Street at <u>12</u>.[34] I don't intend to stay over night in London & in any case wouldn't try to disturb you in your work. Please <u>wire</u> me if ~~whether~~ you can ~~could~~ /easily/ see me either Wednesday or Thursday at Liverpool Street, or elsewhere /wherever you like/. I will then wire you ~~on~~ which day I come. I <u>believe</u> it will be Wednesday.

If I can see you on Thursday & <u>not</u> on Wednesday I'll come on Thursday. I needn't say that, apart from everything else, I'd love to see your old face. If you can't see me at all, please wire what you know about the dates of your London exam, so I know when we can sail. — I looked up the prescription of Mucilago Salep[26] & it is: P.T.O.

Mucilago Salep   100.0
Tannigen[27]   5.0
<u>Syr. Cort. Aurant.</u>[28]   . 20.0

---

22 Richards added '4/6/50' to the letter, which was a Sunday.
23 Knut Erik Tranøy (1918–2012) was a Norwegian philosopher who had come to Cambridge for the 1949–50 academic year. He and his wife lodged in rooms in the von Wright home, and he got to know Wittgenstein during the time that Wittgenstein had stayed with the von Wrights (see Johannessen, Larsen, & Åmås 1994: 174).
24 Wittgenstein and Richards were planning a joint trip – that coming summer – to Skjolden (in western Norway), where Wittgenstein had had a mountainside cabin since 1914.
25 Anna Gripstad (née Tranøy).
26 A mucilage (i.e. a gelatinous substance) made from salep (i.e. dried and ground orchid tubers). This was then made into a drink which was traditionally used to help with indigestion, heartburn, flatulence, diarrhoea, and other conditions.
27 A compound of tannin and acetyl, which was used to reduce intestinal inflammation and improve symptoms of diarrhoea.
28 Stands for: Syrup Corticum Auratiorum: a syrup made from the peels of bitter oranges.

If you can't see me in town but <u>can</u> see me at 63 Glenmore Rd I'll come out there, talk things over with you, & go again. I promise I won't keep you, & if you can't see me at all I'll understand entirely.

God bless you! & help you! I l. y. <u>a.</u> & t. o. y. <u>c.</u>.[29]

                              Ludwig

Ludwig Wittgenstein to Ben Richards, Telegram, June 6, 1950

                      POST OFFICE
                        TELEGRAM

Prefix. Time handed in. Office of Origin and Service Instructions. Words.
CB A 7273 11.35 PM CAMBRIDGE T 17 =
BENEDICT RICHARDS 63 GLENMORE RD LONDON-NW 3 =
ARRIVING THURSDAY 12.34 WAITING FOR YOU WAITING ROOM
LIVERPOOLSTREET LOVE = LUDWIG +
63 NW 3 12.34 LUDWIG +

Ludwig Wittgenstein to Ben Richards, June 8, 1950[30]

                                            Strand Palace
                                                      Hotel
                                                   Thursday at
                                                        4 p.m.

                            Read this <u>very</u> carefully!

Dearest Ben,

I'm afraid I have rather unfavorable news. <u>All</u> the steamship lines to Bergen <u>& to Oslo</u> are completely booked up for July. The <u>only</u> reservation I could make was 2 <u>third class</u> tickets for the 2nd of August.

I made these <u>provisionally</u>, subject to your approval, & I also asked the Cook's representative to have us transferred, <u>in case</u> there is any cancelation, to 2nd class & if possible to an earlier boat. What the likelihood of such a cancelation is, it's impossible to say. – If you agree to go on August 2nd (if necessary) please phone the Cook's[31] representative at Strand Palace Hotel. Her name is M^{iss} Brandrick & her telephone nr

---

29 Stands for: 'I love you <u>always</u> & think of you <u>constantly</u>.'
30 Richards added '8/6/50' to the letter, which was a Thursday.
31 Thomas Cook & Son was an old travel agency with a branch in the Strand Palace Hotel in London.

is Grovenor[32] 4000 extension 500. Ring her up, give her your & my name, & tell her to cancel the reservation, or to go through with it. I hope you will decide on the latter. Also please write me a line /straight away/ just saying what you've decided. I'm terribly sorry there are these difficulties. (They are of course not my making.) If you decide that Aug 2nd is too late for you we'll do something else, & I'll be happy whatever we do, but I think Norway would be a good idea if it's possible.

Dear Ben, it was good to see you. I wish I needn't bother you at this moment with all this business, but it's necessary. We could of course fly to Stavanger, but that's very expensive. If you come decide by to-morrow (~~Saturday~~ ring up the Cook's lady either before 12, or between 2 & 4; on Saturday she knocks off at 12.

God bless you! & help you!
I l y a & t. o. y. w. l. c ..[33]

Ludwig

Ludwig Wittgenstein to Ben Richards, June 11, 1950[34]

27 St. John Street
Oxford
Sunday

Dear Ben, d. H.,

I don't know exactly what day your birthday is but I think it's one of these days.[35] Also the card says "Good luck" & that's what I want to say.

Con wrote to me a few days ago: "Please give my very best wishes to Ben. I believe he is right to take all the papers providing he treats the mid-wifery & surgery just as an exercise & doesn't worry about how well he does."

I thought you'd like to know what he thinks about it. – God bless you & good luck! I hope you won't suffer too terribly from the heat! I think of you with love always.

Ludwig

---

32 Presumably: 'Grosvenor'.
33 Stands for: 'I love you always & think of you with love constantly.'
34 Richards added '11/6/50' to the letter, which was a Sunday.
35 Richards' birthday was June 23.

Ludwig Wittgenstein to Ben Richards, Birthday Card, June 11, 1950[36]

Birthday Greetings – GOOD LUCK

"Here's a horseshoe for the best of Luck –
A fountain in full play
For a Birthday bright with sunny hours
And friendship's Flowers for aye!"
GRAV STEVENS.

A Happy Birthday Wish

With love from Ludwig

Ludwig Wittgenstein to Angela Richards (postmarked: June 16, 1950)[37]

27 St John Street
Oxford
Friday

Dear Angela,
I saw the Midsummernights Dream, or rather the first act of it, on Tuesday, & I wondered if you'd mind discussing the performance with me one of these days.[38] I imagine you're very busy, & you mayn't like the idea anyhow.

---

36 Richards' birthday was June 23.
37 The original letter is in the possession of Gabriel Citron.
38 William Shakespeare's play, *A Midsummer Night's Dream* (1595/96). Angela Richards had herself taken part in the performance on Tuesday June 13. On the same day as he wrote this letter, Wittgenstein also wrote to his friend Rudolf Koder with some of his (rather negative) impressions: "A few days ago, I saw a terrible performance of A Midsummer Night's Dream. I only went because a friend's sister was in it. The direction was so awful that even good acting talent would have been lost. It was an open-air performance & the characters ran around on the lawn like tennis players & shouted their lines because otherwise they wouldn't have been heard" (Wittgenstein to Koder, June 16, 1950).

The only thing that may be said for it is that you'd hear someone who doesn't flatter you & /who/ doesn't think that young people running about on a lawn are in themselves so charming that they shouldn't hear a word of criticism. – If you'd rather not talk about it, or have no time don't bother to reply. If you like to have a talk, either just drop in & if you find me out leave a note on my table, or else write a line saying when you'll come. I'm free all next week except maybe Saturday 24th, & I may be away on the 25th & 26th. I'm also free most of this Sunday (18th). – Some weeks ago Ben wrote to me to give you his love.

   Good luck!
   Yours
     Ludwig Wittgenstein

Ludwig Wittgenstein to Ben Richards, June 17, 1950[39]

27 St. John Street
Oxford
Saturday

Dearest Ben,

Thanks for your letteretu /[a new word][40]/ of 16.th July.[41] <u>Don't worry</u>. I hope your papers were all right & I hope you'll do well in your vivas. Try to be articulate /thereby helping the examiner/. But first & foremost don't worry! (Luck can fail one; & <u>if</u> it does you'll be able to take it.)

God bless you. I think of you with love constantly & hold my thumbs for you.[42]

Ludwig

I saw Miss Anscombe yesterday; I'm glad you saw her too. Please don't have <u>any</u> discussions with her while your exam's on. Get as much rest /& fresh air/ as you can.

   With love
    L.

If you like me to, I shall come to Cambridge next weekend. I shan't come on the Sunday /as you suggested/ but on Saturday afternoon. If you're engaged then you

---

39 Richards added '17/6/50' to the letter, which was a Saturday.
40 The square brackets are Wittgenstein's own. It's not clear whether the strange ending to the word 'letter' was a mistake (a slip of the pen), or an intentional joke. But next to the word, running up the margin, he added "a new word" in square brackets by way of playful 'explanation'.
41 Wittgenstein presumably meant '16th *June*' rather than '16th July'. This letter of Richards' has not been preserved.
42 See Wittgenstein's letter to Richards of May 29, 1950, and the relevant footnote there.

needn't see me until Sunday. (I could stay in M^{iss} Anscombes house or possibly at an address in Clare Street off Barton Rd.)

If you find time send me a wire, saying if you like me to come & how you are.

L. L.

G. bl. y.

Ben Richards to Ludwig Wittgenstein, June 20, 1950

~~ABERNETHIAN ROOM,~~

~~ST BARTHOLOMEW'S HOSPITAL,~~

~~LONDON, E.C.1~~

King's College

Cambridge

20/6/50

Dear Ludwig

Thanks a lot for your letter. Let me know when you arrive on Saturday, and I will meet you. I have no other engagements. The Conjoint exam[43] begins on Wednesday June 28th in London, so I ought to go back to Belsize Park on Monday.

I have failed part 1, but not by very much I think. Part 2 has not been too bad so far except for one viva to-day in Pharmacology, which went badly.

---

43 The 'Conjoint' exam was the basic qualification for medical students in the United Kingdom at the time, consisting of a series of sub-examinations on anatomy, physiology, pharmacology, pathology, and the like.

It will be good to see you again when this is over. I hope Miss Anscombe has been able to make arrangements for your room to be quiet. Have you been able to work?

    Love always,

        Ben

Ludwig Wittgenstein to Ben Richards, June 21, 1950[44]

27 St. John Street
Oxford
Wednesday

Dearest Ben,

Sorry about Part 1. I <u>hope</u> Part 2 will be all right– but <u>if</u> it isn't don't let it get you down. <u>You'll be all right & you won't give up.</u> –

I'm arriving on Saturday at **5.28** p.m. It will be good to see you! God bless you. <u>Don't worry. Keep your head up!</u> I love you <u>always</u>

        Ludwig

Ludwig Wittgenstein to Ben Richards, Telegram, June 23, 1950

POST OFFICE
TELEGRAM

Prefix. Time handed in. Office of Origin and Service Instructions. Words.

+ RG A 0138 8.31 OXFORD RG 11

R B O RICHARDS KINGS COLLEGE CAMBRIDGE =

ARRIVING 5.18 LOVE = LUDWIG

++ R B O 5.18 LUDWIG

Ludwig Wittgenstein to Ben Richards, June 27, 1950[45]

27 St. John Street
Oxford
Tuesday evening

Dear Ben, d. H.,

I've just arrived at Oxford & it's too late for this letter to reach you before the exam. But you know any how what I feel & what my wishes & hopes are. It was lovely seeing you at Cambridge. – <u>Don't worry, & good luck!</u>

---

44 Richards added '21/6/50' to the letter, which was a Wednesday.
45 Richards added '27/6/50' to the letter, which was a Tuesday.

I think of you with love <u>always</u>.
$$\text{Ludwig}$$
M^{iss} Anscombe travelled here with me, so it wasn't dull. I'm looking forward to seeing you as always.
$$\text{L. L.}$$

Ludwig Wittgenstein to Ben Richards, July 1, 1950[46]

$$\text{27 St. John Street}$$
$$\text{Oxford}$$
$$\text{Saturday}$$

Dear Ben, d. H. –

I <u>hope</u> it isn't a serious cause, like illness or great depression, that has kept you from letting me know about Wednesday.[47] That it should have been negligence & a lack of consideration for me, whose feelings you know, I won't believe. May you be well & <u>courageous</u>, & not let failure (if that's what it was) get you down!! G. bl. y..! <u>Remember that I'm thinking of you with love, always</u>.

Don't ever lose hope! Ludwig

Ludwig Wittgenstein to Ben Richards, July 3, 1950[48]

$$\text{27 St. John Street}$$
$$\text{Oxford}$$
$$\text{Monday}$$

Dear Ben,

Thanks for your letter. Perhaps, after all, you didn't do as badly as you think. – Please don't worry!

How you could have waited with writing till Sunday,[49] knowing that this would give me many days of constant anxiety, worry & disappointment, which 2 lines from you could have saved me, I <u>can't</u> understand. Or if I can, I don't want to. – I think it may be better if I don't come to London this week. I have an idea that Mrs Rhees couldn't put me up, & that I would not be a cheerful companion & able to give you the relaxation you need.

---

46 Richards added '1/7/50' to the letter, which was a Saturday.
47 Namely, letting Wittgenstein know how the first of his conjoint exams had gone, which began on Wednesday June 28 (see Richards' letter to Wittgenstein on June 20, 1950, and the relevant footnote there).
48 Richards added '3/7/50' to the letter, which was a Monday.
49 This letter from Richards has not been preserved.

My thoughts & wishes are with you <u>as they always are.</u> May you work quietly & steadily, & have luck!!
<u>God bless you!</u>
    With love
       Ludwig
If you want anything write or wire.
      L. L.

Ludwig Wittgenstein to Ben Richards, July 3, 1950[50]

              Monday

Dear Ben, o. H.
A few hours ago I posted a letter to you which contained a reproach. I can't say whether that reproach was justified or not, but <u>if</u> it was I want you to know that I forgive you, <u>gladly</u>; & I want you to be quite clear about one thing: <u>love</u> isn't measured by what a person <u>feels</u> when the other is with him, but by what he /feels &/ will <u>do</u> for the other when they aren't together. – If my reproach was unjustified I want you to forgive me, now & always, & just go on l . . . g me.
  <u>Work well!!</u>
    <u>I love you always.</u>
      Ludwig
If my coming can <u>help</u> you I will come up for a day.
      L. L.

Ludwig Wittgenstein to Ben Richards, Telegram, July 5, 1950

      POST OFFICE
      TELEGRAM

Prefix. Time handed in. Office of Origin and Service Instructions. Words.
OF + 7087 11.45 OXFORD 15
BENEDICT RICHARS 63 GLENMORE RD LONDONNW 3
= COMING WEEKEND WIRE ARRIVAL LATER DONT WORRY LOVE =
LUDWIG + 63 NW 3 + OF +

---

50 As with the previous letter, Richards also added '3/7/50' to this letter, which was a Monday.

Ludwig Wittgenstein to Ben Richards, Telegram, July 7, 1950
POST OFFICE
TELEGRAM
Prefix. Time handed in. Office of Origin and Service Instructions. Words.
OF A 7116 12.58 OXFORD 16
BENEDICT RICHARDS 63 GLENMORE RD LONDON-NW 3 =
ARRIVING UXBRIDGE 12.44 TUBE TO SWISS COTTAGE LOVE = LUDWIG +
63 NW 3 12.44 LUDWIG +

Ludwig Wittgenstein to Ben Richards, July 11, 1950[51]

> 27 St. John Street
> Oxford
> Tuesday

Dear Ben, o. H. –
This is chiefly to say: Good luck! & God bless you.[52]
Don't worry, please. Think that the examiner tries to find out what you know, & that he can't do it unless you <u>talk</u>. Amplify your statements as much as possible. But mainly: <u>don't worry & don't lose hope.</u>
I'm thinking of you with love constantly.

> Ludwig

It's been <u>lovely</u> seeing you. Last night Angela came to see me & we had a little talk. – I wrote to M[iss] Anscombe that you're planning to come to Oxford on Sunday & to go to Cambridge Wednesday next.
Don't forget that I'm thinking of you always & be of good cheer. L. L.

---

51 Richards added '11/7/50' to the letter, which was a Tuesday.
52 In addition to written components, the conjoint medical exams also included clinical and oral examinations. Wittgenstein was referring to these, which were upcoming for Richards (see Richards' letter to Wittgenstein on June 20, 1950, and the relevant footnote there).

Ludwig Wittgenstein to Ben Richards, July 12, 1950[53]

27 St John Street
Oxford
Wednesday

Dear Ben, d. H.,

I have just received your wire.[54] Please don't let depression get hold of you. I <u>know</u> how you must feel, but what has happened isn't the tragedy it may now seem to be. Remember you only went into digs in March, & that didn't give you quite enough time. Hold your head high! – I'm looking forward to seeing you on Sunday. Never forget that I'm thinking of you

    with love

        always.

           Ludwig

Ludwig Wittgenstein to Ben Richards, July 22, 1950[55]

27 St. John Street
Oxford
Saturday

Dear Ben,

It is not easy for me to write to you to-day. I'm still under the influence of the shock of yesterday.[56] I must write because there are a few things I can't postpone saying.

1) Don't work for M^iss Anscombe till Wednesday, but take a few days off, if possible in the fresh air. You could, e.g., come here for 2–3 days & just <u>take it easy</u>. This might be good for both of us. /It certainly would for me /(but do whatever is best for you)//. I still think what you're proposing to do utterly unwise, but if you're <u>determined</u> to go through with it then it's your <u>duty</u> to do it with as much sense & as little gambling as possible. (I consider it your duty also towards me.)

---

53 Richards added '12/7/50' to the letter, which was a Wednesday.
54 It seems that Richards had telegrammed to tell Wittgenstein that he had failed some elements of his conjoint exams (see Richards' letter to Wittgenstein on June 20, 1950, and the relevant footnote there).
55 Richards added '22/7/50' to the letter, which was a Saturday.
56 The shock was presumably that Richards had written to tell Wittgenstein they would have to cancel their planned trip to Norway that summer, so that Richards could study to retake the conjoint exams he had just failed. A few days later Wittgenstein wrote to Jean Rhees: "My Norwegian journey is off. Ben Richards decided to take his London exam again at the end of September. So he's got to cram & can't have a holiday. I've cancelled the passages. Maybe we'll go in October" (Wittgenstein to Rhees, around July 29, 1950; and see also Wittgenstein's letters to Norman Malcolm of July 30 and to Rush Rhees of August 3, 1950).

2) Don't try just to make repairs in your knowledge but plough through your text book steadily, so that if you should fail in September /none of/ your ~~work~~ effort will have been lost.

3) Don't work at Ickenham. I hope you'll get your digs back. (If the worst came to the worst ask M^iss A.,[57] or Smythies[58] to put you up here. I promise I won't disturb you.)

Write to me what your plans are /in detail/ <u>as soon as possible</u>! May you be guided /in what you're doing/ by something better than ~~fear~~ /timidity/ & folly, & may your friendship for me consist not merely in <u>words</u>!

   With love, as always,
    Ludwig

Ludwig Wittgenstein to Ben Richards, July 30, 1950[59]

            27 St. John Street
            Oxford
            Sunday

Dearest Ben,

I've written to Mrs Rhees asking her, could she put me up next weekend I hope to get an answer soon.[60] No telegram has come here from Mr Keillor,[61] unless you found one just before you left for Cambridge on Thursday morning. Please let me know without delay as soon as you know where you're staying. Miss Anscombe who arrived yesterday didn't know, & she thought you were a bit vague about ~~when~~ /what day/ you'd start cramming. I hope this isn't so. Please don't lose a single day! You know how great the stake is & how great the sacrifice was. Please let <u>nothing</u> divert you from your purpose. I don't want to preach to you /o. H./! but it means <u>everything</u> to me, & I know what the dangers are. I <u>hope</u> your health is good. You know it was wonderful for me to see you. I think of you with love always. Ludwig
/I hope you won't find it too difficult to settle down again to work. God bless you & help you! My thoughts & wishes are with you constantly. L. L./

---

57 Elizabeth Anscombe, i.e. in the house in which Wittgenstein was lodging.
58 Yorick Smythies also lived in Oxford, at 22 Banbury Road.
59 Richards added '30/7/50' to the letter, which was a Sunday.
60 In the same letter to Jean Rhees as Wittgenstein had reported their change of Norway plans, he asked: "Could you put me up next weekend? I.e., from Sat. to Monday? If not, please write me a line. Hope to see you soon" (Wittgenstein to Rhees, around July 29, 1950).
61 Mr Keillor rented out rooms for short-term guests in London (see Richards' letter to Wittgenstein of September 5, 1950).

Ben Richards to Ludwig Wittgenstein, July 31, 1950

63 Glenmore Road
N.W.3.
31/7/50

Dear Ludwig,

I am back in my room again and I have started work. I borrowed Conybeare[62] from Willy[63] yesterday and have started reading it.

I had a wonderful time in Oxford, and I am looking forward to seeing you next week-end. I took all day cycling home from Cambridge and didn't hurry. I had lunch on the way and ~~did~~ went to sleep for about an hour on a hill. I was less tired after it than when I went to Oxford, though the distance is much more.

Perhaps I am in better training. They said I looked fitter when I got home.

How are you? Can you work reasonably well? Bring Eduards Traum[64] when you come – we might be able to read a little.

Love always
Ben.

Ludwig Wittgenstein to Ben Richards, August 2, 1950[65]

27 St. John Street
Oxford
Wednesday

Dear Ben, o. H. –

Thanks for your letter. I'm <u>ever</u> so glad, that you're back in your old digs! I'm coming by bus on Saturday, arriving at Uxbridge about **11**.15 & at Swiss Cottage /probably/ about 12. I shall come straight to you. I wish you luck with your work & I hope you can concentrate & be methodical /& that you're in good health/. God bless you! I'm looking forward to seeing you, <u>as you know</u>.

With love, <u>as always</u>
Ludwig

Mrs Rhees is putting me up. L. L.

---

62 This refers to the classic *Textbook of Medicine*, multiply authored, and edited by John Josias Conybeare. It was first published in 1929 and was issued in new editions for many decades thereafter.

63 A friend of Richards' from university (see Richards' letter to Wittgenstein of September 15, 1950).

64 *Eduards Traum* [*Edward's Dream*] is a late work by Wilhelm Busch (1832–1908) published in 1891, which Wittgenstein thought very highly of (see Engelmann 1967: 116 [and fn. 1], and Wittgenstein's letter to Georg Henrik von Wright of November 6, 1947).

65 Richards added '2/8/50' to the letter, which was a Wednesday.

Ben Richards to Ludwig Wittgenstein, August 10, 1950

63 Glenmore Road,
N.W.3.
August 10th 1950

Dear Ludwig,

I called on Miss Brandrick,[66] and she had a letter written which she was about to send you, saying she had cancelled the passages to Norway and back and that £5 could be refunded, or count as a deposit towards the October fare.

I booked us a good second-class berth from Newcastle to Bergen on October 11th (I think on the Astrea, which I travelled on before) and a return for about a month later – she will have to write to find out the exact date. She says it will not be hard to change the dates at that time of year if we want to later. She is writing to tell you all this.

I have arranged to have coaching with a man at Bart's twice a week – partly clinical, examining patients. I saw him on Tuesday and spent an hour profitably, he asking me questions. He seems decent.

I have been working pretty steadily but rather slowly. I have tried asking myself questions and explaining things to myself, but I find it extremely difficult to make myself do it.

I love seeing you as you know and am looking forward to the next time. I think of you constantly.

    Love always,
    Ben.

Ludwig Wittgenstein to Ben Richards, August 11, 1950

27 St. John Street
Oxford
11. 8. 50.

Dear Ben, d. H. –

I got to the coach station in plenty of time & the journey wasn't bad. A few days ago I got a letter from Cook's, saying that you'd rung up & booked two passages to Bergen for the 11.10.. I had a letter from Tranøy in reply to one of mine in which I told him about our changed plans.[67] He is rather pessimistic about our going to Norway in

---

66 This was the representative of the Thomas Cook & Son travel agency at the Strand Palace Hotel, London (see Wittgenstein's letter to Richards of June 8, 1950).
67 Tranøy's letter has not been preserved (see Wittgenstein's letter to Richards of June 4, 1950).

October. I'm myself not quite clear as to whether it's a wise thing to do & I want to talk it over with you when I see you end of next week. I've written to two people in Skjolden[68] & asked them about the state my hut's in & also about other accommodation. I should hear from them next week, or the week after that. Anyhow, don't worry. We'll get decent holidays somewhere, – & perhaps Norway is a good idea. I /also/ want to see the Norwegian Railways people on Cockspur Street Monday after next. – I hope you have been able to work well and steadily! When I see you next time we'll take a good rest, God being willing! You know how much I loved being with you last weekend.

I think of you constantly with love.
Ludwig

P.S. I haven't been working too badly this week, though with little result.[69] But I'm not discontented. Good luck! G. b. y.. L. a. L.

Ludwig Wittgenstein to Ben Richards, August 13, 1950[70]

27 St. John Street
Oxford
Sunday

Dear Ben o. H.,

Thanks for your letter. I'm very glad you're being coached & made to examine patients. Please tell the man who coaches you not to be too patient with you, not to allow you, to stand /there/ endlessly before you answer a question. Make him train you in giving prompt answers if possible. I hope travelling to /& from/ the hospital won't take too much of your time /& strength/.

---

68 Wittgenstein had written to Anna Rebni and Kari Holme (see his letter to Richards of August 24, 1950). Anna Rebni (1869–1970) was one of Wittgenstein's close friends in Skjolden; she owned the Eide farm and also ran a guesthouse there where Wittgenstein often stayed (see Vatne 2016: 70). Kari Holme was the daughter of Hans and Sofia Klingenberg (and Sofia, née Drægni, was the sister of Wittgenstein's other very close Skjolden friend, Arne Drægni). During his first stay in Skjolden in 1912–13, Wittgenstein had lodged with the Klingenberg family.
69 At this time Wittgenstein was working in MSS 174 and 175. A week and a half earlier he had reported on his work to Malcolm as follows: "I'm pretty well, & I'm working but not particularly well. I get tired soon. The climate here, too, is very relaxing. (But I'm not making that responsible.) . . . I have hardly any philosophical discussions. I could see students if I wanted, but I don't want to. I've got all sorts of unclear thoughts in my old head which perhaps will remain there for ever in this unsatisfactory state" (Wittgenstein to Malcolm, July 30, 1950).
70 Richards added '13/8/50' to the letter, which was a Sunday.

I know you're having a pretty hard time now, but please don't get discouraged & don't get slack. I want you to have a proper rest when I come on Saturday. If nothing unexpected happens I'll arive by tube at Swiss Cottage about **12.**15, & I hope you'll be there because I may have a rather heavy parcel which I'd like you to help me to carry. – God bless you. May your health keep all right! Lots of luck!
I think of you always with love. Ludwig

Ludwig Wittgenstein to Ben Richards, August 14, 1950[71]

27 St John Street
Oxford
Monday

Dear Ben, d. H.

The third letter within a week! I had a note from Mrs Rhees to-day, saying she ~~couldn't~~ /can't/ after all put me up next weekend (as she had promised) & in fact not any more before Sept. 25th, because she's going away for all that time. So now I'm homeless again in London. Smythies is going to try to find me accommodation for this weekend, but the success is doubtful. If you can without wasting too much time, make some enquiries, also. Perhaps Slater[72] knows something or a room in your house may be free over the weekend. If you find something wire me. If I find I can stay somewhere I'll arrive /on Saturday/ at Swiss Cottage at approx. 12.15. Good luck & I hope I'll see you next Saturday. Work well! I think of you with love constantly.

    G. bl. y.

        Ludwig

If the worst came to the worst you could come to Oxford on Sat. & return Sunday night. You could take a book to read in the train. But this is only if you think you can afford the time.

L. a. L.

---

71 Richards added '15/8/50' to the letter, which was a Tuesday; and since Wittgenstein wrote 'Monday' on the letter, Richards was presumably noting the date the letter was received.
72 It is not known who this was.

Ludwig Wittgenstein to Ben Richards, August 24, 1950[73]

27 St. John Street
Oxford
Thursday

Dear Ben, d. H.

I have good & bad news to-day. In London at the Norwegian railway Co. ~~people~~ I couldn't find out much that was useful, but the day after coming back here I had a letter from Anna Rebni, saying that we'd be welcome to stay in the little hotel near her farmyard & that, of course, there would be no tourists in October. She also spoke to the man who owns my hut now & he said that it was in good repair & that we could live there if we liked.[74] – I haven't yet heard from Kari Holme, the other woman I wrote to. – The bad news is that I can't come to London on the Saturday after next. I had forgotten that a man, Townsend, a friend of Con's and mine,[75] is coming here on Friday 1st Sept. for a week. This was arranged about 6 or 8 weeks ago but I didn't realize when I saw you last weekend that it would interfere with our plans. <u>Needless to say</u>, if you want /to see/ me that weekend particularly, I mean, if you were ill or something, I'd come in spite of Townsend; but otherwise I'm afraid ~~I~~ we'll have to change our arrangement. Would it be all right /with you/ if I came the weekend after the one T. is staying with me, i.e., Saturday September 9th? It's a <u>long</u> time for me to wait! – I <u>like</u> to see Townsend, I haven't seen him for some years, but I wish I had arranged to see him after <u>our</u> weekend. – The weather is being terribly oppressive here & I'm more stupid & dull than ever & can hardly work at all.[76] I'm glad to say, others, e.g. M^{iss} Anscombe & Smythies, feel it too. – Con sends you his good wishes. – I think of you <u>constantly</u> with love. Seeing you the other day was wonderful. <u>Work well</u>! Write soon!

G. b. y. With love, always Ludwig

/I hope your health is good! Please look after yourself. <u>I miss you.</u>

L. L./

---

73 Richards added '24/8/50' to the letter, which was a Thursday.
74 This was Arne Bolstad. When Wittgenstein returned from the First World War he divested himself of all his wealth and assets – including the cabin he'd had built in Skjolden only a few years beforehand, which he gifted to Bolstad (see Wittgenstein's letter to Halvard Drægni of October 30, 1919). At the time Wittgenstein thought he would never return to Norway. In later years, when Wittgenstein did return to Skjolden, Bolstad – who did not live in the cabin – would let Wittgenstein stay in it whenever he wanted (see Vatne 2016: 53–58 & 103–105).
75 Raymond Townsend (1902–1986) was a student of Wittgenstein's in the early 1930s, at the same time as Maurice O'Connor Drury. Thereafter Townsend remained a friend of Wittgenstein's and a very close friend of Drury's (see Drury 2017: 430).
76 A few days later Wittgenstein wrote to his friend Rudolf Koder: "There's nothing at all to report from me. I'm vegetating & seem to be getting stupider and stupider" (Wittgenstein to Koder, August 26, 1950).

Ben Richards to Ludwig Wittgenstein, August 27, 1950

63 Glenmore Road
N.W.3.
August 27th 1950

Dear Ludwig

I am very sorry you can't come next week-end. I thought of your coming during the following week, but I think you are right and that we'd have more time together the next week-end. I'll miss you, and think of you constantly.

Your news about Norway is very good. You do not say if there will be a boat to row to and from the cottage /(hut)/ in.[77] If there is, I'd rather be there than anywhere else. It won't spoil it for me if the weather isn't fine.

My work has been going quite well this week – a bit better even than before.

I am writing on very special paper called "Society Club".[78] A I made myself a stew on Friday of sliced lamb's hearts with potatoes carrots onions and pearl barley in the double saucepan. I made one mistake by putting in some dripping and it was a bit too greasy. Otherwise it was very good. It made three very good meals. I haven't quite finished all the bread you bought last time, but as what's left is like a stone I am buying ~~some~~ a new loaf. It was wonderful to see you last week-end.

    Love always
        Ben

Ludwig Wittgenstein to Ben Richards, August 29, 1950

27 St. Johns Street
Oxford
29. 8. 50.

Dear Ben, d. H.

Thanks for your letter. I'm glad your work is going all right. May it go on like that!! I hope, that coach of yours really lets you examine patients.[79] There isn't too much time & he must get on with it. Please <u>pester</u> him. –

---

77 Wittgenstein's cabin was on the eastern end of the small Lake Eidsvatnet, with the village of Skjolden on the western end. By this time there was a small road running along the southern length of the lake, leading from near Wittgenstein's cabin into the village – but Wittgenstein's cabin was cut off from that road by a river which then had no nearby bridge. On the other hand, the northern length of the lake could not be walked, as it was a steep mountainside coming right up to the water's edge. Thus, the only way to access Wittgenstein's cabin (or to return to the village to get food and supplies once there) was by rowing across the lake in the summer or by walking across the lake's frozen surface in the winter.

78 Richards used high quality paper for this letter, which had watermarked stripes running up and down it.

79 See Richards' letter to Wittgenstein of August 10, 1950.

Anna Rebni wrote in her letter that the man who owns my hut[80] told her he would see to it that we had a boat, & that he would repair the little path that leads from the lake /up/ to the hut.[81] But: – that man's a nice man & a pleasant man, but not reliable. He may easily forget about it, or find it too much trouble; also we need a good many things in the hut if we want to live there, & I don't know if they're there, nor if we can get them without spending too much money. Therefore, please don't be too sure that we'll be able to live there, – although I feel just like you about it! – The weather here is most depressing, & I am completely stupid. – Please try to get me somewhere to stay the weekend after next. So far I haven't anything. Smythies is making enquiries too. I think of you with love constantly. I miss you! G. bl. y.

Ludwig

P.S. In a window of Burton's (the taylor of taste) I saw a big poster & on it in a separate little frame the words: "Direct Trade Epic."[82] L. L.
/One day you must make me a stew too. Not that the food we have isn't always lovely! L. L./

Ludwig Wittgenstein to Ben Richards, September 2, 1950[83]

27 St John Street
Oxford
Saturday

Dearest Ben,

Smythies told me yesterday that he couldn't find any place for me to stay in London next weekend. So I hope you'll be able to suggest something.
I've been feeling rather low for some days with back-ache & weakness. I hope I'll be all right /again/ by next weekend. – I think of you constantly. It would be a blow for me if I couldn't see you next week.

---

80 Arne Bolstad (see the relevant footnote to Wittgenstein's letter to Richards of August 24, 1950).
81 Wittgenstein's cabin sat on a small ledge on the mountainside, about 30 meters above the water, and a small switchback path led steeply up from the lakeshore to the cabin.
82 'Montague Burton, The Tailor of Taste Ltd' was the full name of one of the largest chains of high street tailors in the United Kingdom at the time. It was more commonly known simply as 'Burton's'. Wittgenstein often joked with friends – and especially with his friend Gilbert Pattisson – about the ridiculous self-importance of many companies and their advertisements. As Ray Monk writes: "At Cambridge, Pattisson and Wittgenstein would read together magazines like the Tatler ... enjoying particularly the ludicrous advertisements that used to appear in such journals. They were avid readers, too, of the 'Letters from a satisfied customer' which used to be displayed in the windows of Burton's, 'The Tailor of Taste', and to which Pattisson and Wittgenstein would give exaggerated attention during their shopping trips to buy Wittgenstein's clothes" (Monk 1990: 265; see also Wittgenstein's letter to Pattisson of February 14, 1937).
83 Richards added '2/9/50' to the letter, which was a Saturday.

I hope you're well & working well! G. bl. y..
<u>I love you always.</u>
   Ludwig

Ben Richards to Ludwig Wittgenstein, September 5, 1950

63 Glenmore Road
N.W.3.
5/9/50

Dear Ludwig,

I have been missing you. Keillor's front room has now been taken and he did not know of anyone who might put you up. Miss Williams[84] is having a lot of plumbing and redecorating done and cannot have you yet. I rang up Dr. Marshall and she suggested the Benbridge Hotel, Dorset Square which is near Baker-Street station. She knew people who had stayed there, and she said it would be quiet. I rang them up and they had one room in what they called the annex – another house in the same square which they said would be particularly quiet; so I booked it. I shall expect you about noon on Saturday. I went to Wittering on Saturday evening, where my family are staying, and spent Sunday there, and went for a sail. The weather wasn't good, but it was pretty windy, and it was quite exciting.

My supervisor has been making me examine some patients each week, and the supervisors are a bit more businesslike; my work on my own has been going quite well too.

I hope you had a good time with Townsend.[85]

  Love always,
    Ben

Ludwig Wittgenstein to Ben Richards, September 6, 1950[86]

27 St John Street
Oxford
Wednesday

Dear Ben,

Thanks for reserving a room for me. I wish it could have been at a bed & breakfast place <u>near you</u>. I also wish I'd heard from you /more than/ just once in all these 3

---

84 It is not known who this was.
85 See Wittgenstein's letter to Richards of August 24, 1950, and the relevant footnote there.
86 Richards added '6/9/50' to the letter, which was a Wednesday.

weeks. – I'll come by bus & will be at Swiss Cottage on Saturday about 12.15 . – I hope you've been lucky with your work & with your health!

>With love, as always
>
>Ludwig

Ben Richards to Ludwig Wittgenstein, September 7, 1950

>63 Glenmore Road,
>
>N.W.3.
>
>September 7th 1950

Dear Ludwig,

Thanks for your letter. I'm sorry you don't care for the idea of Benbridge Hotel. I hope it isn't too stuffy, and that we'll find something better next time. It is close to Baker Street Station, and to the 74 bus route which goes to Camden Town, and the 2 & 13 /& 113/ routes which go to Swiss Cottage.

I hope the weather improved, and you felt better, and able to work a bit.

>I think of you constantly
>
>with love, always
>
>Ben.

Ludwig Wittgenstein to Ben Richards, September 12, 1950[87]

>27 St. John Street
>
>Oxford
>
>Tuesday

Dear Ben, d. H.,

The journey yesterday wasn't too bad, although a few spoilt children made a hell of a noise most of the time, with their stupid father smiling enchanted at them. I don't know yet when I'll see Bevan. On the one hand I'd like to see him soon, on the other hand I think he may be able to tell me more if I wait a bit & see how things develop. I think I shan't wait longer than till the middle of next week.[88]

I hope you're working <u>hard</u> & <u>steadily</u> & <u>well</u>.

---

87 Richards added '12/9/50' to the letter, which was a Tuesday.

88 At around this time Wittgenstein wrote to Bevan, to refill some of his existing prescriptions and arrange a meeting: "So could you send me prescriptions for some more of these things? Unless you prefer sending me a bottle of some nice poison, that is. As I know you, you'll take the long and troublesome way. I go on vegetating as before. At that rate I'll never die! ... P.S. I'm planning to go to Norway about Oct. 10th & may come to Cambridge & ask you look at me, if you will be kind enough, before I go" (Wittgenstein to Bevan, undated, 1950).

I had a letter from Con, confirming that he'd come on the 29th (a Friday).[89]
If you think it would be good if we /saw/ each other before your exam I could always come to London just for the day or one night. But it may be better for you not to see me until after the exam. Do whatever you think is the best. Your exam matters more than anything now. Also to me. Except of course your health!
You know how much I loved being with you. Thanks for everything. – God bless you. Good luck! I love you always.

      Ludwig

I was glad that you read to me the story "Ivan the fool".[90] If it really spurs you on you'll be all right. I think of you constantly.

      L. a. L.

Ben Richards to Ludwig Wittgenstein, September 15, 1950

           63 Glenmore Road
           N.W.3.
           September 15th 1950

Dear Ludwig,

Thanks for your letter. I should see Bevan right away if I were you.
I am working quite well and I saw some patients with my supervisor this week.
I loved reading, eating, listening to the gramophone, going to the pictures and the walk over Primrose Hill and along the canal.[91]
You didn't ought to of left me your bacon ration.[92] I'm afraid I've eaten it now, and enjoyed it very much.
I hope you can work and sleep enough and that Bevan is helpful.

  Love always,
    Ben.

---

89 Maurice O'Connor Drury was planning on staying in London for two or three days – on his way from Exeter back to his home in Dublin – and was presumably writing to Wittgenstein in the hopes that they could arrange to see each other during his stay (see Wittgenstein's letter to Jean Rhees of September 25, 1950).

90 Leo Tolstoy's short story 'The Story of Ivan the Fool' (1885). Wittgenstein thought very highly of Tolstoy's 'tales', and he often recommended to friends (or bought them as gifts) the volume in which this tale appears in translation: Leo Tolstoy, *Twenty-Three Tales*, trans. L & A Maude, London, Oxford University Press, 1906. He once said to Maurice Drury: "Those short stories of Tolstoy's will live for ever. They were written for all peoples" (Drury 1984: 86).

91 Primrose Hill is a park to the north of Regent's Park, and just a few minutes south of Belsize Park where Richards lived. It is bordered on the south by Regent's Canal.

92 After the Second World War meat remained rationed in the United Kingdom until 1954.

P.S. It is raining cats & dogs. I started a game of tennis with Willy on Monday, but it came on to rain.

Richards' drawing at the end of his letter of Sept. 15, 1950:

Ludwig Wittgenstein to Ben Richards, September 17, 1950[93]

My Cambridge address	27 St. John Street
will be: c/o Dr Bevan	Oxford
3 Trinity Street.	Sunday

Dear Ben, o. H.

Thanks for your letter. I must say, /some of/ your cats look like mice! Still — . I'm going to Cambridge to-morrow. I postponed going because I thought that Bevan might see more now than he'd have seen a week ago. I'm sure there's nothing serious the matter with me. <u>Perhaps</u> I'm a bit anaemic.

– I can't work at all, but I sleep fairly well.[94]

I'm ever so glad that you're working well. Go on & work like hell /The rhyme is unintentional/. But don't work /at all/ the day before the exam! – I think I shall be back from Cambridge on Thursday. I'll write to you what Bevan says. I hope it won't interfere with our journey. I think of you constantly with love & good wishes! G. bl. y..

    Love <u>always</u>,

        Ludwig

---

93 Richards added '17/9/50' to the letter, which was a Sunday.
94 A few days later Wittgenstein wrote to his friend Rudolf Koder: "I'm fine, at least physically; I often feel very stupid & drowsy & weak, but maybe that will pass" (Wittgenstein to Koder, September 22, 1950).

Ben Richards to Ludwig Wittgenstein, September 21, 1950

63 Glenmore Road,
N.W.3.
November[95] 21st 1950

Dear Ludwig,

I have just heard from the Conjoint Board that my written papers are on Wednesday 27th, which I knew; and that my clinical & oral examinations are on <u>Friday, October 6th</u>. So we can go on Wednesday 11th as arranged.[96]

I hope you are feeling better; and that if Bevan finds anything wrong, it is something he can help you about.

I think of you all the time, and look forward to seeing you after the papers. It will be good to see Con again.[97]

Shall I try to book you a room, and has Con somewhere to stay?

It was good to get your letter on Monday. I hope you'll be able to work again soon.

  Love always,
   Ben.

Ludwig Wittgenstein to Ben Richards, September 22, 1950[98]

27 John Street
Oxford
Friday

Dearest Ben,

Thanks for your letter of Sept. 21st (you wrote "November 21st"!) – I only came back from Cambridge yesterday. Bevan says there is nothing serious the matter with me at all & that ~~he thinks~~ a change of atmosphere, e.g. going to Norway, will do me good I dare say he's right. He was <u>extremely</u> nice, as he always is. He talked about you & told me to give you his very best wishes. So does Con in a letter I got from him to-day. He writes that he'll come to London next Friday (29th) arriving at Waterloo at 2.28 p.m.[99]

---

95 Richards mistakenly wrote 'November' instead of 'September' (as Wittgenstein noted in his reply of September 22, 1950).

96 This was the date of their rescheduled trip to Norway; as Wittgenstein wrote the next day – with a little uncertainty – to his friend Rudolf Koder: "I plan to travel to Norway on October 11th. If it really comes to that, I will write you my address" (September 22, 1950).

97 See the relevant footnote to Wittgenstein's letter to Richards of September 12, 1950.

98 Richards added '22/9/50' to the letter, which was a Friday.

99 See the relevant footnote to Wittgenstein's letter to Richards of September 12, 1950.

If you can manage it, you might meet me on Friday at Swiss Cottage as usual at 12.^{15} & we could have a little lunch & then meet Con at Waterloo together.
But there's plenty of time to decide about that after Sept 27th. – Dear Ben, d. H., You know I think of you constantly, with <u>all</u> the best wishes. Be explicit in your papers & show them what you know! Don't think, a <u>hint</u> is enough & the examiners ought to know what you mean! – I'm glad your oral exam is on the 6th Oct & we can get away, D. v.,[100] on the 11th. <u>Please</u> look after yourself, don't do anything rash that might be bad for your health. God bless you! I love you always.
Ludwig

Ludwig Wittgenstein to Ben Richards, September 25, 1950[101]

27 St. John Street
Oxford
Monday

Dear Ben, d. H. –

This is only to say <u>Good Luck</u>! to you Don't get rattled; remember that you've worked hard & know a lot.[102] –

Please do not work at all to-morrow to <u>rest</u> & to get your nerves ship-shape. That's much more important than the tiny bit of knowledge you may still cram into your head. – I think of you the whole time & will hold my thumbs for you.[103]

God bless you. Don't let anything depress you! I love you <u>always.</u>

Ludwig

I'm looking forward to seeing you on Friday noon.
L. a. L.

---

100 Stands for: 'Deo volente' (Latin: God willing).
101 Richards added '25/9/50' to the letter, which was a Monday.
102 Wittgenstein was referring to Richards' upcoming re-sit of his written conjoint exams (see Richards' letter to Wittgenstein of September 21, 1950). On the same day as he wrote this letter, Wittgenstein wrote to Jean Rhees: "Ben Richards has his written exam on Wednesday. He's worked hard & I hope to God he'll pass, but one can't be sure" (Wittgenstein to Rhees, September 25, 1950).
103 See Wittgenstein's letter to Richards of May 29, 1950, and the relevant footnote there.

Ludwig Wittgenstein to Ben Richards, Good Luck Card (postmarked: September 26, 1950)

 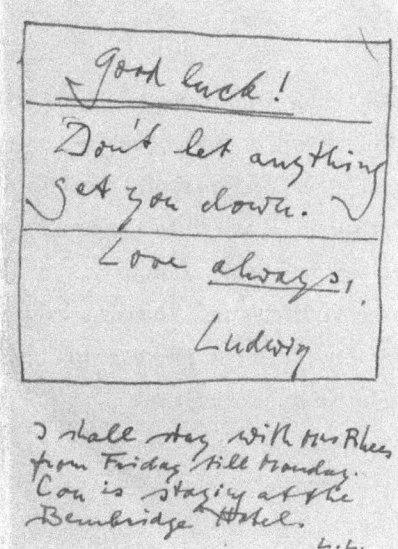

GOOD LUCK

Good luck!

Don't let anything get you down.

    Love <u>always</u>,

        Ludwig

I shall stay with Mrs Rhees from Friday till Monday.[104] Con is staying at the Bembridge Hotel.[105]

    L. L.

---

[104] The previous day Wittgenstein had written to Jean Rhees: "I wonder if you could put me up Friday next, Sept. 29th, until either Sunday or Monday … If it's inconvenient for you, I am sure I'll be able to find a room elsewhere … Please let me know, if possible by wire, whether you can put me up. I'd be very grateful, but that doesn't make it less of a nuisance for you" (Wittgenstein to Rhees, September 25, 1950).

[105] See the relevant footnote to Wittgenstein's letter to Richards of September 12, 1950, and Richards' letter to Wittgenstein of September 21, 1950.

Ben Richards to Ludwig Wittgenstein, September 26, 1950

63 Glenmore Road
N.W.3.
26/9/50

Dear Ludwig

Thanks for your letter. I am very glad Bevan found nothing serious wrong. The Norwegian holiday will do both of us good.

I will meet you at 12.^{15} on Friday and I will be glad to see Con.[106] I have arranged to see my supervisor at 5.0 on Friday afternoon at Bart's.

I am taking it easy before my exam to-morrow.

The weather here is pretty dim. The gas pressure is so low that it is impossible to get hot water out of the geyser and we have to do without baths.

I am looking forward to seeing you

  Love always
    Ben.

Ludwig Wittgenstein to Ben Richards (postmarked: October 5, 1950)

27 St. John Street
Oxford
Thursday

Dear Ben, d. H. –

Good luck![107]

Answer <u>courageously</u> & <u>audibly</u>. Don't be stingy with words, especially if you have to correct yourself.

God bless you.

I am thinking of you with love, as always.

    Ludwig

---

106 See the relevant footnote to Wittgenstein's letter to Richards of September 12, 1950, and see Wittgenstein's letter to Richards of September 22, 1950.

107 Wittgenstein was referring to Richards' upcoming re-sit of his clinical and oral conjoint exams (see Richards' letter to Wittgenstein of September 21, 1950).

Ludwig Wittgenstein to Ben Richards, Telegram (undated, around October 6, 1950)[108]

POST OFFICE
TELEGRAM

Prefix. Time handed in. Office of Origin and Service Instructions. Words.
RG A   6301 9.15 PM OXFORD RG 36
BENEDICT RICHARDS 40 SWAKELEYS RD ICKENHAMUXBRIDGE
DOCTOR ADVISES ME AGAINST GOING LONDON TOMORROW SATURDAY
PLEASE COME OXFORD INSTEAD IF POSSIBLE AND STAY TILL SUNDAY
BRING MY SUITCASES FROM MRS RHEES LETTER ON THE WAY LOVE =
LUDWIG +
40

Ludwig Wittgenstein to Ben Richards (postmarked: October 6, 1950)

27 St. John Street
Oxford
Friday

Dear Ben, o. H. –

I have been feeling very rotten & weak all this week. I wrote my symptoms to Bevan & then had a talk with him over the 'phone. He told me that I seemed to have a mild dysentry & should go to a physician here & ask him to prescribe sulphoguanidine[109] (I think that's the name) for me. I went to a doctor who makes quite a good impression, & he prescribed the tablets for me, & I took them for 2 days. Bevan thought they'd make me feel better straight away but they haven't. I believe that any movement is bad for me, /it certainly makes me feel bad/, & that travelling to London to-morrow ~~would~~ /might/ make me incapable of going to London again on Tuesday & to Norway on Wednesday.

I hate asking this of you – but could you possibly come to Oxford tomorrow (<u>Saturday</u>) instead /of my coming to London/.

---

108 Though this telegram is undated, it's clear from the content that it was sent on the same day as Wittgenstein's letter to Richards of October 6, 1950, intended to be followed up by that letter (this is confirmed by the fact that October 6, was a Friday, and in this telegram he described Saturday as being the next day).

109 Wittgenstein presumably meant: Sulfaguanidine (which was introduced in 1940 for the treatment of bacillary dysentery).

Mrs Rhees will be ~~at~~ in her flat about 1p.m or 2p.m /tomorrow/; could you ring her up (Maidavale 7207) & tell her that you'll fetch my two suitcases? One is almost empty & the other isn't heavy either. Then come to Oxford with them & stay the night. I must see you & talk things over. E.g., I want to know if, in case I were not well enough to travel on Wednesday, we could take a boat a few days later.

I'm seeing my doctor to-night & will write what he sais as a P.S. to this letter.

I wish I knew how your exam went. Please keep your chin up whatever the result is.

I think of you with love <u>always</u>.

Ludwig

P.S. If you can't come to Oxford, please wire & I will ~~try~~ come to London on Sunday, if I can. – In case you can't reach Mrs Rhees, I could borrow a suitcase from Smythies, but his have either no locks or no keys to them.

P.P.S. I saw the doctor just now & he strongly advised me against going to London tomorrow, but he said that I'd <u>probably</u> be able to go to Norway on Wednesday. Please come if you possibly can & if it's not too much of a strain for you.

Ludwig Wittgenstein to Ben Richards, Telegram, October 10, 1950
POST OFFICE
TELEGRAM

Prefix. Time handed in. Office of Origin and Service Instructions. Words.
OF A 608 8 11.50 OXFORD 12
BENEDICT RICHARDS 40 SWAKELEYS RD ICKENHAM UXBRIDGE =
ARRIVING PADDINGTON 5.55 LOVE = LUDWIG +
+ 40 5.55 LUDWIG +

Ludwig Wittgenstein to Ben Richards (undated, end of October 1950)[110]

Dear Ben, D. H.,

I talked to the doctor over the phone in the afternoon & he said he thought you were getting on fine.[111] I don't yet know for certain if I can come to Lyster to-morrow,[112] but the day after I shall certainly come. God bless you! <u>I miss you</u>.

With love, as always

Ludwig P.T.O.

Please be obedient to the sister & the doctor. I think of you all the time with longing.

Ludwig Wittgenstein to Ben Richards, November 26, 1950[113]

27 St John Street
Oxford
Sunday

Dear Ben, d. o. H –

Thanks for being with me & taking me to the station the other day. Bevan was kind as always. I had an injection & am to have another one next Thursday. So far it hasn't improved things but perhaps the next one will. – I saw Miss Anscombe to-day. She is up & can go out for a short time & she's all right except that she still sees double if she looks through the operated eye, & that makes her feel sick. But if one talks to her she forgets about it & doesn't feel the nausea.[114]

---

110 Wittgenstein did not date this letter and Richards didn't add a date either, but the content makes clear that this letter was written while Richards was receiving medical attention in Luster (a small town near Skjolden, Norway, in the municipality of Luster, which had previously been spelt 'Lyster'.) So the letter must have been written when Richards took ill, shortly into the month-long trip that he and Wittgenstein took to Norway, which was between October 15th and November 13th (see Vatne 2016: 81, and the following footnotes to this letter).

111 Shortly after arriving in Skjolden – and moving into Wittgenstein's cabin – Richards developed bronchitis, and had to be treated for a few days at a small hospital in the nearby village of Luster. The physician who treated Richards was a Dr. J. Devoid. Knut Erik Tranøy – who corresponded with Dr. Devoid about this incident – later wrote: "Even in 1950, on his last visit to Norway (which I helped him arrange), his Norwegian was good enough for him to serve as an interpreter when his friend was taken ill and needed a doctor. It was not so much that Dr. Devoid needed an interpreter; Wittgenstein wanted to make sure 'that everything should become clear and there should be no misunderstanding with regard to the facts about the illness' " (Tranøy 2016: 1019). Tranøy also recounted from Dr. Devoid that "When, in 1950, his friend was taken to the little local hospital for treatment, Wittgenstein gave him [Henrik Ibsen's] *Brand* to read, in Norwegian" (Tranøy 2016: 1020). While Richards was in the hospital Wittgenstein left his cabin and moved into Anna Rebni's guesthouse instead, and after Richards was released from the hospital they both stayed in the guesthouse for the remainder of their trip (see Monk 1990: 574).

112 Luster is a small village located about 6 miles (10km) southwest of Skjolden, along the Sognefjord.

113 Richards added '26/11/50' to the letter, which was a Sunday.

114 At the end of October 1950 Elizabeth Anscombe had undergone an operation to save the sight of one of her eyes, and for ten days after the operation she had to stay in bed in a darkened room (see Mac Cumhaill & Waisman 2022: 250).

I am almost certain now that I'll go to Norway in a fortnight or so.[115] What I'll feel like there, so far from you, I don't know, I'll wait until you've had your exams anyhow, so we can see each other comfortably before I go. – I asked M^iss Anscombe to-day how she would pronounce the word LAPEL(L) & she answered immediately láppel, just as I pronounced it. She also agreed /with me/ that 'lapéll' sounded like a high class taylors expression. On the other hand the Oxford Dictionary only gives your pronunciation. But you see I'm not alone. –

Dear Ben, I hope you're feeling well & find you can read for your Cambridge exam.[116] Not that it matters a d . . . whether you pass it or not.

God bless you. I think of you a lot & hope to see you soon.

  As always, with love
    Ludwig

Ben Richards to Ludwig Wittgenstein, November 27, 1950

                63 Glenmore Road
                N.W.3.
                November 27th 1950

Dear Ludwig

Thanks for your letter. I was not sure whether you would be still in Cambridge, or in Oxford by now.

I hope the next injection is successful. I am very glad Miss Anscombe is getting over her operation. Do her doctors expect her to learn to see single using both eyes? Give her my love.

I am revising surgery by going through the questions of the correspondence course, which I never finished – trying to answer them and looking it up afterwards. My exam starts on Tuesday December 12th.

---

115 A few days later Wittgenstein wrote to his friend Ludwig Hänsel: "I was in Norway & was partly very lucky, partly not. My friend who went with me was ill twice, first in Bergen, then in Skjolden. But it was very, very beautiful & the weather was excellent. I must confess to you that I am half & half planning to go again, indeed more than half & half. I have more peace there than anywhere else; & if I am able to write at all (which is doubtful) it will be better there than anywhere else. If I go, it will not be with a light heart. But here my life has damn little meaning" (Wittgenstein to Hänsel, December 1, 1950; and see also Wittgenstein's letter to Norman Malcolm from the same day).

116 Richards had to take a number of further exams in Cambridge in December 1950, presumably for his Final M.B. (*Medicinae Baccalaureus*) qualification from King's College. On December 12, he had written exams in surgery and midwifery, and some time not too long thereafter he had oral exams, presumably on the same subjects (see both Wittgenstein's and Richards' following few letters).

It has been foggy here but I am quite well. I went for a longish walk yesterday with Ralf Hagman,[117] and felt the better for it.

I shall miss you very much in Norway, but I think it is your best plan. – I hope you can really work again there. I shall write regularly.

    love always

        Ben.

P.S. I enclose Arne Draegne's[118] photograph while I remember, and kr.12.[119]

Ludwig Wittgenstein to Ben Richards, December 7, 1950[120]

                              27 St. John Street

                                      Oxford

                                      Thursday 7th?

Dear Ben,

I have changed my plans. I have decided to go to Norway on Dec. 30th. There is no boat on /Saturday/ 23rd, only one on the 22nd, & that would mean that I'd have to go to London on the day after your exam ends. There is no boat between the 23rd & 30th. I talked on /the/ phone to-day with the Bergenske D.S.[121] & they told me so. I'd written to Cooks at the Strand Palace before, but Miss Brandrick[122] was on holiday & the man who is ~~there~~ /in charge/ now seems to be an ass. – I don't know whether, this being so /I mean my sailing on the 30th/, you still want me to come to Cambridge on the 20th or 21st. An alternative would be for you to stay for a few days in Oxford at 27 St John Street. You've plenty of time to decide that. I don't mind /very much/ going to Norway later as I'm not particularly well just now. The effects of my injection are still bothering me a good deal.

The other day I saw Angela. She looks very pale & tired. Otherwise she's nice as ever. We went together into the forestry library & had Smythies show us round[123] (I wish

---

117 It is not known who this was.
118 Arne Drægni (1871–1946) had been Wittgenstein's closest friends in Skjolden (see Wittgenstein's letter to Richards of August 3, 1946, and the relevant footnote there).
119 Norwegian Krone.
120 Richards added 'Dec. '50' to the letter, just beneath Wittgenstein's incomplete date; and December 7, 1950, was indeed a Thursday.
121 'Bergenske Dampskibsselskab' – also known as 'The Bergen Steamship Company' or 'Bergen Line' (BDS) – was a large Norwegian shipping company, which existed from 1851 until 1988.
122 Regarding Miss Brandrick, see Wittgenstein's letter to Richards of June 8, 1950, and Richards' letter to Wittgenstein of August 10, 1950, and the relevant footnotes there.
123 Yorick Smythies worked as a librarian at the Forestry Library in Oxford from 1947 until 1951.

you could see all the monstrosities there). We also bought ~~together~~ a very nice head square for Anna Rebni.[124] I.e., I bought it & Angela helped me choose it.

You know how <u>lovely</u> it was for me being with you last Saturday. I hope you're well! I hope the damn climate doesn't get you down, nor the damn work. Please try to be sensible. I think of you with love & good wishes constantly, & love you <u>always</u>. Ludwig

Ludwig Wittgenstein to Ben Richards, December 9, 1950[125]

27 St. John Street
Oxford
Saturday

Dear Ben, d. H,

Thanks for your letter.

This is only to wish you

<u>good luck</u>.[126]

Dont get rattled, make your answers clear, & don't be stingy with explanations.

<u>God bless you.</u>

I think of you constantly with love.

Ludwig

Ben Richards to Ludwig Wittgenstein, December 12, 1950

King's College
Cambridge
12/12/50

Dear Ludwig,

Thanks for your letters. I have just had my papers in surgery and midwifery. They didn't seem too bad once I had started, but I have no real idea how well I did: it so often turns out quite differently from what I had expected.

I made a short call on Geach.[127] He said Miss Anscombe is coming here on Thursday evening.

---

124 The headscarf was presumably intended as a gift for Anna Rebni, to be given to her on Wittgenstein's planned return to Skjolden at the end of December 1950.

125 Richards added '9/12/50' to the letter, which was a Saturday.

126 Wittgenstein was referring to Richards' upcoming written exams (see Richards' following letter to Wittgenstein of December 12, 1950).

127 Peter Geach (1916–2013), a philosopher and logician who was married to Elizabeth Anscombe, but who lived and worked in Cambridge during these years, while Anscombe lived and worked in Oxford – with each travelling frequently to the other's city.

I went home before I came here and saw Angela who is rather pale, and also Ann Phillips[128] who is back from Canada and called on us. She hasn't decided yet whether she is back for good or will return to Canada later.

I look forward to seeing you after my exam, and after Christmas.

It is very cold here, but the rooms are comfortable now they have installed gas fires.

Love always,

Ben.

Ludwig Wittgenstein to Ben Richards, December 15, 1950[129]

27 St. John Street

Oxford

Friday

Dear Ben, d. H.

Thanks for your letter. I <u>hope</u> you did well in your papers, & I have no reason for doubting it. Work steadily, but not <u>too</u> much, for your viva!

Rest the day before the viva, & I mean <u>rest</u>. – I've had a good deal of trouble after my injection, but its just painful, not serious.

– The other day I bought a "New Statesman" & there is a review in it of a new book by Russell, called "Unpopular Essays", where he is compared with Plato.[130]

---

128 Ann Phillips was a housekeeper for the Richards family before she moved to Canada (see the letter from Richards to Wittenstein of February 8, 1947).

129 Wittgenstein wrote 'Friday', but did not date this letter. Given its content, it's clear that this letter was written after Richards' written exams (which were on December 12) and before his oral exams (which were certainly before Christmas), so it must have been written on either Friday 15 or 22. Since it seems to be a direct reply to Richards' letter to Wittgenstein of December 12, it is most likely that this letter was written on Friday December 15, 1950.

130 The book was Bertrand Russell's *Unpopular Essays*, published in 1950 (simultaneously by Allen and Unwin in London, and by Simon and Schuster in New York). The review of Russell's book (alongside three other recent books) was by R. H. S. Crossman and was entitled 'The Age of Terror' (*New Statesman and Nation*, vol. XL, no. 1031, December 9, 1950, pp. 592–4). The relevant passage reads: "Bertrand Russell's pattern of values does not differ greatly from Cole's. Both are rationalists and agnostics, libertarian Socialists with an extreme distaste of organized stupidity and organized cruelty. Cole is a very much better historian than Russell, an important matter when the subject under discussion is political theory. But Russell remains pre-eminent as the only living philosopher with a literary style. Though he will hate to hear it – for Plato is his *bête noire* – the writing of *Unpopular Essays* is as limpid, as mischievious and occasionally, as sublime as that of *The Republic*. Indeed it is ironical that Russell like Plato writes so well and thinks so elegantly that he exposes his own fallacies to the wary reader. The man who demonstrated the logical case for pacifism in the 1930s demonstrates in the 1950s the logical case for the forcible creation by Americans of a world super-state. Both demonstrations are brilliantly done. The difference between them is due, I think, to Russell's dwindling confidence in the influence of human reason in human affairs. He is still a rationalist; but doubting whether many other men are likely to become so, he now feels, like Plato, that instead of trying to overthrow power in order to free mankind, philosophers must advise kings to use their power in order to save civilisation" (p. 594).

I shall probably come to Cambridge on the 19th but I shan't disturb you; I just want Dr Bevan to have a good look at me before long & <u>before</u> the end of your exam. God bless you.

   I think of you with love always.
        Ludwig

Ludwig Wittgenstein to Ben Richards, January 1, 1951[131]

                27 St. John Street
                      Oxford
                      Monday

Dear Ben, d. H.

I arrived here this evening by car. A friend of the Bevans who was going this way took me with him. I'm feeling pretty well just now & I hope that it may last. – In my room I found your lovely handkerchiefs. <u>Thanks</u>! Thanks also for your 2nd Christmas card.[132] It made me feel good when I arrived. I also found a card from Kari Holme.[133] She sends you all good wishes. She didn't reply to my letter.[134] Obviously it hadn't yet reached her. – Please send me my ration book by return of post. You remember you

---

131 Richards added '2/1/51' to the letter, which was a Tuesday; and since Wittgenstein wrote 'Monday' on the letter, Richards was presumably noting the date the letter was received.
132 Three undated Christmas cards from Richards to Wittgenstein have survived (see Chapter VII). These are possibly two of those.
133 Kari Holme (née Klingenberg) was one of Wittgenstein's friends in Skjolden, whom he had contacted ahead of his trip with Richards to enquire about lodgings, and whom Richards had subsequently met during their stay in Skjolden in October and November 1950 (see Wittgenstein's letter to Richards of August 11, 1950 and the relevant footnote there).
134 Wittgenstein's letter to Holme most likely referred to his intention to return to Skjolden in the near future and enquired about whether she knew of somewhere he could stay (as he neither wanted to stay in his cold and isolated cabin in mid-winter nor at the small local hotel). He had thought he would be able to stay in Anna Rebni's guesthouse (as he had done in October and November, with Richards), but that plan had fallen through – as he wrote the next day to Norman and Leonida Malcolm: "I don't know if I wrote to you that when I was in Norway in October I thought of going back there to do some work. I asked a friend there who has a farm could I come back & stay over the winter, or longer. I was told that I could. It would have been a <u>very</u> cheap & very quiet place. I booked a passage on a steamer Newcastle-Bergen on Dec. 30th. Shortly before Christmas I heard that my friend could not put me up after all & at the same time I fell ill & so couldn't have gone anyway. I'm very much better now & I'm waiting for some news from some other people in Norway to whom I wrote, asking them if they knew a suitable place for me. So far I haven't heard from them & I'm <u>not</u> optimistic" (Wittgenstein to the Malcolms, January 2, 1951). Harald Vatne points out that Anna Rebni was already 81 years old at the time and did not feel able to host Wittgenstein – who was in poor health – over the winter, when it would be both an effort and an expense to keep the guesthouse properly heated. However, she offered to put him up after Easter, when it would be warmer, if he would be able to come then (see Vatne 2016: 82).

took it with the emergency cards to get rations for the Bevans, but now I need it. Or did you leave it with Miss Anscombe? Please let me know as soon as you can. – I am thinking of you constantly. God bless you. I hope I can see you before long. Happy New Year!

    With love as always,

        Ludwig

P.S. Give Angela my love. It was wonderful to be with you. Good luck! L. a. L. Thanks again for the <u>lovely</u> presents!

Ben Richards to Ludwig Wittgenstein, January 3, 1951

GREENOGE
40 SWAKELEYS ROAD
ICKENHAM
UXBRIDGE
RUISLIP 2114
January 3rd 1950[135]

Dear Ludwig,

Thank you for your letter. I enclose the ration book. Thanks for the wonderful slippers – they are just the right size, and very warm and comfortable. Thanks for the two Christmas cards too.[136]

It was wonderful seeing you every day. I was very sorry the time was so short.

It is very good news that you are feeling better: may it last.

Did you ask Bevan the reason for applying for only one job at first, as opposed to several?

I hope you find living in Oxford again tolerable, and your room isn't noisy.

Wishing you a very happy New Year,

    with love always,

        Ben.

---

135 Given the content, it is clear that this is a response to Wittgenstein's letter of January 1, 1951, but Richards made the common January mistake of dating to the previous year.

136 Three undated Christmas cards from Wittgenstein to Richards have survived (see Chapter VII). These are possibly two of those.

Ludwig Wittgenstein to Ben Richards, January 6, 1951

27 St. John Street
Oxford
6.1.51.

Dearest Ben,

Thanks for your letter. I asked Bevan for his reason for his advice. He said he thought that it was perhaps not quite fair to apply for several jobs at the same time: because if they decided in one place to take you &you after seeing you & you then replied that you had made other arrangements you would thereby let them down, & if at a later date you wanted to apply for a job there they might not consider you again. (I hope this monstrous sentence has made clear to you what he meant.) I agreed with him & said that, from the way <u>you</u> described the procedure, both you & the hospital were free to make up their your minds after you'd seen the hospital & and the hospital people had looked at you. Bevan seemed in the end to be convinced by me that it would be all right if you applied for, say, two jobs at the same time. I wish you could talk to Drury about it. I'm sure he would give you some good advice. Please let me know if you got your testimonies & if you're going to have an interview somewhere. Even a place that sounds pretty bad off hand /in the advertisement/ may turn out to be good for you. May you be lucky!

/Please/ Ddon't get depressed! – My health isn't too good just now. I was fairly well for 2–3 days after I came back from Cambridge but then got worse again.[137] But I'm not unhappy. I think of you <u>a lot</u>. Don't forget that I think of you <u>constantly</u> with love.

Ludwig

P.S. I'm looked after very well.[138] Mrs. Goodridge does my shopping for me.[139] God bless you!

---

[137] A few days later – on January 11 – O. K. Bouwsma wrote in his diary: "Yesterday afternoon I went to see W. to carry him the bottle of Christmas port, and a jar of applesauce. Miss Anscombe had called the day before to tell us that he was sick. He has quite severe pains that begin in the morning and cease about four in the afternoon. He was in bed and looked amazingly sweet and mild. He invited me to sit down and stay and when I thought I should leave he urged me to stay longer. The doctor does not know or will not say what ails him" (Bouwsma 1986: 72).

[138] In a letter to his friend Ludwig Hänsel from a few days later, Wittgenstein wrote: "Miss Anscombe, who, as you know, lives in the same house, is very good to me & I am surrounded by too much kindness" (Wittgenstein to Hänsel, January 12, 1951).

[139] Beatrice May Gillian (Gill) Goodridge (1926–2022) and her husband Jonathan Francis (Frank) Goodridge (1924–1984) were among the other lodgers at 27 St John Street. The Goodridges lived on the ground floor, while Wittgenstein lived on the second floor.

I haven't yet heard from Norway.[140] I discovered the other day that the postage for an ordinary letter to Norway is now 4d[141] instead of 3d, & I put 3d on my letters /to Arne B. & to Kari/.[142] I wonder whether that accounts in some way for a delay. L. L.

Ben Richards to Ludwig Wittgenstein, January 9, 1951

GREENOGE
40 SWAKELEYS ROAD
ICKENHAM
UXBRIDGE
RUISLIP 2114
January 9th 1951.

Dear Ludwig,

Thanks for your letter. I have been busy typing out copies of testimonials from Bart's staff, and I have sent in applications ~~for~~ /to/ seven hospitals. So far I have been asked to go for an interview at Derby City Hospital on Thursday.

I am very sorry you are ill again. Is it the same kind of thing as you had in Cambridge? I hope you are better now. I suppose Bevan is coming back this week-end, and that you will go back to stay with him if you are not better.[143] In what way are you well looked after at 27 St. John Street, apart from Mrs Goodridge doing your shopping? My mother has been in bed with bronchitis for several days, and is getting better now.

---

140 See Wittgenstein's letter to Richards of January 1, 1951, and the relevant footnote there.

141 Stands for: 4 pence.

142 These were two friends – Arne Bolstad and Kari Holme – to whom Wittgenstein had written so as to arrange accommodation for his planned return trip to Skjolden in the near future. Bolstad was the man to whom Wittgenstein had given his cabin back in 1919 (see the relevant footnote to the letter from Wittgenstein to Richards of August 24, 1950). Just under three weeks earlier, Wittgenstein had written to Bolstad as follows: "When I was last in Skjolden, I asked Miss Rebni if she could let me stay at Eide again if it turned out that I could come back to Skjolden to work, i.e. write. She said that I could stay with her. About two weeks ago, I wrote to Miss Rebni that I would like to come to Skjolden at the beginning of January. She telegraphed back that I cannot come to Eide before Easter. But that is too late for me. I don't think I can manage to live on "Østerrike" [i.e. Wittgenstein's cabin]; I'm not strong enough. Can you recommend someone to me who could let me have a warm and quiet apartment in winter. It shouldn't be too expensive. I don't want to stay in a hotel. Please be so kind as to write to me if you know of anything that might suit me" (Wittgenstein to Bolstad, December 18, 1950; thanks to Harald Vatne for providing this letter to us, which is not included in the *Collected Correspondence*). Regarding Wittgenstein's communications with Kari Holme see Wittgenstein's letters to Richards of August 11 and 24, 1950, and January 1, 1951, and the relevant footnotes there.

143 Wittgenstein had ended up unexpectedly spending the Christmas holidays until New Year with the Bevans – his doctor Edward, Edward's wife Joan, and their children – in Cambridge. As Wittgenstein had written to Norman Malcolm a week earlier: "I spent Christmas in Cambridge in my doctors house. I'd gone to see him to have an examination before travelling to Norway & I fell ill in his house & had to stay there" (Wittgenstein to Malcolm, January 2, 1951).

Virginia went back to St. Andrew's on Sunday; Tazza returns to school to-day, and Angela to Oxford on Friday.

I am very well.

> Love always,
>
> Ben.

Ludwig Wittgenstein to Ben Richards, January 17, 1951[144]

> 27 St. John Street
>
> Oxford
>
> Wednesday

Dear Ben, d. H.

Thanks for your note. I'm lying in bed on by back – hence the pencil.[145] I am looking forward to seeing you on Saturday. Don't come too late, please, & don't make your visit too short. That's /only/ <u>my</u> wish of course. But if you can't stick it long with me I can't blame you, for I'm rotten company now. I <u>hope</u> I shan't be too bad when you're here. At times I get very bad.[146] <u>However</u> bad I am, <u>your</u> being with me will always be good for me. Come <u>only</u>, though, if you still l.[147] me as you did, & if your feeling hasn't in any way changed. You know I really mean this. If you come, the Smythies will put you up.[148]

> I love you always
>
> Ludwig

---

144 Richards added '17/1/51' to the letter, which was a Wednesday.

145 It was due to his illness that Wittgenstein had to lie down, as he had written a few days earlier to his friend Ludwig Hänsel: "But in Cambridge I began to feel unwell & had to lie down & in the end give up my journey. – Here I am very well cared for & nothing is wrong with me. I have to lie down for part of the day, but I don't mind. I hope to get back on my feet before too long. (But if not, it doesn't matter!)" (Wittgenstein to Hänsel, January 12, 1951).

146 O.K. Bouwsma's diary entry from the previous day presents a vivid picture of Wittgenstein's physical and mental state at the time: "On Saturday [January 13] I saw W. He was in pain, and had been since morning. He was obviously quite despondent. At one point he said: 'I'd not mind now if . . .' and then he turned to me and said he wouldn't finish the sentence. He said he would write to his doctor in Cambridge about seeing a specialist. But he would not go to an English hospital. He would rather die here in his own room. Today he should have a letter from Cambridge. . . . Later he managed to sit on the edge of the bed and felt some better. On Sunday [January 14] Gretchen and I went to see him. She brought four eggs. He was not in such pain, but I think he was weaker. He grew tired as he tried to pay us some attention. . . . Yesterday [January 15] Miss Anscombe said that he was growing weaker. No wonder. On Sunday he said he was not going to eat any more porridge. He eats almost nothing at all. No one says a word about cancer. On Saturday in the very act of turning to avoid a pain he asked if I had ever heard of Couéism. I had: 'Every day in every way I am feeling better and better.' He remembered the sentence. I said I thought it might help if you could believe it. He said: Yes, since fear is a part of one's ailment, saying this might help to allay fear. His mind was still as clear as could be" (Bouwsma 1986: 73–5; January 16, 1951).

147 Presumably: 'love'.

148 That is, Yorick Smythies and his wife Diana ('Polly') Pollard, who lived at 22 Banbury Road, Oxford.

Ludwig Wittgenstein to Ben Richards, January 23, 1951[149]

27 St John Street
Oxford
Tuesday

Dear Ben, dearest Heart

You know what it meant to me to be with you last weekend. <u>Thanks</u> for coming to me & for being so wonderfully kind to me. – I haven't changed much. I haven't got a very great deal of pain but am feeling pretty low & exceedingly weak.

I hope that you will soon get to know the ropes in your new job[150] & that you will soon loose the feeling of utter homelessness which one gets at the beginning of a new job in a new surrounding.

I am thinking of you <u>constantly</u>. God bless you & keep you.

  With love always

    Ludwig

P.S. I find it difficult to eat /anything/ & so M^{iss} Anscombe /gave me/ raw egg mixed with a little brandy & sugar, & that was <u>grand</u>, or should I say 'the cats pyjamas'[151]

  L. a. L.

Ben Richards to Ludwig Wittgenstein, January 26, 1951

Derby City Hospital
Derby
26/1/51

Dear Ludwig,

Thanks for your letter. It was wonderful to be able to see you and read Busch & Grimm again.[152] Let me know how you are.

---

149 Richards added '24/1/51' to the letter, which was a Wednesday; and since Wittgenstein wrote 'Tuesday' on the letter, Richards was presumably noting the date the letter was received.

150 Richards had taken up a job as a 'house officer' Derby City Hospital (see his following letter to Wittgenstein of January 26, 1951). House officer was – at that time – the most junior role for a qualified doctor, and the only position available for doctors who had just received their medical degree.

151 Wittgenstein delighted in American slang phrases such as this. In one of his conversations with Peter Daniel – another of the lodgers at 27 St John Street at this time – Wittgenstein said: "The English language is dead – not even decaying properly. American slang is living" (Daniel 1993: 54).

152 Wittgenstein and Richards had read Wilhelm Busch's *Edward's Dream* (1891) together the previous year (see Richards' letter to Wittgenstein of July 31, 1950); and they had read Jacob and Wilhelm Grimm's *Children's and Household Tales* (1812ff) together in Ireland two years previously (see Wittgenstein's letter to Richards of February 23, 1949).

I am well, and I have quite a comfortable small room, and the food is quite good. I have not really made friends with the other house officers yet. ~~But~~ The medical registrar seems to be a decent & capable man. I find the work confusing and tiring, but I am getting to understand my duties better as I go on. I have to make responsible decisions which I am not used to. I hope the job will do me good – I think it may.

    Love always,

      Ben

Ludwig Wittgenstein to Ben Richards, January 29, 1951

27 St. John Street
Oxford
29.1.51

Dearest Ben,

Thanks for your letter. I'll write about myself first. I'm feeling a good deal better than when you last saw me. On Friday, though I had hardly any pain, I still felt pretty ill; on Saturday I felt better, & yesterday I got up & stayed up for a good many hours. – I'm writing this in bed now because I have a slight pain, but apart from that I feel comfortable.[153]

I am very glad that your room & the food isn't too bad & that the registrar seems decent. That you find your work confusing & tiring doesn't surprise me a bit. That's bound to be so & it's good, if you can win the battle. Dearest Ben, <u>perhaps I'm a fool</u>, but I praise the fate which sent you away from Barths[154] & from London. It's like an operation, & an operation is <u>very</u> disagreeable, but I can't help thinking that <u>good</u> doctors had to do that.[155]

I am thinking of you no end. God bless you & keep you.

    I love you <u>always</u>

        Ludwig

---

[153] A few days later Wittgenstein summed up his condition to his friend Ludwig Hänsel, as follows: "I am now out of bed for a few hours almost every day & have only very slight pain during the painful period. Miss Anscombe is untiring in her kindness & generally helps me from all sides, which does not prevent me from sometimes being impatient & cruel. How things will go on & whether I will still be able to travel to Vienna or Norway, cannot be said." (Wittgenstein to Hänsel, February 2, 1951).

[154] Wittgenstein meant: Bart's (i.e. St Bartholomew's Hospital in London, where Richards had been interning).

[155] Compare Wittgenstein's letter to his friend Paul Engelmann from some thirty years earlier: "A lot has happened; I've performed some operations that were <u>very</u> painful, but they went well. I.e. I'm missing a limb here and there, but better a few limbs less, & the ones you have, healthy" (Wittgenstein to Engelmann, October 11, 1920).

P.S. Three handkerchiefs of yours are still here, but they will be sent before long. Look after yourself, please! I <u>hope</u> your health is good & stays that way.
M^{iss} A.[156] sends her love.

L. a. L.

Ludwig Wittgenstein to Ben Richards, February 2, 1951[157]

27 St. John Street
Oxford
Friday

Dear Ben, d. H.
These are your handkerchiefs. If there was a fourth one I can't find it just now.
My health hasn't changed. There are ups & downs. I have no <u>severe</u> pain & I'm up for some hours every day. I think of you <u>constantly</u> with love & with good wishes. I wish my wishes could help you! God bless you.

With love <u>always</u>
Ludwig

Ben Richards to Ludwig Wittgenstein, February 4, 1951

Derby City Hospital,
4/2/51

Dear Ludwig,
I am very glad you are feeling better. I hope it lasts. Are you going to Cambridge?
I am beginning to feel less lost, but I am still terribly ignorant about treatment of symptoms – for instance sleeplessness. What is that mixture of a quick and a slow-acting barbiturate in red & blue capsules called that you sometimes use? I still find the work pretty tiring, but I am quite well so far.
Give my love to Miss Anscombe and to Angela if you see her – has she been round? And also the Smythies.

Love always,
Ben

---

156 Elizabeth Anscombe.
157 Richards added '3/2/51' to the letter, which was a Saturday; and since Wittgenstein wrote 'Friday' on the letter, Richards was presumably noting the date the letter was received.

Ludwig Wittgenstein to Ben Richards, February 5, 1951[158]

27 St. John Street
Oxford
Monday

Dearest Ben,

Thanks for your note.

I intend to go to Cambridge on Thursday.[159] I <u>hope</u> I'll stick the journey all right. I have no severe pain & generally feel pretty comfortable in a horizontal position. I'll travel 1st class so I can lie down on the seat. M^{iss} Anscombe will go with me as she wants to spend the next weekend at Cambridge. – I'm glad you're feeling "less lost" now. You <u>couldn't</u> expect anything else at the beginning. Your ignorance, too, is just what you'd expect – though this doesn't make it more easy /for you/ to bear. I <u>hope</u> you aren't having <u>too</u> rough a time of it! – You may <u>not</u> have liked what I wrote in my last letter, i.e., that I was glad that you had to leave London /etc./ Perhaps I was wrong, – or at any rate wrong in telling you that I felt that way. But I <u>wasn't</u> callous about your having a tough time! I only hoped, <u>as I still hope</u>, that the toughness of having responsibility thrust on you would do you good. If by any chance I sounded light-hearted /about it/, I certainly never felt it.

I think of you with love & hope. And I hope you still . . . . . – That red & blue sleeping drug is called Tuinal /TUINAL/, ~~I believe~~ but I may get the spelling all wrong.[160] As you know it's important for you to know what the difficulty is: whether to fall asleep, or to ~~stay~~ /remain/ asleep, or both. You also know that it's impossible to foretell which sleeping drug will work with a patient. What makes one man sleep sometimes keeps the other awake. Don't forget the existence of sedobrol.[161] Forgive all this <u>unnecessary</u> advise. – I haven't seen yet Angela, & I have an idea that she won't come either. – M^{iss} A.[162] sends you her love. I haven't seen Smythies yet; he had a <u>bad</u> flu but has now recovered & I'll probably see him soon.[163]

---

158 Richards added '5/2/51' to the letter, which was a Monday.
159 A few days earlier Wittgenstein had written to his friend, Ludwig Hänsel, of his intention to visit Dr. Bevan in Cambridge: "I will probably be travelling to Cambridge in about a week, staying with my wonderful doctor & he will try to see if anything can be done. (Like radiotherapy.) I trust him <u>completely</u>, & have good reason to. He is good, clever & a real friend" (Wittgenstein to Hänsel, February 2, 1951).
160 'Tuinal' was the brand name of a sleeping pill introduced by Eli Lilly in the late 1940s. Each pill capsule was bright red at one tip, then had a band of deep burgundy and a band of light blue.
161 A sleeping pill developed by Hoffmann-LaRoche in 1912.
162 Elizabeth Anscombe.
163 In Wittgenstein's letter to Roy Fouracre of a few days earlier, he wrote: "I hope you won't get the flu'; there's a regular epidemic here" (Wittgenstein to Fouracre, February 1, 1951; and see also his letter to Hänsel of the same date).

I haven't been out so far. I have so far had so[164] spend a good many hours in bed every day. – Please don't lose <u>courage</u> & <u>hope</u>!! May God bless you & help you. Be patient with yourself! I think of you with love, constantly.
   Ludwig

Ludwig Wittgenstein to Ben Richards (undated, probably between June and December 1950)[165]

Dear Ben, o. H.,

This is Studentenfutter.[166] The idea isn't to cram it into your mouth all at once, but to take it in small quantities while you're cramming for the exam. – This somehow reminds me that I gave you a wrong information once when I said that my suppositories contain 'butter of cocoa'. They contain:

  Bismuth Subgallicum 3 grains

  Resorcin 1 gr.

  Ephedrin Hydrochlor. 1/10 gr

  Benzocaine 2 gr.

There are, however, some that contain 'butter of Cocoa' though I don't know what that is.

G. bl. y.! With love, always
   Ludwig

Ludwig Wittgenstein to Angela Richards (undated, between April 1950 and February 1951)[167]

Dear Angela,

I came here thinking you might possibly be in. I'm staying in M[iss] Anscombe's house at 27 St John Street. If any day you wouldn't mind seeing me, just say so. So long.

L. Wittgenstein

---

164 Wittgenstein presumably meant: 'to'.

165 Given the content, this letter is presumably from one of the periods in which Richards was revising for his various medical exams – so: June/July 1949, June/July 1950, September/October 1950, or December 1950.

166 German: 'students' feed' (a mix of nuts and dried fruit), a German snack that had traditionally been particularly popular with students. Wittgenstein had sent some to Richards as an aid for his exam revision.

167 Wittgenstein did not date this note, but he gives his address as 27 St John Street, so it must have been written between April 1950 and February 1951, which was the only period Wittgenstein lived there. The original letter is in the possession of Gabriel Citron.

VI. With the Bevans in Cambridge
(February – April 1951)

Wittgenstein "had a horror of the idea of dying in an English hospital"[1] (in particular "[h]e... loathed" the thought of "being washed with a flannel – smeared with a flannel, as he said, by a nurse when one couldn't wash oneself in bed"[2]). So with remarkable generosity, Wittgenstein's doctor – Edward Bevan – invited him to come and spent his final weeks or months in his family's home, 'Storey's End', at 76 Storey's Way, in Cambridge.

And so – on Thursday February 8, 1951 – Wittgenstein set out from Oxford to Cambridge, accompanied by Elizabeth Anscombe, to move in with Edward and Joan Bevan and their children. He was getting ready to die. Anscombe recalled their journey:

> "Wittgenstein was very frail then. We took a 1st class carriage so that he could lie on the seat, and there was some complication about paying extra for a ticket I already had. The inspector came to alter the charge that had been made, and explained that it was a matter of interpretation of rules. With rules, he said, the thing was, there was always more than one way you could take them. 'Yes, yes' Wittgenstein said and tried to wave him away, but he laboured the point for all it was worth. I was very much amused and Wittgenstein mildly so; he muttered something about not escaping lectures in philosophy. – We were reading *Der Prinz von Homburg* on that journey."[3]

A few weeks after Wittgenstein moved in – towards the end of February – he stopped taking the hormones which he'd been taking to slow the growth and spread of his tumours. He'd been taking them since November 1949, but they were now no longer of any use. Instead, Dr Bevan arranged for Wittgenstein to receive X-ray treatment at Addenbrooke's Hospital – under the supervision of the renowned radiologist and cancer specialist Joseph S. Mitchell – largely intended to help reduce his pain. This lasted for a few weeks, and helped a great deal.

---

1 Drury 1984: 169.
2 Anscombe 2025: 182.
3 Anscombe 2025: 182; the book referred to is Heinrich von Kleist's 1809/10 play, *The Prince of Homburg*.

Around March 10, 1951, something changed: Wittgenstein found that he could philosophize again. This was most likely because he had discontinued the hormone therapy, which had been clouding his mind.[4] Wittgenstein had not made any entries in his working notebooks since September 23, 1950[5] – but in these last seven weeks of his life he suddenly wrote hundreds of pages of philosophical remarks. In mid-April he described what had happened, as follows, to Norman Malcolm:

> "An extraordinary thing has happened to me. About a month ago I suddenly found myself in the right frame of mind for doing philosophy. I had been absolutely certain that I'd never again be able to do it. It's the first time after more than 2 years that the curtain in my brain has gone up. – Of course, so far I've only worked for about 5 weeks & it may be all over by tomorrow; but it bucks me up a lot now."[6]

Joan Bevan recalled that when his philosophical capacities came back to him, Wittgenstein said to her: "I will now work as I have never worked before".[7] And he did. His notes from this period were made in what are now known as manuscripts 175, 176, and 177, and they revolve around the themes of certainty and doubt.

Shortly after Wittgenstein moved into Storey's End, Richards moved to Derby to take up a position as a 'house physician' at Derby City Hospital. He was responsible for many more patients than he was used to, so he was very busy and also felt somewhat out of his depth. This made it hard for him to take any time off to make the four-hour train trip to visit Wittgenstein. In the end, he managed to leave for the long Easter weekend – heading to Cambridge on Good Friday (when he finished early) and staying until Monday. This was to be the last time he saw Wittgenstein before he sat by him at his death bed.

On Thursday April 26, 1951, Wittgenstein turned 62. Joan Bevan gave him an electric blanket as a birthday present and wished him 'many happy returns'. He stared at her and said "There will be no returns".[8] The next day – April 27 – Wittgenstein made his final entry in his philosophical notebook.[9] That evening he became very ill and took to bed. Dr. Bevan told him that he would live for only a few more days, to which Wittgenstein replied: "Good".[10] The next day – April 28 – Dr. Bevan called Elizabeth Anscombe and

---

4 See Anscombe 2025: 185; and see Rhees 1984: 225, fn. 50.
5 See MS 175, p. 31r.
6 Wittgenstein to Malcolm, April 16, 1951.
7 Bevan 2016: 1031.
8 Bevan 2016: 1031.
9 See MS 177, pp. 9r-11r.
10 Bevan 2016: 1031.

Yorick Smythies to come from Oxford, Maurice Drury to come from Dublin, and Richards to come from Derby, so that they could be with Wittgenstein at the end. By that evening, however – before any of his friends had arrived – Wittgenstein had largely slipped out of consciousness. He never fully woke up again. His friends arrived the next day – Sunday April 29 – by which time Wittgenstein was mostly lying with his eyes shut. He died later that day, surrounded by his friends, with Richards holding his hand.[11]

Ludwig Wittgenstein to Ben Richards, February 10, 1951[12]

'Storeys End'[13]
Storeys Way
Cambridge
Saturday

Dear Ben, d. H.

This is only to say that I've moved to Cambridge.

I'm pretty well, on the whole. Are you?? I think of you no end; & I imagine that your life must be a string of great difficulties.[14] I'd give a lot to know how you feel about them, I mean how far you're cheerful & in good spirits. And I'd give still more of course to be able to see you & just say cheer up to you.

 I love you <u>always.</u>

    Ludwig

<u>If</u> <u>you can</u>, let me know something about what's going on in you while you work, & also at other times. – I <u>hope</u> your health is all right!

    L. L.

---

11 See Anscombe 2025: 185.

12 This date was added by Richards; and since February 10 was a Saturday in 1951, this must be the day it was written, rather than – or as well as – the day it was received.

13 'Storey's End' was the name of the Bevans' house at 76 Storey's Way, Cambridge (the road is named after Edward Storey, and has an apostrophe).

14 Wittgenstein is referring to Richards' new job at Derby City Hospital, which involved moving to Derby and taking on a lot more responsibility for patients than he had previously held (see Richards' letters to Wittgenstein of January 26 and February 4, 1951).

Ben Richards to Ludwig Wittgenstein, February 12, 1951

Derby City Hospital
February 12th 1951

Dear Ludwig,

Thanks for your letter. I hope you are comfortable at the Bevans's.

I know my way about much better now, but I have a lot of responsibility – more than I should have at Bart's. I can get the registrar when I am worried badly about a patient but I sometimes feel very incompetent if a rapid decision has to be made. I think I am getting valuable experience, and I learn a bit from the registrar, but I hope I shan't make mistakes with serious consequences while I am learning. I am rather disappointed in my chief. He does not seem to take real interest in what happens to his patients, nor does he give me great confidence in his ability as a physician. He gets impatient if a patient is at all slow in answering, or misunderstands his questions; and he changes his mind about treatment on different days without giving reasons. He ~~do~~ comes twice a week for a ward round and I may be misjudging him, as I have not seen a great deal of him yet. It is worrying, but on the whole I am happy here.

I think of you constantly, and it cheers me up to get your letters.

    Love always,
        Ben.

Ludwig Wittgenstein to Ben Richards, February 13, 1951[15]

'Storeys End'
Storeys Way
Cambridge
Tuesday

Dearest Ben,

Thanks for your letter of Feb. 12th & for writing to me about your work & the people you're dealing with. I was, of course, <u>most</u> interested. – Dear Ben, you're <u>bound</u> to make <u>serious</u> mistakes while you're learning & you'll be learning for a <u>long</u> time. You will also be very unhappy indeed about your mistakes. But I hope you'll be happy in <u>spite</u> of that. That's the real happiness, not the one when you're having a 'good time'. I mean this seriously. – When I read in your letter that, on the whole, you were feeling happy, that

---

15 Richards added '14/2/51' to the letter, which was a Wednesday; and since Wittgenstein wrote 'Tuesday' on the letter, Richards was presumably noting the date the letter was received.

made me feel <u>very</u> good; although I knew that you'd sometimes feel anything but happy. May you have <u>luck</u>, & lots of courage when you've ~~had~~ got bad luck!

"Seid fromm im Glück

Und seid dem Leid

Mit Mut bereit."[16] I don't know if you remember that.

I'm very comfortable here though it's not as quiet as my room in Oxford. I have very little pain or discomfort just now & everybody is very kind to me. – To-day I went to see Professor Mitchell who is a cancer specialist.[17] He made an <u>excellent</u> impression on me. The way he examined me, the questions he asked & the way he listened to what I'd to say made me trust him a <u>lot</u>. He thought that my rectal pain was due, on the one hand to the effect of various troubles I've had in that region, <u>e.g.</u> the cauterisation 20 years ago,[18] on the other hand to a secondary groth[19] in /a certain region of/ lumbar spine. He found that I was tender round about certain vertebrae & wants me to get some more X-rays done which might show a groth. The connection with former trouble (e.g. cauterisation) ~~seems to be~~ he explained in this /way/ that ~~the condition is~~ if I had not scars my present condition would not give me these rectal pains. He also wants me to have deep X-ray treatment. His prognosis was not good. He said, though <u>very</u> tentatively, that I may live for <u>five</u> more years. A long, long time! – That's about all. I'm writing you terribly long letters. If you want them shorter, <u>say so</u>.

I think of you constantly & love you always. God bless you!

Ludwig

P.S. Re your boss. You'll find <u>lots & lots</u> of doctors whose <u>obtuseness</u>, <u>lack of interest</u>, etc. etc. will – rightly – disgust you. You'll suffer from that too /I mean from observing it/. The point is that you <u>mustn't</u> imitate them.

G. b. y. <u>a.</u>

May I see you before too long!

---

16 German: 'Be pious in good fortune / And be ready for suffering / With courage'. This is the (slightly misremembered) ending of the motto with which Robert Schumann prefaced the first edition of his 'Davidsbündlertänze' ['Dances of the League of David'] (op. 6). The full original is: 'Alter Spruch: / In all und jeder Zeit / Verknüpft sich Lust und Leid / Bleibt fromm in Lust und seyd / Dem Leid mit Mut bereit' ('Old saying: / In each and every age / pleasure and suffering are intertwined / Remain pious in pleasure and be / ready for suffering with courage'). Wittgenstein mentioned this also in his letters to Richards of December 28, 1946 and January 19, 1950.

17 Joseph Stanley Mitchell (1909-1987) was a radiologist and cancer specialist, and at that time the director of the Radiotherapeutic Centre at Addenbrooke's Hospital in Cambridge.

18 This is probably a reference to a painful operation which Wittgenstein underwent towards the end of 1928 (probably for his recurrent hernias) – so, about 22 years earlier (see Prokop 2003: 174-5).

19 That is: 'growth'.

Ben Richards to Ludwig Wittgenstein, February 19, 1951

City Hospital
Derby
February 19th 1951

Dear Ludwig

It is good news to hear you are very comfortable – I hope that has lasted. Are you in the same room you were in at Christmas?

I am very sorry it isn't quiet and I hope the noise isn't a wireless. Let me know if the deep x-rays are helping. A colleague of mine here treated a woman with bad rectal pain due to constipation by putting some Nupercaine cream (a local anaesthetic) on a glycerine suppository which he said relieved the pain. I do not know if suppositories are made containing local anaesthetic.

Thank you very much for writing all you did about my letter. Of course I don't want shorter letters. I have of course made mistakes, but none, I think, with very serious consequences so far. But ~~it~~ often if a patient gets more ill or doesn't improve I don't know if it is because I have made a mistake. I suppose as you say I must expect to make bad mistakes (with bad consequences which I'll know /afterwards/ are due to them) – may they be as few as possible.

    Love always,
        Ben.

Ludwig Wittgenstein to Ben Richards, February 21, 1951

76 Storeys Way
Cambridge
21.2.51.

Dearest Ben,

Thanks for your letter. I feel definitely better now. I think the deep X-ray treatment is helping me. The X-ray picture which was taken of my spine (around D7) showed very little, so Dr Mitchell told me to-day; but he says that small changes in a thick bone don't show much on an X-ray & he is certain that there is a growth there. This, he says, produces an exitation of the rectum, & the bowels in general.

The irritability of my bowels & rectum is certainly much less since I started the treatment, though on the day of a treatment ~~it's~~ always gets slightly worse; but not bad enough /for me/ to go to bed.

Suppositories containing local anaesthetics don't help me in the slightest. I imagine they <u>only</u> do if the cause of the pain is <u>local</u>. They did, e.g., when I had a fissure. I tried suppositories containing Benzocaine[20] ("Supol" suppositories do) &, on my request, my Oxford G.P.[21] prescribed me suppositories containing Novocaine.[22] Also Nupercaine[23] ointment, which a doctor puts on his finger when he examines one's rectum, has no effect. – I'm so frightfully explicit about all this because my experience may conceivably come in useful to you. – – I can't think at all but I'm reading a fair amount.[24] Among other things I'm rereading Moby Dick by H. Melville.[25] Do you know it? I think some of it is <u>great</u>. When he gets humorous I often can't follow him. – Have you got your gramophone with you, & do you sometimes play it? I haven't heard any music since the day I heard Haydn with you in Glenmore Rd.. To-day they're playing on the wireless a concerto for trumpet & strings by Timmy Moore.[26] I don't think I'll hear it though. –

When I go to Addenbrooks for treatment I generally see Prof. Mitchell & am impressed by the way in which he listens to <u>anything</u> the patient has to say. I thought: the more patiently ~~he~~ you listen to all a patient says – even though lots if it is <u>bound</u> to be irrelevant – the more you will learn. The more a doctor /in his heart/ just pooh-poohs what the patient tells him, /& therefore doesn't really listen carefully/, the less he learns about medicine. (I know it must be difficult to pick out of all this mass all that might be relevant.) So be very patient with your patients; & also with yourself when you make mistakes.

I think of you constantly & love you <u>always</u>.
Ludwig

---

20 A topical local anaesthetic.
21 Stands for: 'General Practitioner'.
22 Brand name of the local anaesthetic Procain.
23 Brand name of the local anaesthetic Dibucaine.
24 Wittgenstein described his current reading to Rush Rhees in a letter from just a few weeks later: "The books I read recently were: "Studies in Classic American Literature" by D.H. Lawrence (Smythies lent it to me & I <u>liked</u> it, inspite of what seems to me lots of childishness & immaturity), some Hamann (which is terribly difficult for me), "Moby Dick" (which I reread because of some of Lawrence's illuminating remarks – & I got more out of it the second time), bits of the Old Testament, "Rommel" by Brigadier Young (which I definitely like)" (Wittgenstein to Rhees, March 14, 1951).
25 Wittgenstein had reported to Richards that he was reading parts of *Moby Dick* – the first time around – back in his letter of October 1, 1949.
26 Timothy Moore (1922-2003) – son of Wittgenstein's friend and colleague, G. E. Moore – was a composer and pianist, and Director of Music at Dartington Hall School, Devon, from 1950-82. His Concerto for Trumpet and Strings was composed in 1948 and premiered in London in May 1949. This was its first radio broadcast.

Ben Richards to Ludwig Wittgenstein, February 25, 1951

> City Hospital
> Derby
> 25/2/51

Dear Ludwig,

Thanks for your letter. It is good to hear the deep x-rays help. I hope you will get well enough to do some more work. How do you feel apart from your illness? Do you like being where you are better than Oxford or not? Can you get out a bit?

I am very well and pretty busy. I have never read Melville. I have just started the Mill on the Floss[27] but it has not made much impression on me good or bad, so far. I have only read 8 pages.

I have played the gramophone 2 or 3 times since I came here [　][28] Schubert's impromptu, a little [　] Monteverdi and last night I played the other Haydn quartet of the 3 you gave me (not the Emperor, nor the one we heard last at Glenmore Road.) Otherwise I have heard no music. There is an out of tune piano in the sitting room which I have tried once or twice.

I miss you terribly. Let me know as arranged if you specially want to see me. I hope I can arrange to get away to see you in about a month.

> Love always,
> Ben.

Ludwig Wittgenstein to Ben Richards, February 27, 1951

> 76 Storeys Way
> Cambridge
> 27.2.51.

Dear Ben, d. o. H.

I'm not quite as well now as when I wrote to you last, but I'm not <u>bad</u>. Yesterday I developed a ~~little~~ /mild/ cystitis. Bevan thinks it isn't connected with my illness. I went to bed in the early afternoon & after a short time felt much better. I'm up now. Have you ever drunk lemon barley water? I think it's <u>foul</u>. And on the label there's that ghastly head one used to see in the tube, saying something like "Just a <u>little</u> patience". I'm supposed to drink lots of the stuff. Apart from my trouble I feel moderately well

---

27　A novel by George Eliot (the pseudonym of Mary Ann Evans) from 1860.

28　The upper right corner of the sheet has been torn off, so the last word or so of this line and the next (as they appear on the original manuscript) is missing. The empty square brackets mark the missing words.

here, perhaps a little less so than in Oxford – but I don't really know. I rather wonder what would happen if I got really ill /in this place/; sometimes I feel a bit apprehensive. – – I don't think that I'll ever be able to work again. I occasionally ~~tried~~ try to think about a certain problem[29] & I find that my thoughts don't <u>move</u>. I can't <u>handle</u> a problem any more; just as I can't go for a walk. My longest walk ~~has~~ was from the Addenbrookes to Great St Mary's/last week/.[30] But this isn't a complaint! – D.H., a month is a long time to wait, but I'll stick it if I've got to. If I were to get worse & thought that I shouldn't wait so long, I'll let you know.

It felt good to read that you miss me, because that makes us a little more equal.[31] I rarely see anyone here because it tires me a lot, but I <u>always</u> want to see you & I long to see your face again! – Perhaps, if you can come here, we could hear some records together, unless the children & other inmates of the house make it impossible. What ever we do will be wonderful for me, & I hardly dare to hope that it'll come about at all. Please look after yourself. I'm <u>glad</u> you can hear a little music. God bless you. With love always,

    Ludwig

P.S. Is the Mill on the Floss by one of the Brontés?[32]

Good luck with your work! The <u>deeper</u> you get into it the better. Don't be afraid & G. bl. y. <u>a</u>.

                                                L. L.

Ben Richards to Ludwig Wittgenstein, March 5, 1951

                                            City Hospital,
                                                    Derby.
                                                    5/3/51

Dear Ludwig

Thanks for your letter and the primrose.

---

29 Wittgenstein's thinking does not seem to have led to his writing down any of his thoughts (MS 175 has no entries between September 23, 1950, and March 10, 1951, which is when Wittgenstein had a final – and very intensive – writing period; see MS 175, pp. 31r & 35r).

30 A church in the centre of Cambridge; given the location of the hospital at that time, this is a walk of about half a mile (approximately 850m).

31 Wittgenstein had long expressed great concern that their feelings for one another were not equally balanced (see, for example, his letter to Richards of June 16, 1948, and the Introduction).

32 See the relevant footnote to Richards' previous letter, of February 25, 1951.

We've had some sunny weather here at last but I wasn't in very good shape to enjoy it. I had a sore throat last week which got better – and then I was sick one night (I think it was /due to/ the supper) and felt queer all next day – but I am O.K. again now.

I'm very sorry you're not so well. I once used to like lemon barley water, and I don't object strongly to it now. But why must you drink it? Surely water or some other fruit drink would do as well.

How is Bevan? This must be the worst time of the year for him. Give him & Mrs Bevan my kind regards.

I long to see you again, and read or go for a walk – 100 yards would be wonderful. Or if that couldn't be I'd love just to sit in your room.

The Mill on the Floss is by George Eliot (the woman). I haven't got much further – I am reading very little now – but there are some things I like in it now.

I played the first 2 movements of Schubert's C major quintet last night and thought of you.[33]

  Love always,
  Ben

Ludwig Wittgenstein to Ben Richards, March 8, 1951

76 Storeys Way
Cambridge
8.3.51.

Dear Ben, o. H.!

Thanks for your letter. I'm sorry to hear you haven't been well. I know how bad the food in hospitals can be. In Newcastle at the Royal Infirmary[34] one whole group was ill several times because of some rotten fish or something we'd had for lunch. Perhaps you should buy yourself some decent unrationed cheese or something so you can eat in your room if it isn't safe to eat the official supper. – My own health is very variable, or at least the degree to which I feel well or ill is variable. My cystitis disappeared /shortly after I wrote to you/, came again, & /has/ disappeared again. I'm very weak now & I don't think it's <u>likely</u> that I shall be able to walk with you even a 100 yards when you come (though God knows). Thanks for saying that it's all right with you

---

33 Franz Schubert's String Quintet in C major (D 956). Some years earlier – in his letter to Richards of April 24, 1947 – Wittgenstein had asked Richards to think of him when listening to that piece.

34 During the Second World War – from mid-April 1943 until February 1944 – Wittgenstein worked as a technician in a medical research team at the Royal Victoria Infirmary in Newcastle.

if we just <u>sit</u> together! You know as well as I do that one can't foretell what may happen. Yesterday, e.g. I had to go to bed, I felt so rotten, & to-day I'm up again.[35] Oh Ben, I <u>hope</u> I'll be well enough for us to read & talk, though even <u>seeing</u> you will be a blessing for me. – I'm reading a fair amount even when I'm in bed, & oddly enough, not detective stories. (Though, if I had any fairly good ones, I'd read them) – I wish there was a better recording of the Schubert string quintet.[36] Yours is just good enough to show one how wonderful it <u>would</u> be if it were played as it should be. – I think of you <u>constantly</u>. God bless you. Please take care yourself! I love you
<u>always.</u>
Ludwig

P.S. You're quite right: it isn't necessary to drink lemon barley water, any non alcoholic drink will do, & I very soon switched over to other drinks.
This snowdrop comes from our garden but I didn't pick it myself.

L. L.

Ben Richards to Ludwig Wittgenstein, March 12, 1951

City Hospital,
Derby.
March 12th 1951

Dear Ludwig,

Thanks very much for your letter and the flower.

I am quite well again now. I am quite busy as one of the other house physicians is away on holiday and I am looking after half of his patients. I wish I could plan my work better – I find I spend more time on some patients I am interested in and not enough on others. I have always been bad at organising my time. Of course I may be interrupted at any time by a new patient arriving or by an emergency in the hospital, but I get unduly disturbed and waste a lot of time. I have no fixed time-table apart from the rounds with my chief. I think I'll try writing one down, but I shall probably have to keep changing it at short notice.

---

35 The next day Wittgenstein wrote to Rush Rhees: "I'm up every day a bit & often the whole day. I'm very weak physically & mentally & have all sorts of discomforts but <u>very</u> little pain... A fortnight ago, when I felt particularly well for a bit, I walked from Addenbrookes to Great St. Mary's" (Wittgenstein to Rhees, March 9, 1951).
36 See Richards' previous letter regarding this quintet.

Let me know how you are. I hope you'll be able to get out again when weather's finer. It has been foul here: dull, damp & foggy.

I look forward to seeing you in about a fortnight – I'll let you know. I wonder which way I'll get from here to Cambridge, cross-country or via London. It will be wonderful for me as you know.

   Love always,
    Ben.

Ludwig Wittgenstein to Ben Richards, March 12-14, 1951[37]

76 Storeys Way
Cambridge
Monday

Dearest Ben,

I think of you a <u>lot</u>. To-day I went for a little walk, from the house to the entrance to the /astronomical/ observatory & back.[38] I thought I might find some flowers on the wayside but there were none. You see I was unnecessarily pessimistic when I wrote that it was unlikely that we'd be able to walk 100 yards. – I enclose a cutting from the New Statesman in lieu of a flower.[39] [Tuesday][40] I went to see Prof. Mitchell this morning. He said he doesn't want to give me any more treatment; also that he thought I had widely spread deposits, that he'd give me deep X-rays again if I should again feel ~~violent~~ /severe/ pain in my rectum. He was, to my great surprise, in favour of my

---

37 Richards added '14/3/51' to the letter, which was a Wednesday in 1951. Wittgenstein began this letter on the Monday prior to that (March 12) and wrote it over three consecutive days until that Wednesday.

38 This was presumably the Cambridge University Observatory Building on Madingley Road. The walk is about half a mile (approximately 850m) each way. On the same day Wittgenstein wrote to Rush Rhees: "This is only to tell you that I've been feeling <u>very</u> much better the last few days. I went for short walks yesterday & the day before, & they had no ill consequences. I imagine that this improvement is due to the x-ray treatment".

39 This issue of *The New Statesman* (March 3, 1951) had contained an article which had rather annoyed Wittgenstein – a review by Mary Scrutton of a volume of essays edited by A.G.N. Flew, entitled *Logic and Language* (Oxford, Basil Blackwell, 1951). On the same day that he posted this letter to Richards, he wrote as follows to Rush Rhees: "The other day I saw in the New Statesman a review of a book which seems to be a collection of articles by various Logical Positivists: Wisdom, Ryle, Waisman, etc.. It particularly praised Waisman for a remark which comes straight from me. Whenever I see an obvious theft I very much dislike it; although I really ought by now to be entirely used to it. I wish some reviewer would debunk these humbugs" (Wittgenstein to Rhees, March 14, 1951).

40 The square brackets are Wittgenstein's own.

stopping the stilboestrol[41] (I stopped it some weeks ago). I feel pretty well, took quite a walk in town to-day & have no pain except a <u>little</u> back ache. I even think about philosophy[42] – but <u>don't</u> say you're glad, because it may have ceased before you can say it! – I sent you a book to-day, "Rommel" by Brigadier Young.[43] I read in it again yesterday & found it interesting & liked it. Had it been written by a German, or by an Englishman about an <u>Englishman</u>, it wouldn't interest me much. What interests me & what I like so much is that it was written about an 'enemy'. You <u>may</u> not find it interesting at all, partly perhaps because you haven't been in a war; or it may just not appeal to you. I'd like to know what you think. I hope you won't mind that I wrote something inside. – I still want to say that Prof. Mitchell always gives me an excellent impression, I like him. [Wednesday] Thanks for your letter. Yes, I <u>think</u> I understand your difficulties in distributing your time fairly among all your jobs. Am I wrong in imagining that it is briefly a difficulty in denying yourself things that you'd like to do at the moment. I often called you a "dawdler". I am <u>sorry</u> you should have to undergo such a hard training now! May it do you good only & no harm. I mean, I hope it will

---

41 Diethylstilboestrol, a synthetic nonsteroidal estrogen developed in 1938 and used – at the time – in the treatment of prostate and breast cancers (amongst other things). Wittgenstein had been taking this medication since November 1949.

42 Three days before writing this comment – on March 10, 1951 – Wittgenstein had made the first philosophical entry in his manuscript notebook after a long hiatus (since September 23, 1950). And in just the few weeks between that entry and his death, he filled hundreds of pages of his notebooks on topics revolving around doubt and certainty (see MSS 175, 176, and 177). His final entry was made on April 27, 1951, just two days before his death (see MS 177, pp. 9r ff). It's possible that his ability to do fruitful philosophical work was due to having discontinued the medication a few weeks earlier, as Rush Rhees later reported: "About six weeks before his death... Wittgenstein found he was able to do good work again. From the end of November 1949 to, roughly, the end of February 1951, he was, as he wrote to me, 'letting the hormones do their work', and more often than not he felt that he could not write anything worth putting down. He recovered his power of mind when he left off the hormones" (Rhees 1984: 225, fn. 50). See also the letter from Wittgenstein to Norman Malcolm (of April 16, 1951) quoted in the introduction to this chapter.

43 Desmond Young's *Rommel: The Desert Fox*, New York, Harper, 1950. Wittgenstein much admired this book, and around this time he wrote about, recommended, or gifted Young's *Rommel* to a number of his friends, including Norman Malcolm (to whom he had sent it as a belated Christmas gift in January) and Rush Rhees (to whom he mentioned the book in a number of letters). To Malcolm he wrote just a few days later saying "I'm very glad you liked the Rommel book. I looked at it quite recently again & was impressed again by the thoroughly <u>decent</u> way in which it's written. Such books are few & far between. The author, where he disagrees with other people of high rank (as on p.p. 160-161), expresses himself very cautiously, but one always knows what he thinks & what he would say if he could let himself go" (Wittgenstein to Malcolm, March 19, 1951). Similarly, to Rush Rhees he wrote: "I don't know if I told you that I had made the acquaintance of a book which I like & admire a lot. It's a book called "Rommel" by one Brigadier Desmond Young. It's a kind of biography of Rommel & describes his exploits in France & Africa. It is <u>extremely</u> interesting, seems to me <u>very</u> well written & with complete fairness & without a trace of meanness" (Wittgenstein to Rhees, March 30, 1951).

/gradually/ teach you something & yet not deaden your interest. All this sounds pretty much like a talk of a hypocritical person (which is roughly what I am). But yet I mean what I say, even though I don't express it well. And I always knew that some day you'd have to learn to allocate your time more according to duty than to your inclination at the moment. I wish you'd understand what I say in the spirit in which it's meant: I <u>love</u> your dawdling; but one can love the branches & twigs of a tree & yet think that the tree will have to be <u>pruned</u> /but not so that it dies/. God bless you & keep your <u>heart</u> as it is.

I will make enquiries here as to the best way of getting from Derby to Cambridge & will let you know the result. The weather here is <u>mostly foul</u>. Wind, rain & cold. But if I'm as well in a fortnight as I'm now we'll be able to go out if the weather permits. – Take good care of yourself! I think of you constantly & love you always.

Ludwig

P.S. I <u>know</u> that you know all that I've said anyhow, & what I write wasn't meant to tell you anything you don't know but simply to pour out my own thoughts etc. about it.

L.a.

L.

Enclosure included with the letter of March 12-14, 1951:[44]

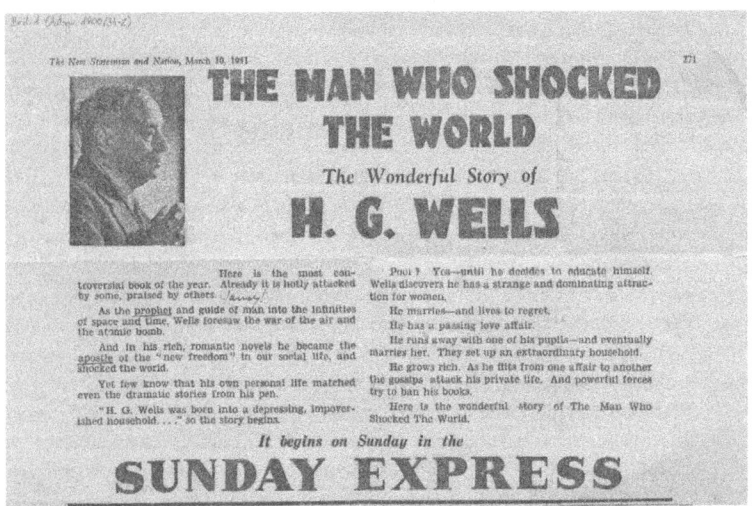

---

44 After the first paragraph Wittgenstein added by hand: 'Fancy!' (presumably in mock astonishment). And in the second and third paragraphs he underlined the religious epithets 'prophet' and 'apostle' (presumably to highlight their absurdity in this context).

Ludwig Wittgenstein to Ben Richards, March 17, 1951[45]

76 Storeys Way
Cambridge
Saturday

Dearest Ben,

I enquired yesterday at the railway office in Town about the connection between Derby & Cambridge. The best way on weekends is via Kettering.

    Derby dep. 12.5 noon

    arr. Kettering 1.30, dep Kettering 2.10

    arr. here 3.45 p.m. (check up on that)

On Sunday, & <u>probably</u> on Bank Holiday, you've got to go via London. — I heard a wonderful record yesterday & got it for you. I'm not telling you what it is.[46] – I long to see you. I hope you won't be here <u>too terribly</u> short! /I'm afraid this isn't English/ God bless you! <u>Whatever</u> you do. – I walked about in Town a good deal yesterday, perhaps a bit too much. I'll rest to-day. – I can still think. I'd never have expected that to happen again. But let me not <u>crow</u>![47]

    I love you always.

    Ludwig

P.S. You can stay here ~~either~~ either with Miss A.[48] or with the Bevans, both told me they'd like to have you. That shows you – –. I. l. y. a. & t. o. y. <u>c</u>.[49]
May nothing prevent our seeing each other!

---

45 This date was added by Richards; and since March 17 was a Saturday in 1951, this must be the day it was written, rather than – or as well as – the day it was received.

46 Two days earlier, Wittgenstein had written to his sister, Helene Salzer: "The other day I read that there is now a recording of Bach's C major concerto for 3 pianos... Edwin Fischer plays the one piano & also conducts" (Wittgenstein to Helene Salzer, March 15, 1951). Then, on the same day as he wrote this letter to Richards, he followed up to his sister: "This is just a P.S. to my letter of yesterday. I have heard the three-piano concerto & it is beautifully performed. (There is only one passage in the first movement that does not strike me as good.) I have the feeling that Fischer is a great artist" (Wittgenstein to Helene Salzer, March 17, 1951). The record that Wittgenstein bought for Richards therefore seems likely to have been a recording of Bach's Concerto in C major for three Pianos and Orchestra (BWV 1064) by the London Philharmonic – conducted by Edwin Fischer, and with Fischer, Ronald Smith, and Denis Matthews, on the three pianos (recorded for HMV in 1950).

47 A couple of days later Wittgenstein expanded on his situation to Norman Malcolm: "I'm feeling much better now than I did a month ago. I have hardly any pain. The improvement is probably due to the deep x-ray treatment I took for a few weeks. (This time it wasn't my shoulders but my spine that got the rays). I am of course very weak & there seems no doubt that this isn't going to change for the better as time goes on. I hardly think that I'll be on this earth when you come to Cambridge in Autumn '52. Still, one doesn't know. I am not depressed in the least, by the way... I saw Moore yesterday & we talked philosophy. But it was no good because I was far too dull & hazy. When I'm alone I am sometimes a bit brighter" (Wittgenstein to Malcolm, March 19, 1951).

48 Elizabeth Anscombe lived mainly in Oxford during term time, but she spent the university vacations in Cambridge where her husband and children lived, at 19 Fitzwilliam Street.

49 Stands for: 'I love you always & think of you <u>constantly</u>'.

Ben Richards to Ludwig Wittgenstein, March 19, 1951

City Hospital,
Derby.
March 19th 1951

Dear Ludwig,

Thanks for your letter and the book.[50] Since reading it with you I have been wondering if I could get a copy somewhere, as what we read I was very interested in and it made me want to read more.

I can get off about lunch-time on Good Friday.[51] I rang the station and they told me there was a train at 3.45 changing at Bedford and reaching Cambridge at 8.19 P.M. (the same service as on Sunday). I can stay till Monday when there is a train from Cambridge at 4.55 via Kettering and Trent reaching Derby at 8.58.

I should feel more at home staying with Miss Anscombe, but if you are sure /that/ the Bevan's really mean what they say and that my staying with them wouldn't put them out, I'd rather stay with them – as time is so short and I should then have a bit more time to see you.

I look forward to next week-end as you do. If nothing prevents our meeting, it will be wonderful for me whatever your health does.

God bless you:
love always,
Ben.

Ludwig Wittgenstein to Ben Richards, Telegram, March 22, 1951

POST OFFICE
TELEGRAM

Prefix. Time handed in. Office of Origin and Service Instructions.   Words.
CB A 1137 2.40 CAMBRIDGE 19
DR BENEDICT RICHARDS CITY HOSPTIAL DERBY =
YOU WILL STAY STOREYS WAY WILL TRY TO MEET YOUR TRAIN LOVE =
LUDWIG +

---

50 Wittgenstein had sent Richards Desmond Young's *Rommel: The Desert Fox* (see Wittgenstein's letter to Richards of March 12-14, 1951).
51 That year Good Friday fell on March 23.

Ludwig Wittgenstein to Ben Richards, March 27, 1951[52]

76 Storeys Way
Cambridge
Tuesday

Dear Ben, dear o. H.

There is no news since I said good-bye to you yesterday. So this is only to tell you what you know anyhow: that every moment I was with you was wonderful for me. Thanks for everything you did & for your patience & for all your kindness. I hope you got to Derby safely & that the journey wasn't too awful. I also hope you are a *little* rested by your *short* holiday, & that you find some peace in your work & not only difficulties. I needn't tell you that my thoughts are with you constantly. You know *all* that I can tell you. You are still with me in this room.

God bless you. I love you always.

Ludwig

Ben Richards to Ludwig Wittgenstein, April 2, 1951

City Hospital,
Derby.
April 2nd 1951

Dear Ludwig,

Thanks for your letter. I had quite a good journey back, though I had to change twice. You can guess what it meant to me to be with you again. Thank you again for the wonderful record – I have played it once since I got back.[53] It didn't come out quite so clearly on my gramophone, but that didn't matter. I loved listening to it, and reading Rommel[54] and Busch.[55] I long for the next time I can see you.

I have been very busy this week and feel rather tired. I have a cold coming on again – I hope nothing comes of it.

Give my best wishes to the Bevans and thank them for their great kindness. Give my love to Miss Anscombe too, and let me know how she is.

Love always,
Ben.

---

52 Richards added '28/3/51' to the letter, which was a Wednesday; and since Wittgenstein wrote 'Tuesday' on the letter, Richards was presumably noting the date the letter was received.
53 See Wittgenstein's letter to Richards of March 17, 1951, and the relevant footnote.
54 See Wittgenstein's letter to Richards of March 12-14, 1951, and the relevant footnote.
55 See Wittgenstein's letter to Richards of January 26, 1951, and the relevant footnote.

Ludwig Wittgenstein to Ben Richards, April 4, 1951

76 Storeys Way
Cambridge
4.4.51.

Dear Ben, dear H.

Thanks for your letter. I <u>hope</u> you won't get a cold! The weather's awful. I find it terribly trying. <u>Please</u> look after yourself. I know it's very difficult for you to look after yourself. Just don't do <u>unnecessarily</u> foolish things, please.

M^{iss} Anscombe is pretty well, considering. She left the hospital about 4 days ago & she's at home now & up. If she knew I was writing to you she would send you her love. So take it as sent. – I'm moderately well, rather weak /& very tired/ & my brain has practically ceased to work. I have walked very little indeed since you left. – I'm afraid I <u>miss</u> you. Dearest Ben, I hope you will be able to ward off that damned cold. Is there by any chance anything that I can send you? Please write if there is. I think of you <u>constantly</u>, as always & love you always.

  Ludwig

P.S. The other day I got a book from Rhees in Swansea, called "Time of fallen blossoms" by a man Allan Clifton.[56] It's about Japan & the allied occupation. I found it interesting & courageously written, but I don't really like it.[57] And that brings me to an awful thing I did: I wrote a letter to Brigadier D. Young! expressing my admiration for the Rommel book.[58] This is all the more asinine as he ~~can't~~ doesn't know me from Adam. I sent it to him % his publishers. I suppose it's the second childhood, – or is it still the first?

God Bless you. I wish you luck! Please don't overwork.

L. a. L.

---

56 Allan S. Clifton, *Time of Fallen Blossoms*, New York, Alfred A. Knopf, 1951. Clifton was an Australian officer during the Second World War, and this is a memoir of his time in Japan after the war, serving as an interpreter in the British Commonwealth Occupation Forces. He was stationed in Hiroshima, and the book not only describes the devastation wrought on Hiroshima and its people by the atomic bomb, but also the Australian soldiers' mistreatment of the Japanese prisoners of war and their many sexual assaults on civilian women (among various other crimes).

57 A few days earlier Wittgenstein had written to Rush Rhees: "Thank you ever so much for sending me the book about Japan. It arrived yesterday & I immediately began to read in it; first the beginning & then a bit in the middle. It interests me <u>very</u> much. I don't know if I always like the <u>way</u> it's written. But of course I can't tell from the little I've read so far" (Wittgenstein to Rhees, March 30, 1951).

58 See Wittgenstein's letter to Richards of March 12-14, 1951, and the relevant footnote. The letter to Young has not been located and has probably not been preserved.

Ludwig Wittgenstein to Ben Richards, April 7, 1951[59]

76 Storeys Way
Cambridge
Saturday

Dearest Ben,

I want to tell you how much I love you & how much I need you. I am getting rather weak these days & I think it's not unlikely that our walk, when you were here, was our last one. I think of you <u>constantly</u>, with good wishes & with longing.

I hope the cold which threatened you didn't actually develop. Take care of yourself! Thanks again for the <u>lovely</u> days you gave me.

I love you always,

    Ludwig

P.S. I have <u>no</u> pain. G. b. y.

Ben Richards to Ludwig Wittgenstein, April 9, 1951

City Hospital,
Derby
April 9th 1951

Dear Ludwig

Thanks for your letter. I am sorry you were feeling tired & weak, and I hope you are getting no bad pain. It was a great blessing your being so well when I came, but I should have loved being with you quite as much if you hadn't been.

There has been some very fine weather here on & off lately. I had a walk yesterday for about an hour across the fields opposite the hospital. There was nobody about as it is just fields and farms and a railway in a cutting which goes into a tunnel. It was fine and I wished I could have been walking there with you, though I had to cross quite a few fences and streams.

Why is it so awful to have written to Brigadier Young?[60] Do you now regret having done it? What did you say and did he answer? Surely there is nothing wrong in telling him how much pleasure his book has given.

---

59 Richards added '9/4/51' to the letter, which was a Monday; and since Wittgenstein wrote 'Saturday' on the letter, Richards was presumably noting the date the letter was received.

60 Richards is responding to Wittgenstein's letter to him of April 4, 1951, in which Wittgenstein had written: "[T]hat brings me to an awful thing I did: I wrote a letter to Brigadier D. Young! expressing my admiration for the Rommel book."

I am fairly well. I have an irritating cough which is dragging on rather, but I have had no asthma.

Give my love to Miss Anscombe if you see her. I expect she will go back to Oxford as soon as she is well enough.

 Love always,

  Ben.

Ludwig Wittgenstein to Ben Richards, April 11, 1951

76 Storeys Way

Cambridge

Wednesday 11.4.

Dear Ben, dear H.

Thanks for your letter. I know I am selfish: I wish it had been a little longer. When I get a letter from you, do you know what I do? I look for those bits which seem to say that you . . . . . ., & then I read <u>them</u> more often than the rest.

There is one thing I want to tell you. Whatever happens to me now, I want you to know that you have given me more than I could <u>possibly</u> ever have hoped for. You have given me happiness & joy which I never deserved & made my life different <u>altogether</u> from what it would have been without you. <u>Thanks</u> for all you did to me. /You are at the background of <u>all</u> my happiness./ I can't express /completely/ what I want to say, but if I could, I know you wouldn't dislike it. I <u>long</u> to see you again, & I hope that I shall at least <u>once</u> more be with you, see your old face, <u>etc. etc.</u>. – I have no pain, just a <u>little</u> ache now & then, but when I sit still I'm all right & I can even work a little![61] Moving about seems to get increasingly difficult /but perhaps that will get better again/ & my nights aren't very good because I alternately feel cold & sweat. – Dr Bevan went to America to-day /for 10 days/, <u>officially</u> in order to look after the Cambridge boat crew who are rowing two races, against Harvard & Yale.[62] I'm <u>sorry</u> he went; it was a bad time for him to leave. – Con is coming here for the day on Apr. 22nd (without his wife). – It isn't at all 'awful' to have written to Brigadier Young, &

---

61 At this time Wittgenstein was working in MS 176 (see around pp. 40v ff). A few days later Wittgenstein wrote to Norman Malcolm: "It's the first time after more than 2 years that the curtain in my brain has gone up. - Of course, so far I've only worked for about 5 weeks & it may be all over by tomorrow; but it bucks me up a lot now" (Wittgenstein to Malcolm, April 16, 1951).

62 Bevan had been a part of Trinity College's rowing crew when he was a student at the college. Indeed, Bevan won a gold medal in the coxless four in the 1928 Olympics (along with the rest of his Trinity College rowing crew). After his student days Bevan remained deeply involved with rowing at the university. He became the senior treasurer of the Cambridge University Boat Cub and helped coach the university rowing crew for many years.

I don't for a moment regret having done it. You say "Surely there is nothing wrong in telling him . . . . . .", & I absolutely agree with you. (So what more do you want?)[63] Forgive me what I wrote in the beginning of this letter. It was /just/ an expression of <u>hunger</u>! – God bless you.
<u>I love you always</u> & think of you all the time.

Ludwig

Ben Richards to Ludwig Wittgenstein, April 16, 1951

City Hospital,
Derby
16/4/51

Dear Ludwig
Thanks for your letter. It made me feel happier, as I always do when I get a letter from you. I am very glad Con is coming to see you. I should like to have news of him. Give him my love.
My cough seems to have gone. One of the house physicians has finished his appointment and there are only two of us at the moment. The other one leaves at the end of April. No one has been appointed yet to replace them.
I don't know yet how soon I shall be able to get time off to come and see you. Not until the new house physicians come and know there way about a bit I'm afraid. I long to see you again and think of you constantly.
    Love always,
        Ben.

Ludwig Wittgenstein to Ben Richards, April 19, 1951

76 Storeys Way
Cambridge
19.4.51.

Dear Ben, o. H.
Thanks for your letter.
I wish I knew a little more about how happy, &/or unhappy, you're feeling in your work. I imagine there must always be reasons for both. <u>If</u> you can say something about it, please do when you write to me. – I am a good deal stronger again than I was when

---

63 Presumably Wittgenstein had forgotten that – in his earlier letter of April 4, 1951 – he himself had described writing to Young as "an awful thing I did", such that it was Wittgenstein's own concern that Richards was reacting to.

I wrote my last pessimistic letter to you. I walked about quite a lot in the town yesterday & people tell me I look better, too. So you see you can't rely on what I tell you when I'm feeling low. My work doesn't go as well as it did a fortnight ago, /I'm sorry to say/, but perhaps it'll improve again.

My nights aren't very good; that may be one of the reasons. – I'm longing to see you. I hope those house-physicians will arrive soon & be broken in in record time. – There are many things I'd like to talk to you about. – May you still xxxx me!! & think of me with kind thoughts.

I love you always & think of you constantly.

Ludwig

I wish I could put a flower in this letter, but I couldn't find one though I looked out for one.

L. L.

Ben Richards to Ludwig Wittgenstein, April 23, 1951[64]

City Hospital,
Derby.
April 23rd 1951

Dear Ludwig

Thanks for your letter. It is good to hear you have been able to walk about again.

I have been less busy than I was but I expect there will be a lot of work in the next few days. I get different moods – for no real reason: sometimes I am enthusiastic about my work, and other times I wonder if it does any good, and have to force myself to keep on with it.

The weather has been really fine lately, but I have not been out much.

I wish I could see you and talk about my work – it would encourage me.

I hope you can still do some work, and that you don't feel too ill. I miss you terribly.

Love always,
    Ben.

---

64 An undated draft of this letter has been preserved:
"Dear Ludwig,
Thanks for your letter. It is good to hear you have been able to walk about again. I am not so busy as I was. I wish I were not so moody. Sometimes I am more enthusiastic & other times I wonder if my work does any good, & have to force myself to keep on with it. I am in the latter mood now – for no reason that I can find. I know it will pass but it is depressing." The draft ends here.

Ludwig Wittgenstein to Ben Richards, April 25, 1951

76 Storeys Way
Cambridge
25.4.51.

Dearest Ben,

Thanks for your letter. I confess, I rather imagined that your mood might be variable, because your last letter but one seemed, somehow, to me to /have/ been written in a depressed state.[65] (Perhaps I was wrong.) I think everybody has such changes, & in your case they seem to me most natural because you're sensitive. I think enthusiasm is a special gift, I mean a <u>present</u>, for which you should be grateful but which you can't always expect. That you sometimes have to force yourself to keep on with your work <u>isn't</u> anything degrading – or something that shows that ~~this~~ /medicine/ isn't really your job. To be able to do your work when you're not enthusiastic about it has it's special great value.

I wish you <u>lots</u> of enthusiasm, but don't make the mistake to think that drudgery is just something foul. – It's like <u>getting</u> presents & <u>giving</u> presents:- if you can't get any, ~~y~~ then find your joy in giving them. – I'm writing just like a bl... parson – forgive me! Try to find what's true in what I say & throw the rest away. —— I'm pretty well on the whole, just very weak. But I still go out for short crawls & I still work moderately to pretty hard & not too badly, which I find very astonishing. —— I think of you a terrible lot & I hope you still ....[66] me.

Dear Ben, I know very well how odd that sounds & that there is no earthly reason why you should, now or ever. – If you see that I am in a false belief, or hope, <u>please open my eyes,</u> even if it hurts. – I <u>long</u> to be with you & love you always. God bless you & keep you.

      Ludwig

P.S. Con was here on Sunday. He looks healthy & brown. He sends you his love. I think he isn't changed, as I was afraid he might be.[67] – Rhees wrote to me a few days ago & mentioned the picture which I enclose.[68] Don't throw it away, please

    I miss you a <u>lot!</u>

        L. L.

---

65 Namely, Richards' letter to Wittgenstein of April 16, 1951.
66 Presumably: 'love'.
67 Maurice O'Connor Drury had married Eileen Herbert (the head nurse at St. Patrick's Hospital), on March 28, 1951 (see Hayes 2017: 48), and they had honeymooned in Italy. Drury had come to visit Wittgenstein on his way back from Italy to Dublin. It was presumably Drury's now married status that Wittgenstein had feared may change him.
68 Neither the picture nor Rhees' letter have survived.

P.P.S. Please don't regard what I wrote about enthusiasm as a piece of advice that I think I can give you from the hight of my wisdom, & as though I could cope with such a situation as yours. I know I would feel just like you; but would try to tell myself roughly what I told you. Just, please, don't lose patience. (With the circumstances & with me.) – The weather was nice here, too, & Mrs Bevan occasionally took me for a ride in the car. I wish you could have got into the open air more. You must try to. It will do youre /nerves/ good. The nicest weather will come for me when I can see you again! G. bl. Y. Today is my birthday;[69] wish me luck!

---

[69] Wittgenstein's birthday was April 26, so presumably he had started – and dated – this letter the day before, and then taken until the next day to finish it.

VII. Undatable letters and cards, & notes from 'John Smith'

Finally, this chapter contains a number of letters and cards which were not dated, and which contain no clues allowing us to assign them to any particular period. These are from Wittgenstein to Ben Richards, from Ben Richards to Wittgenstein, and from Wittgenstein to Angela Richards.

Some of these are regular letters, but most of them are Christmas and Easter cards. Wittgenstein liked kitschy greetings cards, and especially ones containing pre-printed sentimental messages. Norman Malcolm's observation that "Wittgenstein always bought extremely florid Xmas and Easter cards: they had to be 'soupy' " is certainly borne out here.[1]

Another unusual type of letter included here are the notes for Ben Richards which Wittgenstein signed from 'John Smith' – a 'King's Counsel' and ostensibly Wittgenstein's attorney. This was the playful pseudonym that Wittgenstein sometimes used when he left notes for Richards in the living room, if Wittgenstein was going to be in the bathroom when Richards arrived at Wittgenstein's lodgings. He likely wrote the first of these notes in late September 1946, when Richards was visiting him in Swansea.[2] That note appears in chapter I,[3] while two others are included in this chapter. It seems likely that these latter two undatable 'John Smith' letters are also from Richards' visit to see Wittgenstein in Swansea in 1946 (and perhaps in 1947 too), but it's impossible to know.

---

1 Malcolm 1984: 101, fn. 2.
2 See Wittgenstein's letters to Richards of September 12, 1946, and the following one of (probably) late September 1946, and see also Richards' letter to Wittgenstein of October 23, 1946.
3 Wittgenstein's letter to Richards of (probably) late September 1946.

Undatable letters and cards from Wittgenstein to Ben Richards

Ludwig Wittgenstein to Ben Richards (undated)

Dear Ben,
I shall be on /one of/ the 'invalide benches' at 4 p.m. . We can then either have a short tea in town or go to Ickenham & have it there. I have told your mother that we shall be in for supper (because of your cold). On the whole I should prefer having tea with you in town to having it in Ickenham but we can decide the matter at 4 p.m. .
With love
Ludwig

Ludwig Wittgenstein to Ben Richards (undated)

D. B., o. H –
In case I don't come to-morrow it is because my cold has got worse. It's rather on the up-grade & should by to-morrow be 'running'. If it is, it might be better for me to stay home; thereby obviating . . . .
G. b. y.. A. a., w. l.[4]
L.

Ludwig Wittgenstein to Ben Richards, Christmas Card (undated)

 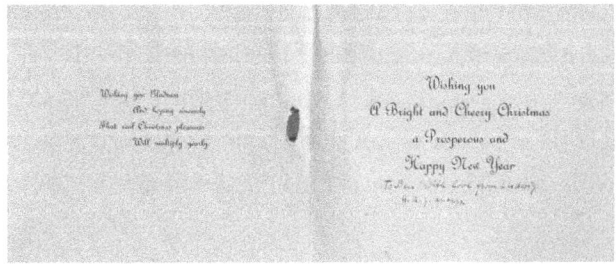

Christmas Wishes

Wishing you Gladness
    And hoping sincerely

---

4 Stands for: 'God bless you. As always, with love'.

That real Christmas pleasures
   Will multiply yearly.

Wishing you
A Bright and Cheery Christmas
a Prosperous and
Happy New Year

To Ben with love from Ludwig
G. b. y. always.

Ludwig Wittgenstein to Ben Richards, Christmas Card (undated)

 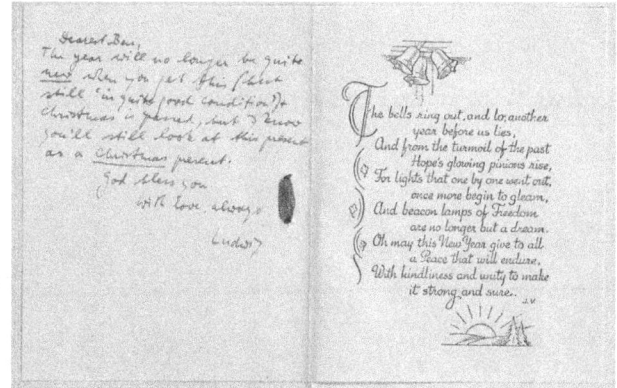

KIND THOUGHTS
and
BEST WISHES

Dearest Ben,
The year will no longer be quite <u>new</u> when you get this (but still 'in quite good condition') & Christmas is passed, but I know you'll still look at this present as a <u>Christmas</u> present.
God bless you.
With love, always
Ludwig

The bells ring out, and lo, another
    year before us lies,
And from the turmoil of the past
    Hope's glowing pinions rise,
For lights that one by one went out,
    once more begin to gleam,
And beacon lamps of Freedom
    are no longer but a dream.
Oh may this New Year give to all
    a Peace that will endure,
With kindliness and unity to make
    it strong and sure.
            J.V.

Ludwig Wittgenstein to Ben Richards, Christmas Card (undated)

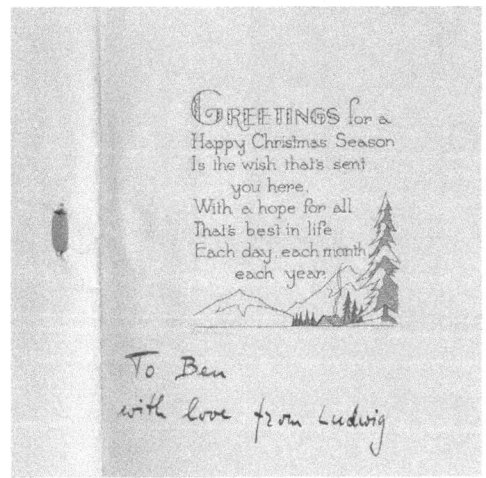

The SEASON'S GREETINGS

GREETINGS for a
Happy Christmas Season
Is the wish that's sent you here.
With a hope for all

That's best in life
Each day, each month each year.

To Ben
with love from Ludwig

Ludwig Wittgenstein to Ben Richards, Easter Card (undated)

 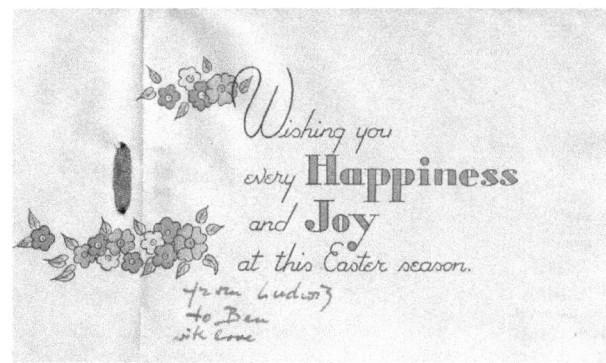

Easter Joy

Wishing you
every Happiness
and Joy
at this Easter season.

from Ludwig
to Ben
with love

Ludwig Wittgenstein to Ben Richards, Easter Card (undated)

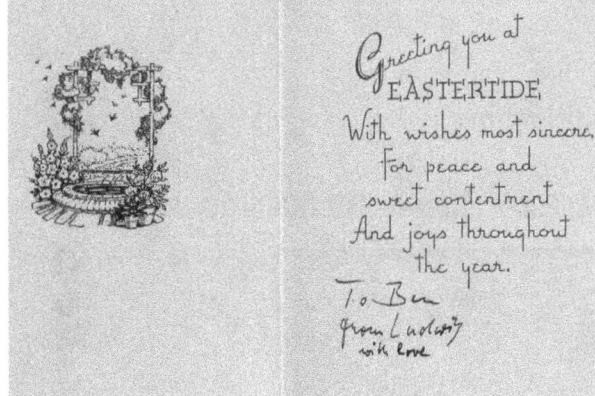

All
Easter
Happiness

Greeting you at
EASTERTIDE
With wishes most sincere,
For peace and
sweet contentment
And joys throughout
the year.

To Ben
from Ludwig
with love

Undatable notes from Wittgenstein (in his persona of 'John Smith') to Ben Richards

Ludwig Wittgenstein to Ben Richards (undated)

Dear Sir,

Professor Wittgenstein, with Schopenhauer,[5] considers it wrong to have his face surrounded, & partly hidden, by dead matter. He is at present in his bathroom removing same. He is /greatly/ looking forward to seeing your bloody old face.
Sincerely yours
J. S.

Ludwig Wittgenstein to Ben Richards (undated)

Dear Sir,

Professor Wittgenstein has had an <u>urgent</u> call to the lavatories, vomitories & baths. He regrets not to be able to welcome you at your arrival, but hopes you will be quite comfortable in his absence, even more so than in his presence.
I remain, dear Sir
your obedient servant
J. Smith K. C.[6]

---

5 This is an allusion to one of Arthur Schopenhauer's (multiple) objections to beards: "The ferocity and atrocity that the beard bestows on the physiognomy rests on the fact that an always *inanimate* mass occupies half of the face, namely the half that expresses what is moral" (Schopenhauer 2016: 158 [188]), and "A *beard*, being a half mask, should be forbidden by the police" (Schopenhauer 2017: 404 [478]). In the autumn of 1949, Richards' growing of a beard led to serious tension between him and Wittgenstein (see Wittgenstein's letters of October 10 and 19, 1949, and the discussion of this incident in the Introduction).

6 The post-nominal initial standing for 'King's Counsel'. This (or 'Queen's Counsel' when the monarch is a woman) is the most senior rank of barrister or solicitor advocate in the United Kingdom and some Commonwealth countries.

Undatable letters and cards from Ben Richards to Wittgenstein

Ben Richards to Ludwig Wittgenstein (undated)

GREENOGE
40, SWAKELEYS ROAD
ICKENHAM
UXBRIDGE
RUISLIP 2114

Dear Ludwig,

Thank you <u>very</u> much for the week-end. I went to the Strand Palace Hotel and they haven't a single room for the week-end after this. We have no visitors then and my parents would be very pleased indeed for you to come. My work at the hospital finishes at mid-day on Saturday. We could stay in London & perhaps go to the pictures or something, or down here there are some walks which are not too bad in the "green belt".

Please let me know when you are coming and I shall look forward to meeting your train, and seeing you.

Love always

Ben.

Ben Richards to Ludwig Wittgenstein, Christmas Card (undated)

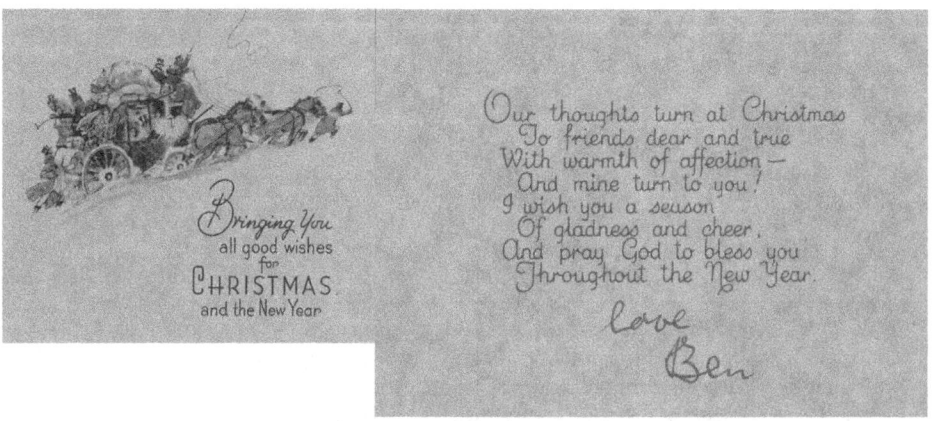

Our thoughts turn at Christmas
To friends dear and true
With warmth of affection —
And mine turn to you!
I wish you a season
Of gladness and cheer,
And pray God to bless you
Throughout the New Year.

love
Ben

Bringing you
all good wishes
for
CHRISTMAS
and the New Year

Our thoughts turn at Christmas
   To friends dear and true
With warmth of affection –
   And mine turn to you!
I wish you a season
   Of gladness and cheer,
And pray God to bless you
   Throughout the New Year.

love
Ben

Ben Richards to Ludwig Wittgenstein, Christmas Card (undated)

 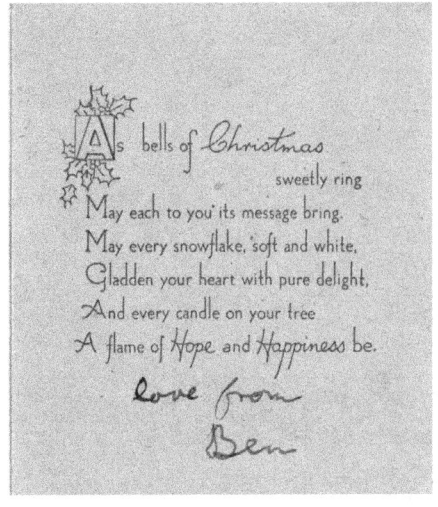

Best Wishes

As bells of Christmas sweetly ring
May each to you its message bring.

May every snowflake, soft and white,
Gladden your heart with pure delight.
And every candle on your tree
A flame of Hope and Happiness be.

love from
Ben

Ben Richards to Ludwig Wittgenstein, Christmas Card (undated)

BEST WISHES

"Happy Christmas! Happy Christmas!"
   All our hearts to-day are singing.
While the holly berries glisten
   And the bells are gaily ringing:
May this season, glad and merry
   Many a joy to you be bringing!
love
Ben

Undatable cards from Wittgenstein to Angela Richards

Ludwig Wittgenstein to Angela Richards, Postcard (undated)[7]

Wien XIII, Schloss Schönbrunn mit Gloriette[8]

IV. Argentinierstr. 16
Wien

Dear Angela,

This is not, as you might suppose, my little summer-residence.[9]

Give my good wishes to everybody including yourself.

Ludwig Wittgenstein

---

7 This Viennese postcard was presumably sent during one of Wittgenstein stays in Vienna – namely, September 1948, or April 1949, or between December 1949 and March 1950.
8 German: Vienna, 13[th district], Schönbrunn Palace with Gloriette..
9 Schönbrunn Palace was the Habsburgs' summer residence in Vienna. It was partly based on plans by Johann Bernhard Fischer von Erlach, an architect whom Wittgenstein greatly admired (see Wijdeveld 1994: 159 & 223).

Ludwig Wittgenstein to Angela Richards, Christmas Card (undated)[10]

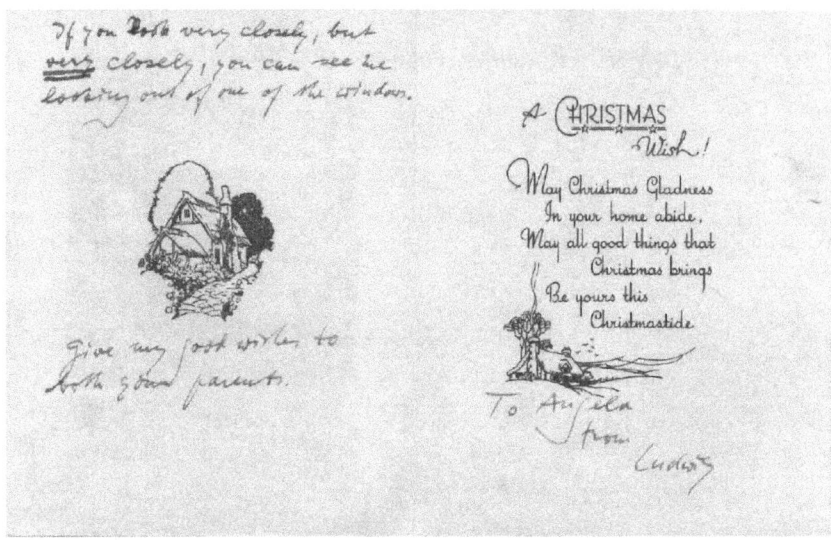

If you look very closely, but <u>very</u> closely, you can see me looking out of one of the windows.

Give my good wishes to both your parents.

---

10 The original is in the possession of Gabriel Citron.

A <u>CHRISTMAS</u> Wish!
May Christmas Gladness
In your home abide,
May all good things that
Christmas brings
Be yours this
Christmastide

To Angela
from
Ludwig

Ludwig Wittgenstein to Angela Richards, Christmas Card (undated)[11]

The church inside burns candles bright,
    And stars behold a peaceful night;
The window gives a perfect scene
    Of snow that covers hills once green.
May your star guide you all the way
    And cheer you on this Christmas Day.

---

11 The original is in the possession of Gabriel Citron.

To wish you Happiness
at Christmas
and throughout
the New Year . . .

To Angela
from Ludwig Wittgenstein

Ludwig Wittgenstein to Angela Richards, Christmas Card (undated)[12]

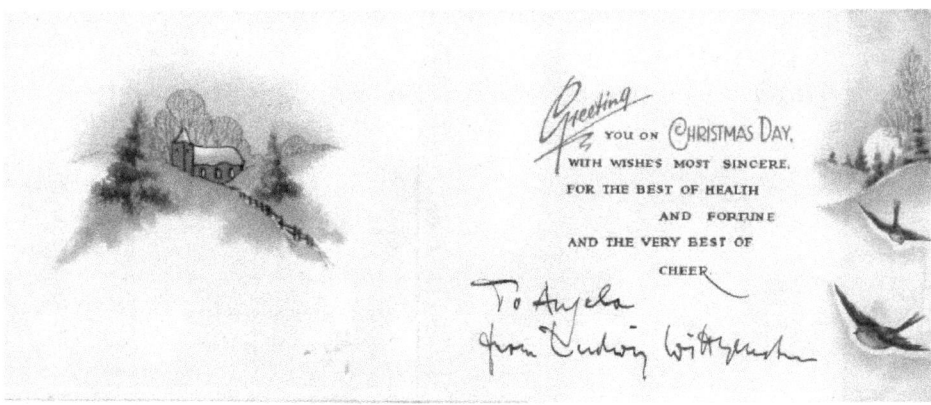

Greeting YOU ON CHRISTMAS DAY,
WITH WISHES MOST SINCERE,
FOR THE BEST OF HEALTH AND FORTUNE
AND THE VERY BEST OF CHEER

To Angela
from Ludwig Wittgenstein

---

12 The original is in the possession of Gabriel Citron.

Timeline[1]

November 1942 – June 1945	Richards undertakes Part I of the Natural Sciences Tripos (focusing on medicine) at King's College, Cambridge, and receives a B.A. degree with a second class pass.[2]
October 1944	After some time away (engaging in war work and writing), Wittgenstein moves back to Cambridge and resumes teaching.[3]
October 1945 – June 1946	Richards undertakes Part II of the Moral Sciences Tripos (focusing on Psychology) and is awarded a lower second pass.[4]
October 1945	Wittgenstein starts teaching a course on the philosophy of psychology, in which Ben Richards is a student.[5]
July 12-18 1946	Wittgenstein and Richards spend five days in Exeter, visiting Maurice O'Connor Drury.
July 22 1946	Richards is mentioned for the first time in one of Wittgenstein's manuscript notebooks.[6]
July 24 1946 – August 1946	Richards goes on a climbing holiday to Turtagrø (Norway), not far from Skjolden where Wittgenstein had lived periodically since 1913, and Richards meets Anna Rebni.
September 12-30, 1946	Wittgenstein and Richards spend two weeks together in Swansea.[7]
December 1946 – January 10, 1947	Wittgenstein spends the Christmas vacation in Swansea.

---

1 The footnotes contain selected sources which have been used outside of this correspondence; but where the information has been derived from the correspondence in this volume, no specific reference is given.
2 Cambridge University Archives.
3 Monk 1990: 471.
4 Cambridge University Archives.
5 Klagge 2019: 54; *King's College Annual Report* 1995: 73; and Wittgenstein's MS 130, p. 185.
6 MS 130, p. 185.
7 See Wittgenstein, MS 132, pp. 85 &147.

May 1947 – March 1948	Richards interns at St. Bartolomew's (Bart's) Hospital in London. When Wittgenstein is in the country, they regularly meet up on weekends, in either Cambridge or in London.
July 1947	Wittgenstein spends the vacation in Swansea, with Richards visiting for two weeks.[8]
August 6-19, 1947	Wittgenstein spends two weeks in Dublin (mainly at Ross's Hotel), visiting Maurice O'Connor Drury.[9]
August 19, 1947 – September 12, 1947	Wittgenstein spends three weeks with Richards and his family in their home in Ickenham (London).[10]
September 12, 1947 – October 4 or 6, 1947	Wittgenstein spends three weeks in Vienna, staying with his niece, Marie Stockert.
October 8, 1947	Wittgenstein tenders his resignation as Professor of Philosophy at Cambridge. He is allowed the Michaelmas Term as a sabbatical, with his resignation to take official effect at the end of the year.
October – November 1947	Wittgenstein stays in Cambridge to dictate to a typist from his manuscripts so as to generate a typescript.
November 25, 1947 – June 18, 1949	Wittgenstein is largely in Ireland (with two principal breaks).
November 25 – December 11, 1947	Wittgenstein is in Dublin, looking for suitable accommodation.
December 9, 1947 – April 20, 1948	Wittgenstein lodges at Kilpatrick House, just outside Redcross, in County Wicklow.[11]
December 26-31, 1947	Richards and Maurice Drury come – from London and Dublin respectively – to stay with Wittgenstein in Kilpatrick House.[12]
April – November 1948	Richards interns at St. Andrew's Hospital in London.
April 20-27, 1948	Wittgenstein is back in Dublin (at Ross's Hotel), preparing for his move to the west coast of Ireland.
April 28 – July 29, 1948	Wittgenstein stays in the Drury family's cottage in Rosroe (Connemara), on the west coast of Ireland.
May 15-23, 1948	Richards visits Wittgenstein in Rosroe.

---

8 Monk 1990: 516.
9 Wittgenstein to Rush Rhees, July 26, 1947, and to Yorick Smythies, July 27, 1947.
10 See Wittgenstein, letter to Yorick Smythies, July 27, 1947, and to Rush Rhees September 21, 1947.
11 Kilpatrick House *Visitors Book*, entry for April 20, 1948 (owned by the Kingston family).
12 Wittgenstein to Leonida Malcolm, January 4, 1948.

July 29 or 30 – August 3, 1948	Wittgenstein is in Dublin (in Ross's Hotel) preparing for his upcoming trips to England and to Vienna.
August 3-15, 1948	Wittgenstein flies from Dublin to London, briefly sees Richards in London, and then travels to Oxford to stay with Yorick Smythies for just under two weeks.
August 14 or 15 – September 8, 1948	Wittgenstein stays with Richards and his family in their home in Ickenham (London).
September 8 or 9 – 29, 1948	Wittgenstein visits Vienna, staying in the family mansion at Argentinierstrasse 16, to spend time with his oldest sister – Hermine – who is very ill.
September 30 – October 15, 1948	Wittgenstein stays in Cambridge to dictate to a typist from his manuscripts.
October 16, 1948 – March 1949	Wittgenstein is back in Dublin, staying at Ross's Hotel.
Mid-November 1948	Richards visits Wittgenstein in Dublin.
December 1948	Elizabeth Anscombe visits Wittgenstein in early December, and Rush Rhees visits him for Christmas.
December 1948 – Summer 1949	Richards interns at Hill End Hospital in St. Albans.
March 5-14, 1949	Richards comes to Ireland, and he and Wittgenstein spend ten or so days in Howth, on the east coast of Ireland.[13]
April 11 – May 15, 1949	Wittgenstein visits Vienna, staying in the family mansion at Argentinierstrasse 16, to spend time with his oldest sister – Hermine – whose condition is worsening.
May 17 – June 18, 1949	Wittgenstein is back in Dublin, at Ross's Hotel.
June 20 or 21 – July 2 or 3, 1949	Wittgenstein stays with the von Wright family in their home in Cambridge.
July 2 or 3 – 21, 1949	Wittgenstein stays with the Richards family in their home in Ickenham (London).[14]
July 21-26, 1949	Wittgenstein on board the Queen Mary, sailing from Southampton to New York.

---

13 Wittgenstein to Rudolf Koder, March 9, 1949, and to Rush Rhees, March 16, 1949; and see also Wittgenstein's MS 138, p. 30a.

14 Wittgenstein to Helene Salzer, July 3, 1949.

July 26 – October 17, 1949	Wittgenstein stays with the Malcolm family in their home in Ithaca, NY.
August 1 – September 15, 1949	Richards and his family are on holiday in Ventimiglia, Italy.
October 17-20, 1949	On his way back from Ithacan to his ship in New York, Wittgenstein stays with Oets K Bouwsma and his family for a couple of days at Smith College, then he travels down to New York and meets up with his sister, Margaret Stonborough-Wittgenstein.[15]
October 20-27, 1949	Wittgenstein is on board the Queen Mary, sailing from New York back to Southampton.
October 27 – November 9, 1949	Wittgenstein falls ill upon arriving back in London, so he stays for a couple of weeks with Jean Rhees, in her London flat.
November 9 – December 22, 1949	Wittgenstein stays with the von Wright family in their home in Cambridge; shortly after arriving he is diagnosed with prostate cancer, and begins a hormone therapy to slow its advance.
December 24, 1949 – March 23, 1950	Wittgenstein visits Vienna, staying in the family mansion at Argentinierstrasse 16, to see his dying sister, Hermine. She dies – during his stay – on February 11, 1950.
January 15 – end of May, 1950	Elizabeth Anscombe comes to Vienna, staying with Wittgenstein's friends – the Hänsels – and meeting with Wittgenstein regularly.
April – November, 1950	Richards moves out of his family's home in Ickenham and into a student flat in Belsize Park, London.
April 4-26, 1950	Wittgenstein stays with the von Wright family in their home in Cambridge.
April 26, 1950 – February 8, 1951	Wittgenstein moves into a room in Elizabeth Anscombe's house in Oxford (though Anscombe herself only moves back in – after her trip to Vienna and then Italy – on June 16, 1950).[16]
August 1950	Wittgenstein's and Richards' planned August trip to Skjolden (Norway) together, to stay in Wittgenstein's cabin, has to be postponed because Richards failed his final exams and has to revise for the autumn re-sit.[17]
September 27 & October 6, 1950	Richards re-sits – and passes – the written and oral exams he had previously failed.

---

15 Pinch & Swedberg 2013: 18–21.
16 Berkman 2025: 69–70.
17 Wittgenstein to Rhees, August 3, 1950.

October 11 – November 13, 1950	Wittgenstein and Richards spend almost five weeks together in Skjolden (Norway), staying briefly in Wittgenstein's cabin overlooking Eidsvatnet Lake, and then for the remainder of the stay in Anna Rebni's guesthouse.
February 8 – April 29, 1951	Wittgenstein spends his last two and a half months living with the Bevans – his doctor, Edward Bevan, Edward's wife, Joan, and their children – who offered to look after him as he approached death.
March 1951	Richards starts an internship at Derby City Hospital taking up a position as 'house physician'.
March 23-26, 1951	Richards manages to get away from the hospital to spend a few days with Wittgenstein in Cambridge.
April 29, 1951	Wittgenstein dies in in the Bevans' house, with Richards – and a handful of other close friends – by his side (though they only arrived after Wittgenstein had mostly lost consciousness).

Bibliography

All references to 'MS' (followed by a number) are to Ludwig Wittgenstein's manuscript notebooks. These are referred to using the manuscript numbers and page numbers as they appear in the *Interactive Dynamic Presentation (IDP) of Ludwig Wittgenstein's philosophical Nachlass* (ed. Alois Pichler, Bergen, Wittgenstein Archives at the University of Bergen, 2016ff). This can be found at: http://wittgensteinonline.no/

Other than his correspondence with Richards, all correspondence to and from Ludwig Wittgenstein is quoted from the online edition: *Wittgenstein: Gesamtbriefwechsel (Complete Correspondence), Innsbrucker Electronic Edition* (2nd Release), eds. Monika Seekircher et al., Charlottesville Va., InteLex Corporation, 2011.

* * * * * *

Anscombe, G. E. M. (1981): *The Collected Papers of G.E.M. Anscombe, Volume Two: Metaphysics and the Philosophy of Mind*, Oxford, Basil Blackwell

Anscombe, Elizabeth (2025): *Anscombe on Wittgenstein: Reminiscences of a Philosophical Friendship*, eds. John Berkman & Roger Teichmann, Oxford University Press

Békássy, Ferenc (2016): *The Alien in the Chapel – Ferenc Békássy, Rupert Brooke's Unknown Rival: Poems and Letters*, eds. George Gömöri & Mari Gömöri, Bloxham, Skyscraper Publications

Benson, S. Vere (1937): *The Observer's Book of British Birds*, London, Frederick Warne & Co

Berkman, John (2025): 'Anscombe's Relationship with Wittgenstein: Contextualizing the *Reminiscences*', in Anscombe 2025: 1–91.

Bevan, Joan (2016): 'Wittgenstein's Last Year', in Flowers III & Ground 2016: 1030–31

Bouwsma, O. K. (1986): *Wittgenstein: Conversations, 1949–1951*, eds. J. L. Craft & Ronald E. Hustwit, Indianapolis, Hackett Publishing Company

Conradi, Peter J. (2001): *Iris Murdoch: A Life*, New York, WW Norton & Company

Cornell Alumni News (1942): 'Enlarge Medical Staff', Vol 45, No. 5 (October 22), p. 64a–b

Daniel, Peter (1993): 'Afternoons with Wittgenstein', *Edinburgh Review*, Vol. 89 (Spring), pp. 52–5

Delany, Paul (1987): *The Neo-Pagans: Rupert Brooke and the Ordeal of Youth*, New York, The Free Press

Deutsch Arnold, Gitta (2016), 'Recollections of Wittgenstein', in Flowers III & Ground 2016: 755–6

Drury, M. O'C. (1984), 'Some Notes on Conversations with Wittgenstein' and 'Conversations with Wittgenstein', in Rhees 1984: 76–171

Drury, Maurice O'Connor (2017): *The Selected Writings of Maurice O'Connor Drury: On Wittgenstein, Philosophy, Religion, and Psychiatry*, ed. John Hayes, London, Bloomsbury Academic

Edmonds, David & John Eidinow (2001): *Wittgenstein's Poker: The Story of a Ten-Minute Argument Between Two Great Philosophers*, New York, Ecco (Harper Collins)

Engelmann, Paul (1967): *Letters from Ludwig Wittgenstein with a Memoir*, Oxford, Basil Blackwell

Ewing, A.C. (1948): 'Is Metaphysics Impossible?', *Analysis*, Vol 8, No. 3 (January), pp. 33–38

Faderman, Lillian (1993): 'Nineteenth-Century Boston Marriage as a Possible Lesson for Today', in Rothblum & Brehony 1993: 29–42

Flowers III, F. A. & Ian Ground (eds.) (2016): *Portraits of Wittgenstein*, Volumes I & II (2nd edition), London, Bloomsbury Academic

Gamper, Verena & Hans-Peter Wipplinger (eds.) (2021): *Ludwig Wittgenstein: Fotografie als analytische Praxis / Photography as Analytical Practice*, Köln, Verlag der Buchhandlung Walther und Franz König (Leopold Museum Wien)

Goethe, Johann Wolfgang von (1987): *Verse Plays and Epic (Goethe's Collected Works, Volume 8)*, eds. Cyrus Hamlin & Frank Ryder, trans. Michael Hamburger, Hunter Hannum, & David Luke, Princeton, Princeton University Press

Goldhill, Simon (2025): *Queer Cambridge: An Alternative History*, Cambridge, Cambridge University Press

Hausmann, Luise & Eugene C. Hargrove (2016): 'Wittgenstein in Austria as an Elementary-School Teacher', in Flowers III & Ground 2016: 379–95

Hayes, Hohn (2017): 'Drury and Wittgenstein: Kindred Souls', in Drury 2017: 1–86

Johannessen, Kjell S., Rolf Larsen, & Knut Olav Åmås (eds.) (1994): *Wittgenstein and Norway*, Oslo, Solum Forlag

Judge, Tony (2016): *Radio Philosopher: The Radical Life of Cyril Joad*, London, Alpha House

King's College Annual Report (1995): 'Robert Benedict Oliver Richards (1942)', pp. 73–4

Kinlen, Leo (2016): 'Wittgenstein in Newscastle', in Flowers III & Ground 2016: 717–729

Klagge, James (2019): 'The Wittgenstein Lectures, Revisited', *Nordic Wittgenstein Review*, Vol. 8, Nos. 1–2, pp. 11–82

Korstvedt, Benjamin M. (2000): *Anton Bruckner: Symphony No. 8*, Cambridge, Cambridge University Press

Lee, H. D. P. (1979): 'Wittgenstein 1929-1931', *Philosophy*, Vol 54, No. 208 (April), pp. 211–20

Lewis, C. S. (2004): *The Collected Letters of C. S. Lewis, Vol III: Narnia, Cambridge, and Joy 1950-1963*, ed. Walter Hooper, San Franciso, Harper

Mac Cumhaill, Clare & Rachael Wiseman (2022). *Metaphysical Animals: How Four Women Brought Philosophy Back to Life*, New York, Doubleday

Malcom, Norman (1984): *Ludwig Wittgenstein: A Memoir (with a Biographical Sketch by G. H. von Wright), Second Edition with Wittgenstein's Letters to Malcolm*, Oxford, Oxford University Press

McGuinness, Brian (2005): *Young Ludwig: Wittgenstein's Life, 1889-1921*, Oxford, Clarendon Press

Monk, Ray (1990): *Wittgenstein: The Duty of Genius*, London, Jonathan Cape

Moore, George Edward & Norman Malcolm (2001/2): 'Correspondence (1937–1958)', eds. Josef G. F. Rothhaupt, Aidan Seery, & Denis McManus, *Wittgenstein-Jahrbuch*, 2001/2002, pp. 245–95

Munz, Volker A. (2001): 'Ludwig Wittgenstein and Yorick Smythies: A Hitherto Unknown Relationship', Wittgenstein und die Zukunft der Philosophie: Eine Neubewertung nach 50 Jahren / Wittgenstein and the Future of Philosophy: A Reassessment after 50 Years, Rudolf Haller & Klaus Puhl (eds.), Kirchberg am Wechsel, Austrian Ludwig Wittgenstein Society, pp. 92–7

Nedo, Michael (ed.) (2012): *Ludwig Wittgenstein: Ein biographisches Album*, München, C. H. Beck

Pinch, Trevor & Richard Swedberg (2013): 'Wittgenstein's visit to Ithaca in 1949: On The Importance of Details', *Distinktion: Scandinavian Journal of Social Theory*, Vol. 14, No. 1, pp. 2–29

Prokop, Ursula (2003): *Margaret Stonborough-Wittgenstein: Bauherrin, Intellektuelle, Mäzenin*, Wien, Böhlau Verlag

Rhees, Rush (ed.) (1984): *Recollections of Wittgenstein: Hermine Wittgenstein, Fania Pascal, F. R. Leavis, John King, M. O'C. Drury*, Oxford, Oxford University Press

Rhees, Rush (2001): 'On Religion: Notes on Four Conversations with Wittgenstein', ed. D. Z. Phillips, *Faith and Philosophy*, Vol. 18, No. 4 (October), pp. 409–15

Richards, Tara & Alec Benjamin (1995): 'Robert Benedict Olivier ("Ben") Richards', *BMJ: British Medical Journal*, Vol. 311, No. 7009 (September 30), p. 870

Rosenbaum, S. P. (1998): *Aspects of Bloomsbury: Studies in Modern English Literary and Intellectual History*, Houndmills, Macmillan Press

Rothblum, Esther D. & Kathleen A. Brehony (1993): *Boston Marriages: Romantic but Asexual Relationships Among Contemporary Lesbians*, Amherst, The University of Massachusetts Press

Rowe, M. W. (2023): *J. L. Austin: Philosopher and D-Day Intelligence Officer*, Oxford, Oxford University Press

Schopenhauer, Arthur (2016): *Parerga and Paralipomena: Short Philosophical Essays (Vol I)*, ed. & trans. Sabine Roehr & Christopher Janaway, Cambridge, Cambridge University Press

Schopenhauer, Arthur (2017): *Parerga and Paralipomena: Short Philosophical Essays (Vol II)*, ed. & trans. Adrian del Caro & Christopher Janaway, Cambridge, Cambridge University Press

Somavilla, Ilse (2010): 'Wittgenstein's Coded Remarks in the Context of His Philosophizing', in Venturinha 2010: 30–50

Stockton, Jim & Benjamin J. B. Lipscomb (2021): 'The Anscombe-Lewis Debate: New Archival Sources Considered', *Journal of Inklings Studies*, Vol. 11, No. 1, pp. 35–57

Sullivan, Matthew Barry (1979): *Thresholds of Peace: Four Hundred Thousand German Prisoners and the People of Britain, 1944–1948*, London, Hamish Hamilton

Taddeo, Julie Anne (2002): *Lytton Strachey and the Search for Modern Sexual Identity: The Last Eminent Victorian*, New York, Harrington Park Press

Tolstoy, Leo (1904) *What is Art?* trans. Aylmer Maude, New York, Funk & Wagnalls Company

Tranøy, Knut E. (2016): 'Wittgenstein in Cambridge, 1949–1951: Some Personal Recollections', in Flowers III & Ground 2016: 1018–1025

Vatne, Harald (2016). *Ludwig Wittgenstein and the People of Skjolden / Ludwig Wittgenstein og skjoldingane*, trans. Elianne Eggum, Jon Bech, & Harald Vatne, Skjolden [no publisher]

Venturinha, Nuno (ed.) (2010): *Wittgenstein After His Nachlass*, London, Palgrave Macmillan

Venturinha, Nuno & Jonathan Smith (2018): 'Wittgenstein on British Anti-Nazi Propaganda: A Fragment', *Nordic Wittgenstein Review*, Vol. 7, No. 2, pp. 195–208

Villon-Lechner, Alice (1989): 'Es brauchte Mut, mit Ludwig auszugehen: Der Philosoph Wittgenstein und seine Freundin Marguerite – neue Zugänge zu einem Denker', *Die Weltwoche*, No. 24, June 15, 1989, pp. 57 & 59

Wang-Kathrein, Joseph (2021): 'Ludwig Wittgensteins *Nonsense Collection* / Ludwig Wittgenstein's *Nonsense Collection*', in Gamper & Wipplinger 2021: 258–67

Weeks, Jeffrey (2018): *Sex, Politics and Society: The Regulation of Sexuality Since 1800 (Fourth Edition)*, Abingdon, Routledge

Wijdeveld, Paul (1994): *Ludwig Wittgenstein: Architect*, Cambridge Mass., The MIT Press

Wittgenstein, Ludwig (1966), *Lectures & Conversations on Aesthetics, Psychology, and Religious Belief: Compiled from Notes Taken by Yorick Smythies, Rush Rhees and James Taylor*, ed. Cyril Barrett, Oxford, Blackwell

Wittgenstein, Ludwig (1977): *Remarks on Colour*, ed. G. E. M. Anscombe, trans. Linda L. McAlister & Margarete Schättle, Oxford, Basil Blackwell

Wittgenstein, Ludwig (1979): *Wittgenstein's Lectures, Cambridge, 1932–1935: from the Notes of Alice Ambrose and Margaret Macdonald*, ed. Alice Ambrose, Oxford, Basil Blackwell

Wittgenstein, Ludwig (1988): *Wittgenstein's Lectures on Philosophical Psychology: 1946–47, Notes by P. T. Geach, K. J. Shah, A. C. Jackson*, ed. P. T. Geach, New York, Harvester Wheatsheaf

Wittgenstein, Ludwig (1980): *Wittgenstein's Lectures, Cambridge 1930-1932: from the Notes of John King and Desmond Lee*, ed. Desmond Lee, Chicago, University of Chicago Press

Wittgenstein, Ludwig (1993): *Ludwig Wittgenstein: Philosophical Occasions*, eds. James Klagge & Alfred Nordmann, Indianapolis, Hackett Publishing Company

Wittgenstein, Ludwig (1998): *Culture and Value*, eds. GH von Wright, Heikki Nyman, & Alois Pichler, trans. Peter Winch, Oxford, Blackwell

Wittgenstein, Ludwig & Rush Rhees (2001): 'On Religion: Notes on Four Conversations with Wittgenstein', ed. D. Z. Phillips, *Faith and Philosophy*, Vol. 18, No. 4 (October)

Wittgenstein, Ludwig (2003): *Ludwig Wittgenstein: Public and Private Occasions*, eds. & trans. James C. Klagge & Alfred Nordmann, Lanham, Rowman & Littlefield

Wittgenstein, Ludwig (2009): *Philosophische Untersuchungen. Philosophical Investigations (Revised Fourth Edition)*, trans. G. E. M. Anscombe, P. M. S. Hacker, & Joachim Schulte, Oxford, Wiley-Blackwell

Wittgenstein, Ludwig, & Rush Rhees (2015): 'Wittgenstein's Philosophical Conversations with Rush Rhees (1939-50): From the Notes of Rush Rhees', ed. Gabriel Citron, *Mind*, Vol. 124, No. 493 (January)

Wright, Georg H. von (2016): 'The Strongest Impression Any Man Ever Made on Me', in Flowers III & Ground 2016: 1026-29

Index of Names

Aitken, Kate 66
Ambrose, Alice 94
Anscombe, G. E. M. xviii, xxvii, xxxiii, xl, xlii, xliv, xlv, xlviii, l, li, 20, 46, 62, 79, 81, 94, 99, 109, 111–113, 118, 146, 155, 157–158, 162, 146–167, 169, 194–195, 211–212, 236–237, 247, 251–252, 256–257, 259, 261, 263, 267, 270–271, 282–285, 287–289, 294, 307–308, 310, 313–314, 316–321, 323–323, 337–340, 342, 363–364
Attlee, Clement 148
Augustine of Hippo xxxiii
Austin, J. L. xliv, 25–26, 269

Bach, Johann Sebastian xli, 45, 53, 115, 118, 121, 132, 156, 249, 260, 268, 337
Barbrooke (family) xxxiv, 136, 138, 175, 178
Beecham, Sir Thomas 88
Beethoven, Ludwig van 39, 60, 80, 86, 88, 132, 212
Beinum, Eduard Alexander van (Beynum) 264
Békássy, Ferenc xvii
Benett, Dr. 250
Bevan, Aneurin 148
Bevan, Edward xxxix, xl, xli, xlviii, 235, 242, 249–253, 257, 262, 270, 272, 298–301, 304–305, 307, 312–315, 320, 323, 325–326, 330, 332, 337–339, 342
Bevan, Joan xxxix, xli, xlviii, 237, 270, 315, 323–324, 365
Black, Max 207–208, 213
Böhler, Otto 99, 100
Bolstad, Arne 124, 269, 294, 296, 315
Born, Max 113

Bouwsma, Oets K. 207, 209, 212–213, 218, 222, 252, 314, 316, 364
Brady, Dr. 114, 118–119, 124
Brahms, Johannes xli, 156
Braithwaite, Richard B. 25, 26, 59
Brandrick, Miss 279, 291, 209
Broad C. D. 26, 63–64, 86, 91
Bronte, Sisters (Charlotte, Emily, & Anne) 331
Brooke, Rupert xvi
Brown, Stuart 207, 213
Bruckner, Anton xli, xlii, 86, 102–106, 138, 243, 245, 264
Burton, Montague 296
Busch, Wilhelm xl, xli, xlii, 60, 156, 211, 290, 317, 339

Campbell, Charles Arthur 107
Catterall, Arthur 156
Cheyney, Peter 244–245, 247
Christie, Agatha xlii, 226
Clement (family) 2, 36, 39–40, 47, 52, 54–56, 71–73, 148
Clifton, Allan S. 340
Conybeare, John 290
Curran, Desmond 118

Daniel, Peter 267, 317
Davies (family) 36–37, 39, 56, 71
Deutsch Arnold, Gitta 104, 158
Devoid, Dr. J. 307
Dickens, Charles 94
Doney, Willis 207, 213, 222
Draegni (family) 11–12, 124, 292, 294, 309
Drury, Maurice O'Connor (Con) xxxiii, xl, xlvi, xlviii, 43, 46–50, 54–58, 61, 78–82, 84, 94, 97–99, 101–102, 105, 107, 110–111, 114–115,

118, 124–126, 128, 130–131, 133, 135, 144, 147–148, 151, 154, 158, 161–157, 170–171, 173, 175–179, 181–182, 186, 198, 217, 226, 235, 237, 240, 248, 265, 294, 299, 301, 314, 323, 345, 361–362
Dürer, Albrecht xlvi
Dyson, Freeman 20

Edwards, Gilbert Harris 26, 46
Eliot, George (Mary Ann Evans) 330, 332
Eliot, T. S. 213, 217
Elizabeth II, Queen 72
Engelmann, Paul 180, 318
Erlach, Johann Bernhard Fischer von 357
Evangelos, Christou 46
Evangelos, Jani 46
Ewing, A. C. 57, 59

Fawcus, Mr. 95
Fischer, Edwin 337
Fischer, Emanuel 258
Fischer, J. B. 258
Flew, A. G. N. 334
Forster, E. M. 179
Fouracre, Roy xlvii
Frege, Gottlob 269
Freud, Sigmund xvii, 120–121
Fuchs, Wolfgang 144, 207

Garnett (family) 82, 90, 249
Geach, Peter 46, 158, 267, 310
Goethe, Johann Wolfgang von xxvi, 247, 252, 277
Goodridge, Frank 112, 314
Goodridge, Gillian 267, 270, 314–315
Grimm, Brothers (Jacob & Wilhelm) xl, xli, xlii, 181, 277, 317
Gripstad, Anna 278
Guter, Eran 103
Guter, Inbal 103
Guttman, Eric 118

Habsburg family 357
Hansel, Ludwig 236, 242, 251, 308, 314, 316, 318, 320, 364
Harris, Pippa xvi
Haydn, Joseph 211, 329–330

Herbert, Eileen 345
Herbert, Eileen 345
Hijab, Wasfi 20, 25, 46
Holme-Klingenberg, Kari 12, 292, 294, 312, 315
Horus (god) xxxiii
Hume, David 113
Hunt, E. Bruce 46
Hutt, Rowland xxxiv

Ingres, Jean-Auguste-Dominique 90

Jackson, A. C. 46
James, William 16
Joad, C. E. M. xlvi, 129, 134
John, Augustus Edwin 177
Jones, J. R. 46

Karajan, Herbert von 156, 211
Keillor, Mr. 289, 297
Keysser, Christian 252
Kingston (family) 98, 100–101, 104, 107, 109, 110, 362
Keynes, John Maynard xvii
Kirk, Keith xv
Klingenberg, Hans 195
Koder, Rudolf xxii, 86, 157, 159, 161, 181, 183, 189, 199, 219, 227, 246, 248, 264, 281, 294, 300–301, 363
Kreisel, Georg 46
Kubelik, Rafael 264

Labor, Josef 127
Lake, Dr. 211, 222
Lazerowitz, Morris 94
Lenau, Nikolaus 110
Lewis, C. S. xliv, 109, 111–112

MacNab, Donald G. C. 113
Mahler, Gustav 99–100
Mahler-Werfel, Alma 99
Malcolm, Leonida (Lee) xxxv, xlix, 102–103, 138, 183, 185, 200, 207, 227, 235, 212, 362, 364
Malcolm, Norman xxviii, xxxv, xlvi, xlvii, xlix, 4, 10, 17, 20, 28, 46, 79, 89, 94, 105, 125, 134, 162, 176, 180, 183, 185, 187, 189, 194,

    199–200, 202, 207–213, 217, 221–224, 229, 235–237, 240, 242, 247, 252, 257, 263, 270, 288, 292, 308, 312, 315, 324, 335, 337, 342, 347, 364
Marshall, Dr. Joyce 259, 297
Martini, Miss H. 46
Matthew (Apostle) xxiv
Matthews, Denis 337
McGuinness, Brian xvii
Melville, Herman 229, 329–330
Mendelssohn Bartholdy, Felix 120, 125, 127
Meyer, Eduard 94
Mitchell, Joseph S. 323, 327–329, 334–335
Monk, Ray xi, xii, xvii, xix
Montgomery, General Bernhard 60
Mooney, Dr. Louise C. 208, 222
Moore, G.E. xvii, xlii, xlix, li, 94, 162, 170, 224, 329, 337
Moore, John Norman Parker 54, 57, 130, 171
Moore, Timothy 329
Morgan, Reverend Wynford 2, 5–8, 10, 18, 36–40, 47
Moss, Mr. 249
Mozart, Wolfgang Amadeus xli, xlii, 36, 39, 88, 132–133, 175–177, 182, 211, 248
Mulkerrins, Mrs. 128, 143
Mulkerrins, Tommy 79, 128, 133, 142, 143
Munz, Peter 46

Nelson, John 207–208, 213
Nicolai, Otto 120
Norton, Henry xvii

Olivier, Brynhild xvi
Olivier, Daphne xvi
Olivier, Margery xvi
Olivier, Sydney H. (Baron) 42

Parker, Miss xxx, 54, 130, 156, 159
Pattison, Gilbert 24, 296
Philip, Prince 72
Phillips, Ann 47, 53, 63, 82, 121, 311
Pichler, Alois 119
Pink, Barry 267
Pinsent, David xi, xv, xxxiii
Plaister, Stephen 46
Plato 208, 311

Pollard, Diana (Polly) l
Popper, Sir Karl 26
Prokop, Ursula xxi
Priestley, John Boynton 119

Quiller-Couch, Arthur 45

Ramsey, Frank Plumpton 404
Ramsey, Lettice 119
Raphael, Santi 127
Raven, Charles Earle 91
Rebni, Anna 1, 11–14, 125, 269–270, 292, 294, 296, 307, 310, 312, 315, 361, 365
Reinecke, Carl xlii, 139, 144–145
Respinger, Marguerite xi, xv, xxi, xxxi, xxxii, xxxix
Rex (the Kingston family's dog) 106
Rhees, Jean xlix, 230, 234–237, 241, 256, 259–260, 262–263, 271, 285, 288–290, 293, 299, 302–303, 305–306, 364
Rhees, Rush xlviii, xlix, l, li, 100, 105, 127, 132, 138, 170–172, 183–184, 189, 202–203, 210, 236–237, 240, 242, 246–247, 271–271, 288–290, 324, 329, 333–335, 340, 345, 362–363
Richards, Angela vi, xvii, xxviii, l, 54, 56, 58, 60, 63, 82, 87–88, 101–102, 119, 124, 128, 132, 135–136, 214, 221, 226, 231, 246, 265, 268, 271, 273, 275–276, 281, 309–311, 313, 316, 319–321, 347, 357–360
Richards, Isabella (Tazza) xvii, l, 58, 63, 82, 205, 214, 226, 228, 231, 316
Richards, Julia (Heshe) xvii, xlix, l, 25, 42, 45, 50, 63, 82, 92, 139, 147, 214, 226
Richards, Miranda vi, xviii
Richards, Noel (née Olivier) xvi, xvii, xxvii, xxviii, 42, 43, 44, 45, 46, 52, 58, 63, 71, 82, 87, 98, 101, 102, 127, 141, 149, 172, 175, 178, 180, 183, 184, 185, 187, 190, 191, 195, 196, 212, 214, 217, 219, 315, 348
Richards, Tara vi, xviii
Richards, Virginia (Jinny) xvii, xlix, l, 58, 63, 82, 88, 205, 214, 221, 228, 316
Richards, William Arthur xvi, xvii, 48, 214
Rijn, Rembrandt van 177
Rommel, Erwin 329, 335, 338–341
Rosenbaum, S. P. xvii

Russell, Bertrand xvii, 17, 311
Ryle, Gilbert 252, 334
Ryle, John A. 114, 179, 265

Sachs, Hans 145
Salzer, Helene l, 39, 84, 105, 109, 120, 155, 184, 189, 210–211, 248, 257, 337, 363
Salzer, Max l
Sandry, Alan 133
Sargant, William 118
Schopenhauer, Arthur 232, 353
Schubert, Franz xli, 4, 8, 16, 57–58, 60, 133, 145, 330, 332–333
Schumann, Robert xli, xlv, 37, 39, 132, 246, 248, 327
Shah, Kanti 46
Shakespeare, William 145, 281
Sjögren, Talla xxxii
Skinner Francis xi, xv, xix, xxxii, xxxiii, xxxiv, xxxix, 78, 110, 136
Slater, Eliot 118, 293
Smith, John (pseudonym of L. Wittgenstein) vii, xlvi, lii, 18, 24, 232, 347, 353
Smith, Ronald 337
Smythies, Yorick xl, l, 20, 46, 62, 72, 77, 79, 96–97, 112–113, 146, 154–155, 162, 194, 252, 262, 265, 267, 274, 276, 289, 293–294, 296, 306, 309, 316, 318–320. 325, 329, 362, 363
Sraffa, Irma 115
Stevens, Grav 281
Stockert, Marie 77, 84, 86, 89, 155, 157, 362
Stonborough, Jerome l
Stonborough-Wittgenstein, Margaret l, 21, 67, 85, 96, 122, 156, 209, 246, 253, 257, 364
Strachey, James xvii
Strachey, Lytton xvii
Strauss, Richard 88
Synge, Victor Millington 80, 177, 179, 196–199, 208

Taylor, George 110
Tolstoy, Leo xlii, 17, 132, 171, 180, 299
Toulmin, Stephen 46

Townsend, Raymond xxxiv, 30, 294, 297
Tranøy, Knut Erik 278, 291, 307
Trevelyan, George Macaulay 91

Uhland, Ludwig 180

Vatne, Harald 315
Vinelott, John 46
Vlastos, Gregory 207–208

Waismann, Friedrich 334
Walter, Bruno 86
Watling, Sarah xvi
Watson, William Heriot 66
Wedgwood, Dorothy 249
Wedgwood, John 249–250, 253, 257
Weingartner, Felix 104
Wells, H. G. 336
Wilkinson, Naomi 33–35, 71–72
Williams, Miss 297
Winkler, R. O. C. 46
Wisdom, John 26, 334
Withycombe, Dr. 249
Wittgenstein, Hermine li, 79, 86, 155, 181, 184, 189, 191. 236, 242, 244, 254, 363, 364
Wittgenstein, Karl 155
Wittgenstein, Paul 66
Wodehouse, Sir Pelham Grenville 248
Wood, Oscar 62
Woods, Rex xlviii
Woolf, Virginia xvi
Wright, Anita von 241, 263
Wright, Benedict von 241
Wright, Georg Henrik von xviii, xlviii, l, li, 2, 46, 59, 77, 84, 89, 94, 100, 113, 120, 191, 197, 199–200, 202, 204, 235, 237, 244, 247, 257, 262–263, 267–269, 271, 277–278, 296, 363, 364
Wright, Maria Elisabeth von li

Young, Brigadier Desmond 329, 335, 338, 340–343
Young, Desmond xlii